GHOSTS
AND
THREE OTHER PLAYS

HENRIK IBSEN, the most influential dramatist since Shakespeare, was born at Skien, Norway, in 1828. After years of failure and poverty, he emigrated at the age of thirty-six to Italy, and there wrote *Brand*, which brought him immediate fame. He remained in self-imposed exile for twenty-seven years, living in Rome, Dresden and Munich. In 1891 he returned to Norway, and spent the last fifteen years of his life in Christiania (now Oslo). He died there in 1906 at the age of seventy-eight. Ibsen wrote twenty-six plays, sixteen of which are still performed in England and America.

MICHAEL MEYER, the translator, was born in London in 1921. After studying at Oxford he was for three years Lecturer in English Literature at Uppsala University in Sweden, and now lives partly in Stockholm and partly in London. Author of one novel, two plays and several television plays, he is best known as a translator from the Scandinavian languages and has established a unique reputation for himself in this field in England. In 1964 he was awarded the Gold Medal of the Swedish Academy, the first time that this rarely given and coveted honour has been bestowed upon a translator.

THE PLAYS OF HENRIK IBSEN
(1828–1906)

WITH THEIR DATES OF COMPOSITION

Cataline (1849)

The Warrior's Barrow
   (1849–50)

Norma (1851)

St. John's Eve (1852)

Lady Inger of Oestraat
   (1854)

The Feast at Solhaug
   (1855)

Olaf Liljekrans (1856)

The Vikings at Helgeland
   (1857)

Love's Comedy (1862)

The Pretenders (1863)

Brand (1865)

Peer Gynt (1867)

The League of Youth
   (1868–69)

Emperor and Galilean
   (1864–73)

The Pillars of Society
   (1875–77)

A Doll's House (1879)

Ghosts (1881)

An Enemy of the People
   (1882)

The Wild Duck (1884)

Rosmersholm (1886)

The Lady from the Sea
   (1888)

Hedda Gabler (1890)

The Master Builder (1892)

Little Eyolf (1894)

John Gabriel Borkman
   (1896)

When We Dead Awaken
   (1899)

A DOLL'S HOUSE
GHOSTS
AN ENEMY OF THE PEOPLE
ROSMERSHOLM

BY

HENRIK IBSEN

NEWLY TRANSLATED FROM
THE NORWEGIAN BY
MICHAEL MEYER

Anchor Books
Doubleday & Company, Inc.
Garden City, New York

The Anchor Books edition is the first publication
of *Ghosts and Three Other Plays*.

The quotation from Sigmund Freud's "Some Character-Types Met
with in Psycho-Analytic Work" (1916) which appears in the Introduction to *Rosmersholm* is reprinted with permission of Sigmund
Freud Copyrights Ltd., Mr. James Strachey and The Hogarth Press
Ltd., London, and Basic Books, Inc., New York. It appears in Volume XIV of the Standard Edition of *The Complete Works of Sigmund Freud;* Translation, copyright 1957 Mr. James Strachey,
The Hogarth Press Ltd. and The Institute of Psycho-Analysis; and in
The Collected Papers of Sigmund Freud, Volume IV, translation
supervised by Joan Riviere (New York: Basic Books, Inc. 1959),
pp. 335–40.

Anchor Books edition: 1966

These translations of *A Doll's House, Ghosts, An Enemy of the
People* and *Rosmersholm* are the sole property of the translator
and are fully protected by copyright. They may not be acted by
professionals or amateurs without formal permission and the payment of a royalty. All rights, including professional, amateur, stock,
radio and television broadcasting, motion picture, recitation, lecturing, public reading and the rights of translation in foreign languages are reserved. All American and Canadian enquiries should
be addressed to the translator's agent: Harold Freedman, Brandt &
Brandt Dramatic Department, Inc., 101 Park Avenue, New York
17, N.Y. Application for performance in any other part of the world
should be made to Margaret Ramsay, Ltd., 14 Goodwin's Court,
London W.C. 2, England.

FOREWORD

Ibsen wrote the four plays contained in this volume during his fifties; *A Doll's House* (1879) at fifty-one, *Ghosts* (1881) at fifty-three, *An Enemy of the People* (1882) at fifty-four, and *Rosmersholm* (1886) at fifty-eight. *A Doll's House* was the first play to make him internationally famous. Prior to that he had been known in Scandinavia principally as a poet who wrote plays to be read rather than acted, the author of *Brand* and *Peer Gynt*. *The Pillars of Society* (1877) had spread his fame to Germany, but no further; *A Doll's House*, on the other hand, very soon became the subject of world-wide discussion, and so, once theatrical managers had plucked up the courage to put it on, did *Ghosts*.

Many people, even today, think of Ibsen mainly as the author of these two plays, and still speak glibly of him as a "social dramatist," a description which his next play, *An Enemy of the People*, seemed to confirm. It was a description which Ibsen himself resented. In these plays, as in *The Pillars of Society*, he had deliberately suppressed the poet within him and was, as William Archer put it, "trying to act the essentially uncongenial part of the prosaic realist. . . . He was introduced to the world at large through two plays which showed his power, indeed, almost in perfection, but left the higher and subtler qualities of his genius for the most part unrepresented." Yet today, when the social content of *A Doll's House*, *Ghosts*, and *An Enemy of the People* is no longer topical and interests us only as history, their power is, if anything, greater, because we can see their true theme more clearly; the need of every individual to discover the kind of person he or she really is, and to become that person.

Women may have become emancipated, syphilis been rendered curable, typhoid been virtually eliminated, but man's quest for his identity remains; it is a theme that will never date. That is why these plays are as riveting in a theatre now as when they first astonished audiences nearly a century ago.

Rosmersholm is an example of Ibsen's later method; like all of his plays from *The Wild Duck* onwards, it bewildered contemporary critics and readers in a way that *The Pillars of Society*, *A Doll's House*, *An Enemy of the People*, and even *Ghosts* had not. In *Rosmersholm*, as in *The Lady from the Sea*, *The Master Builder* and *Little Eyolf*, Ibsen probed the then uncharted depths of man's unconsciousness, and of all Ibsen's plays *Rosmersholm* is the one which especially interested Sigmund Freud, who made it the subject of one of his most fascinating analyses.

A Doll's House, *Ghosts*, and *Rosmersholm* were all reviled when they first appeared, even in supposedly enlightened quarters. *A Doll's House* was described by the *Observer* as "dreary and sterilizing"; *Ghosts* by the *Daily Telegraph* as "an open drain; a loathsome sore unbandaged; a dirty act done publicly"; *Rosmersholm* by the *Saturday Review* as "provincial and quite contemptible." This should not surprise us, any more than it surprised Ibsen. He might, like Freud a decade later, have written: "I understood that from now onward I belonged to those who have 'troubled the sleep of the world,' as Hebbel says, and that I could not reckon upon objectivity and tolerance."

M. M.

CONTENTS

CONTENTS

A DOLL'S HOUSE

INTRODUCTION

Ibsen wrote *A Doll's House* in Rome and Amalfi during the summer of 1879, at the age of fifty-one. It was his first real international success. *Brand* (1865) and *Peer Gynt* (1867) had been written to be read, not acted, and had established him only in Scandinavia. *The Pillars of Society* (1877) had spread his fame to Germany. But *A Doll's House* immediately became a subject of world-wide discussion. Books and pamphlets were written about it, public meetings were held to dissect it, sermons were preached on it, it aroused extraordinary controversy wherever it was staged or read. By the end of the eighties, there was scarcely a civilised country where it had not been performed.

The problem of women's rights was particularly topical just then in Norway. Many books had been published on the subject since John Stuart Mill's *The Subjection of Women* had been translated in 1869; Ibsen had returned to Norway himself briefly in 1874, and had noted the unrest. His wife, Suzannah, was an outspoken champion of the feminist cause; so was the Norwegian novelist Camilla Collett, who had seen a good deal of Ibsen in Dresden in 1871, and had been scandalised at what she regarded as the old-fashionedness of his ideas about woman's place in society. His previous heroines, such as Svanhild in *Love's Comedy*, Agnes in *Brand*, and Solveig in *Peer Gynt*, had accepted their position with the placidity of Dickensian maidens. However, Selma Bratsberg, a minor character in *The League of Youth* (1869), had complained to her husband: "You dressed me up like a doll; you played with me as one plays with a child;" Georg Brandes suggested to Ibsen that she, or a character like her, might make a good central theme for a later play; and in his next work, *The Pillars of Society*, Ibsen created two more women, Lona Hessel and Dina Dorf, who rebelled violently against the subordinate position to which a man-dominated society was trying to degrade them.

Nine years before he wrote *A Doll's House*, in 1870, Ibsen had become acquainted with a young Norwegian girl named Laura Petersen, who had written, and sent him, a sequel to *Brand*. He took a great fancy to her, and nicknamed her his "skylark." In 1872 she married a Danish schoolmaster named Victor Kieler. He fell ill, and the doctor said he must go to a warmer climate. Since they were very poor, she arranged a loan secretly, and took him to Switzerland and Italy; this was in 1876. On their way home, they stopped in Munich, and visited Ibsen, in whom she confided the truth. She had still not dared to tell her husband. Finally, in despair, she forged a bill of exchange. When this was discovered, the husband learned the full story, became furious and demanded a divorce. Laura had a nervous breakdown, and had to enter a mental home. This incident seemed to Ibsen to crystallize woman's, and indeed mankind's fight against conventional morality and prejudice. The battle between the individual's inner compulsion towards freedom and the external pressures of society was not confined to women—he insisted later that *A Doll's House* was written on behalf, not of women, but of humanity in general—but women, he said, share with artists and children "that instinctive genius that unconsciously hits on the right answer."

The first reference to *A Doll's House* in Ibsen's letters occurs on 5 May 1878. "I have begun to busy myself," he wrote to his publisher, Frederik Hegel of Gyldendals, from Munich, where he had been living since 1875, "with plans for a new play with a contemporary setting; it will, like the last one, be in four acts. When it will be ready, however, I can as yet have no idea." Two months later, on 2 August 1878, he writes again to Hegel: "Towards the middle of this month we shall be leaving for the south; we plan to spend the winter in Rome, where I hope to find time and peace to complete my new work. The weather here [i.e., in Munich] has been beastly all the time, so that we have had no real summer. I greatly long to get across the Alps. . . . Mrs. Laura Kieler, as you probably know, has suffered a sad calamity. Her husband informed us rather curtly that she had been admitted into a mental clinic. Do you know the exact circumstances of this, and whether she is still there?"

On their way south, the Ibsens stopped for a few days in Gossensass, the little village in the Tyrol[1] which he had visited, and liked, in 1876. They had also planned to spend a while in Florence, but decided against this and proceeded directly to Rome "since (8 October 1878) I longed greatly for familiar surroundings so as to find real peace to work." Within three weeks of his arrival there, on 19 October 1878, he jotted down the following *Notes for a Modern Tragedy:*

There are two kinds of spiritual laws, two kinds of conscience, one for men and one, quite different, for women. They don't understand each other; but in practical life, woman is judged by masculine law, as though she weren't a woman but a man.

The wife in the play ends by having no idea what is right and what is wrong; natural feelings on the one hand and belief in authority on the other lead her to utter distraction.

A woman cannot be herself in modern society. It is an exclusively male society, with laws made by men and with prosecutors and judges who assess female conduct from a male standpoint.

She has committed forgery, which is her pride; for she has done it out of love of her husband, to save his life. But this husband of hers takes his standpoint, conventionally honourable, on the side of the law, and sees the situation with male eyes.

Spiritual conflict. Weighed down and confused by her trust in authority, she loses faith in her own morality, and in her fitness to bring up her children. Bitterness. A mother in modern society, like certain insects, goes away

[1] It now lies on the Italian side of the frontier, and has been renamed Colle Isarco.

and dies once she has done her duty by propagating the
race. Love of life, of home, of husband and children and
family. Now and then, as women do, she shrugs off her
thoughts. Suddenly anguish and fear return. Everything
must be borne alone. The catastrophe approaches, mer-
cilessly, inevitably. Despair, conflict, and defeat.

On the sheet of paper on which these notes end, Ibsen,
possibly somewhat later, added a cast list. This corresponds
exactly to his final list of characters, apart from the names;
Helmer is "Stenborg, a civil servant," Mrs. Linde is Miss Lind
(corrected to Mrs. . . . , widow), Dr. Rank is, unattractively
to English and American ears, Dr. Hank, and the nurse
Karen instead of Anne-Marie. There is also a detailed scenario
of each act; the only substantial difference from the play as
we know it is the absence of the tarantella scene.[2]

It was, though, to be another six months before he actually
sat down to write the dialogue; it was his method to ponder
a theme at length and then write the play swiftly in a matter
of weeks. He was touchy and nervous that winter in Rome,
keeping more to himself and mixing much less with other
Scandinavians than had been his practice during his previous
stay there in 1864–68. "We live, in general, pretty quietly"
he wrote on 22 January 1879 to Markus Groenvold. "Lunch is
brought in to us, and our landlady prepares our breakfast and
dinner. Everything is much cheaper here than in Munich,
and wine in particular is to be had for practically nothing this
winter."

Six days later he emerged from his shell to place two
proposals before the Scandinavian Club of Rome; firstly, that
the post of paid librarian should be thrown open to women,
and secondly, that women should have the right to vote in

---

[2] But William Archer may have been right in suggesting that
Ibsen originally schemed a "happy ending," to be achieved by
Krogstad's return of the forged document, the rest to be "a more or
less conventional winding-up" (how otherwise, asks Archer, explain
"the invention, to that end alone, of Mrs. Linde's relation to, and
influence over, Krogstad?"). As Professor Didrik Arup Seip has
shown, Ibsen wrote the scenario for each act only *after* he had
finished the draft of the previous act.

all matters concerning the Club. The former motion was accepted, but the latter failed by a single vote to get the necessary two-thirds majority. Ibsen was furious; he left the Club immediately, sat alone in a café, and refused to speak to anyone who had voted against him. Some days later, however, to the general amazement, he attended the Club's gala evening. One of those present, Gunnar Heiberg, has left a picturesque account of what happened:

No one would have anticipated it—but Ibsen came. He looked magnificent, in full panoply, with medals to boot. He ran his hand ceaselessly through his rich, grizzled hair, greeting no one in particular, but everyone in general. There was a deep peace in his face, but his eyes were watchful, so watchful. He sat alone. We all thought he had forgiven his fellow-mortals, and some even supposed him penitent. This helped to make the atmosphere unusually gay and euphoric. Then, suddenly, he rose and stepped forward to a big table, so that he was facing the whole ballroom with its dancing couples.

"Ladies and gentlemen!" It was a tense and dramatic moment. What was going to happen? Was he about to admit the error of his ways? Surely he was not intending to propose a toast? . . . He stroked his hair calmly. Then he began, softly, but with a terrifying earnestness. He had recently wished to do the Club a great service, he might almost say a great favour, by bringing its members abreast of contemporary ideas. No one could escape these mighty developments. Not even here—in this community—in this duckpond! He did not actually use the word duckpond, but the contempt around his mouth proclaimed it loudly. And how had his offer been received? As a criminal attempt! Rejected by a paltry vote or two. And how had the women reacted—the women for whom his gift was intended? They had intrigued and agitated against him. They had thrown his gift into the mud. What kind of women are these? They are worse— worse than the dregs, worse than scum—

Now he was no longer speaking calmly, no longer thoughtfully stroking his hair. He shook his head with its grey mane. He folded his arms across his breast. His eyes shone. His voice shook, his mouth trembled, and he thrust out his underlip. He resembled a lion, nay, more— he resembled that future enemy of the people, Dr. Stockmann. He repeated and repeated: what kind of women are these, what kind of ladies, what kind of a sex, ignorant, in the truest sense ill-bred, immoral, dreg-like, contemptible—

Thump! A lady, Countess B., fell to the floor. She, like the rest of us, feared to hear the unspeakable. So she took time by the forelock, and swooned. She was carried out. Ibsen continued. Perhaps slightly more calmly. But eloquently and lucidly, never searching for a word. He intoxicated himself with his rhetoric against the ignorant, contemptible, and rigid resistance that mankind, especially women, was attempting to offer to these new ideas whose purpose was to make people bigger, richer, and better. He looked remote, ecstatic. As his voice thundered it was as though he were clarifying his own thoughts, as his tongue chastised it was as though his spirit were scouring the darkness in search of his present spiritual goal, his poem—as though he were personally living out his theories, incarnating his characters. And when he was done, he went out into the hall, took his overcoat and walked home. Calm and silent.

"My new dramatic work occupies all my thoughts and all my interest," he wrote to Hegel on 18 February 1879; but still he had not written a line of dialogue. It was not until 2 May that he began his first draft; but then, as usual once he had started, the work went quickly. Act One occupied him from 2–24 May, and on 22 May he was able to write to Hegel: "My new work is so far advanced that I hope to be able to send you the first part of the manuscript around 8 July, and the remainder shortly afterwards." On 25 May he wrote even more optimistically to Jonas Lie that he hoped to have his new play ready in a month. In the event, Act Two took him, even in draft, nearly six weeks; he began it on 4 June and did not complete it until 14 July. However, he had a good excuse. "For reasons of health," he explained to

Hegel on 19 June, "we have decided to change our original plan for our summer holiday. We had at first thought to go to one of the mountain villages around Rome; but the sanitary conditions there leave much to be desired, so we have decided to retire to Amalfi, on the coast south of Naples, where there are facilities for sea-bathing. This will in some measure delay the completion of my play; in addition to which I have, in order to perfect as far as possible the language and the dialogue, decided to rewrite it once again, making various improvements and alterations, before sending you the final fair copy. It is therefore highly probable that you will receive nothing from me before August; but this will be soon enough. Once I start sending you the manuscript, the rest will follow very quickly."

In Amalfi he took rooms in the Albergo della Luna, an old monastery converted into a hotel which still stands on a cliff overlooking a sheer drop into the sea. Here he could bathe and take long walks in the hills. He always worked well in the heat, and he began Act Three on 18 July, four days after finishing Act Two. He completed it in less than three weeks on 3 August. By 2 September he had finished fair-copying Act One and posted it off to Hegel. "Since this work deals with problems that cannot but be regarded as exceptionally topical," he declared in his accompanying letter, "I think it can be assured of a large sale." Act Two followed on 13 September, and Act Three shortly afterwards (we do not know the exact date). On 15 September he wrote to Hegel: "I cannot recall any work of mine that has given me more satisfaction in the solving of specific problems." He left Amalfi at the end of September, stayed a little over a week in Sorrento, then a week in Rome, and finally, in mid-October, returned to Munich.

A Doll's House was published by Gyldendals of Copenhagen on 4 December 1879 in an impression of eight thousand copies, the largest printing to that date of any of Ibsen's plays. It was exhausted within the month; a second impression appeared on 4 January 1880, and a third on 8 March. Halvdan Koht has described the effect: "*A Doll's House* exploded like a bomb into contemporary life. . . . It sounded the crack of doom on prevailing social ethics. . . . Ibsen was hailed, not only as the revolutionary champion of intellectual liberty, but as the especial champion of women, and those who were against revolution, against social and moral upheaval, against female emancipation, came to see in Ibsen their greatest and most dangerous enemy."

The first performance of *A Doll's House* took place at the Royal Theatre in Copenhagen on 21 December 1879. Stockholm followed suit on 8 January 1880, Bergen on 18 January, and Christiania on 20 January. March saw the first German production, at Flensburg, under curious circumstances. Frau Hedwig Niemann-Raabe, who was to play Nora, refused to perform the final scene as written. "I would never leave *my* children!" she explained indignantly. Since, in those days, there was no international copyright convention, and Ibsen was powerless to prevent any theatre from acting as it wished, he decided that a "happy" ending written by himself would be preferable to one by another hand which could be published and repeated at other German theatres. "To forestall any such possibility," he explained in an open letter dated 17 February 1880 to the Danish newspaper *Nationaltidende,* "I sent my translator and agent for use in emergency a drafted emendation, in which Nora does not leave the house, but is forced by Helmer to the doorway of the children's bedroom; here a few lines are exchanged, Nora sinks down by the door, and the curtain falls. This emendation I have myself described to my translator as a "barbaric outrage" on the play. . . . But if any such outrage is threatened, I prefer, on the basis of previous experience, to commit it myself rather than submit my work to the treatment and adaptation of less tender and competent hands."

Frau Niemann-Raabe subsequently acted this distorted version in Hamburg, Dresden, Hanover, and Berlin, where there was a public protest at the perversion of the original. Other German theatres copied the "happy ending," but the play was never a success in this form, and eventually even Frau Niemann-Raabe returned to the original text. The first unbowdlerized German production had meanwhile taken place in Munich on 3 March 1880, with Ibsen himself among the audience.

In 1881 *A Doll's House* was performed in Vienna and in St. Petersburg (in Polish, with Helena Modjeska). In 1882 Modjeska played it in Warsaw, and the following year she gave a single performance in Louisville, Kentucky. The real breakthrough, however, came at the end of the eighties, when *A Doll's House* took its place in the permanent repertory of almost every civilized country. Paris, curiously behind the times, did not see it until 1894, when Nora was acted by Gabrielle Réjane.

According to Bernard Shaw, the first performance of *A Doll's House* in England took place "on the first floor in a Bloomsbury lodging-house. Karl Marx's youngest daughter played Nora Helmer; and I impersonated Krogstad at her request, with a very vague notion of what it was all about." The date of this interesting occasion unfortunately remains unrecorded. The first public performance in England was on 3 March 1884, when an adaptation by Henry Arthur Jones and H. Herman entitled *Breaking a Butterfly* was staged at the Prince's Theatre in Coventry Street (now the Prince of Wales's). "To fit the play for the English stage," noted William Archer, "the adaptors had been forced, not only to reconstruct and rewrite it, but absolutely to reverse its motive, making the husband an ideal hero, instead of the sensual, self-righteous weakling of Ibsen! The result was a nice little play, standing somewhat in the relation of Mr. Gilbert's *Gretchen* to Goethe's *Faust,* and even so, it did not succeed." Flora (*sic*) was played by Alice Lingard, and a young actor named Beerbohm Tree took "Dunkley, a cashier" (i.e., Krogstad).

In 1885 some amateurs called The Scribblers performed *A Doll's House* for charity at a drama school in Argyle Street, but the first proper production in England took place on 7 June 1889 at the Novelty Theatre (later the Kingsway), when Charles Charrington directed it with his wife, Janet Achurch, as Nora, and Herbert Waring as Helmer. Archer

later recorded: "It was this production that really made Ibsen
known to the English-speaking public. In other words, it
marked his second stride towards world-wide, as distinct from
merely national renown—if we reckon as the first stride the
success of *The Pillars of Society* in Germany." "The Ibsen
controversy indeed," Archer commented elsewhere, "did not
break out [in England] in its full virulence until 1891, when
Ghosts and *Hedda Gabler* were produced in London; but
from the date of the Novelty production onwards, Ibsen was
generally recognized as a potent factor in the intellectual and
artistic life of the day." And Granville Barker recalled (in
The Coming of Ibsen): "The play was talked of and written
about—mostly abusively, it is true—as no play had been for
years."

In an article entitled "The Mausoleum of Ibsen" (1894),
Archer collected some examples of critical comments upon
this production:

> "This foolish, fitful, conceited, selfish and unlovable
> Nora is to drive off the stage the loving and noble hero-
> ines who have adorned it and filled all hearts with ad-
> miration from the time of Shakespeare to the time of
> Pinero. . . . The noble women of drama and fiction, the
> Andromaches and Penelopes, and the Iphigenias and
> Unas and Imogens and Constances and Jeannie Deans,
> are to be thrust aside for deformed and stunted and love-
> less creatures, whose unnatural selfishness the modern
> dramatist extols, and with whose puny natures the mod-
> ern essayist professes to be in love."
>
> (Clement Scott in the *Daily Telegraph*)

> "*A Doll's House*, with its almost total lack of dramatic
> action, is certainly not an enlivening spectacle."
>
> (*The Times*)

> "It would be a misfortune were such a morbid and un-
> wholesome play to gain the favour of the public."
>
> (*Standard*)

> "Strained deductions, lack of wholesome human na-
> ture, pretentious inconclusiveness. . . . Cannot be al-

lowed to pass without a word of protest against the
dreary and sterilizing principle which it seeks to embody."   (*Observer*)

"Unnatural, immoral and, in its concluding scene, essentially undramatic."   (*The People*)

"The works of the Norwegian playwright are not suitable for dramatic representation—at any rate on the English stage."   (*St. James's Gazette*)

The *Sporting and Dramatic News* commented: "I never sat
out a play more dreary or more illogical as a whole, or in its
details more feeble and commonplace. . . . It is as though
someone had dramatized the cooking of a Sunday dinner."

Janet Achurch repeated her performance of Nora in Lon-
don in 1892, 1893, and 1897, and toured the world with it
for two years, playing in, among other countries, America,
Egypt, and Australia. Seventeen actresses have subsequently
acted the part professionally on the London stage: Marie
Fraser (1891), Rose Norreys (1891), Eleonora Duse (in
Italian, 1893), Eleonore von Driller (in German, 1894),
Irene Triesch (in German, 1900), Lydia Yavorska (1911),
Muriel Pratt (1921), Doris Lloyd (1922), Madge Titheradge
(1925), Gillian Scaife (1928), Gwen Ffrangcon-Davies
(1930), Ludmilla Pitoëff (in French, 1933), Lydia Lopo-
kova (1934 and 1936), Lucie Mannheim (1939), Jenny
Laird (1945), Angela Baddeley (1946), and Mai Zetterling
(1953). Which was the greatest? James Agate wrote in 1930
that "by general consent the finest of all Noras was Janet
Achurch. And I agree, always with this reservation, that it
was a magnificent whole made up out of totally unrelated
parts. Janet would enter in the first act and behave in the
traditional manner of Frou-Frou in Meilhac and Halévy's
comedy. In the next act, at Dr. Rank's declaration, Janet
would throw a fit of dignity and say the words: 'Let me pass,
please' in a manner not to be exceeded by a chorus-girl
turned Duchess. And in the last act this great actress would
magnify herself into the magnitude of Boadicea, Brunnhilde
and the Statue of Liberty rolled into one." J. T. Grein, how-

ever, on witnessing Madge Titheradge's performance in 1925, declared: "I have seen them all who made the play and were made by it in the days of Ibsen's advent, from Janet Achurch to Agnes Sorma, and Miss Titheradge's is the most moving of them all."

The first American production of *A Doll's House* took place on 2 June 1882 in Milwaukee, when a translation by William M. Lawrence entitled *The Child Wife* was given with the "happy ending." The translator, we are told, "introduced an Irish widow to give the play some humour, and in the second act one of Nora's children sang a pretty solo, which the audience enjoyed so much that she had to repeat it."[3] The following year, on 7 December 1883, Helena Modjeska gave the single performance at Louisville, Kentucky, referred to above. On this occasion the play and principal character were for some reason renamed *Thora;* it was not well received. "Thora's" husband was acted by Maurice Barrymore (the father of Ethel, Lionel, and John).

On 30 October 1889, Beatrice Cameron (the wife of Richard Mansfield, who was to be a famous Peer Gynt in 1906), "encouraged," according to Archer, "by the success of the London production," presented and played Nora at the Globe Theatre, Boston, and later in New York, Philadelphia, Washington, Baltimore, Chicago, and St. Louis. These performances "mark the first serious attempt to bring Ibsen before the American public, and aroused considerable notice and discussion."[4] The same year, Charles Charrington and Janet Achurch brought their London production to America in the course of their world tour, visiting New York, Boston, San Francisco, and other cities. In 1894 Minnie Maddern-Fiske played it for a single performance at the Empire Theatre, New York, with Courtenay Thorpe as Helmer; she was very successful in the role, and made it part of her permanent repertoire when she went on the road in 1895-96. It has been said that her performance "cracked the solid front

[3] *Ibsen in America,* by Einar Haugen (*Edda,* 1956).
[4] *Henrik Ibsen on the American Stage,* by R. H. Fife and A. Anstensen (*American-Scandinavian Review,* xvi, 1928).

of American opposition to Ibsen." Janet Achurch acted it
again in New York in 1895; so, that year, did Gabrielle Réjane, followed in 1897 by the German actress Agnes Sorma.
In 1905 Ethel Barrymore achieved a great personal triumph
as Nora at the Lyceum Theatre, New York, which was
equalled three years later at the Princess Theatre (and later
also at the Bijou) by the Russian actress Alla Nazimova, playing in English with Lionel Atwill as Helmer and Walter
Hampden as Dr. Rank.

Of the many contemporary attacks launched against *A
Doll's House,* the most (indeed, almost the only) valid one is
August Strindberg's, contained in his foreword to the volume
of short stories, *Marriage,* which he published (in French) in
1885. But after a spirited and ingenious, if not altogether
convincing defence of Helmer (if Nora blames her heredity
and upbringing for her shortcomings, asks Strindberg, why
may not her husband do the same?), he admits: "Nevertheless, *A Doll's House* did bring the question of unhappy marriages into the daylight. Every wife suddenly saw her husband as a tyrant and herself, with varying degrees of
justification, as a doll. Thus we had a whole succession of
fictitious husbands who forged bills of exchange and were
humbled by their wives in the final act, without the author-
esses of these pieces being as honourable as Ibsen in suggesting a hereditary tendency to forge as an excuse. Thus, too,
we saw husbands who squandered their wives' money, but
never, to balance the picture, wives who squandered their
husbands'. Disregarding, however, all the nonsense that came
to be written, this much was gained, that marriage was revealed as being a far from divine institution, people stopped
regarding it as an automatic provider of absolute bliss, and
divorce between incompatible parties came at last to be accepted as conceivably justifiable. And that was something."

A Doll's House has been performed more often in both
England and the United States than any other of Ibsen's plays,
save only, in both countries, *Ghosts.* In the early days, especially, these two were automatically thought of when Ibsen's

name was mentioned. William Archer, in his introduction to the play (1906), noted the consequence. "The fact that for many years he was known to thousands of people solely as the author of *A Doll's House,* and its successor *Ghosts,* was largely responsible for the extravagant misconceptions of his genius and character which prevailed during the last decade of the nineteenth century, and are not yet entirely extinct. In these plays he seemed to be delivering a direct assault on marriage, from the standpoint of feminine individualism; wherefore he was taken to be a preacher and a pamphleteer rather than a poet. In these plays, and in these only, he made physical disease a considerable factor in the action; whence it was concluded that he had a morbid predilection for 'nauseous' subjects. In these plays he laid special and perhaps disproportionate stress on the influence of heredity; whence he was believed to be possessed by a monomania on the point. In these plays, finally, he was trying to act the essentially uncongenial part of the prosaic realist. The effort broke down at many points, and the poet reasserted himself; but these flaws in the prosaic texture were regarded as mere bewildering errors and eccentricities. In short, he was introduced to the world at large through two plays which showed his power, indeed, almost in perfection, but left the higher and subtler qualities of his genius for the most part unrepresented. Hence the grotesquely distorted vision of him which for so long haunted the minds even of intelligent people. Hence, for example, the amazing opinion, given forth as a truism by more than one critic of great ability, that the author of *Peer Gynt* was devoid of humour."

Ibsen himself repeatedly protested against *any* of his plays being regarded as social or moral tracts. Nineteen years after he wrote *A Doll's House,* he was invited to address the Norwegian Association for Women's Rights at Christiania. He accepted; but his speech must sadly have disappointed that militant audience. "I am not a member of the Association for Women's Rights," he stated (26 May 1898). "I have never written any play to further a social purpose. I have been more of a poet and less of a social philosopher than most people seem inclined to believe. I thank you for your good wishes, but I must decline the honour of being said to have worked for the Women's Rights movement. I am not even very sure what Women's Rights really are." *A Doll's House*, in other words, was not about female emancipation any more than *Ghosts* was about syphilis or *An Enemy of the People* about bad hygiene. Its theme was the need of every individual to find out the kind of person he or she really is, and to strive to *become* that *person*. Ibsen knew what Freud and Jung were later to assert, that liberation can only come from within; which was why he expressed to Georg Brandes his lack of interest in "special revolutions, revolutions in externals, in the political sphere. . . . What is really wanted" he declared, "is a revolution of the spirit of man."

M. M.

CHARACTERS

TORVALD HELMER, a lawyer
NORA, his wife
DR. RANK
MRS. LINDE
NILS KROGSTAD, also a lawyer
The HELMERS' three small children
ANNE-MARIE, their nurse
HELEN, the maid
A PORTER

The action takes place in the HELMERS' *apartment.*

This translation of A DOLL's HOUSE *was first performed on 16 October 1964 at the Oxford Playhouse with the following cast:*

TORVALD HELMER	Richard Gale
NORA	Barbara Young
DR. RANK	James Cairncross
MRS. LINDE	Pamela Lane
KROGSTAD	John Warner
ANNE-MARIE	Gabrielle Hamilton
HELEN	Yvette Byrne

Directed by Robert Chetwyn

ACT ONE

A comfortably and tastefully, but not expensively furnished room. Backstage right a door leads out to the hall; backstage left, another door to HELMER's *study. Between these two doors stands a piano. In the middle of the left-hand wall is a door, with a window downstage of it. Near the window, a round table with armchairs and a small sofa. In the right-hand wall, slightly upstage, is a door; downstage of this, against the same wall, a stove lined with porcelain tiles, with a couple of armchairs and a rocking-chair in front of it. Between the stove and the side door is a small table. Engravings on the wall. A what-not with china and other bric-a-brac; a small bookcase with leather-bound books. A carpet on the floor; a fire in the stove. A winter day.*

A bell rings in the hall outside. After a moment, we hear the front door being opened. NORA *enters the room, humming contentedly to herself. She is wearing outdoor clothes and carrying a lot of parcels, which she puts down on the table right. She leaves the door to the hall open; through it, we can see a* PORTER *carrying a Christmas tree and a basket. He gives these to the* MAID, *who has opened the door for them.*

NORA. Hide that Christmas tree away, Helen. The children mustn't see it before I've decorated it this evening. (*To the* PORTER, *taking out her purse.*) How much—?
PORTER. A shilling.
NORA. Here's half a crown. No, keep it.

The PORTER *touches his cap and goes.* NORA *closes the door. She continues to laugh happily to herself as she removes her coat, etc. She takes from her pocket a bag containing maca-*

*roons and eats a couple. Then she tiptoes across and listens
at her husband's door.*

NORA. Yes, he's here. (*Starts humming again as she goes over
to the table, right.*)

HELMER (*from his room*). Is that my skylark twittering out
there?

NORA (*opening some of the parcels*). It is!

HELMER. Is that my squirrel rustling?

NORA. Yes!

HELMER. When did my squirrel come home?

NORA. Just now. (*Pops the bag of macaroons in her pocket
and wipes her mouth.*) Come out here, Torvald, and see
what I've bought.

HELMER. You mustn't disturb me! (*Short pause; then he
opens the door and looks in, his pen in his hand.*) Bought,
did you say? All that? Has my little squanderbird been
overspending again?

NORA. Oh, Torvald, surely we can let ourselves go a little this
year! It's the first Christmas we don't have to scrape.

HELMER. Well, you know, we can't afford to be extravagant.

NORA. Oh yes, Torvald, we can be a little extravagant now.
Can't we? Just a tiny bit? You've got a big salary now, and
you're going to make lots and lots of money.

HELMER. Next year, yes. But my new salary doesn't start till
April.

NORA. Pooh; we can borrow till then.

HELMER. Nora! (*Goes over to her and takes her playfully
by the ear.*) What a little spendthrift you are! Suppose I
were to borrow fifty pounds today, and you spent it all over
Christmas, and then on New Year's Eve a tile fell off a roof
on to my head—

NORA (*puts her hand over his mouth*). Oh, Torvald! Don't
say such dreadful things!

HELMER. Yes, but suppose something like that did happen?
What then?

NORA. If anything as frightful as that happened, it wouldn't
make much difference whether I was in debt or not.

HELMER. But what about the people I'd borrowed from?

NORA. Them? Who cares about them? They're strangers.

HELMER. Oh, Nora, Nora, how like a woman! No, but seriously, Nora, you know how I feel about this. No debts! Never borrow! A home that is founded on debts can never be a place of freedom and beauty. We two have stuck it out bravely up to now; and we shall continue to do so for the short time we still have to.

NORA (*goes over towards the stove*). Very well, Torvald. As you say.

HELMER (*follows her*). Now, now! My little songbird mustn't droop her wings. What's this? Is little squirrel sulking? (*Takes out his purse.*) Nora; guess what I've got here!

NORA (*turns quickly*). Money!

HELMER. Look. (*Hands her some banknotes.*) I know how these small expenses crop up at Christmas.

NORA (*counts them*). One—two—three—four. Oh, thank you, Torvald, thank you! I should be able to manage with this.

HELMER. You'll have to.

NORA. Yes, yes, of course I will. But come over here, I want to show you everything I've bought. And so cheaply! Look, here are new clothes for Ivar—and a sword. And a horse and a trumpet for Bob. And a doll and a cradle for Emmy —they're nothing much, but she'll pull them apart in a few days. And some bits of material and handkerchiefs for the maids. Old Anne-Marie ought to have had something better, really.

HELMER. And what's in that parcel?

NORA (*cries*). No, Torvald, you mustn't see that before this evening!

HELMER. Very well. But now, tell me, you little spendthrift, what do you want for Christmas?

NORA. Me? Oh, pooh, I don't want anything.

HELMER. Oh, yes, you do. Now tell me, what, within reason, would you most like?

NORA. No, I really don't know. Oh, yes—Torvald—!

HELMER. Well?

NORA (*plays with his coat-buttons; not looking at him*). If

you really want to give me something, you could—you
could—

HELMER. Come on, out with it.

NORA (*quickly*). You could give me money, Torvald. Only
as much as you feel you can afford; then later I'll buy
something with it.

HELMER. But, Nora—

NORA. Oh yes, Torvald dear, please! Please! Then I'll wrap up
the notes in pretty gold paper and hang them on the
Christmas tree. Wouldn't that be fun?

HELMER. What's the name of that little bird that can never
keep any money?

NORA. Yes, yes, squanderbird; I know. But let's do as I say,
Torvald; then I'll have time to think about what I need
most. Isn't that the best way? Mm?

HELMER (*smiles*). To be sure it would be, if you could keep
what I give you and really buy yourself something with it.
But you'll spend it on all sorts of useless things for the
house, and then I'll have to put my hand in my pocket
again.

NORA. Oh, but Torvald—

HELMER. You can't deny it, Nora dear. (*Puts his arm round
her waist.*) The squanderbird's a pretty little creature, but
she gets through an awful lot of money. It's incredible what
an expensive pet she is for a man to keep.

NORA. For shame! How can you say such a thing? I save
every penny I can.

HELMER (*laughs*). That's quite true. Every penny you can.
But you can't.

NORA (*hums and smiles, quietly gleeful*). Hm. If you only
knew how many expenses we larks and squirrels have,
Torvald.

HELMER. You're a funny little creature. Just like your father
used to be. Always on the look-out for some way to get
money, but as soon as you have any it just runs through
your fingers, and you never know where it's gone. Well, I
suppose I must take you as you are. It's in your blood. Yes,
yes, yes, these things are hereditary, Nora.

NORA. Oh, I wish I'd inherited more of Papa's qualities.

HELMER. And I wouldn't wish my darling little songbird to be any different from what she is. By the way, that reminds me. You look awfully—how shall I put it?—awfully guilty today.

NORA. Do I?

HELMER. Yes, you do. Look me in the eyes.

NORA (looks at him). Well?

HELMER (wags his finger). Has my little sweet-tooth been indulging herself in town today, by any chance?

NORA. No, how can you think such a thing?

HELMER. Not a tiny little digression into a pastry shop?

NORA. No, Torvald, I promise—

HELMER. Not just a wee jam tart?

NORA. Certainly not.

HELMER. Not a little nibble at a macaroon?

NORA. No, Torvald—I promise you, honestly—

HELMER. There, there. I was only joking.

NORA (goes over to the table, right). You know I could never act against your wishes.

HELMER. Of course not. And you've given me your word— (Goes over to her.) Well, my beloved Nora, you keep your little Christmas secrets to yourself. They'll be revealed this evening, I've no doubt, once the Christmas tree has been lit.

NORA. Have you remembered to invite Dr. Rank?

HELMER. No. But there's no need; he knows he'll be dining with us. Anyway, I'll ask him when he comes this morning. I've ordered some good wine. Oh, Nora, you can't imagine how I'm looking forward to this evening.

NORA. So am I. And, Torvald, how the children will love it!

HELMER. Yes, it's a wonderful thing to know that one's position is assured and that one has an ample income. Don't you agree? It's good to know that, isn't it?

NORA. Yes, it's almost like a miracle.

HELMER. Do you remember last Christmas? For three whole weeks you shut yourself away every evening to make flowers for the Christmas tree, and all those other things

you were going to surprise us with. Ugh, it was the most
boring time I've ever had in my life.

NORA. I didn't find it boring.

HELMER (*smiles*). But it all came to nothing in the end, didn't
it?

NORA. Oh, are you going to bring that up again? How could
I help the cat getting in and tearing everything to bits?

HELMER. No, my poor little Nora, of course you couldn't. You
simply wanted to make us happy, and that's all that matters. But it's good that those hard times are past.

NORA. Yes, it's wonderful.

HELMER. I don't have to sit by myself and be bored. And you
don't have to tire your pretty eyes and your delicate little
hands—

NORA (*claps her hands*). No, Torvald, that's true, isn't it—I
don't have to any longer? Oh, it's really all just like a miracle. (*Takes his arm.*) Now, I'm going to tell you what I
thought we might do, Torvald. As soon as Christmas is
over— (*A bell rings in the hall.*) Oh, there's the doorbell.
(*Tidies up one or two things in the room.*) Someone's coming. What a bore.

HELMER. I'm not at home to any visitors. Remember!

MAID (*in the doorway*). A lady's called, madam. A stranger.

NORA. Well, ask her to come in.

MAID. And the doctor's here too, sir.

HELMER. Has he gone to my room?

MAID. Yes, sir.

HELMER *goes into his room. The* MAID *shows in* MRS. LINDE,
who is dressed in travelling clothes, and closes the door.

MRS. LINDE (*shyly and a little hesitantly*). Good evening,
Nora.

NORA (*uncertainly*). Good evening—

MRS. LINDE. I don't suppose you recognize me.

NORA. No, I'm afraid I— Yes, wait a minute—surely— (*Ex-
claims.*) Why, Christine! Is it really you?

MRS. LINDE. Yes, it's me.

NORA. Christine! And I didn't recognize you! But how could

I–? (*More quietly.*) How you've changed, Christine!

MRS. LINDE. Yes, I know. It's been nine years—nearly ten—

NORA. Is it so long? Yes, it must be. Oh, these last eight years have been such a happy time for me! So you've come to town? All that way in winter! How brave of you!

MRS. LINDE. I arrived by the steamer this morning.

NORA. Yes, of course—to enjoy yourself over Christmas. Oh, how splendid! We'll have to celebrate! But take off your coat. You're not cold, are you? (*Helps her off with it.*) There! Now let's sit down here by the stove and be comfortable. No, you take the armchair. I'll sit here in the rocking-chair. (*Clasps* MRS. LINDE's *hands.*) Yes, now you look like your old self. It was just at first that—you've got a little paler, though, Christine. And perhaps a bit thinner.

MRS. LINDE. And older, Nora. Much, much older.

NORA. Yes, perhaps a little older. Just a tiny bit. Not much. (*Checks herself suddenly and says earnestly.*) Oh, but how thoughtless of me to sit here and chatter away like this! Dear, sweet Christine, can you forgive me?

MRS. LINDE. What do you mean, Nora?

NORA (*quietly*). Poor Christine, you've become a widow.

MRS. LINDE. Yes. Three years ago.

NORA. I know, I know—I read it in the papers. Oh, Christine, I meant to write to you so often, honestly. But I always put it off, and something else always cropped up.

MRS. LINDE. I understand, Nora dear.

NORA. No, Christine, it was beastly of me. Oh, my poor darling, what you've gone through! And he didn't leave you anything?

MRS. LINDE. No.

NORA. No children, either?

MRS. LINDE. No.

NORA. Nothing at all, then?

MRS. LINDE. Not even a feeling of loss or sorrow.

NORA (*looks incredulously at her*). But, Christine, how is that possible?

MRS. LINDE (*smiles sadly and strokes* NORA's *hair*). Oh, these things happen, Nora.

NORA. All alone. How dreadful that must be for you. I've three
lovely children. I'm afraid you can't see them now, because
they're out with nanny. But you must tell me everything—

MRS. LINDE. No, no, no. I want to hear about you.

NORA. No, you start. I'm not going to be selfish today, I'm just
going to think about you. Oh, but there's one thing I *must*
tell you. Have you heard of the wonderful luck we've just
had?

MRS. LINDE. No. What?

NORA. Would you believe it—my husband's just been made
manager of the bank!

MRS. LINDE. Your husband? Oh, how lucky—!

NORA. Yes, isn't it? Being a lawyer is so uncertain, you know,
especially if one isn't prepared to touch any case that isn't
—well—quite nice. And of course Torvald's been very firm
about that—and I'm absolutely with him. Oh, you can imagine how happy we are! He's joining the bank in the New
Year, and he'll be getting a big salary, and lots of percent-
ages too. From now on we'll be able to live quite differently
—we'll be able to do whatever we want. Oh, Christine, it's
such a relief! I feel so happy! Well, I mean, it's lovely to
have heaps of money and not to have to worry about anything. Don't you think?

MRS. LINDE. It must be lovely to have enough to cover one's
needs, anyway.

NORA. Not just our needs! We're going to have heaps and
heaps of money!

MRS. LINDE (*smiles*). Nora, Nora, haven't you grown up yet?
When we were at school you were a terrible little spendthrift.

NORA (*laughs quietly*). Yes, Torvald still says that. (*Wags
her finger.*) But "Nora, Nora" isn't as silly as you think. Oh,
we've been in no position for me to waste money. We've
both had to work.

MRS. LINDE. You too?

NORA. Yes, little things—fancy work, crocheting, embroidery
and so forth. (*Casually.*) And other things too. I suppose
you know Torvald left the Ministry when we got married?

There were no prospects of promotion in his department, and of course he needed more money. But the first year he overworked himself quite dreadfully. He had to take on all sorts of extra jobs, and worked day and night. But it was too much for him, and he became frightfully ill. The doctors said he'd have to go to a warmer climate.

MRS. LINDE. Yes, you spent a whole year in Italy, didn't you?

NORA. Yes. It wasn't easy for me to get away, you know. I'd just had Ivar. But of course we had to do it. Oh, it was a marvellous trip! And it saved Torvald's life. But it cost an awful lot of money, Christine.

MRS. LINDE. I can imagine.

NORA. Two hundred and fifty pounds. That's a lot of money, you know.

MRS. LINDE. How lucky you had it.

NORA. Well, actually, we got it from my father.

MRS. LINDE. Oh, I see. Didn't he die just about that time?

NORA. Yes, Christine, just about then. Wasn't it dreadful, I couldn't go and look after him. I was expecting little Ivar any day. And then I had my poor Torvald to care for—we really didn't think he'd live. Dear, kind Papa! I never saw him again, Christine. Oh, it's the saddest thing that's happened to me since I got married.

MRS. LINDE. I know you were very fond of him. But you went to Italy—?

NORA. Yes. Well, we had the money, you see, and the doctors said we mustn't delay. So we went the month after Papa died.

MRS. LINDE. And your husband came back completely cured?

NORA. Fit as a fiddle!

MRS. LINDE. But—the doctor?

NORA. How do you mean?

MRS. LINDE. I thought the maid said that the gentleman who arrived with me was the doctor.

NORA. Oh yes, that's Doctor Rank, but he doesn't come because anyone's ill. He's our best friend, and he looks us up at least once every day. No, Torvald hasn't had a moment's illness since we went away. And the children are fit and

healthy and so am I. (*Jumps up and claps her hands.*) Oh
God, oh God, Christine, isn't it a wonderful thing to be
alive and happy! Oh, but how beastly of me! I'm only talk-
ing about myself. (*Sits on a footstool and rests her arms on*
MRS. LINDE's *knee.*) Oh, please don't be angry with me!
Tell me, is it really true you didn't love your husband?
Why did you marry him, then?

MRS. LINDE. Well, my mother was still alive; and she was
helpless and bedridden. And I had my two little brothers
to take care of. I didn't feel I could say no.

NORA. Yes, well, perhaps you're right. He was rich then, was
he?

MRS. LINDE. Quite comfortably off, I believe. But his business
was unsound, you see, Nora. When he died it went bankrupt, and there was nothing left.

NORA. What did you do?

MRS. LINDE. Well, I had to try to make ends meet somehow,
so I started a little shop, and a little school, and anything
else I could turn my hand to. These last three years have
been just one endless slog for me, without a moment's rest.
But now it's over, Nora. My poor dear mother doesn't need
me any more; she's passed away. And the boys don't need
me either; they've got jobs now and can look after themselves.

NORA. How relieved you must feel—

MRS. LINDE. No, Nora. Just unspeakably empty. No one to
live for any more. (*Gets up restlessly.*) That's why I
couldn't bear to stay out there any longer, cut off from the
world. I thought it'd be easier to find some work here that
will exercise and occupy my mind. If only I could get a
regular job—office work of some kind—

NORA. Oh but, Christine, that's dreadfully exhausting; and
you look practically finished already. It'd be much better
for you if you could go away somewhere.

MRS. LINDE (*goes over to the window*). I have no Papa to
pay for my holidays, Nora.

NORA (*gets up*). Oh, please don't be angry with me.

MRS. LINDE. My dear Nora, it's I who should ask you not to be

angry. That's the worst thing about this kind of situation
—it makes one so bitter. One has no one to work for; and
yet one has to be continually sponging for jobs. One has to
live; and so one becomes completely egocentric. When you
told me about this luck you've just had with Torvald's new
job—can you imagine?—I was happy not so much on your
account, as on my own.

NORA. How do you mean? Oh, I understand. You mean Torvald might be able to do something for you?

MRS. LINDE. Yes, I was thinking that.

NORA. He will too, Christine. Just you leave it to me. I'll lead
up to it so delicately, so delicately; I'll get him in the right
mood. Oh, Christine, I do so want to help you.

MRS. LINDE. It's sweet of you to bother so much about me,
Nora. Especially since you know so little of the worries and
hardships of life.

NORA. I? You say I know little of—?

MRS. LINDE (*smiles*). Well, good heavens—those bits of fancy
work of yours—well, really—! You're a child, Nora.

NORA (*tosses her head and walks across the room*). You
shouldn't say that so patronisingly.

MRS. LINDE. Oh?

NORA. You're like the rest. You all think I'm incapable of
getting down to anything serious—

MRS. LINDE. My dear—

NORA. You think I've never had any worries like the rest of
you.

MRS. LINDE. Nora dear, you've just told me about all your
difficulties—

NORA. Pooh—that! (*Quietly.*) I haven't told you about the big
thing.

MRS. LINDE. What big thing? What do you mean?

NORA. You patronise me, Christine; but you shouldn't. You're
proud that you've worked so long and so hard for your
mother.

MRS. LINDE. I don't patronise anyone, Nora. But you're right
—I am both proud and happy that I was able to make my
mother's last months on earth comparatively easy.

NORA. And you're also proud at what you've done for your brothers.

MRS. LINDE. I think I have a right to be.

NORA. I think so too. But let me tell you something, Christine. I too have done something to be proud and happy about.

MRS. LINDE. I don't doubt it. But—how do you mean?

NORA. Speak quietly! Suppose Torvald should hear! He mustn't, at any price—no one must know, Christine—no one but you.

MRS. LINDE. But what is this?

NORA. Come over here. (*Pulls her down on to the sofa beside her.*) Yes, Christine—I too have done something to be happy and proud about. It was I who saved Torvald's life.

MRS. LINDE. Saved his—? How did you save it?

NORA. I told you about our trip to Italy. Torvald couldn't have lived if he hadn't managed to get down there—

MRS. LINDE. Yes, well—your father provided the money—

NORA (*smiles*). So Torvald and everyone else thinks. But—

MRS. LINDE. Yes?

NORA. Papa didn't give us a penny. It was I who found the money.

MRS. LINDE. You? All of it?

NORA. Two hundred and fifty pounds. What do you say to that?

MRS. LINDE. But Nora, how could you? Did you win a lottery or something?

NORA (*scornfully*). Lottery? (*Sniffs.*) What would there be to be proud of in that?

MRS. LINDE. But where did you get it from, then?

NORA (*hums and smiles secretively*). Hm; tra-la-la-la!

MRS. LINDE. You couldn't have borrowed it.

NORA. Oh? Why not?

MRS. LINDE. Well, a wife can't borrow money without her husband's consent.

NORA (*tosses her head*). Ah, but when a wife has a little business sense, and knows how to be clever—

MRS. LINDE. But Nora, I simply don't understand—

NORA. You don't have to. No one has said I borrowed the

money. I could have got it in some other way. (*Throws herself back on the sofa.*) I could have got it from an admirer. When a girl's as pretty as I am—

MRS. LINDE. Nora, you're crazy!

NORA. You're dying of curiosity now, aren't you, Christine?

MRS. LINDE. Nora dear, you haven't done anything foolish?

NORA (*sits up again*). Is it foolish to save one's husband's life?

MRS. LINDE. I think it's foolish if without his knowledge you—

NORA. But the whole point was that he mustn't know! Great heavens, don't you see? He hadn't to know how dangerously ill he was. I was the one they told that his life was in danger and that only going to a warm climate could save him. Do you suppose I didn't try to think of other ways of getting him down there? I told him how wonderful it would be for me to go abroad like other young wives; I cried and prayed; I asked him to remember my condition, and said he ought to be nice and tender to me; and then I suggested he might quite easily borrow the money. But then he got almost angry with me, Christine. He said I was frivolous, and that it was his duty as a husband not to pander to my moods and caprices—I think that's what he called them. Well, well, I thought, you've got to be saved somehow. And then I thought of a way—

MRS. LINDE. But didn't your husband find out from your father that the money hadn't come from him?

NORA. No, never. Papa died just then. I'd thought of letting him into the plot and asking him not to tell. But since he was so ill—! And as things turned out, it didn't become necessary.

MRS. LINDE. And you've never told your husband about this?

NORA. For heaven's sake, no! What an idea! He's frightfully strict about such matters. And besides—he's so proud of being a *man*—it'd be so painful and humiliating for him to know that he owed anything to me. It'd completely wreck our relationship. This life we have built together would no longer exist.

MRS. LINDE. Will you never tell him?

NORA (*thoughtfully, half-smiling*). Yes—some time, perhaps.

Years from now, when I'm no longer pretty. You mustn't
laugh! I mean of course, when Torvald no longer loves me
as he does now; when it no longer amuses him to see me
dance and dress up and play the fool for him. Then it
might be useful to have something up my sleeve. (*Breaks
off.*) Stupid, stupid, stupid! That time will never come.
Well, what do you think of my big secret, Christine? I'm
not completely useless, am I? Mind you, all this has caused
me a frightful lot of worry. It hasn't been easy for me to
meet my obligations punctually. In case you don't know, in
the world of business there are things called quarterly instalments and interest, and they're a terrible problem to
cope with. So I've had to scrape a little here and save a
little there as best I can. I haven't been able to save much
on the housekeeping money, because Torvald likes to live
well; and I couldn't let the children go short of clothes—I
couldn't take anything out of what he gives me for them.
The poor little angels!

MRS. LINDE. So you've had to stint yourself, my poor Nora?

NORA. Of course. Well, after all, it was my problem. Whenever Torvald gave me money to buy myself new clothes,
I never used more than half of it; and I always bought
what was cheapest and plainest. Thank heaven anything
suits me, so that Torvald's never noticed. But it made me a
bit sad sometimes, because it's lovely to wear pretty
clothes. Don't you think?

MRS. LINDE. Indeed it is.

NORA. And then I've found one or two other sources of income. Last winter I managed to get a lot of copying to
do. So I shut myself away and wrote every evening, late
into the night. Oh, I often got so tired, so tired. But it was
great fun, though, sitting there working and earning
money. It was almost like being a man.

MRS. LINDE. But how much have you managed to pay off
like this?

NORA. Well, I can't say exactly. It's awfully difficult to keep
an exact check on these kind of transactions. I only know
I've paid everything I've managed to scrape together.

Sometimes I really didn't know where to turn. (*Smiles.*)
Then I'd sit here and imagine some rich old gentleman had
fallen in love with me—

MRS. LINDE. What! What gentleman?

NORA. Silly! And that now he'd died and when they opened
his will it said in big letters: "Everything I possess is to be
paid forthwith to my beloved Mrs. Nora Helmer in cash."

MRS. LINDE. But, Nora dear, who was this gentleman?

NORA. Great heavens, don't you understand? There wasn't
any old gentleman; he was just something I used to dream
up as I sat here evening after evening wondering how on
earth I could raise some money. But what does it matter?
The old bore can stay imaginary as far as I'm concerned,
because now I don't have to worry any longer! (*Jumps
up.*) Oh, Christine, isn't it wonderful? I don't have to worry
any more! No more troubles! I can play all day with the
children, I can fill the house with pretty things, just the
way Torvald likes. And, Christine, it'll soon be spring, and
the air'll be fresh and the skies blue,—and then perhaps
we'll be able to take a little trip somewhere. I shall be able
to see the sea again. Oh, yes, yes, it's a wonderful thing to
be alive and happy!

The bell rings in the hall.

MRS. LINDE (*gets up*). You've a visitor. Perhaps I'd better go.

NORA. No, stay. It won't be for me. It's someone for Torvald—

MAID (*in the doorway*). Excuse me, madam, a gentleman's
called who says he wants to speak to the master. But I
didn't know—seeing as the doctor's with him—

NORA. Who is this gentleman?

KROGSTAD (*in the doorway*). It's me, Mrs. Helmer.

MRS. LINDE *starts, composes herself and turns away to the
window.*

NORA (*takes a step towards him and whispers tensely*). You?
What is it? What do you want to talk to my husband about?

KROGSTAD. Business—you might call it. I hold a minor post in

the bank, and I hear your husband is to become our new
chief—

NORA. Oh—then it isn't—?

KROGSTAD. Pure business, Mrs. Helmer. Nothing more.

NORA. Well, you'll find him in his study.

*Nods indifferently as she closes the hall door behind him.
Then she walks across the room and sees to the stove.*

MRS. LINDE. Nora, who was that man?

NORA. A lawyer called Krogstad.

MRS. LINDE. It was him, then.

NORA. Do you know that man?

MRS. LINDE. I used to know him—some years ago. He was a
solicitor's clerk in our town, for a while.

NORA. Yes, of course, so he was.

MRS. LINDE. How he's changed!

NORA. He was very unhappily married, I believe.

MRS. LINDE. Is he a widower now?

NORA. Yes, with a lot of children. Ah, now it's alight.

*She closes the door of the stove and moves the rocking-chair
a little to one side.*

MRS. LINDE. He does—various things now, I hear?

NORA. Does he? It's quite possible—I really don't know. But
don't let's talk about business. It's so boring.

DR. RANK *enters from* HELMER's *study.*

RANK (*still in the doorway*). No, no, my dear chap, don't
see me out. I'll go and have a word with your wife. (*Closes
the door and notices* MRS. LINDE.) Oh, I beg your pardon.
I seem to be *de trop* here too.

NORA. Not in the least. (*Introduces them.*) Dr. Rank. Mrs.
Linde.

RANK. Ah! A name I have often heard in this house. I believe
I passed you on the stairs as I came up.

MRS. LINDE. Yes. Stairs tire me; I have to take them slowly.

RANK. Oh, have you hurt yourself?

MRS. LINDE. No, I'm just a little run down.

RANK. Ah, is that all? Then I take it you've come to town to cure yourself by a round of parties?

MRS. LINDE. I have come here to find work.

RANK. Is that an approved remedy for being run down?

MRS. LINDE. One has to live, Doctor.

RANK. Yes, people do seem to regard it as a necessity.

NORA. Oh, really, Dr. Rank. I bet you want to stay alive.

RANK. You bet I do. However miserable I sometimes feel, I still want to go on being tortured for as long as possible. It's the same with all my patients; and with people who are morally sick, too. There's a moral cripple in with Helmer at this very moment—

MRS. LINDE (*softly*). Oh!

NORA. Whom do you mean?

RANK. Oh, a lawyer fellow called Krogstad—you wouldn't know him. He's crippled all right; morally twisted. But even he started off by announcing, as though it were a matter of enormous importance, that he had to live.

NORA. Oh? What did he want to talk to Torvald about?

RANK. I haven't the faintest idea. All I heard was something about the bank.

NORA. I didn't know that Krog—that this man Krogstad had any connection with the bank.

RANK. Yes, he's got some kind of job down there. (*To* MRS. LINDE.) I wonder if in your part of the world you too have a species of human being that spends its time fussing around trying to smell out moral corruption? And when they find a case they give him some nice, comfortable position so that they can keep a good watch on him. The healthy ones just have to lump it.

MRS. LINDE. But surely it's the sick who need care most?

RANK (*shrugs his shoulders*). Well, there we have it. It's that attitude that's turning human society into a hospital.

NORA, *lost in her own thoughts, laughs half to herself and claps her hands.*

RANK. Why are you laughing? Do you really know what society is?

NORA. What do I care about society? I think it's a bore. I was laughing at something else—something frightfully funny. Tell me, Dr. Rank—will everyone who works at the bank come under Torvald now?

RANK. Do you find that particularly funny?

NORA (*smiles and hums*). Never you mind! Never you mind! (*Walks around the room.*) Yes, I find it very amusing to think that we—I mean, Torvald—has obtained so much influence over so many people. (*Takes the paper bag from her pocket.*) Dr. Rank, would you like a small macaroon?

RANK. Macaroons! I say! I thought they were forbidden here.

NORA. Yes, well, these are some Christine gave me.

MRS. LINDE. What? I—?

NORA. All right, all right, don't get frightened. You weren't to know Torvald had forbidden them. He's afraid they'll ruin my teeth. But, dash it—for once—! Don't you agree, Dr. Rank? Here! (*Pops a macaroon into his mouth.*) You too, Christine. And I'll have one too. Just a little one. Two at the most. (*Begins to walk round again.*) Yes, now I feel really, really happy. Now there's just one thing in the world I'd really love to do.

RANK. Oh? And what is that?

NORA. Just something I'd love to say to Torvald.

RANK. Well, why don't you say it?

NORA. No, I daren't. It's too dreadful.

MRS. LINDE. Dreadful?

RANK. Well, then, you'd better not. But you can say it to us. What is it you'd so love to say to Torvald?

NORA. I've the most extraordinary longing to say: "Bloody hell!"

RANK. Are you mad?

MRS. LINDE. My dear Nora—!

RANK. Say it. Here he is.

NORA (*hiding the bag of macaroons*). Ssh! Ssh!

HELMER, *with his overcoat on his arm and his hat in his hand, enters from his study.*

NORA (*goes to meet him*). Well, Torvald dear, did you get rid of him?

HELMER. Yes, he's just gone.

NORA. May I introduce you—? This is Christine. She's just arrived in town.

HELMER. Christine—? Forgive me, but I don't think—

NORA. Mrs. Linde, Torvald dear. Christine Linde.

HELMER. Ah. A childhood friend of my wife's, I presume?

MRS. LINDE. Yes, we knew each other in earlier days.

NORA. And imagine, now she's travelled all this way to talk to you.

HELMER. Oh?

MRS. LINDE. Well, I didn't really—

NORA. You see, Christine's frightfully good at office work, and she's mad to come under some really clever man who can teach her even more than she knows already—

HELMER. Very sensible, madam.

NORA. So when she heard you'd become head of the bank—it was in her local paper—she came here as quickly as she could and—Torvald, you will, won't you? Do a little something to help Christine? For my sake?

HELMER. Well, that shouldn't be impossible. You are a widow, I take it, Mrs. Linde?

MRS. LINDE. Yes.

HELMER. And you have experience of office work?

MRS. LINDE. Yes, quite a bit.

HELMER. Well then, it's quite likely I may be able to find some job for you—

NORA (*claps her hands*). You see, you see!

HELMER. You've come at a lucky moment, Mrs. Linde.

MRS. LINDE. Oh, how can I ever thank you—?

HELMER. There's absolutely no need. (*Puts on his overcoat.*) But now I'm afraid I must ask you to excuse me—

RANK. Wait. I'll come with you.

He gets his fur coat from the hall and warms it at the stove.

NORA. Don't be long, Torvald dear.

HELMER. I'll only be an hour.

NORA. Are you going too, Christine?

MRS. LINDE (*puts on her outdoor clothes*). Yes, I must start to look round for a room.

HELMER. Then perhaps we can walk part of the way together.

NORA (*helps her*). It's such a nuisance we're so cramped here —I'm afraid we can't offer to—

MRS. LINDE. Oh, I wouldn't dream of it. Goodbye, Nora dear, and thanks for everything.

NORA. *Au revoir.* You'll be coming back this evening, of course. And you too, Dr. Rank. What? If you're well enough? Of course you'll be well enough. Wrap up warmly, though.

They go out, talking, into the hall. Children's voices are heard from the stairs.

NORA. Here they are! Here they are!

She runs out and opens the door. ANNE-MARIE, *the nurse, enters with the children.*

NORA. Come in, come in! (*Stoops down and kisses them.*) Oh, my sweet darlings—! Look at them, Christine! Aren't they beautiful?

RANK. Don't stand here chattering in this draught!

HELMER. Come, Mrs. Linde. This is for mothers only.

DR. RANK, HELMER *and* MRS. LINDE *go down the stairs. The* NURSE *brings the children into the room.* NORA *follows, and closes the door to the hall.*

NORA. How well you look! What red cheeks you've got! Like apples and roses! (*The* CHILDREN *answer her inaudibly as she talks to them.*) Have you had fun? That's splendid. You gave Emmy and Bob a ride on the sledge? What, both together? I say! What a clever boy you are, Ivar! Oh, let me hold her for a moment, Anne-Marie! My sweet little baby doll! (*Takes the smallest child from the* NURSE *and dances with her.*) Yes, yes, Mummy will dance with Bob too. What? Have you been throwing snowballs? Oh, I wish I'd been there! No, don't—I'll undress them myself, Anne-

Marie. No, please let me; it's such fun. Go inside and warm yourself; you look frozen. There's some hot coffee on the stove. (*The* NURSE *goes into the room on the left.* NORA *takes off the children's outdoor clothes and throws them anywhere while they all chatter simultaneously.*) What? A big dog ran after you? But he didn't bite you? No, dogs don't bite lovely little baby dolls. Leave those parcels alone, Ivar. What's in them? Ah, wouldn't you like to know! No, no; it's nothing nice. Come on, let's play a game. What shall we play? Hide and seek. Yes, let's play hide and seek. Bob shall hide first. You want me to? All right, let me hide first.

NORA *and the* CHILDREN *play around the room, and in the adjacent room to the left, laughing and shouting. At length* NORA *hides under the table. The* CHILDREN *rush in, look, but cannot find her. Then they hear her half-stifled laughter, run to the table, lift up the cloth and see her. Great excitement. She crawls out as though to frighten them. Further excitement. Meanwhile, there has been a knock on the door leading from the hall, but no one has noticed it. Now the door is half-opened and* KROGSTAD *enters. He waits for a moment; the game continues.*

KROGSTAD. Excuse me, Mrs. Helmer—
NORA (*turns with a stifled cry and half jumps up*). Oh! What do you want?
KROGSTAD. I beg your pardon; the front door was ajar. Someone must have forgotten to close it.
NORA (*gets up*). My husband is not at home, Mr. Krogstad.
KROGSTAD. I know.
NORA. Well, what do you want here, then?
KROGSTAD. A word with you.
NORA. With—? (*To the* CHILDREN, *quietly.*) Go inside to Anne-Marie. What? No, the strange gentleman won't do anything to hurt Mummy. When he's gone we'll start playing again.

She takes the children into the room on the left and closes the door behind them.

NORA (*uneasy, tense*). You want to speak to me?

KROGSTAD. Yes.

NORA. Today? But it's not the first of the month yet.

KROGSTAD. No, it is Christmas Eve. Whether or not you have a merry Christmas depends on you.

NORA. What do you want? I can't give you anything today—

KROGSTAD. We won't talk about that for the present. There's something else. You have a moment to spare?

NORA. Oh, yes. Yes, I suppose so; though—

KROGSTAD. Good. I was sitting in the café down below and I saw your husband cross the street—

NORA. Yes.

KROGSTAD. With a lady.

NORA. Well?

KROGSTAD. Might I be so bold as to ask: was not that lady a Mrs. Linde?

NORA. Yes.

KROGSTAD. Recently arrived in town?

NORA. Yes, today.

KROGSTAD. She is a good friend of yours, is she not?

NORA. Yes, she is. But I don't see—

KROGSTAD. I used to know her too once.

NORA. I know.

KROGSTAD. Oh? You've discovered that. Yes, I thought you would. Well then, may I ask you a straight question: is Mrs. Linde to be employed at the bank?

NORA. How dare you presume to cross-examine me, Mr. Krogstad? You, one of my husband's employees? But since you ask, you shall have an answer. Yes, Mrs. Linde is to be employed by the bank. And I arranged it, Mr. Krogstad. Now you know.

KROGSTAD. I guessed right, then.

NORA (*walks up and down the room*). Oh, one has a little influence, you know. Just because one's a woman it doesn't necessarily mean that— When one is in a humble position, Mr. Krogstad, one should think twice before offending someone who—hm—

KROGSTAD. —who has influence?

NORA. Precisely.

KROGSTAD (*changes his tone*). Mrs. Helmer, will you have the kindness to use your influence on my behalf?

NORA. What? What do you mean?

KROGSTAD. Will you be so good as to see that I keep my humble position at the bank?

NORA. What do you mean? Who is thinking of removing you from your position?

KROGSTAD. Oh, you don't need to play the innocent with me. I realize it can't be very pleasant for your friend to risk bumping into me; and now I also realize whom I have to thank for being hounded out like this.

NORA. But I assure you—

KROGSTAD. Look, let's not beat about the bush. There's still time, and I'd advise you to use your influence to stop it.

NORA. But, Mr. Krogstad, I have no influence!

KROGSTAD. Oh? I thought you just said—

NORA. But I didn't mean it like that! I? How on earth could you imagine that I would have any influence over my husband?

KROGSTAD. Oh, I've known your husband since we were students together. I imagine he has his weaknesses like other married men.

NORA. If you speak impertinently of my husband, I shall show you the door.

KROGSTAD. You're a bold woman, Mrs. Helmer.

NORA. I'm not afraid of you any longer. Once the New Year is in, I'll soon be rid of you.

KROGSTAD (*more controlled*). Now listen to me, Mrs. Helmer. If I'm forced to, I shall fight for my little job at the bank as I would fight for my life.

NORA. So it sounds.

KROGSTAD. It isn't just the money; that's the last thing I care about. There's something else—well, you might as well know. It's like this, you see. You know of course, as everyone else does, that some years ago I committed an indiscretion.

NORA. I think I did hear something—

KROGSTAD. It never came into court; but from that day, every opening was barred to me. So I turned my hand to the kind of business you know about. I had to do something; and I don't think I was one of the worst. But now I want to give up all that. My sons are growing up; for their sake, I must try to regain what respectability I can. This job in the bank was the first step on the ladder. And now your husband wants to kick me off that ladder back into the dirt.

NORA. But my dear Mr. Krogstad, it simply isn't in my power to help you.

KROGSTAD. You say that because you don't want to help me. But I have the means to make you.

NORA. You don't mean you'd tell my husband that I owe you money?

KROGSTAD. And if I did?

NORA. That'd be a filthy trick! (*Almost in tears.*) This secret that is my pride and my joy—that he should hear about it in such a filthy, beastly way—hear about it from you! It'd involve me in the most dreadful unpleasantness—

KROGSTAD. Only—unpleasantness?

NORA (*vehemently*). All right, do it! You'll be the one who'll suffer. It'll show my husband the kind of man you are, and then you'll never keep your job.

KROGSTAD. I asked you whether it was merely domestic unpleasantness you were afraid of.

NORA. If my husband hears about it, he will of course immediately pay you whatever is owing. And then we shall have nothing more to do with you.

KROGSTAD (*takes a step closer*). Listen, Mrs. Helmer. Either you've a bad memory or else you know very little about financial transactions. I had better enlighten you.

NORA. What do you mean?

KROGSTAD. When your husband was ill, you came to me to borrow two hundred and fifty pounds.

NORA. I didn't know anyone else.

KROGSTAD. I promised to find that sum for you—

NORA. And you did find it.

KROGSTAD. I promised to find that sum for you on certain conditions. You were so worried about your husband's illness and so keen to get the money to take him abroad that I don't think you bothered much about the details. So it won't be out of place if I refresh your memory. Well—I promised to get you the money in exchange for an I.O.U., which I drew up.

NORA. Yes, and which I signed.

KROGSTAD. Exactly. But then I added a few lines naming your father as security for the debt. This paragraph was to be signed by your father.

NORA. Was to be? He did sign it.

KROGSTAD. I left the date blank for your father to fill in when he signed this paper. You remember, Mrs. Helmer?

NORA. Yes, I think so—

KROGSTAD. Then I gave you back this I.O.U. for you to post to your father. Is that not correct?

NORA. Yes.

KROGSTAD. And of course you posted it at once; for within five or six days you brought it along to me with your father's signature on it. Whereupon I handed you the money.

NORA. Yes, well. Haven't I repaid the instalments as agreed?

KROGSTAD. Mm—yes, more or less. But to return to what we were speaking about—that was a difficult time for you just then, wasn't it, Mrs. Helmer?

NORA. Yes, it was.

KROGSTAD. Your father was very ill, if I am not mistaken.

NORA. He was dying.

KROGSTAD. He did in fact die shortly afterwards?

NORA. Yes.

KROGSTAD. Tell me, Mrs. Helmer, do you by any chance remember the date of your father's death? The day of the month, I mean.

NORA. Papa died on the twenty-ninth of September.

KROGSTAD. Quite correct; I took the trouble to confirm it. And that leaves me with a curious little problem— (*Takes out a paper*)—which I simply cannot solve.

NORA. Problem? I don't see—

KROGSTAD. The problem, Mrs. Helmer, is that your father signed this paper three days after his death.

NORA. What? I don't understand—

KROGSTAD. Your father died on the twenty-ninth of September. But look at this. Here your father has dated his signature the second of October. Isn't that a curious little problem, Mrs. Helmer? (NORA *is silent.*) Can you suggest any explanation? (*She remains silent.*) And there's another curious thing. The words "second of October" and the year are written in a hand which is not your father's, but which I seem to know. Well, there's a simple explanation to that. Your father could have forgotten to write in the date when he signed, and someone else could have added it before the news came of his death. There's nothing criminal about that. It's the signature itself I'm wondering about. It *is* genuine, I suppose, Mrs. Helmer? It was your father who wrote his name here?

NORA (*after a short silence, throws back her head and looks defiantly at him*). No, it was not. It was I who wrote Papa's name there.

KROGSTAD. Look, Mrs. Helmer, do you realize this is a dangerous admission?

NORA. Why? You'll get your money.

KROGSTAD. May I ask you a question? Why didn't you send this paper to your father?

NORA. I couldn't. Papa was very ill. If I'd asked him to sign this, I'd have had to tell him what the money was for. But I couldn't have told him in his condition that my husband's life was in danger. I couldn't have done that!

KROGSTAD. Then you would have been wiser to have given up your idea of a holiday.

NORA. But I couldn't! It was to save my husband's life. I couldn't put it off.

KROGSTAD. But didn't it occur to you that you were being dishonest towards me?

NORA. I couldn't bother about that. I didn't care about you. I hated you because of all the beastly difficulties you'd put in my way when you knew how dangerously ill my husband was.

KROGSTAD. Mrs. Helmer, you evidently don't appreciate exactly what you have done. But I can assure you that it is no bigger nor worse a crime than the one I once committed, and thereby ruined my whole social position.

NORA. You? Do you expect me to believe that you would have taken a risk like that to save your wife's life?

KROGSTAD. The law does not concern itself with motives.

NORA. Then the law must be very stupid.

KROGSTAD. Stupid or not, if I show this paper to the police, you will be judged according to it.

NORA. I don't believe that. Hasn't a daughter the right to shield her father from worry and anxiety when he's old and dying? Hasn't a wife the right to save her husband's life? I don't know much about the law, but there must be something somewhere that says that such things are allowed. You ought to know about that, you're meant to be a laywer, aren't you? You can't be a very good lawyer, Mr. Krogstad.

KROGSTAD. Possibly not. But business, the kind of business we two have been transacting—I think you'll admit I understand something about that? Good. Do as you please. But I tell you this. If I get thrown into the gutter for a second time, I shall take you with me.

He bows and goes out through the hall.

NORA (*stands for a moment in thought, then tosses her head*). What nonsense! He's trying to frighten me! I'm not that stupid. (*Busies herself gathering together the children's clothes; then she suddenly stops.*) But—? No, it's impossible. I did it for love, didn't I?

THE CHILDREN (*in the doorway, left*). Mummy, the strange gentleman's gone out into the street.

NORA. Yes, yes, I know. But don't talk to anyone about the strange gentleman. You hear? Not even to Daddy.

CHILDREN. No, Mummy. Will you play with us again now?

NORA. No, no. Not now.

CHILDREN. Oh but, Mummy, you promised!

NORA. I know, but I can't just now. Go back to the nursery. I've a lot to do. Go away, my darlings, go away. (*She pushes them gently into the other room, and closes the door behind them. She sits on the sofa, takes up her embroidery, stitches for a few moments, but soon stops.*) No! (*Throws the embroidery aside, gets up, goes to the door leading to the hall and calls.*) Helen! Bring in the Christmas tree! (*She goes to the table on the left and opens the drawer in it; then pauses again.*) No, but it's utterly impossible!

MAID (*enters with the tree*). Where shall I put it, madam?

NORA. There, in the middle of the room.

MAID. Will you be wanting anything else?

NORA. No, thank you. I have everything I need.

The MAID *puts down the tree and goes out.*

NORA (*busy decorating the tree*). Now—candles here—and flowers here. That loathsome man! Nonsense, nonsense, there's nothing to be frightened about. The Christmas tree must be beautiful. I'll do everything that you like, Torvald. I'll sing for you, dance for you—

HELMER, *with a bundle of papers under his arm, enters.*

NORA. Oh—are you back already?

HELMER. Yes. Has anyone been here?

NORA. Here? No.

HELMER. That's strange. I saw Krogstad come out of the front door.

NORA. Did you? Oh yes, that's quite right—Krogstad was here for a few minutes.

HELMER. Nora, I can tell from your face, he's been here and asked you to put in a good word for him.

NORA. Yes.

HELMER. And you were to pretend you were doing it of your own accord? You weren't going to tell me he'd been here? He asked you to do that too, didn't he?

NORA. Yes, Torvald. But—

HELMER. Nora, Nora! And you were ready to enter into such a conspiracy? Talking to a man like that, and making him promises—and then, on top of it all, to tell me me an untruth!

NORA. An untruth?

HELMER. Didn't you say no one had been here? (*Wags his finger.*) My little songbird must never do that again. A songbird must have a clean beak to sing with; otherwise she'll start twittering out of tune. (*Puts his arm round her waist.*) Isn't that the way we want things? Yes, of course it is. (*Lets go of her.*) So let's hear no more about that. (*Sits down in front of the stove.*) Ah, how cosy and peaceful it is here. (*Glances for a few moments at his papers.*)

NORA (*busy with the tree; after a short silence*). Torvald.

HELMER. Yes.

NORA. I'm terribly looking forward to that fancy dress ball at the Stenborgs on Boxing Day.

HELMER. And I'm terribly curious to see what you're going to surprise me with.

NORA. Oh, it's so maddening.

HELMER. What is?

NORA. I can't think of anything to wear. It all seems so stupid and meaningless.

HELMER. So my little Nora's come to that conclusion, has she?

NORA (*behind his chair, resting her arms on its back*). Are you very busy, Torvald?

HELMER. Oh—

NORA. What are those papers?

HELMER. Just something to do with the bank.

NORA. Already?

HELMER. I persuaded the trustees to give me authority to make certain immediate changes in the staff and organization. I want to have everything straight by the New Year.

NORA. Then that's why this poor man Krogstad—

HELMER. Hm.

NORA (*still leaning over his chair, slowly strokes the back of his head*). If you hadn't been so busy, I was going to ask you an enormous favour, Torvald.

HELMER. Well, tell me. What was it to be?

NORA. You know I trust your taste more than anyone's. I'm so anxious to look really beautiful at the fancy dress ball. Torvald, couldn't you help me to decide what I shall go as, and what kind of costume I ought to wear?

HELMER. Aha! So little Miss Independent's in trouble and needs a man to rescue her, does she?

NORA. Yes, Torvald. I can't get anywhere without your help.

HELMER. Well, well, I'll give the matter thought. We'll find something.

NORA. Oh, how kind of you! (*Goes back to the tree. Pause.*) How pretty these red flowers look! But, tell me, is it so dreadful, this thing that Krogstad's done?

HELMER. He forged someone else's name. Have you any idea what that means?

NORA. Mightn't he have been forced to do it by some emergency?

HELMER. He probably just didn't think—that's what usually happens. I'm not so heartless as to condemn a man for an isolated action.

NORA. No, Torvald, of course not!

HELMER. Men often succeed in re-establishing themselves if they admit their crime and take their punishment.

NORA. Punishment?

HELMER. But Krogstad didn't do that. He chose to try and trick his way out of it; and that's what has morally destroyed him.

NORA. You think that would—?

HELMER. Just think how a man with that load on his conscience must always be lying and cheating and dissembling; how he must wear a mask even in the presence of those who are dearest to him, even his own wife and children! Yes, the children. That's the worst danger, Nora.

NORA. Why?

HELMER. Because an atmosphere of lies contaminates and poisons every corner of the home. Every breath that the children draw in such a house contains the germs of evil.

NORA (*comes closer behind him*). Do you really believe that?

HELMER. Oh, my dear, I've come across it so often in my work at the bar. Nearly all young criminals are the children of mothers who are constitutional liars.

NORA. Why do you say mothers?

HELMER. It's usually the mother; though of course the father can have the same influence. Every lawyer knows that only too well. And yet this fellow Krogstad has been sitting at home all these years poisoning his children with his lies and pretences. That's why I say that, morally speaking, he is dead. (*Stretches out his hands towards her.*) So my pretty little Nora must promise me not to plead his case. Your hand on it. Come, come, what's this? Give me your hand. There. That's settled, now. I assure you it'd be quite impossible for me to work in the same building as him. I literally feel physically ill in the presence of a man like that.

NORA (*draws her hand from his and goes over to the other side of the Christmas tree*). How hot it is in here! And I've so much to do.

HELMER (*gets up and gathers his papers*). Yes, and I must try to get some of this read before dinner. I'll think about your costume too. And I may even have something up my sleeve to hang in gold paper on the Christmas tree. (*Lays his hand on her head.*) My precious little songbird!

He goes into his study and closes the door.

NORA (*softly, after a pause*). It's nonsense. It must be. It's impossible. It *must* be impossible!

NURSE (*in the doorway, left*). The children are asking if they can come in to Mummy.

NORA. No, no, no; don't let them in! You stay with them, Anne-Marie.

NURSE. Very good, madam. (*Closes the door.*)

NORA (*pale with fear*). Corrupt my little children—! Poison my home! (*Short pause. She throws back her head.*) It isn't true! It *couldn't* be true!

ACT TWO

The same room. In the corner by the piano the Christmas tree stands, stripped and dishevelled, its candles burned to their sockets. NORA's *outdoor clothes lie on the sofa. She is alone in the room, walking restlessly to and fro. At length she stops by the sofa and picks up her coat.*

NORA (*drops the coat again*). There's someone coming! (*Goes to the door and listens.*) No, it's no one. Of course—no one'll come today, it's Christmas Day. Nor tomorrow. But perhaps—! (*Opens the door and looks out.*) No. Nothing in the letter-box. Quite empty. (*Walks across the room.*) Silly, silly. Of course he won't do anything. It couldn't happen. It isn't possible. Why, I've three small children.

The NURSE, *carrying a large cardboard box, enters from the room on the left.*

NURSE. I found those fancy dress clothes at last, madam.

NORA. Thank you. Put them on the table.

NURSE (*does so*). They're all rumpled up.

NORA. Oh, I wish I could tear them into a million pieces!

NURSE. Why, madam! They'll be all right. Just a little patience.

NORA. Yes, of course. I'll go and get Mrs. Linde to help me.

NURSE. What, out again? In this dreadful weather? You'll catch a chill, madam.

NORA. Well, that wouldn't be the worst. How are the children?

NURSE. Playing with their Christmas presents, poor little dears. But—

NORA. Are they still asking to see me?

NURSE. They're so used to having their Mummy with them.

NORA. Yes, but, Anne-Marie, from now on I shan't be able to spend so much time with them.

NURSE. Well, children get used to anything in time.

NORA. Do you think so? Do you think they'd forget their mother if she went away from them—for ever?

NURSE. Mercy's sake, madam! For ever!

NORA. Tell me, Anne-Marie—I've so often wondered. How could you bear to give your child away—to strangers?

NURSE. But I had to when I came to nurse my little Miss Nora.

NORA. Do you mean you wanted to?

NURSE. When I had the chance of such a good job? A poor girl what's got into trouble can't afford to pick and choose. That good-for-nothing didn't lift a finger.

NORA. But your daughter must have completely forgotten you.

NURSE. Oh no, indeed she hasn't. She's written to me twice, once when she got confirmed and then again when she got married.

NORA (hugs her). Dear old Anne-Marie, you were a good mother to me.

NURSE. Poor little Miss Nora, you never had any mother but me.

NORA. And if my little ones had no one else, I know you would—no, silly, silly, silly! (Opens the cardboard box.) Go back to them, Anne-Marie. Now I must— Tomorrow you'll see how pretty I shall look.

NURSE. Why, there'll be no one at the ball as beautiful as my Miss Nora.

She goes into the room, left.

NORA (begins to unpack the clothes from the box, but soon throws them down again). Oh, if only I dared go out! If I could be sure no one would come, and nothing would happen while I was away! Stupid, stupid! No one will come. I just mustn't think about it. Brush this muff. Pretty gloves, pretty gloves! Don't think about it, don't think about it!

One, two, three, four, five, six— (*Cries.*) Ah—they're
coming—!

She begins to run towards the door, but stops uncertainly.
MRS. LINDE *enters from the hall, where she has been taking
off her outdoor clothes.*

NORA. Oh, it's you, Christine. There's no one else out there,
is there? Oh, I'm so glad you've come.

MRS. LINDE. I hear you were at my room asking for me.

NORA. Yes, I just happened to be passing. I want to ask you
to help me with something. Let's sit down here on the
sofa. Look at this. There's going to be a fancy dress ball
tomorrow night upstairs at Consul Stenborg's, and Torvald
wants me to go as a Neapolitan fisher-girl and dance the
tarantella. I learned it on Capri.

MRS. LINDE. I say, are you going to give a performance?

NORA. Yes, Torvald says I should. Look, here's the dress.
Torvald had it made for me in Italy; but now it's all so torn,
I don't know—

MRS. LINDE. Oh, we'll soon put that right; the stitching's just
come away. Needle and thread? Ah, here we are.

NORA. You're being awfully sweet.

MRS. LINDE (*sews*). So you're going to dress up tomorrow,
Nora? I must pop over for a moment to see how you look.
Oh, but I've completely forgotten to thank you for that
nice evening yesterday.

NORA (*gets up and walks across the room*). Oh, I didn't think
it was as nice as usual. You ought to have come to town a
little earlier, Christine. . . . Yes, Torvald understands
how to make a home look attractive.

MRS. LINDE. I'm sure you do, too. You're not your father's
daughter for nothing. But, tell me. Is Dr. Rank always in
such low spirits as he was yesterday?

NORA. No, last night it was very noticeable. But he's got a
terrible disease; he's got spinal tuberculosis, poor man. His
father was a frightful creature who kept mistresses and so
on. As a result Dr. Rank has been sickly ever since he was
a child—you understand—

MRS. LINDE (*puts down her sewing*). But, my dear Nora, how on earth did you get to know about such things?

NORA (*walks about the room*). Oh, don't be silly, Christine— when one has three children, one comes into contact with women who—well, who know about medical matters, and they tell one a thing or two.

MRS. LINDE (*sews again; a short silence*). Does Dr. Rank visit you every day?

NORA. Yes, every day. He's Torvald's oldest friend, and a good friend to me too. Dr. Rank's almost one of the family.

MRS. LINDE. But, tell me—is he quite sincere? I mean, doesn't he rather say the sort of thing he thinks people want to hear?

NORA. No, quite the contrary. What gave you that idea?

MRS. LINDE. When you introduced me to him yesterday, he said he'd often heard my name mentioned here. But later I noticed your husband had no idea who I was. So how could Dr. Rank—?

NORA. Yes, that's quite right, Christine. You see, Torvald's so hopelessly in love with me that he wants to have me all to himself—those were his very words. When we were first married, he got quite jealous if I as much as mentioned any of my old friends back home. So naturally, I stopped talking about them. But I often chat with Dr. Rank about that kind of thing. He enjoys it, you see.

MRS. LINDE. Now listen, Nora. In many ways you're still a child; I'm a bit older than you and have a little more experience of the world. There's something I want to say to you. You ought to give up this business with Dr. Rank.

NORA. What business?

MRS. LINDE. Well, everything. Last night you were speaking about this rich admirer of yours who was going to give you money—

NORA. Yes, and who doesn't exist—unfortunately. But what's that got to do with—?

MRS. LINDE. Is Dr. Rank rich?

NORA. Yes.

MRS. LINDE. And he has no dependants?

NORA. No, no one. But—

MRS. LINDE. And he comes here to see you every day?

NORA. Yes, I've told you.

MRS. LINDE. But how dare a man of his education be so forward?

NORA. What on earth are you talking about?

MRS. LINDE. Oh, stop pretending, Nora. Do you think I haven't guessed who it was who lent you that two hundred pounds?

NORA. Are you out of your mind? How could you imagine such a thing? A friend, someone who comes here every day! Why, that'd be an impossible situation!

MRS. LINDE. Then it really wasn't him?

NORA. No, of course not. I've never for a moment dreamed of—anyway, he hadn't any money to lend then. He didn't come into that till later.

MRS. LINDE. Well, I think that was a lucky thing for you, Nora dear.

NORA. No, I could never have dreamed of asking Dr. Rank— Though I'm sure that if I ever did ask him—

MRS. LINDE. But of course you won't.

NORA. Of course not. I can't imagine that it should ever become necessary. But I'm perfectly sure that if I did speak to Dr. Rank—

MRS. LINDE. Behind your husband's back?

NORA. I've got to get out of this other business; and *that's* been going on behind his back. I've *got* to get out of it.

MRS. LINDE. Yes, well, that's what I told you yesterday. But—

NORA (*walking up and down*). It's much easier for a man to arrange these things than a woman—

MRS. LINDE. One's own husband, yes.

NORA. Oh, bosh. (*Stops walking.*) When you've completely repaid a debt, you get your I.O.U. back, don't you?

MRS. LINDE. Yes, of course.

NORA. And you can tear it into a thousand pieces and burn the filthy, beastly thing!

MRS. LINDE (*looks hard at her, puts down her sewing and*

gets up slowly). Nora, you're hiding something from me.

NORA. Can you see that?

MRS. LINDE. Something has happened since yesterday morning. Nora, what is it?

NORA *(goes towards her).* Christine! *(Listens.)* Ssh! There's Torvald. Would you mind going into the nursery for a few minutes? Torvald can't bear to see sewing around. Anne-Marie'll help you.

MRS. LINDE *(gathers some of her things together).* Very well. But I shan't leave this house until we've talked this matter out.

She goes into the nursery, left. As she does so, HELMER *enters from the hall.*

NORA *(runs to meet him).* Oh, Torvald dear, I've been so longing for you to come back!

HELMER. Was that the dressmaker?

NORA. No, it was Christine. She's helping me mend my costume. I'm going to look rather splendid in that.

HELMER. Yes, that was quite a bright idea of mine, wasn't it?

NORA. Wonderful! But wasn't it nice of me to give in to you?

HELMER *(takes her chin in his hand).* Nice—to give in to your husband? All right, little silly, I know you didn't mean it like that. But I won't disturb you. I expect you'll be wanting to try it on.

NORA. Are you going to work now?

HELMER. Yes. *(Shows her a bundle of papers.)* Look at these. I've been down to the bank— *(Turns to go into his study.)*

NORA. Torvald.

HELMER *(stops).* Yes.

NORA. If little squirrel asked you really prettily to grant her a wish—

HELMER. Well?

NORA. Would you grant it to her?

HELMER. First I should naturally have to know what it was.

NORA. Squirrel would do lots of pretty tricks for you if you granted her wish.

HELMER. Out with it, then.

NORA. Your little skylark would sing in every room—

HELMER. My little skylark does that already.

NORA. I'd turn myself into a little fairy and dance for you in the moonlight, Torvald.

HELMER. Nora, it isn't that business you were talking about this morning?

NORA (*comes closer*). Yes, Torvald—oh, please! I beg of you!

HELMER. Have you really the nerve to bring that up again?

NORA. Yes, Torvald, yes, you must do as I ask! You must let Krogstad keep his place at the bank!

HELMER. My dear Nora, his is the job I'm giving to Mrs. Linde.

NORA. Yes, that's terribly sweet of you. But you can get rid of one of the other clerks instead of Krogstad.

HELMER. Really, you're being incredibly obstinate. Just because you thoughtlessly promised to put in a word for him, you expect me to—

NORA. No, it isn't that, Helmer. It's for your own sake. That man writes for the most beastly newspapers—you said so yourself. He could do you tremendous harm. I'm so dreadfully frightened of him—

HELMER. Oh, I understand. Memories of the past. That's what's frightening you.

NORA. What do you mean?

HELMER. You're thinking of your father, aren't you?

NORA. Yes, yes. Of course. Just think what those dreadful men wrote in the papers about Papa! The most frightful slanders. I really believe it would have lost him his job if the Ministry hadn't sent you down to investigate, and you hadn't been so kind and helpful to him.

HELMER. But my dear little Nora, there's a considerable difference between your father and me. Your father was not a man of unassailable reputation. But I am; and I hope to remain so all my life.

NORA. But no one knows what spiteful people may not dig up. We could be so peaceful and happy now, Torvald—we could be free from every worry—you and I and the children. Oh, please, Torvald, please—!

HELMER. The very fact of your pleading his cause makes it impossible for me to keep him. Everyone at the bank already knows that I intend to dismiss Krogstad. If the rumour got about that the new manager had allowed his wife to persuade him to change his mind—

NORA. Well, what then?

HELMER. Oh, nothing, nothing. As long as my little Miss Obstinate gets her way—! Do you expect me to make a laughing-stock of myself before my entire staff—give people the idea that I am open to outside influence? Believe me, I'd soon feel the consequences! Besides—there's something else that makes it impossible for Krogstad to remain in the bank while I am its manager.

NORA. What is that?

HELMER. I might conceivably have allowed myself to ignore his moral obloquies—

NORA. Yes, Torvald, surely?

HELMER. And I hear he's quite efficient at his job. But we —well, we were schoolfriends. It was one of those friendships that one enters into over-hastily and so often comes to regret later in life. I might as well confess the truth. We—well, we're on Christian name terms. And the tactless idiot makes no attempt to conceal it when other people are present. On the contrary, he thinks it gives him the right to be familiar with me. He shows off the whole time, with "Torvald this," and "Torvald that." I can tell you, I find it damned annoying. If he stayed, he'd make my position intolerable.

NORA. Torvald, you can't mean this seriously.

HELMER. Oh? And why not?

NORA. But it's so petty.

HELMER. What did you say? Petty? You think I am petty?

NORA. No, Torvald dear, of course you're not. That's just why—

HELMER. Don't quibble! You call my motives petty. Then I must be petty too. Petty! I see. Well, I've had enough of this. (*Goes to the door and calls into the hall.*) Helen!

NORA. What are you going to do?

HELMER (*searching among his papers*). I'm going to settle this matter once and for all. (*The* MAID *enters.*) Take this letter downstairs at once. Find a messenger and see that he delivers it. Immediately! The address is on the envelope. Here's the money.

MAID. Very good, sir. (*Goes out with the letter.*)

HELMER (*putting his papers in order*). There now, little Miss Obstinate.

NORA (*tensely*). Torvald—what was in that letter?

HELMER. Krogstad's dismissal.

NORA. Call her back, Torvald! There's still time. Oh, Torvald, call her back! Do it for my sake—for your own sake—for the children! Do you hear me, Torvald? Please do it! You don't realize what this may do to us all!

HELMER. Too late.

NORA. Yes. Too late.

HELMER. My dear Nora, I forgive you this anxiety. Though it is a bit of an insult to me. Oh, but it is! Isn't it an insult to imply that I should be frightened by the vindictiveness of a depraved hack journalist? But I forgive you, because it so charmingly testifies to the love you bear me. (*Takes her in his arms.*) Which is as it should be, my own dearest Nora. Let what will happen, happen. When the real crisis comes, you will not find me lacking in strength or courage. I am man enough to bear the burden for us both.

NORA (*fearfully*). What do you mean?

HELMER. The whole burden, I say—

NORA (*calmly*). I shall never let you do that.

HELMER. Very well. We shall share it, Nora—as man and wife. And that is as it should be. (*Caresses her.*) Are you happy now? There, there, there; don't look at me with those frightened little eyes. You're simply imagining things. You go ahead now and do your tarantella, and get some practice on that tambourine. I'll sit in my study and close the door. Then I won't hear anything, and you can make all the noise you want. (*Turns in the doorway.*) When Dr. Rank comes, tell him where to find me. (*He nods to her, goes into his room with his papers and closes the door.*)

NORA (*desperate with anxiety, stands as though transfixed, and whispers*). He said he'd do it. He will do it. He will do it, and nothing'll stop him. No, never that. I'd rather anything. There must be some escape—! Some way out—! (*The bell rings in the hall.*) Dr. Rank—! Anything but that! Anything, I don't care—!

She passes her hand across her face, composes herself, walks across and opens the door to the hall. DR. RANK *is standing there, hanging up his fur coat. During the following scene it begins to grow dark.*

NORA. Good evening, Dr. Rank. I recognized your ring. But you mustn't go in to Torvald yet. I think he's busy.

RANK. And—you?

NORA (*as he enters the room and she closes the door behind him*). Oh, you know very well I've always time to talk to you.

RANK. Thank you. I shall avail myself of that privilege as long as I can.

NORA. What do you mean by that? As long as you *can?*

RANK. Yes. Does that frighten you?

NORA. Well, it's rather a curious expression. Is something going to happen?

RANK. Something I've been expecting to happen for a long time. But I didn't think it would happen quite so soon.

NORA (*seizes his arm*). What is it? Dr. Rank, you must tell me!

RANK (*sits down by the stove*). I'm on the way out. And there's nothing to be done about it.

NORA (*sighs with relief*). Oh, it's you—?

RANK. Who else? No, it's no good lying to oneself. I am the most wretched of all my patients, Mrs. Helmer. These last few days I've been going through the books of this poor body of mine, and I find I am bankrupt. Within a month I may be rotting up there in the churchyard.

NORA. Ugh, what a nasty way to talk!

RANK. The facts aren't exactly nice. But the worst is that there's so much else that's nasty to come first. I've only one more test to make. When that's done I'll have a pretty accurate idea of when the final disintegration is likely to begin. I want to ask you a favour. Helmer's a sensitive chap, and I know how he hates anything ugly. I don't want him to visit me when I'm in hospital—

NORA. Oh but, Dr. Rank—

RANK. I don't want him there. On any pretext. I shan't have him allowed in. As soon as I know the worst, I'll send you my visiting card with a black cross on it, and then you'll know that the final filthy process has begun.

NORA. Really, you're being quite impossible this evening. And I did hope you'd be in a good mood.

RANK. With death on my hands? And all this to atone for someone else's sin? Is there justice in that? And in every single family, in one way or another, the same merciless law of retribution is at work—

NORA (holds her hands to her ears). Nonsense! Cheer up! Laugh!

RANK. Yes, you're right. Laughter's all the damned thing's fit for. My poor innocent spine must pay for the fun my father had as a gay young lieutenant.

NORA (at the table, left). You mean he was too fond of asparagus and foie gras?

RANK. Yes; and truffles too.

NORA. Yes, of course, truffles, yes. And oysters too, I suppose?

RANK. Yes, oysters, oysters. Of course.

NORA. And all that port and champagne to wash them down. It's too sad that all those lovely things should affect one's spine.

RANK. Especially a poor spine that never got any pleasure out of them.

NORA. Oh yes, that's the saddest thing of all.

RANK (looks searchingly at her). Hm—

NORA (after a moment). Why did you smile?

RANK. No, it was you who laughed.

NORA. No, it was you who smiled, Dr. Rank!

RANK (gets up). You're a worse little rogue than I thought.

NORA. Oh, I'm full of stupid tricks today.

RANK. So it seems.

NORA (*puts both her hands on his shoulders*). Dear, dear Dr. Rank, you mustn't die and leave Torvald and me.

RANK. Oh, you'll soon get over it. Once one is gone, one is soon forgotten.

NORA (*looks at him anxiously*). Do you believe that?

RANK. One finds replacements, and then—

NORA. Who will find a replacement?

RANK. You and Helmer both will, when I am gone. You seem to have made a start already, haven't you? What was this Mrs. Linde doing here yesterday evening?

NORA. Aha! But surely you can't be jealous of poor Christine?

RANK. Indeed I am. She will be my successor in this house. When I have moved on, this lady will—

NORA. Ssh—don't speak so loud! She's in there!

RANK. Today again? You see!

NORA. She's only come to mend my dress. Good heavens, how unreasonable you are! (*Sits on the sofa.*) Be nice now, Dr. Rank. Tomorrow you'll see how beautifully I shall dance; and you must imagine that I'm doing it just for you. And for Torvald, of course; obviously. (*Takes some things out of the box.*) Dr. Rank, sit down here and I'll show you something.

RANK (*sits*). What's this?

NORA. Look here! Look!

RANK. Silk stockings!

NORA. Flesh-coloured. Aren't they beautiful? It's very dark in here now, of course, but tomorrow—! No, no, no; only the soles. Oh well, I suppose you can look a bit higher if you want to.

RANK. Hm—

NORA. Why are you looking so critical? Don't you think they'll fit me?

RANK. I can't really give you a qualified opinion on that.

NORA (*looks at him for a moment*). Shame on you! (*Flicks him on the ear with the stockings.*) Take that. (*Puts them back in the box.*)

RANK. What other wonders are to be revealed to me?

NORA. I shan't show you anything else. You're being naughty.

She hums a little and looks among the things in the box.

RANK (*after a short silence*). When I sit here like this being so intimate with you, I can't think—I cannot imagine what would have become of me if I had never entered this house.

NORA (*smiles*). Yes, I think you enjoy being with us, don't you?

RANK (*more quietly, looking into the middle distance*). And now to have to leave it all—

NORA. Nonsense. You're not leaving us.

RANK (*as before*). And not to be able to leave even the most wretched token of gratitude behind; hardly even a passing sense of loss; only an empty place, to be filled by the next comer.

NORA. Suppose I were to ask you to—? No—

RANK. To do what?

NORA. To give me proof of your friendship—

RANK. Yes, yes?

NORA. No, I mean—to do me a very great service—

RANK. Would you really for once grant me that happiness?

NORA. But you've no idea what it is.

RANK. Very well, tell me, then.

NORA. No, but, Dr. Rank, I can't. It's far too much—I want your help and advice, and I want you to do something for me.

RANK. The more the better. I've no idea what it can be. But tell me. You do trust me, don't you?

NORA. Oh, yes, more than anyone. You're my best and truest friend. Otherwise I couldn't tell you. Well then, Dr. Rank —there's something you must help me to prevent. You know how much Torvald loves me—he'd never hesitate for an instant to lay down his life for me—

RANK (*leans over towards her*). Nora—do you think he is the only one—?

NORA (*with a slight start*). What do you mean?

RANK. Who would gladly lay down his life for you?

NORA (*sadly*). Oh, I see.

RANK. I swore to myself I would let you know that before I go. I shall never have a better opportunity. . . . Well, Nora, now you know that. And now you also know that you can trust me as you can trust nobody else.

NORA (*rises; calmly and quietly*). Let me pass, please.

RANK (*makes room for her but remains seated*). Nora—

NORA (*in the doorway to the hall*). Helen, bring the lamp. (*Goes over to the stove.*) Oh, dear Dr. Rank, this was really horrid of you.

RANK (*gets up*). That I have loved you as deeply as anyone else has? Was that horrid of me?

NORA. No—but that you should go and tell me. That was quite unnecessary—

RANK. What do you mean? Did you know, then—?

The MAID *enters with the lamp, puts it on the table and goes out.*

RANK. Nora—Mrs. Helmer—I am asking you, did you know this?

NORA. Oh, what do I know, what did I know, what didn't I know—I really can't say. How could you be so stupid, Dr. Rank? Everything was so nice.

RANK. Well, at any rate now you know that I am ready to serve you, body and soul. So—please continue.

NORA (*looks at him*). After this?

RANK. Please tell me what it is.

NORA. I can't possibly tell you now.

RANK. Yes, yes! You mustn't punish me like this. Let me be allowed to do what I can for you.

NORA. You can't do anything for me now. Anyway, I don't need any help. It was only my imagination—you'll see. Yes, really. Honestly. (*Sits in the rocking chair, looks at him and smiles.*) Well, upon my word you *are* a fine gentleman, Dr. Rank. Aren't you ashamed of yourself, now that the lamp's been lit?

RANK. Frankly, no. But perhaps I ought to say—*adieu?*

NORA. Of course not. You will naturally continue to visit us as

before. You know quite well how Torvald depends on your
company.

RANK. Yes, but you?

NORA. Oh, I always think it's enormous fun having you here.

RANK. That was what misled me. You're a riddle to me, you
know. I'd often felt you'd just as soon be with me as with
Helmer.

NORA. Well, you see, there are some people whom one loves,
and others whom it's almost more fun to be with.

RANK. Oh yes, there's some truth in that.

NORA. When I was at home, of course I loved Papa best. But
I always used to think it was terribly amusing to go down
and talk to the servants; because they never told me what
I ought to do; and they were such fun to listen to.

RANK. I see. So I've taken their place?

NORA (*jumps up and runs over to him*). Oh, dear, sweet Dr.
Rank, I didn't mean that at all. But I'm sure you understand—I feel the same about Torvald as I did about Papa.

MAID (*enters from the hall*). Excuse me, madam. (*Whispers
to her and hands her a visiting card.*)

NORA (*glances at the card*). Oh! (*Puts it quickly in her
pocket.*)

RANK. Anything wrong?

NORA. No, no, nothing at all. It's just something that—it's my
new dress.

RANK. What? But your costume is lying over there.

NORA. Oh—that, yes—but there's another—I ordered it specially
—Torvald mustn't know—

RANK. Ah, so that's your big secret?

NORA. Yes, yes. Go in and talk to him—he's in his study—keep
him talking for a bit—

RANK. Don't worry. He won't get away from me. (*Goes into
HELMER's study.*)

NORA (*to the* MAID). Is he waiting in the kitchen?

MAID. Yes, madam, he came up the back way—

NORA. But didn't you tell him I had a visitor?

MAID. Yes, but he wouldn't go.

NORA. Wouldn't go?

MAID. No, madam, not until he'd spoken with you.

NORA. Very well, show him in; but quietly. Helen, you mustn't tell anyone about this. It's a surprise for my husband.

MAID. Very good, madam. I understand. (*Goes.*)

NORA. It's happening. It's happening after all. No, no, no, it can't happen, it mustn't happen.

She walks across and bolts the door of HELMER'*s study. The* MAID *opens the door from the hall to admit* KROGSTAD, *and closes it behind him. He is wearing an overcoat, heavy boots and a fur cap.*

NORA (*goes towards him*). Speak quietly. My husband's at home.

KROGSTAD. Let him hear.

NORA. What do you want from me?

KROGSTAD. Information.

NORA. Hurry up, then. What is it?

KROGSTAD. I suppose you know I've been given the sack.

NORA. I couldn't stop it, Mr. Krogstad. I did my best for you, but it didn't help.

KROGSTAD. Does your husband love you so little? He knows what I can do to you, and yet he dares to—

NORA. Surely you don't imagine I told him?

KROGSTAD. No, I didn't really think you had. It wouldn't have been like my old friend Torvald Helmer to show that much courage—

NORA. Mr. Krogstad, I'll trouble you to speak respectfully of my husband.

KROGSTAD. Don't worry, I'll show him all the respect he deserves. But since you're so anxious to keep this matter hushed up, I presume you're better informed than you were yesterday of the gravity of what you've done?

NORA. I've learned more than you could ever teach me.

KROGSTAD. Yes, a bad lawyer like me—

NORA. What do you want from me?

KROGSTAD. I just wanted to see how things were with you,

Mrs. Helmer. I've been thinking about you all day. Even duns and hack journalists have hearts, you know.

NORA. Show some heart, then. Think of my little children.

KROGSTAD. Have you and your husband thought of mine? Well, let's forget that. I just wanted to tell you, you don't need to take this business too seriously. I'm not going to take any action, for the present.

NORA. Oh, no—you won't, will you? I knew it.

KROGSTAD. It can all be settled quite amicably. There's no need for it to become public. We'll keep it among the three of us.

NORA. My husband must never know about this.

KROGSTAD. How can you stop him? Can you pay the balance of what you owe me?

NORA. Not immediately.

KROGSTAD. Have you any means of raising the money during the next few days?

NORA. None that I would care to use.

KROGSTAD. Well, it wouldn't have helped anyway. However much money you offered me now I wouldn't give you back that paper.

NORA. What are you going to do with it?

KROGSTAD. Just keep it. No one else need ever hear about it. So in case you were thinking of doing anything desperate—

NORA. I am.

KROGSTAD. Such as running away—

NORA. I am.

KROGSTAD. Or anything more desperate—

NORA. How did you know?

KROGSTAD. —just give up the idea.

NORA. How did you know?

KROGSTAD. Most of us think of that at first. I did. But I hadn't the courage—

NORA (*dully*). Neither have I.

KROGSTAD (*relieved*). It's true, isn't it? You haven't the courage either?

NORA. No. I haven't. I haven't.

KROGSTAD. It'd be a stupid thing to do anyway. Once the first little domestic explosion is over. . . . I've got a letter in my pocket here addressed to your husband—

NORA. Telling him everything?

KROGSTAD. As delicately as possibly.

NORA (*quickly*). He must never see that letter. Tear it up. I'll find the money somehow—

KROGSTAD. I'm sorry, Mrs. Helmer, I thought I'd explained—

NORA. Oh, I don't mean the money I owe you. Let me know how much you want from my husband, and I'll find it for you.

KROGSTAD. I'm not asking your husband for money.

NORA. What do you want, then?

KROGSTAD. I'll tell you. I want to get on my feet again, Mrs. Helmer. I want to get to the top. And your husband's going to help me. For eighteen months now my record's been clean. I've been in hard straits all that time; I was content to fight my way back inch by inch. Now I've been chucked back into the mud, and I'm not going to be satisfied with just getting back my job. I'm going to get to the top, I tell you. I'm going to get back into the bank, and it's going to be higher up. Your husband's going to create a new job for me—

NORA. He'll never do that!

KROGSTAD. Oh, yes he will. I know him. He won't dare to risk a scandal. And once I'm in there with him, you'll see! Within a year I'll be his right-hand man. It'll be Nils Krogstad who'll be running that bank, not Torvald Helmer!

NORA. That will never happen.

KROGSTAD. Are you thinking of—?

NORA. Now I *have* the courage.

KROGSTAD. Oh, you can't frighten me. A pampered little pretty like you—

NORA. You'll see! You'll see!

KROGSTAD. Under the ice? Down in the cold, black water? And then, in the spring, to float up again, ugly, unrecognizable, hairless—?

NORA. You can't frighten me.

KROGSTAD. And you can't frighten me. People don't do such

things, Mrs. Helmer. And anyway, what'd be the use? I've got him in my pocket.

NORA. But afterwards? When I'm no longer—?

KROGSTAD. Have you forgotten that then your reputation will be in my hands? (*She looks at him speechlessly.*) Well, I've warned you. Don't do anything silly. When Helmer's read my letter, he'll get in touch with me. And remember, it's your husband who's forced me to act like this. And for that I'll never forgive him. Goodbye, Mrs. Helmer. (*He goes out through the hall.*)

NORA (*runs to the hall door, opens it a few inches and listens*). He's going. He's not going to give him the letter. Oh, no, no, it couldn't possibly happen. (*Opens the door a little wider.*) What's he doing? Standing outside the front door. He's not going downstairs. Is he changing his mind? Yes, he—!

A letter falls into the letter-box. KROGSTAD'S *footsteps die away down the stairs.*

NORA (*with a stifled cry, runs across the room towards the table by the sofa. A pause*). In the letter-box. (*Steals timidly over towards the hall door.*) There it is! Oh, Torvald, Torvald! Now we're lost!

MRS. LINDE (*enters from the nursery with* NORA'S *costume*). Well, I've done the best I can. Shall we see how it looks—?

NORA (*whispers hoarsely*). Christine, come here.

MRS. LINDE (*throws the dress on the sofa*). What's wrong with you? You look as though you'd seen a ghost!

NORA. Come here. Do you see that letter? There—look—through the glass of the letter-box.

MRS. LINDE. Yes, yes, I see it.

NORA. That letter's from Krogstad—

MRS. LINDE. Nora! It was Krogstad who lent you the money!

NORA. Yes. And now Torvald's going to discover everything.

MRS. LINDE. Oh, believe me, Nora, it'll be best for you both.

NORA. You don't know what's happened. I've committed a forgery—

MRS. LINDE. But, for heaven's sake—!

NORA. Christine, all I want is for you to be my witness.

MRS. LINDE. What do you mean? Witness what?

NORA. If I should go out of my mind—and it might easily happen—

MRS. LINDE. Nora!

NORA. Or if anything else should happen to me—so that I wasn't here any longer—

MRS. LINDE. Nora, Nora, you don't know what you're saying!

NORA. If anyone should try to take the blame, and say it was all his fault—you understand—?

MRS. LINDE. Yes, yes—but how can you think—?

NORA. Then you must testify that it isn't true, Christine. I'm not mad—I know exactly what I'm saying—and I'm telling you, no one else knows anything about this. I did it entirely on my own. Remember that.

MRS. LINDE. All right. But I simply don't understand—

NORA. Oh, how could you understand? A—miracle—is about to happen.

MRS. LINDE. Miracle?

NORA. Yes. A miracle. But it's so frightening, Christine. It *mustn't* happen, not for anything in the world.

MRS. LINDE. I'll go over and talk to Krogstad.

NORA. Don't go near him. He'll only do something to hurt you.

MRS. LINDE. Once upon a time he'd have done anything for my sake.

NORA. He?

MRS. LINDE. Where does he live?

NORA. Oh, how should I know—? Oh yes, wait a moment—! (*Feels in her pocket.*) Here's his card. But the letter, the letter—!

HELMER (*from his study, knocks on the door*). Nora!

NORA (*cries in alarm*). What is it?

HELMER. Now, now, don't get alarmed. We're not coming in; you've closed the door. Are you trying on your costume?

NORA. Yes, yes—I'm trying on my costume. I'm going to look so pretty for you, Torvald.

MRS. LINDE (*who has been reading the card*). Why, he lives just round the corner.

NORA. Yes; but it's no use. There's nothing to be done now.
The letter's lying there in the box.

MRS. LINDE. And your husband has the key?

NORA. Yes, he always keeps it.

MRS. LINDE. Krogstad must ask him to send the letter back
unread. He must find some excuse—

NORA. But Torvald always opens the box at just about this
time—

MRS. LINDE. You must stop him. Go in and keep him talking.
I'll be back as quickly as I can.

She hurries out through the hall.

NORA (*goes over to* HELMER'S *door, opens it and peeps in*).
Torvald!

HELMER (*offstage*). Well, may a man enter his own drawing-
room again? Come on, Rank, now we'll see what— (*In the
doorway.*) But what's this?

NORA. What, Torvald dear?

HELMER. Rank's been preparing me for some great transformation scene.

RANK (*in the doorway*). So I understood. But I seem to have
been mistaken.

NORA. Yes, no one's to be allowed to see me before tomorrow
night.

HELMER. But, my dear Nora, you look quite worn out. Have
you been practising too hard?

NORA. No, I haven't practised at all yet.

HELMER. Well, you must.

NORA. Yes, Torvald, I must, I know. But I can't get anywhere
without your help. I've completely forgotten everything.

HELMER. Oh, we'll soon put that to rights.

NORA. Yes, help me, Torvald. Promise me you will? Oh, I'm
so nervous. All those people—! You must forget everything
except me this evening. You mustn't think of business—I
won't even let you touch a pen. Promise me, Torvald?

HELMER. I promise. This evening I shall think of nothing but
you—my poor, helpless little darling. Oh, there's just one
thing I must see to— (*Goes towards the hall door.*)

NORA. What do you want out there?

HELMER. I'm only going to see if any letters have come.

NORA. No, Torvald, no!

HELMER. Why, what's the matter?

NORA. Torvald, I beg you. There's nothing there.

HELMER. Well, I'll just make sure.

He moves towards the door. NORA *runs to the piano and plays the first bars of the tarantella.*

HELMER (*at the door, turns*). Aha!

NORA. I can't dance tomorrow if I don't practise with you now.

HELMER (*goes over to her*). Are you really so frightened, Nora dear?

NORA. Yes, terribly frightened. Let me start practising now, at once—we've still time before dinner. Oh, do sit down and play for me, Torvald dear. Correct me, lead me, the way you always do.

HELMER. Very well, my dear, if you wish it.

He sits down at the piano. NORA *seizes the tambourine and a long multi-coloured shawl from the cardboard box, wraps the latter hastily around her, then takes a quick leap into the centre of the room.*

NORA. Play for me! I want to dance!

HELMER *plays and* NORA *dances.* DR. RANK *stands behind* HELMER *at the piano and watches her.*

HELMER (*as he plays*). Slower, slower!

NORA. I can't!

HELMER. Not so violently, Nora.

NORA. I must!

HELMER (*stops playing*). No, no, this won't do at all.

NORA (*laughs and swings her tambourine*). Isn't that what I told you?

RANK. Let me play for her.

HELMER (*gets up*). Yes, would you? Then it'll be easier for me to show her.

RANK *sits down at the piano and plays.* NORA *dances more and more wildly.* HELMER *has stationed himself by the stove and tries repeatedly to correct her, but she seems not to hear him. Her hair works loose and falls over her shoulders; she ignores it and continues to dance.* MRS. LINDE *enters.*

MRS. LINDE (*stands in the doorway as though tongue-tied*). Ah—!

NORA (*as she dances*). Oh, Christine, we're having such fun!

HELMER. But, Nora darling, you're dancing as if your life depended on it.

NORA. It does.

HELMER. Rank, stop it! This is sheer lunacy. Stop it, I say!

RANK *ceases playing.* NORA *suddenly stops dancing.*

HELMER (*goes over to her*). I'd never have believed it. You've forgotten everything I taught you.

NORA (*throws away the tambourine*). You see!

HELMER. I'll have to show you every step.

NORA. You see how much I need you! You must show me every step of the way. Right to the end of the dance. Promise me you will, Torvald?

HELMER. Never fear. I will.

NORA. You mustn't think about anything but me—today or tomorrow. Don't open any letters—don't even open the letter-box—

HELMER. Aha, you're still worried about that fellow—

NORA. Oh, yes, yes, him too.

HELMER. Nora, I can tell from the way you're behaving, there's a letter from him already lying there.

NORA. I don't know. I think so. But you mustn't read it now. I don't want anything ugly to come between us till it's all over.

RANK (*quietly, to* HELMER). Better give her her way.

HELMER (*puts his arm round her*). My child shall have her way. But tomorrow night, when your dance is over—

NORA. Then you will be free.

MAID (*appears in the doorway, right*). Dinner is served, madam.

NORA. Put out some champagne, Helen.

MAID. Very good, madam. (*Goes.*)

HELMER. I say! What's this, a banquet?

NORA. We'll drink champagne until dawn! (*Calls.*) And, Helen! Put out some macaroons! Lots of macaroons—for once!

HELMER (*takes her hands in his*). Now, now, now. Don't get so excited. Where's my little songbird, the one I know?

NORA. All right. Go and sit down—and you too, Dr. Rank. I'll be with you in a minute. Christine, you must help me put my hair up.

RANK (*quietly, as they go*). There's nothing wrong, is there? I mean, she isn't—er—expecting—?

HELMER. Good heavens no, my dear chap. She just gets scared like a child sometimes—I told you before—

They go out right.

NORA. Well?

MRS. LINDE. He's left town.

NORA. I saw it from your face.

MRS. LINDE. He'll be back tomorrow evening. I left a note for him.

NORA. You needn't have bothered. You can't stop anything now. Anyway, it's wonderful really, in a way—sitting here and waiting for the miracle to happen.

MRS. LINDE. Waiting for what?

NORA. Oh, you wouldn't understand. Go in and join them. I'll be with you in a moment.

MRS. LINDE *goes into the dining-room.*

NORA (*stands for a moment as though collecting herself. Then she looks at her watch*). Five o'clock. Seven hours till midnight. Then another twenty-four hours till midnight tomorrow. And then the tarantella will be finished. Twenty-four and seven? Thirty-one hours to live.

HELMER (*appears in the doorway, right*). What's happened to my little songbird?

NORA (*runs to him with her arms wide*). Your songbird is here!

ACT THREE

The same room. The table which was formerly by the sofa has been moved into the centre of the room; the chairs surround it as before. The door to the hall stands open. Dance music can be heard from the floor above. MRS. LINDE *is seated at the table, absent-mindedly glancing through a book. She is trying to read, but seems unable to keep her mind on it. More than once she turns and listens anxiously towards the front door.*

MRS. LINDE (*looks at her watch*). Not here yet. There's not much time left. Please God he hasn't—! (*Listens again.*) Ah, here he is. (*Goes out into the hall and cautiously opens the front door. Footsteps can be heard softly ascending the stairs. She whispers.*) Come in. There's no one here.

KROGSTAD (*in the doorway*). I found a note from you at my lodgings. What does this mean?

MRS. LINDE. I must speak with you.

KROGSTAD. Oh? And must our conversation take place in this house?

MRS. LINDE. We couldn't meet at my place; my room has no separate entrance. Come in. We're quite alone. The maid's asleep, and the Helmers are at the dance upstairs.

KROGSTAD (*comes into the room*). Well, well! So the Helmers are dancing this evening? Are they indeed?

MRS. LINDE. Yes, why not?

KROGSTAD. True enough. Why not?

MRS. LINDE. Well, Krogstad. You and I must have a talk together.

KROGSTAD. Have we two anything further to discuss?

MRS. LINDE. We have a great deal to discuss.

KROGSTAD. I wasn't aware of it.

MRS. LINDE. That's because you've never really understood me.

KROGSTAD. Was there anything to understand? It's the old story, isn't it—a woman chucking a man because something better turns up?

MRS. LINDE. Do you really think I'm so utterly heartless? You think it was easy for me to give you up?

KROGSTAD. Wasn't it?

MRS. LINDE. Oh, Nils, did you really believe that?

KROGSTAD. Then why did you write to me the way you did?

MRS. LINDE. I had to. Since I had to break with you, I thought it my duty to destroy all the feelings you had for me.

KROGSTAD (*clenches his fists*). So that was it. And you did this for money!

MRS. LINDE. You mustn't forget I had a helpless mother to take care of, and two little brothers. We couldn't wait for you, Nils. It would have been so long before you'd had enough to support us.

KROGSTAD. Maybe. But you had no right to cast me off for someone else.

MRS. LINDE. Perhaps not. I've often asked myself that.

KROGSTAD (*more quietly*). When I lost you, it was just as though all solid ground had been swept from under my feet. Look at me. Now I am a shipwrecked man, clinging to a spar.

MRS. LINDE. Help may be near at hand.

KROGSTAD. It was near. But then you came, and stood between it and me.

MRS. LINDE. I didn't know, Nils. No one told me till today that this job I'd found was yours.

KROGSTAD. I believe you, since you say so. But now you know, won't you give it up?

MRS. LINDE. No—because it wouldn't help you even if I did.

KROGSTAD. Wouldn't it? I'd do it all the same.

MRS. LINDE. I've learned to look at things practically. Life and poverty have taught me that.

KROGSTAD. And life has taught me to distrust fine words.

MRS. LINDE. Then it's taught you a useful lesson. But surely you still believe in actions?

KROGSTAD. What do you mean?

MRS. LINDE. You said you were like a shipwrecked man clinging to a spar.

KROGSTAD. I have good reason to say it.

MRS. LINDE. I'm in the same position as you. No one to care about, no one to care for.

KROGSTAD. You made your own choice.

MRS. LINDE. I had no choice—then.

KROGSTAD. Well?

MRS. LINDE. Nils, suppose we two shipwrecked souls could join hands?

KROGSTAD. What are you saying?

MRS. LINDE. Castaways have a better chance of survival together than on their own.

KROGSTAD. Christine!

MRS. LINDE. Why do you suppose I came to this town?

KROGSTAD. You mean—you came because of me?

MRS. LINDE. I must work if I'm to find life worth living. I've always worked, for as long as I can remember; it's been the greatest joy of my life—my only joy. But now I'm alone in the world, and I feel so dreadfully lost and empty. There's no joy in working just for oneself. Oh, Nils, give me something—someone—to work for.

KROGSTAD. I don't believe all that. You're just being hysterical and romantic. You want to find an excuse for self-sacrifice.

MRS. LINDE. Have you ever known me be hysterical?

KROGSTAD. You mean you really—? Is it possible? Tell me— you know all about my past?

MRS. LINDE. Yes.

KROGSTAD. And you know what people think of me here?

MRS. LINDE. You said just now that with me you might have become a different person.

KROGSTAD. I know I could have.

MRS. LINDE. Couldn't it still happen?

KROGSTAD. Christine—do you really mean this? Yes—you do —I see it in your face. Have you really the courage—?

MRS. LINDE. I need someone to be a mother to; and your children need a mother. And you and I need each other. I believe in you, Nils. I am afraid of nothing—with you.

KROGSTAD (*clasps her hands*). Thank you, Christine—thank you! Now I shall make the world believe in me as you do! Oh—but I'd forgotten—

MRS. LINDE (*listens*). Ssh! The tarantella! Go quickly, go!

KROGSTAD. Why? What is it?

MRS. LINDE. You hear that dance? As soon as it's finished, they'll be coming down.

KROGSTAD. All right, I'll go. It's no good, Christine. I'd forgotten—you don't know what I've just done to the Helmers.

MRS. LINDE. Yes, Nils. I know.

KROGSTAD. And yet you'd still have the courage to—?

MRS. LINDE. I know what despair can drive a man like you to.

KROGSTAD. Oh, if only I could undo this!

MRS. LINDE. You can. Your letter is still lying in the box.

KROGSTAD. Are you sure?

MRS. LINDE. Quite sure. But—

KROGSTAD (*looks searchingly at her*). Is that why you're doing this? You want to save your friend at any price? Tell me the truth. Is that the reason?

MRS. LINDE. Nils, a woman who has sold herself once for the sake of others doesn't make the same mistake again.

KROGSTAD. I shall demand my letter back.

MRS. LINDE. No, no.

KROGSTAD. Of course I shall. I shall stay here till Helmer comes down. I'll tell him he must give me back my letter—I'll say it was only to do with my dismissal, and that I don't want him to read it—

MRS. LINDE. No, Nils, you mustn't ask for that letter back.

KROGSTAD. But—tell me—wasn't that the real reason you asked me to come here?

MRS. LINDE. Yes—at first, when I was frightened. But a day has passed since then, and in that time I've seen incredible things happen in this house. Helmer must know the truth. This unhappy secret of Nora's must be revealed. They must come to a full understanding; there must be an end of all these shiftings and evasions.

KROGSTAD. Very well. If you're prepared to risk it. But one thing I can do—and at once—

MRS. LINDE (*listens*). Hurry! Go, go! The dance is over. We aren't safe here another moment.

KROGSTAD. I'll wait for you downstairs.

MRS. LINDE. Yes, do. You can see me home.

KROGSTAD. I've never been so happy in my life before!

He goes out through the front door. The door leading from the room into the hall remains open.

MRS. LINDE (*tidies the room a little and gets her hat and coat*). What a change! Oh, what a change! Someone to work for—to live for! A home to bring joy into! I won't let this chance of happiness slip through my fingers. Oh, why don't they come? (*Listens.*) Ah, here they are. I must get my coat on.

She takes her hat and coat. HELMER's *and* NORA's *voices become audible outside. A key is turned in the lock and* HELMER *leads* NORA *almost forcibly into the hall. She is dressed in an Italian costume with a large black shawl. He is in evening dress, with a black cloak.*

NORA (*still in the doorway, resisting him*). No, no, no—not in here! I want to go back upstairs. I don't want to leave so early.

HELMER. But my dearest Nora—

NORA. Oh, please, Torvald, please! Just another hour!

HELMER. Not another minute, Nora, my sweet. You know what we agreed. Come along, now. Into the drawing-room. You'll catch cold if you stay out here.

He leads her, despite her efforts to resist him, gently into the room.

MRS. LINDE. Good evening.

NORA. Christine!

HELMER. Oh, hullo, Mrs. Linde. You still here?

MRS. LINDE. Please forgive me. I did so want to see Nora in her costume.

NORA. Have you been sitting here waiting for me?

MRS. LINDE. Yes. I got here too late, I'm afraid. You'd already gone up. And I felt I really couldn't go back home without seeing you.

HELMER (*takes off* NORA's *shawl*). Well, take a good look at her. She's worth looking at, don't you think? Isn't she beautiful, Mrs. Linde?

MRS. LINDE. Oh, yes, indeed—

HELMER. Isn't she unbelievably beautiful? Everyone at the party said so. But dreadfully stubborn she is, bless her pretty little heart. What's to be done about that? Would you believe it, I practically had to use force to get her away!

NORA. Oh, Torvald, you're going to regret not letting me stay —just half an hour longer.

HELMER. Hear that, Mrs. Linde? She dances her tarantella— makes a roaring success—and very well deserved—though possibly a trifle too realistic—more so than was aesthetically necessary, strictly speaking. But never mind that. Main thing is—she had a success—roaring success. Was I going to let her stay on after that and spoil the impression? No, thank you. I took my beautiful little Capri signorina—my capricious little Capricienne, what?—under my arm—a swift round of the ballroom, a curtsey to the company, and, as they say in novels, the beautiful apparition disappeared! An exit should always be dramatic, Mrs. Linde. But unfortunately that's just what I can't get Nora to realize. I say, it's hot in here. (*Throws his cloak on a chair and opens the door to his study.*) What's this? It's dark in here. Ah, yes, of course—excuse me. (*Goes in and lights a couple of candles.*)

NORA (*whispers swiftly, breathlessly*). Well?

MRS. LINDE (*quietly*). I've spoken to him.

NORA. Yes?

MRS. LINDE. Nora—you must tell your husband everything.

NORA (*dully*). I knew it.

MRS. LINDE. You've nothing to fear from Krogstad. But you must tell him.

NORA. I shan't tell him anything.

MRS. LINDE. Then the letter will.

NORA. Thank you, Christine. Now I know what I must do. Ssh!

HELMER (*returns*). Well, Mrs. Linde, finished admiring her?

MRS. LINDE. Yes. Now I must say good night.

HELMER. Oh, already? Does this knitting belong to you?

MRS. LINDE (*takes it*). Thank you, yes. I nearly forgot it.

HELMER. You knit, then?

MRS. LINDE. Why, yes.

HELMER. Know what? You ought to take up embroidery.

MRS. LINDE. Oh? Why?

HELMER. It's much prettier. Watch me, now. You hold the embroidery in your left hand, like this, and then you take the needle in your right hand and go in and out in a slow, easy movement—like this. I am right, aren't I?

MRS. LINDE. Yes, I'm sure—

HELMER. But knitting, now—that's an ugly business—can't help it. Look—arms all huddled up—great clumsy needles going up and down—makes you look like a damned Chinaman. I say, that really was a magnificent champagne they served us.

MRS. LINDE. Well, good night, Nora. And stop being stubborn. Remember!

HELMER. Quite right, Mrs. Linde!

MRS. LINDE. Good night, Mr. Helmer.

HELMER (*accompanies her to the door*). Good night, good night! I hope you'll manage to get home all right? I'd gladly—but you haven't far to go, have you? Good night, good night. (*She goes. He closes the door behind her and returns.*) Well, we've got rid of her at last. Dreadful bore that woman is!

NORA. Aren't you very tired, Torvald?

HELMER. No, not in the least.

NORA. Aren't you sleepy?

HELMER. Not a bit. On the contrary, I feel extraordinarily exhilarated. But what about you? Yes, you look very sleepy and tired.

NORA. Yes, I am very tired. Soon I shall sleep.

HELMER. You see, you see! How right I was not to let you stay longer!

NORA. Oh, you're always right, whatever you do.

HELMER (*kisses her on the forehead*). Now my little song-bird's talking just like a real big human being. I say, did you notice how cheerful Rank was this evening?

NORA. Oh? Was he? I didn't have a chance to speak with him.

HELMER. I hardly did. But I haven't seen him in such a jolly mood for ages. (*Looks at her for a moment, then comes closer.*) I say, it's nice to get back to one's home again, and be all alone with you. Upon my word, you're a distractingly beautiful young woman.

NORA. Don't look at me like that, Torvald!

HELMER. What, not look at my most treasured possession? At all this wonderful beauty that's mine, mine alone, all mine.

NORA (*goes round to the other side of the table*). You mustn't talk to me like that tonight.

HELMER (*follows her*). You've still the tarantella in your blood, I see. And that makes you even more desirable. Listen! Now the other guests are beginning to go. (*More quietly.*) Nora—soon the whole house will be absolutely quiet.

NORA. Yes, I hope so.

HELMER. Yes, my beloved Nora, of course you do! Do you know—when I'm out with you among other people like we were tonight, do you know why I say so little to you, why I keep so aloof from you, and just throw you an occasional glance? Do you know why I do that? It's because I pre-tend to myself that you're my secret mistress, my clandes-tine little sweetheart, and that nobody knows there's any-thing at all between us.

NORA. Oh, yes, yes, yes—I know you never think of anything but me.

HELMER. And then when we're about to go, and I wrap the shawl round your lovely young shoulders, over this won-

derful curve of your neck—then I pretend to myself that
you are my young bride, that we've just come from the
wedding, that I'm taking you to my house for the first time
—that, for the first time, I am alone with you—quite alone
with you, as you stand there young and trembling and
beautiful. All evening I've had no eyes for anyone but
you. When I saw you dance the tarantella, like a huntress,
a temptress, my blood grew hot, I couldn't stand it any
longer! That was why I seized you and dragged you down
here with me—

NORA. Leave me, Torvald! Get away from me! I don't want
all this.

HELMER. What? Now, Nora, you're joking with me. Don't
want, don't want—? Aren't I your husband—?

There is a knock on the front door.

NORA (*starts*). What was that?

HELMER (*goes towards the hall*). Who is it?

RANK (*outside*). It's me. May I come in for a moment?

HELMER (*quietly, annoyed*). Oh, what does he want now?
(*Calls.*) Wait a moment. (*Walks over and opens the door.*)
Well! Nice of you not to go by without looking in.

RANK. I thought I heard your voice, so I felt I had to say
goodbye. (*His eyes travel swiftly around the room.*) Ah,
yes—these dear rooms, how well I know them. What a
happy, peaceful home you two have.

HELMER. You seemed to be having a pretty happy time yourself upstairs.

RANK. Indeed I did. Why not? Why shouldn't one make the
most of this world? As much as one can, and for as long as
one can. The wine was excellent—

HELMER. Especially the champagne.

RANK. You noticed that too? It's almost incredible how much
I managed to get down.

NORA. Torvald drank a lot of champagne too, this evening.

RANK. Oh?

NORA. Yes. It always makes him merry afterwards.

RANK. Well, why shouldn't a man have a merry evening after a well-spent day?

HELMER. Well-spent? Oh, I don't know that I can claim that.

RANK (*slaps him across the back*). I can, though, my dear fellow!

NORA. Yes, of course, Dr. Rank—you've been carrying out a scientific experiment today, haven't you?

RANK. Exactly.

HELMER. Scientific experiment! Those are big words for my little Nora to use!

NORA. And may I congratulate you on the finding?

RANK. You may indeed.

NORA. It was good, then?

RANK. The best possible finding—both for the doctor and the patient. Certainty.

NORA (*quickly*). Certainty?

RANK. Absolute certainty. So aren't I entitled to have a merry evening after that?

NORA. Yes, Dr. Rank. You were quite right to.

HELMER. I agree. Provided you don't have to regret it to-morrow.

RANK. Well, you never get anything in this life without paying for it.

NORA. Dr. Rank—you like masquerades, don't you?

RANK. Yes, if the disguises are sufficiently amusing.

NORA. Tell me. What shall we two wear at the next masquerade?

HELMER. You little gadabout! Are you thinking about the next one already?

RANK. We two? Yes, I'll tell you. You must go as the Spirit of Happiness—

HELMER. You try to think of a costume that'll convey that.

RANK. Your wife need only appear as her normal, everyday self—

HELMER. Quite right! Well said! But what are you going to be? Have you decided that?

RANK. Yes, my dear friend. I have decided that.

HELMER. Well?

RANK. At the next masquerade, I shall be invisible.

HELMER. Well, that's a funny idea.

RANK. There's a big, black hat—haven't you heard of the invisible hat? Once it's over your head, no one can see you any more.

HELMER (*represses a smile*). Ah yes, of course.

RANK. But I'm forgetting what I came for. Helmer, give me a cigar. One of your black Havanas.

HELMER. With the greatest pleasure. (*Offers him the box.*)

RANK (*takes one and cuts off the tip*). Thank you.

NORA (*strikes a match*). Let me give you a light.

RANK. Thank you. (*She holds out the match for him. He lights his cigar.*) And now—goodbye.

HELMER. Goodbye, my dear chap, goodbye.

NORA. Sleep well, Dr. Rank.

RANK. Thank you for that kind wish.

NORA. Wish me the same.

RANK. You? Very well—since you ask. Sleep well. And thank you for the light. (*He nods to them both and goes.*)

HELMER (*quietly*). He's been drinking too much.

NORA (*abstractedly*). Perhaps.

HELMER *takes his bunch of keys from his pocket and goes out into the hall.*

NORA. Torvald, what do you want out there?

HELMER. I must empty the letter-box. It's absolutely full. There'll be no room for the newspapers in the morning.

NORA. Are you going to work tonight?

HELMER. You know very well I'm not. Hullo, what's this? Someone's been at the lock.

NORA. At the lock—?

HELMER. Yes, I'm sure of it. Who on earth—? Surely not one of the maids? Here's a broken hairpin. Nora, it's yours—

NORA (*quickly*). Then it must have been the children.

HELMER. Well, you'll have to break them of that habit. Hm, hm. Ah, that's done it. (*Takes out the contents of the box and calls into the kitchen.*) Helen! Helen! Put out the light on the staircase. (*Comes back into the drawing-room*

with the letters in his hand and closes the door to the hall.)
Look at this! You see how they've piled up? (*Glances
through them.*) What on earth's this?

NORA (*at the window*). The letter! Oh, no, Torvald, no!

HELMER. Two visiting cards—from Rank.

NORA. From Dr. Rank?

HELMER (*looks at them*). Peter Rank, M.D. They were on
top. He must have dropped them in as he left.

NORA. Has he written anything on them?

HELMER. There's a black cross above his name. Look. Rather
gruesome, isn't it? It looks just as though he was announcing his death.

NORA. He is.

HELMER. What? Do you know something? Has he told you
anything?

NORA. Yes. When these cards come, it means he's said goodbye to us. He wants to shut himself up in his house and
die.

HELMER. Ah, poor fellow. I knew I wouldn't be seeing him
for much longer. But so soon—! And now he's going to slink
away and hide like a wounded beast.

NORA. When the time comes, it's best to go silently. Don't
you think so, Torvald?

HELMER (*walks up and down*). He was so much a part of
our life. I can't realize that he's gone. His suffering and
loneliness seemed to provide a kind of dark background to
the happy sunlight of our marriage. Well, perhaps it's best
this way. For him, anyway. (*Stops walking.*) And perhaps
for us too, Nora. Now we have only each other. (*Embraces
her.*) Oh, my beloved wife—I feel as though I could never
hold you close enough. Do you know, Nora, often I wish
some terrible danger might threaten you, so that I could
offer my life and my blood, everything, for your sake.

NORA (*tears herself loose and says in a clear, firm voice*).
Read your letters now, Torvald.

HELMER. No, no. Not tonight. Tonight I want to be with you,
my darling wife—

NORA. When your friend is about to die—?

HELMER. You're right. This news has upset us both. An ugliness has come between us; thoughts of death and dissolution. We must try to forget them. Until then—you go to your room; I shall go to mine.

NORA (*throws her arms round his neck*). Good night, Torvald! Good night!

HELMER (*kisses her on the forehead*). Good night, my darling little songbird. Sleep well, Nora. I'll go and read my letters.

He goes into the study with the letters in his hand, and closes the door.

NORA (*wild-eyed, fumbles around, seizes* HELMER's *cloak, throws it round herself and whispers quickly, hoarsely*). Never see him again. Never. Never. Never. (*Throws the shawl over her head.*) Never see the children again. Them too. Never. Never. Oh—the icy black water! Oh—that bottomless—that—! Oh, if only it were all over! Now he's got it—he's reading it. Oh, no, no! Not yet! Goodbye, Torvald! Goodbye, my darlings!

She turns to run into the hall. As she does so, HELMER *throws open his door and stands there with an open letter in his hand.*

HELMER. Nora!

NORA (*shrieks*). Ah—!

HELMER. What is this? Do you know what is in this letter?

NORA. Yes, I know. Let me go! Let me go!

HELMER (*holds her back*). Go? Where?

NORA (*tries to tear herself loose*). You mustn't try to save me, Torvald!

HELMER (*staggers back*). Is it true? Is it true, what he writes? Oh, my God! No, no—it's impossible, it can't be true!

NORA. It *is* true. I've loved you more than anything else in the world.

HELMER. Oh, don't try to make silly excuses.

NORA (*takes a step towards him*). Torvald—

HELMER. Wretched woman! What have you done?

NORA. Let me go! You're not going to suffer for my sake. I won't let you!

HELMER. Stop being theatrical. (*Locks the front door.*) You're going to stay here and explain yourself. Do you understand what you've done? Answer me! Do you understand?

NORA (*looks unflinchingly at him and, her expression growing colder, says*). Yes. Now I am beginning to understand.

HELMER (*walking round the room*). Oh, what a dreadful awakening! For eight whole years—she who was my joy and my pride—a hypocrite, a liar—worse, worse—a criminal! Oh, the hideousness of it! Shame on you, shame!

NORA *is silent and stares unblinkingly at him.*

HELMER (*stops in front of her*). I ought to have guessed that something of this sort would happen. I should have foreseen it. All your father's recklessness and instability—be quiet!—I repeat, all your father's recklessness and instability he has handed on to you. No religion, no morals, no sense of duty! Oh, how I have been punished for closing my eyes to his faults! I did it for your sake. And now you reward me like this.

NORA. Yes. Like this.

HELMER. Now you have destroyed all my happiness. You have ruined my whole future. Oh, it's too dreadful to contemplate! I am in the power of a man who is completely without scruples. He can do what he likes with me, demand what he pleases, order me to do anything—I dare not disobey him. I am condemned to humiliation and ruin simply for the weakness of a woman.

NORA. When I am gone from this world, you will be free.

HELMER. Oh, don't be melodramatic. Your father was always ready with that kind of remark. How would it help me if you were "gone from this world," as you put it? It wouldn't assist me in the slightest. He can still make all the facts public; and if he does, I may quite easily be suspected of having been an accomplice in your crime. People may think that I was behind it—that it was I who encouraged you! And for all this I have to thank you, you whom I have carried on my hands through all the years of our marriage! Now do you realize what you've done to me?

NORA (*coldly calm*). Yes.

HELMER. It's so unbelievable I can hardly credit it. But we must try to find some way out. Take off that shawl. Take it off, I say! I must try to buy him off somehow. This thing must be hushed up at any price. As regards our relationship—we must appear to be living together just as before. Only *appear*, of course. You will therefore continue to reside here. That is understood. But the children shall be taken out of your hands. I dare no longer entrust them to you. Oh, to have to say this to the woman I once loved so dearly—and whom I still—! Well, all that must be finished. Henceforth there can be no question of happiness; we must merely strive to save what shreds and tatters— (*The front door bell rings.* HELMER *starts.*) What can that be? At this hour? Surely not—? He wouldn't—? Hide yourself, Nora. Say you're ill.

NORA *does not move.* HELMER *goes to the door of the room and opens it. The* MAID *is standing half-dressed in the hall.*

MAID. A letter for madam.

HELMER. Give it me. (*Seizes the letter and shuts the door.*) Yes, it's from him. You're not having it. I'll read this myself.

NORA. Read it.

HELMER (*by the lamp*). I hardly dare to. This may mean the end for us both. No. I must know. (*Tears open the letter hastily; reads a few lines; looks at a piece of paper which is enclosed with it; utters a cry of joy.*) Nora! (*She looks at him questioningly.*) Nora! No—I must read it once more. Yes, yes, it's true! I am saved! Nora, I am saved!

NORA. What about me?

HELMER. You too, of course. We're both saved, you and I. Look! He's returning your I.O.U. He writes that he is sorry for what has happened—a happy accident has changed his life—oh, what does it matter what he writes? We are saved, Nora! No one can harm you now. Oh, Nora, Nora—no, first let me destroy this filthy thing. Let me see—! (*Glances at the I.O.U.*) No, I don't want to look at it. I shall merely regard the whole business as a dream. (*He tears the I.O.U. and both letters into pieces, throws them into the stove and watches them burn.*) There. Now they're destroyed. He wrote that ever since Christmas Eve you've been—oh, these must have been three dreadful days for you, Nora.

NORA. Yes. It's been a hard fight.

HELMER. It must have been terrible—seeing no way out except—no, we'll forget the whole sordid business. We'll just be happy and go on telling ourselves over and over again: "It's over! It's over!" Listen to me, Nora. You don't seem to realize. It's over! Why are you looking so pale? Ah, my poor little Nora, I understand. You can't believe that I have forgiven you. But I have, Nora. I swear it to you. I have forgiven you everything. I know that what you did you did for your love of me.

NORA. That is true.

HELMER. You have loved me as a wife should love her husband. It was simply that in your inexperience you chose the wrong means. But do you think I love you any the less because you don't know how to act on your own initiative? No, no. Just lean on me. I shall counsel you. I shall guide you. I would not be a true man if your feminine helplessness did not make you doubly attractive in my eyes. You mustn't mind the hard words I said to you in those first dreadful moments when my whole world seemed to be tumbling about my ears. I have forgiven you, Nora. I swear it to you; I have forgiven you.

NORA. Thank you for your forgiveness.

She goes out through the door, right.

HELMER. No, don't go— (*Looks in.*) What are you doing there?

NORA (*offstage*). Taking off my fancy dress.

HELMER (*by the open door*). Yes, do that. Try to calm yourself and get your balance again, my frightened little songbird. Don't be afraid. I have broad wings to shield you.

(*Begins to walk around near the door.*) How lovely and peaceful this little home of ours is, Nora. You are safe here; I shall watch over you like a hunted dove which I have snatched unharmed from the claws of the falcon. Your wildly beating little heart shall find peace with me. It will happen, Nora; it will take time, but it will happen, believe me. Tomorrow all this will seem quite different. Soon everything will be as it was before. I shall no longer need to remind you that I have forgiven you; your own heart will tell you that it is true. Do you really think I could ever bring myself to disown you, or even to reproach you? Ah, Nora, you don't understand what goes on in a husband's heart. There is something indescribably wonderful and satisfying for a husband in knowing that he has forgiven his wife—forgiven her unreservedly, from the bottom of his heart. It means that she has become his property in a double sense; he has, as it were, brought her into the world anew; she is now not only his wife but also his child. From now on that is what you shall be to me, my poor, helpless, bewildered little creature. Never be frightened of anything again, Nora. Just open your heart to me. I shall be both your will and your conscience. What's this? Not in bed? Have you changed?

NORA (*in her everyday dress*). Yes, Torvald. I've changed.

HELMER. But why now—so late—?

NORA. I shall not sleep tonight.

HELMER. But, my dear Nora—

NORA (*looks at her watch*). It isn't that late. Sit down here, Torvald. You and I have a lot to talk about.

She sits down on one side of the table.

HELMER. Nora, what does this mean? You look quite drawn—

NORA. Sit down. It's going to take a long time. I've a lot to say to you.

HELMER (*sits down on the other side of the table*). You alarm me, Nora. I don't understand you.

NORA. No, that's just it. You don't understand me. And I've never understood you—until this evening. No, don't inter-

rupt me. Just listen to what I have to say. You and I have
got to face facts, Torvald.

HELMER. What do you mean by that?

NORA (*after a short silence*). Doesn't anything strike you
about the way we're sitting here?

HELMER. What?

NORA. We've been married for eight years. Does it occur to
you that this is the first time that we two, you and I, man
and wife, have ever had a serious talk together?

HELMER. Serious? What do you mean, serious?

NORA. In eight whole years—no, longer—ever since we first
met—we have never exchanged a serious word on a serious
subject.

HELMER. Did you expect me to drag you into all my worries—worries you couldn't possibly have helped me with?

NORA. I'm not talking about worries. I'm simply saying that
we have never sat down seriously to try to get to the bottom of anything.

HELMER. But, my dear Nora, what on earth has that got to
do with you?

NORA. That's just the point. You have never understood me.
A great wrong has been done to me, Torvald. First by
Papa, and then by you.

HELMER. What? But we two have loved you more than anyone in the world!

NORA (*shakes her head*). You have never loved me. You just
thought it was fun to be in love with me.

HELMER. Nora, what kind of a way is this to talk?

NORA. It's the truth, Torvald. When I lived with Papa, he
used to tell me what he thought about everything, so that
I never had any opinions but his. And if I did have any of
my own, I kept them quiet, because he wouldn't have
liked them. He called me his little doll, and he played with
me just the way I played with my dolls. Then I came here
to live in your house—

HELMER. What kind of a way is that to describe our marriage?

NORA (*undisturbed*). I mean, then I passed from Papa's

hands into yours. You arranged everything the way you wanted it, so that I simply took over your taste in everything—or pretended I did—I don't really know—I think it was a little of both—first one and then the other. Now I look back on it, it's as if I've been living here like a pauper, from hand to mouth. I performed tricks for you, and you gave me food and drink. But that was how you wanted it. You and Papa have done me a great wrong. It's your fault that I have done nothing with my life.

HELMER. Nora, how can you be so unreasonable and ungrateful? Haven't you been happy here?

NORA. No; never. I used to think I was; but I haven't ever been happy.

HELMER. Not—not happy?

NORA. No. I've just had fun. You've always been very kind to me. But our home has never been anything but a playroom. I've been your doll-wife, just as I used to be Papa's doll-child. And the children have been my dolls. I used to think it was fun when you came in and played with me, just as they think it's fun when I go in and play games with them. That's all our marriage has been, Torvald.

HELMER. There may be a little truth in what you say, though you exaggerate and romanticize. But from now on it'll be different. Playtime is over. Now the time has come for education.

NORA. Whose education? Mine or the children's?

HELMER. Both yours and the children's, my dearest Nora.

NORA. Oh, Torvald, you're not the man to educate me into being the right wife for you.

HELMER. How can you say that?

NORA. And what about me? Am I fit to educate the children?

HELMER. Nora!

NORA. Didn't you say yourself a few minutes ago that you dare not leave them in my charge?

HELMER. In a moment of excitement. Surely you don't think I meant it seriously?

NORA. Yes. You were perfectly right. I'm not fitted to educate them. There's something else I must do first. I must educate myself. And you can't help me with that. It's something I must do by myself. That's why I'm leaving you.

HELMER (*jumps up*). What did you say?

NORA. I must stand on my own feet if I am to find out the truth about myself and about life. So I can't go on living here with you any longer.

HELMER. Nora, Nora!

NORA. I'm leaving you now, at once. Christine will put me up for tonight—

HELMER. You're out of your mind! You can't do this! I forbid you!

NORA. It's no use your trying to forbid me any more. I shall take with me nothing but what is mine. I don't want anything from you, now or ever.

HELMER. What kind of madness is this?

NORA. Tomorrow I shall go home—I mean, to where I was born. It'll be easiest for me to find some kind of a job there.

HELMER. But you're blind! You've no experience of the world—

NORA. I must try to get some, Torvald.

HELMER. But to leave your home, your husband, your children! Have you thought what people will say?

NORA. I can't help that. I only know that I must do this.

HELMER. But this is monstrous! Can you neglect your most sacred duties?

NORA. What do you call my most sacred duties?

HELMER. Do I have to tell you? Your duties towards your husband, and your children.

NORA. I have another duty which is equally sacred.

HELMER. You have not. What on earth could that be?

NORA. My duty towards myself.

HELMER. First and foremost you are a wife and a mother.

NORA. I don't believe that any longer. I believe that I am first and foremost a human being, like you—or anyway, that I must try to become one. I know most people think as you do, Torvald, and I know there's something of the sort to be found in books. But I'm no longer prepared to accept what people say and what's written in books. I must think things out for myself, and try to find my own answer.

HELMER. Do you need to ask where your duty lies in your own home? Haven't you an infallible guide in such matters —your religion?

NORA. Oh, Torvald, I don't really know what religion means.

HELMER. What are you saying?

NORA. I only know what Pastor Hansen told me when I went to confirmation. He explained that religion meant this and that. When I get away from all this and can think things out on my own, that's one of the questions I want to look into. I want to find out whether what Pastor Hansen said was right—or anyway, whether it is right for me.

HELMER. But it's unheard of for so young a woman to behave like this! If religion cannot guide you, let me at least appeal to your conscience. I presume you have some moral feelings left? Or—perhaps you haven't? Well, answer me.

NORA. Oh, Torvald, that isn't an easy question to answer. I simply don't know. I don't know where I am in these matters. I only know that these things mean something quite different to me from what they do to you. I've learned now that certain laws are different from what I'd imagined them to be; but I can't accept that such laws can be right. Has a woman really not the right to spare her dying father pain, or save her husband's life? I can't believe that.

HELMER. You're talking like a child. You don't understand how society works.

NORA. No, I don't. But now I intend to learn. I must try to satisfy myself which is right, society or I.

HELMER. Nora, you're ill; you're feverish. I almost believe you're out of your mind.

NORA. I've never felt so sane and sure in my life.

HELMER. You feel sure that it is right to leave your husband and your children?

NORA. Yes. I do.

HELMER. Then there is only one possible explanation.

NORA. What?

HELMER. That you don't love me any longer.

NORA. No, that's exactly it.

HELMER. Nora! How can you say this to me?

NORA. Oh, Torvald, it hurts me terribly to have to say it, because you've always been so kind to me. But I can't help it. I don't love you any longer.

HELMER (*controlling his emotions with difficulty*). And you feel quite sure about this too?

NORA. Yes, absolutely sure. That's why I can't go on living here any longer.

HELMER. Can you also explain why I have lost your love?

NORA. Yes, I can. It happened this evening, when the miracle failed to happen. It was then that I realized you weren't the man I'd thought you to be.

HELMER. Explain more clearly. I don't understand you.

NORA. I've waited so patiently, for eight whole years—well, good heavens, I'm not such a fool as to suppose that miracles occur every day. Then this dreadful thing happened to me, and then I *knew*: "Now the miracle will take place!" When Krogstad's letter was lying out there, it never occurred to me for a moment that you would let that man trample over you. I *knew* that you would say to him: "Publish the facts to the world." And when he had done this—

HELMER. Yes, what then? When I'd exposed my wife's name to shame and scandal—

NORA. Then I was certain that you would step forward and take all the blame on yourself, and say: "I am the one who is guilty!"

HELMER. Nora!

NORA. You're thinking I wouldn't have accepted such a sacrifice from you? No, of course I wouldn't! But what would my word have counted for against yours? That was the miracle I was hoping for, and dreading. And it was to prevent it happening that I wanted to end my life.

HELMER. Nora, I would gladly work for you night and day, and endure sorrow and hardship for your sake. But no man can be expected to sacrifice his honour, even for the person he loves.

NORA. Millions of women have done it.

HELMER. Oh, you think and talk like a stupid child.

NORA. That may be. But you neither think nor talk like the man I could share my life with. Once you'd got over your fright—and you weren't frightened of what might threaten me, but only of what threatened you—once the danger was past, then as far as you were concerned it was exactly as though nothing had happened. I was your little songbird just as before—your doll whom henceforth you would take particular care to protect from the world because she was so weak and fragile. (*Gets up.*) Torvald, in that moment I realized that for eight years I had been living here with a complete stranger, and had borne him three children—! Oh, I can't bear to think of it! I could tear myself to pieces!

HELMER (*sadly*). I see it, I see it. A gulf has indeed opened between us. Oh, but Nora—couldn't it be bridged?

NORA. As I am now, I am no wife for you.

HELMER. I have the strength to change.

NORA. Perhaps—if your doll is taken from you.

HELMER. But to be parted—to be parted from you! No, no, Nora, I can't conceive of it happening!

NORA (*goes into the room, right*). All the more necessary that it should happen.

She comes back with her outdoor things and a small travelling-bag, which she puts down on a chair by the table.

HELMER. Nora, Nora, not now! Wait till tomorrow!

NORA (*puts on her coat*). I can't spend the night in a strange man's house.

HELMER. But can't we live here as brother and sister, then—?

NORA (*fastens her hat*). You know quite well it wouldn't last. (*Puts on her shawl.*) Goodbye, Torvald. I don't want to see the children. I know they're in better hands than mine. As I am now, I can be nothing to them.

HELMER. But some time, Nora—some time—?

NORA. How can I tell? I've no idea what will happen to me.

HELMER. But you are my wife, both as you are and as you will be.

NORA. Listen, Torvald. When a wife leaves her husband's house, as I'm doing now, I'm told that according to the law he is freed of any obligations towards her. In any case, I release you from any such obligations. You mustn't feel bound to me in any way, however small, just as I shall not feel bound to you. We must both be quite free. Here is your ring back. Give me mine.

HELMER. That too?

NORA. That too.

HELMER. Here it is.

NORA. Good. Well, now it's over. I'll leave the keys here. The servants know about everything to do with the house—much better than I do. Tomorrow, when I have left town, Christine will come to pack the things I brought here from home. I'll have them sent on after me.

HELMER. This is the end then! Nora, will you never think of me any more?

NORA. Yes, of course. I shall often think of you and the children and this house.

HELMER. May I write to you, Nora?

NORA. No. Never. You mustn't do that.

HELMER. But at least you must let me send you—

NORA. Nothing. Nothing.

HELMER. But if you should need help—?

NORA. I tell you, no. I don't accept things from strangers.

HELMER. Nora—can I never be anything but a stranger to you?

NORA (*picks up her bag*). Oh, Torvald! Then the miracle of miracles would have to happen.

HELMER. The miracle of miracles?

NORA. You and I would both have to change so much that—oh, Torvald, I don't believe in miracles any longer.

HELMER. But I want to believe in them. Tell me. We should have to change so much that—?

NORA. That life together between us two could become a marriage. Goodbye.

She goes out through the hall.

HELMER (*sinks down on a chair by the door and buries his face in his hands*). Nora! Nora! (*Looks round and gets up.*) Empty! She's gone! (*A hope strikes him.*) The miracle of miracles—?

The street door is slammed shut downstairs.

GHOSTS

INTRODUCTION

On completing *A Doll's House* Ibsen returned, in the autumn of 1879, from Italy to Munich, and spent the winter there. Next summer he holidayed in Berchtesgaden, dressed like a German tourist, with a Tyrolean hat on his head. There was much rain and fog that summer, even more than usual for Berchtesgaden, and when his friend John Paulsen asked him what he was busy with, Ibsen replied: "It is a family history—grey and gloomy as this rainy day."

He did no actual writing in Berchtesgaden, merely brooding upon the theme and characters. In the autumn of 1880 he returned to Munich and there received a note from the Norwegian Ecclesiastical Department, which was also responsible for education, informing him that his son Sigurd could not graduate in law in Norway without first taking certain elementary Norwegian examinations. Ibsen was furious at this example of what he regarded as typical Norwegian pig-headedness. "To the black gang of theologians which at present rules the Norwegian Ecclesiastical Department," he wrote to his publisher, Frederik Hegel of Gyldendals, "I shall in good time raise a fitting memorial." The immediate effect was that his son decided to continue his studies in Italy, and on 2 November 1880 Ibsen moved to Rome, where he took a house at 75 Via Capo le Case. From there, on 26 November 1880, he wrote to Edmund Gosse that he was "busy pondering a new play, which I hope to complete during the summer."

This play seems, however, not to have been *Ghosts*, for on 18 June 1881 he wrote to Hegel: "There has been a change in my literary plans for the summer. The work[1] about which I previously wrote you has temporarily been shelved, and early this month I started on a theme which has long occupied my thoughts and which at length forced itself upon me so insistently that I could no longer ignore it. I hope to be able to send you the manuscript by the middle of October. I will tell you the title later; today I shall merely state that I describe it as 'a domestic drama in three acts.' I need hardly add that this play has no kind of connection with *A Doll's House*."

On 28 June, Ibsen and his family moved to Sorrento, and by 23 September he had completed a first draft of the play, which has unfortunately not survived. A week later he wrote to Hegel: "I take advantage of a free moment to tell you briefly that on the 23rd instant I finished the draft of my new play and on the 25th began my fair copy. The play is called *Ghosts, a Domestic Drama in Three Acts*. If possible, you shall have the whole thing by the end of October." This "fair copy" in fact took the form of a new draft, the various stages of which he dated, enabling us to chart its progress. Act One took him from 25 September to 4 October; Act Two from 13 to 20 October; and Act Three from 21 to 24 October. After completing Act One he made a fair copy of it; on 16 October he wrote again to Hegel: "As promised I enclose the fair copy of Act 1. Act 2, which will be somewhat shorter, will follow in a fortnight, and the remainder in the early days of next month, so that the book will, I trust, be able to be in the shops in the beginning of December, as *A Doll's House* was." Ibsen kept to this schedule, for on 4 November, still from Sorrento, he wrote: "Yesterday I sent off the manuscript

[1] Possibly *An Enemy of the People*, which Ibsen completed with unwonted speed the following year. Within a month of finishing *Ghosts* he wrote to Hegel: "I am already busy planning a new four-act comedy which I had thought about before but put aside to make way for *Ghosts*, which was obsessing me and monopolising my thoughts." Some critics, however, believe that Ibsen had been planning another play which never got written, and his remark to Paulsen quoted above suggests that he had a more sombre work than *An Enemy of the People* in mind.

of Act 2, plus the first page of Act 3. This last act is much shorter than the others. . . . The remainder will be sent to you with all speed from Rome, whither we return tomorrow." On 23 November, writing from Rome, he uttered a mild warning to Hegel: "*Ghosts* will probably cause alarm in some circles; but that can't be helped. If it didn't, there would have been no necessity for me to write it."

Ghosts was duly published by Gyldendals of Copenhagen on 13 December 1881, and at once aroused a consternation and hostility beyond anything Ibsen had envisaged. At first he accepted this calmly; he knew there were small prospects of getting it performed in either Scandinavia or Germany, but reckoned it would, like *Brand* and *Peer Gynt*, have its effect on the reading public. On 22 December he wrote to one of his German translators, Ludwig Passarge: "My new play has now come out and has created a violent commotion in the Scandinavian press. Every day I receive letters and newspaper articles, some for, some against. A copy will be sent to you very shortly; but I feel it's quite impossible that this play should be performed in any German theatre at this time; I hardly think they'll dare to stage it even in Scandinavia for some little while. Incidentally, it has been printed in an edition of 10,000 copies, and there is every prospect that a new impression will be required soon."

That Christmas, replying to a toast at the Scandinavian Club in Rome, he remarked that Christmas, which to most people brought joy and peace, to him usually brought battle, since it was at this season that his books appeared; but that to him battle was joy, and peace merely a breathing-space until he could take up the struggle anew.

On 2 January 1882 he wrote in the same mood to Hegel: "The violent criticisms and insane attacks which people are levelling against *Ghosts* don't worry me in the least. I was expecting this. When *Love's Comedy* appeared, there was just as hysterical an outcry in Norway as there is now. They moaned about *Peer Gynt* too, and *The Pillars of Society* and *A Doll's House*, just as much. The commotion will die away this time as it did before." But he added: "One thing worries me a little when I think how big an edition you printed. Has all this fuss damaged the sales of the book?"

It had indeed. The scandal created by the critics in Norway was so great that people were afraid to buy *Ghosts;* it was not a book to have about the house. It attacked the most sacred principles of the age—the sanctity of marriage, the commandment that a man must honour his father and mother —it defended free love, and suggested not only that a woman had the right to leave her husband, but that even incest might under certain circumstances be justifiable. Hegel was forced to take back enormous quantities of the book from the shops; and Ibsen's other books sold noticeably less than usual that Christmas.[2]

In the other Scandinavian capitals it was the same. August Lindberg, the Swedish actor, has described the scene in Stockholm when *Ghosts* appeared in the bookshops. "People were expecting something from Ibsen after the controversial *A Doll's House,* which had appeared the previous year (*sic*). There was a rush to the bookshops. But the excitement vanished in silence. Absolute silence. The newspapers said nothing and the bookshops sent the book back to the publisher. It was contraband. Something which could not be decently discussed." When Lindberg asked his chief at Nya Teatern, Ludwig Josephson, if he would not consider presenting *Ghosts,* Josephson refused point blank. "The play," he said, "is one of the filthiest things ever written in Scandinavia."

It was, however, in Norway itself that *Ghosts* was attacked most violently. Ibsen had expected the right-wing papers to dislike it, but he was shocked to discover that the radical press denounced it with even greater fervour. The left-wing *Oplandenes Avis* set the tone when it declared that "complete silence would, in our opinion, be the most fitting reception for this work." The reviewer went on to describe it as "the most unpleasant book we have read for a long while," but drew some comfort from the fact that it was "in our humble

[2] Even when the scandal had died down, and the play was being performed before respectful audiences, it was thirteen years before a fresh printing was required.

opinion at least, much worse written than the author's previous works." Ironically enough, these words were penned by a prominent novelist, Arne Garborg, who had just published a story entitled *The Freethinker*—a point Ibsen was to remember when he wrote *An Enemy of the People*. Andreas Munch, writing in *Morgenbladet*, dismissed Ibsen as "a fallen star . . . a spent, quenched meteor," and Ibsen's old admirer Henrik Jaeger went round the country lecturing against the play. Even such "progressive" writers as Alexander Kielland and Jonas Lie, in their private letters, raised their eyebrows. Almost the only Norwegians to defend *Ghosts* publicly were Bjoernson, Camilla Collett, and P. O. Schjoett, who wrote in *Nyt Tidsskrift:* "When the dust which ignorant criticism has raised has subsided, which we trust will happen soon, Ibsen's latest drama, with its pure bold contours, will stand not only as his noblest deed but as the greatest work of art which he, or indeed our whole dramatic literature, has yet produced." In Denmark, Georg Brandes, faithful to his old friend, praised the poet's courage; but even he confidentially expressed the opinion that he found the play "dramatically weak."

In Rome, Ibsen read these reviews with increasing indignation. "What is one to say of the attitude taken by the so-called liberal press?" he wrote to Brandes on 3 January 1882. "These leaders who talk and write of freedom and progressiveness and who at the same time let themselves be the slaves of the supposed opinions of their subscribers? . . . Under no circumstances will I ever link myself with any party that has the majority behind it. Bjoernson says: 'The majority is always right.' As a practising politician he has to say so. But I say: 'The minority is always right.'" He was to develop this theme in his next play, *An Enemy of the People*, using these very words. Three days later he wrote to Sophus Schandorph: "I was prepared for some such commotion. If for nothing else, certain of our Norwegian reviewers have an undeniable talent for completely misunderstanding and misinterpreting the authors whose books they presume to judge." After denying that the views expressed by the characters in *Ghosts* were necessarily his own ("In none of my plays is the

author so wholly detached and uncommitted as in this"), he
went on to deny that *Ghosts* advocated nihilism. "The play is
not concerned with advocating anything. It merely points to
the fact that nihilism is fermenting beneath the surface in
Norway as everywhere else. It is inevitable. A Pastor Manders will always sting some Mrs. Alving into existence. And
she, simply because she is a woman, will, once she has
started, go to the ultimate extreme."

On 28 January he wrote to Otto Borschenius: "It may well
be that in some respects this play is somewhat audacious.
But I thought the time had come when a few boundary
marks had to be shifted. And it was much easier for me, as
an elder writer, to do this job than for the many younger
writers who might want to do something of the kind. I was
prepared for a storm to break over me; but one can't run
away from such things. That would have been cowardice.
What has most depressed me has been not the attacks themselves, but the lack of guts which has been revealed in the
ranks of the so-called liberals in Norway. They are poor stuff
with which to man the barricades."

On 16 March he told Hegel of his plans for a new work.
"This time it will be a peaceful play, which can be read by
cabinet ministers and wholesale merchants and their ladies,
and from which the theatres will not need to shrink. . . . As
far as *Ghosts* is concerned, comprehension will seep into the
minds of the good people of our country, and that in the not
too distant future. But all these fading and decrepit figures
who have spat upon this work will some time bring upon
their heads the crushing judgment of future literary histori-
ans. . . . My book belongs to posterity."

On 24 June he wrote to Countess Sophie Adlersparre, who
had lectured in defence of *Ghosts:* "I am entirely in agreement with you when you say that further than *Ghosts* I dare
not go. I myself felt that the general state of mind in our
country would not admit of it; nor do I feel any urgency to
go further. A writer has not the right to set such a distance
between himself and his public that there is no longer any
understanding between them and him. But I *had* to write

Ghosts; I couldn't stop at *A Doll's House;* after Nora, I had to create Mrs. Alving."

Before publication, towards the end of November 1881, *Ghosts* had been offered to the Royal Theatre in Copenhagen, but had been rejected by the theatre's censor, Erik Boegh. "It takes as the main theme of its action," he wrote in his report, using words that would not have sounded amiss in Pastor Manders's mouth, "a repulsive pathological phenomenon, at the same time undermining the morality which forms the foundation of our social order." The Christiania Theatre and the Royal Theatre in Stockholm also refused to stage it. On 20 May 1882 *Ghosts* received its world premiere in, of all places, Chicago, where it was presented in the original language before an audience of Scandinavian immigrants with the Danish actress Helga von Bluhme as Mrs. Alving, the rest of the parts being played by Danish and Norwegian amateurs. This production subsequently toured Minneapolis and other cities of the Middle West which contained a large Scandinavian population.

The main Scandinavian theatres still fought shy, but at last August Lindberg, having failed to convince Ludwig Josephson of the need to present it, obtained Ibsen's permission to stage the play himself. He organized a company to tour it through the three Scandinavian kingdoms, and on 22 August 1883 he presented it in the Swedish city of Hälsingborg, on the west coast opposite Elsinore. Lindberg himself played Oswald, having visited a hospital in Copenhagen to study patients who had inherited syphilis and lost their reason, and Mrs. Alving was taken by Hedvig Charlotte Winter-Hjelm, a once-famous actress who had been persuaded out of retirement. The occasion passed off without disturbance, and six days later Lindberg took his company across the Sound and gave ten performances at the Folketeater in Copenhagen. In performance the play aroused none of the hostility which it had caused in its printed form. Ludwig Josephson, his fears allayed, allowed the production to visit Nya Teatern in Stockholm, and on 17 October 1883 Lindberg presented

Ghosts for the first time in Ibsen's own country at the Moeller-
gaten Theatre in Christiania. William Archer attended this
performance, and wrote:

> I was present, and well remember the profound im-
> pression it made on the crowded and enthusiastic audi-
> ence. By this time the reaction in favour of the play had
> fairly set in. It happened that on the same evening a
> trivial French farce, *Tête de Linotte* (known in Eng-
> land as *Miss Featherbrain*) was being played at the
> Christiania Theatre; and the contrast could not but strike
> people. They saw a masterpiece of Norwegian literature
> acted by a foreign (Swedish) company at a minor play-
> house, while the official theatre of the capital was given
> over to a piece of Parisian frivolity. The result was that
> on the following evening, and for some nights after-
> wards, demonstrations were made at the Christiania
> Theatre against the policy of the management in reject-
> ing Ibsen's play. . . . Fru Winter-Hjelm's performance
> of Mrs. Alving was exceedingly powerful, and Lindberg
> seemed to me an almost ideal Oswald. In his make-up,
> I remember, there was a strong suggestion of the por-
> traits of Edgar Allan Poe.

Lindberg himself has left an interesting impression of the
Christiania premiere as it seemed to someone on the other
side of the footlights. "When the curtain was raised, it felt as
though the public held its breath. The scenes of the play un-
folded in a silence worthy of a spiritual séance. When the
final curtain fell, the silence continued for a good while, before the ovations started."

Altogether, Lindberg's company performed *Ghosts* seventy-
five times during this tour, a remarkable record for those
days. He returned with the production to Christiania several
times during the next few years; in 1891 Ibsen himself attended a performance, and expressed unqualified approval of
Fru Winter-Hjelm's interpretation.

In 1883 the Royal Theatre in Stockholm and the Swedish
Theatre in Helsinki both staged the play; and Olaus Olsen's
Danish-Norwegian company toured it through the Norwe-
gian provinces. It was not, however, until 1890, nine years

after its publication, that *Ghosts* was played by a completely Norwegian company, at the National Theatre in Bergen. Schroeder, who had originally rejected it, steadfastly refused to allow the Christiania Theatre to perform it as long as he remained in charge, and it was not presented there until 1900, when Bjoern Bjoernson became director. H. A. T. Dedichen, who attended the opening performance of this production on 5 March, remarked that "it passed as easily as a letter through the post. . . . The assemblage of the 'upper ten' which filled the boxes and stalls sat and marvelled that the play could ever have excited such paroxysms of horror."

In Germany, surprisingly, *Ghosts* had to wait five years for its first production, which occurred on 19 April 1886[3] at the Stadttheater in Augsburg. This was a private performance, the local censor having vetoed the play, and Ibsen himself was present. William Archer, in the 1900 introduction to his translation of the play, noted: "The acting does not seem to have been altogether fortunate, for one of the leading critics of Germany has related to me how the poet, at the dress-rehearsal, expressed his opinions in an oft-repeated comment, '*O nein!*' When Regina made her appearance in something that purported to be a Norwegian peasant costume (a ridiculous error which almost all non-Scandinavian Reginas commit), Ibsen's '*O nein!*' was particularly emphatic."

Later that year, on 21 December 1886, *Ghosts* was more worthily presented at the Court Theatre of Meiningen—a production that, according to Archer, "is said to have elicited warm praise from Ibsen himself." A few weeks later, on 9 January 1887, a private performance was given at the Residenz Theater, Berlin, and interest in the play was now so great that there were over 14,000 applications for tickets. A more significant production, however, was that of 29 September 1889 with which the Berlin Freie Bühne opened its first season at the Lessing Theater. Archer, writing in 1900, observed: "This performance is destined to hold a conspicuous place in German literary history, for the Freie Bühne, which it inaugurated, gave the strongest impulse to the recent

[3] Not 14 April, as stated in some records.

renascence of the German drama. . . . Before another ten
years had elapsed [Ibsen's] influence, operating largely
through the Freie Bühne, and the movement it set on
foot, had practically created a new dramatic literature in
Germany."

On 29 May 1890 André Antoine produced *Ghosts* at the
Théâtre des Menus Plaisirs in Paris, the first recorded performance of any Ibsen play in France. George Moore was
present among the audience, and has left a vivid description
of the occasion in his *Impressions and Opinions*. The German
censorship now withdrew its veto, and in 1894 no less than
three separate productions of *Ghosts* were mounted at different theatres in Berlin, to say nothing of a visit by Antoine
with the Théâtre Libre production.

In 1890 *Ghosts* was performed in Vienna and Amsterdam.
The following year London was scandalized by J. T. Grein's
famous production for the Independent Theatre Society, and
the play was acted in New York (in German) and Tiflis (in
Armenian). In 1892 it was staged in Milan, and in 1894 in
New York in (at last) English. By the close of the century,
Ghosts was known throughout Europe, the United States
(where the 1894 production visited numerous cities, without
undue incident), and even in South America, where the
great Italian actor Ermete Novelli and his company toured
the play in Italian. It has been the most frequently performed
of all Ibsen's plays in England, London having seen twenty-
five separate professional productions to date, including one
in German, one in Italian, and one in Yiddish.

Of Grein's London production, William Archer noted: "The
shriek of execration with which this performance was received by the newspapers of the day has scarcely its counter-
part in the history of criticism." Three weeks after the performance, on 8 April 1891, he published in the *Pall Mall
Gazette* an anthology of the choicest comments, and it is
worth quoting in full:

"GHOSTS" AND GIBBERINGS
DESCRIPTIONS OF THE PLAY

"An open drain; a loathsome sore unbandaged; a dirty act done publicly; a lazar-house with all its doors and windows open . . . Candid foulness . . . Kotzebue turned bestial and cynical. Offensive cynicism . . . Ibsen's melancholy and malodorous world . . . Absolutely loathsome and fetid . . . Gross, almost putrid indecorum"—*Daily Telegraph* (leading article). "This mass of vulgarity, egotism, coarseness and absurdity"—*Daily Telegraph* (criticism). "Unutterably offensive . . . Prosecution under Lord Campbell's Act . . . Abominable piece . . . Scandalous"—*Standard*. "Naked loathsomeness . . . Most dismal and repulsive production"—*Daily News*. "Revoltingly suggestive and blasphemous . . . Characters either contradictory in themselves, uninteresting or abhorrent"—*Daily Chronicle*. "A repulsive and degrading work"—*Queen*. "Morbid, unhealthy, unwholesome and disgusting story . . . A piece to bring the stage into disrepute and dishonour with every right-thinking man and woman"—*Lloyd's*. "Merely dull dirt long drawn out"—*Hawk*. "Morbid horrors of the hideous tale . . . Ponderous dullness of the didactic talk . . . If any repetition of this outrage be attempted, the authorities will doubtless wake from their lethargy"—*Sporting and Dramatic News*. "Just a wicked nightmare"—*The Gentlewoman*. "Lugubrious diagnosis of sordid impropriety . . . Characters are prigs, pedants and profligates . . . Morbid caricatures . . . Maunderings of nook-shotten Norwegians . . . It is no more of a play than an average Gaiety burlesque"—*Black and White*. "Most loathsome of all Ibsen's plays . . . Garbage and offal"—*Truth*. "Ibsen's putrid play called *Ghosts* . . . so loathsome an enterprise"—*Academy*. "As foul and filthy a concoction as has ever been allowed to disgrace the boards of an English theatre . . . Dull and disgusting . . . Nastiness and malodorousness laid on thickly as with a trowel"—*Era*. "Noisome corruption"—*Stage*.

DESCRIPTIONS OF IBSEN

"An egotist and a bungler"—*Daily Telegraph*. "A crazy fanatic . . . A crazy, cranky being . . . Not only consistently dirty but deplorably dull"—*Truth*. "The Norwegian pessimist *in petto* (*sic*)—*Black and White*. "Ugly,

nasty, discordant and downright dull . . . A gloomy sort
of ghoul, bent on groping for horrors by night, and blink-
ing like a stupid old owl when the warm sunlight of the
best of life dances into his wrinkled eyes"—*Gentlewoman.* "A teacher of the aestheticism of the Lock Hospital"—*Saturday Review.*

DESCRIPTIONS OF IBSEN'S ADMIRERS

"Lovers of prurience and dabblers in impropriety who
are eager to gratify their illicit tastes under the pretence
of art"—*Evening Standard.* "Ninety-seven per cent of the
people who go to see *Ghosts* are nasty-minded people
who find the discussion of nasty subjects to their taste in
exact proportion to their nastiness"—*Sporting and Dramatic News.* "The sexless . . . the unwomanly woman,
the unsexed females, the whole army of unprepossessing
cranks in petticoats . . . Educated and muck-ferreting
dogs . . . Effeminate men and male women . . . They
all of them—men and women alike—know that they are
doing not only a nasty but an illegal thing . . . The Lord
Chamberlain left them alone to wallow in *Ghosts* . . .
Outside a silly clique, there is not the slightest interest in
the Scandinavian humbug or all his works . . . A wave
of human folly"—*Truth.*

One of the few critics courageous enough to defend the
play was A. B. Walkley. Writing in the *Star* over the pseud-
onym of "Spectator," he asked: "Do these people really find
nothing in *Ghosts* but a mere hospital ward play? Is it really
for them nothing but a painful study of disease? Have they
no eyes for what stares them in the face: the plain, simple
fact that *Ghosts* is a great spiritual drama? Like nearly all
other great masterpieces of the stage, it is a drama of revolt
—the revolt of the "joy of life" against the gloom of hide-
bound, conventional morality, the revolt of the natural man
against the law-made, law-bound puppet, the revolt of the
individual against the oppression of social prejudice . . .
This is the spiritual drama which I see in *Ghosts.*"

Mrs. Alving was played on this occasion by a well-known
amateur named Mrs. Theodore Wright. Mrs. J. T. Grein, in

her biography of her husband (*J. T. Grein,* by "Michael Orme," London, 1936) has told how Mrs. Wright came to be chosen for the part. "One day she wandered into J. T.'s rooms and said she had heard of the intended production. He was immediately struck by the timbre of her voice, detecting in it his conception of the maternal accent to perfection. He asked her to read the third act and, when she had finished, said to her: 'I know nothing about you, but you will play Mrs. Alving, and you will be famous next morning.'" Bernard Shaw later described her performance as "an achievement quite beyond the culture of any other actress of her generation." Subsequent Mrs. Alvings in London include Bessie Hatton (in the first licensed production of the play in 1914), Letitia Darragh (1917), Eleonora Duse (in Italian, 1923), Anna Appel (in Yiddish, 1924), Mrs. Patrick Campbell (1928), Sybil Thorndike (1930), Louise Hampton (1933), Nancy Price (1935), Marie Ney (1937), Katina Paxinou (1940, and 1962 on television), Beatrix Lehmann (1943 and 1951), Mary Hinton (1948), Cathleen Nesbitt (1951, on television), Flora Robson (1958), and Catherine Lacey (1965). Almost certainly the finest, however, was Janet Achurch, who acted the part in Manchester in 1907 and excited C. E. Montague to a memorable tribute:

"Where Mrs. Alving in *Ghosts* stands behind Oswald's chair to hide the despair in her face, and struggles to cheer him with hopeless lies about hope, the beauty of tenderness in Miss Janet Achurch's acting was a thing not to be figured in words, for one art cannot re-do the masterpieces of another. To see it was to grow in experience and bring to life more of your mind; you were born into new, truer knowledge of what the word 'tenderness' means. And a praise almost as tall was due to the giant effort of imagination with which Mr. Courtenay Thorpe, as Oswald, lent every corporal agent to the dramatist's purpose. At the most poignant parts of his revelation of his own destruction, you lost consciousness even of the technical brilliancy of the dramatist and of the individual power and subtlety of the two actors. As happens at rare moments in the theatre, the emotion rose to the

heat at which it first fuses into one whole, and then, to
your sense, consumes clean away the very means of its
own presentation—the force or music of words, the fine
flexure of gesture and tone, the aptness of surroundings;
tragedy burned up the lamp that had held it, and flamed
like a star, unconditioned and absolute."

Of Duse's performance, James Agate wrote: "This weeping, tender lady, bending over Oswald like some sad willow,
is not the woman whom Ibsen drew, gazing speechless upon
her stricken son and twining her hands among horrific hairs.
This exquisite creature, moving from grief to grief in some
saraband of woe, was not Ibsen's still rebellious woman whose
egotism, hardly baulked, breaks out again in bitter mockery
of Pastor Manders. . . . Her performance was instinct with
resignation, whereas Ibsen's character battled it out to the
end. . . . Far truer, in my opinion, was the Mrs. Alving of
Janet Achurch. This was Ibsen's heroine, a mountain of fierce
egotism, of warped, twisted self-assertiveness. . . . She did
not soothe you into accepting grief as a part of human heritage to be expressed in beauty. She brought you face to face
with unbearable shock." On Mrs. Campbell in the part, Agate
commented: "The performance gave us only the shell of Ibsen's character, and as a projection of the artist's personal
genius never rose, until the third act, above the perfunctory.
. . . It was magnificent, but it was not this particular play of
Ibsen. When the curtain went up for the third act we saw a
different Mrs. Campbell. Now at last the great play had got
hold of her. . . . From this point until the end, her playing
was perfect." None of the later English interpreters of the
role have been wholly successful. The best Oswald, after
Courtenay Thorpe, was probably either Leon Quartermaine
in 1914 or the young John Gielgud in 1928.

The first American production after that of 1882 in Chicago
seems to have been in 1887, when an adaptation entitled
Phantoms, or the Sins of His Father was presented in several
of the larger cities; it was widely advertised as "Forbidden
in Germany." The first authentic performance in the States
in English took place on 5 January 1894 at the Berkeley

Lyceum, New York, with Ida Jeffreys as Mrs. Alving and
Courtenay Thorpe as Oswald. In 1899 Mary Shaw played it
at the Carnegie Lyceum in New York; she was much ac-
claimed, and toured it for thirty-seven weeks as far west as
Colorado. Other early Mrs. Alvings in New York included
Alla Nazimova (in Russian, 1905), Mary Shaw again (1917),
Duse (at the Metropolitan Opera House, 1923) and Minnie
Fiske (1928).

As has already been stated, Ibsen's original draft for *Ghosts*
has not been preserved, and the differences between his second draft and the final version as we know it are few and
insignificant. After Ibsen's death, however, six brief sets of
notes presumably relating to *Ghosts* were discovered among
his papers, some (nos. 1–4) on two sheets of quarto, some
(no. 5) on the back of an envelope, and some (no. 6) on a
torn newspaper wrapper. They are undated, but probably
belong to the winter and spring of 1881:

1. The play to be a realistic picture of life. Faith undermined—but people daren't admit it. The "Orphanage"—for the sake of others. They want to be happy—
but this, too, is only an illusion— Everything is ghosts—
An important point: She has been a believer and a romantic—and this can't completely be eradicated by the
attitude she has subsequently adopted—"Everything is
ghosts."
To marry for the wrong reasons, even though they be
religious or moral, brings a Nemesis on the children.
She, the illegitimate child, can be saved by being
married to—the son—but then—?
2. He in his youth was depraved, a debauchee; then
she appeared, a woman who had "seen the light"; she
saved him; she was rich. He had wanted to marry a girl
who was thought unworthy. His wife bore him a son;
then he turned back to the girl; a daughter—
3. These modern women, misused as daughters, as
sisters, as wives, not educated according to their talents,
barred from their vocation, robbed of their inheritance,
their minds embittered—these are the women who are to

provide the mothers for the new generation. What will
be the consequence?

4. She became passionately religious in her youth;
partly because of this, but partly also from affection, she
married him, the "bright genius," the "prodigal." They
move away from town; he "gets on," eventually becomes
a judge, a model public servant, a model man in every
way, religious too. They had a son, then another who
died young. Very early in his life the eldest was put to
lodge with a clergyman, then sent to a boarding school,
was seldom allowed to visit his home. The judge performed his duties for many years, much honoured and
respected; she too was honoured as his "good genius,"
who had been worthily rewarded for her magnanimity.
Then he died; a large part of the fortune into which he
unexpectedly came after his marriage has been formed
into a trust, and now this memorial is about to be dedicated.

Here the play begins.

5. The main theme must be: the fine flowering of our
spiritual life *via* literature, art, etc.—and, in contrast, all
mankind wandering blindly on the wrong track.

6. The perfect man is no longer a natural product, he
is something cultivated like corn and fruit-trees and the
Creole race and thoroughbred horses and breeds of
dogs, vines, etc.—

The trouble is that mankind as a whole is a failure. If
a human being demands to live and develop according to
his nature as a human being, it's regarded as megalomania. All humanity, especially Christians, suffers from
megalomania.

We raise monuments to the *dead;* because we feel a
duty towards them; we allow lepers to marry; but their
offspring—? The unborn—?

Ibsen's contemporaries saw *Ghosts* primarily as a play
about inherited physical illness; for some years Oswald, not
Mrs. Alving, was regarded as the chief character. They did
not realize that what *Ghosts* is really about is the devitalizing
effect of inherited convention. Oswald's syphilis is not the
theme of *Ghosts,* any more than Dr. Rank's inherited disease

is the theme of *A Doll's House*. To quote Halvdan Koht:
"Oswald was branded with disease, not because his father
was a beast, but because Mrs. Alving had obeyed the immoral ethics of society. . . . *Ghosts* is a play about ethical,
not physical debility." The importance of waging war against
the past, the need for each individual to find his or her own
freedom, the danger of renouncing love in the name of duty
—these are the real themes of *Ghosts*, as they are the themes
of every play Ibsen wrote from *A Doll's House* onwards. And
the targets are the same as those which he had attacked in
A Doll's House and, before that, in *The Pillars of Society*,
and which he was to go on attacking until the end of his life
—the hollowness of great reputations, provincialism of outlook, the narrowness of small-town life, the suppression of
individual freedom from within as well as from without, and
the neglect of the significance of heredity. The problem of
the connection between heritage and decadence was much
discussed in the Scandinavian group in Rome around 1880.
J. P. Jacobsen had translated Darwin's *The Origin of Species*
into Danish in 1872, and *The Descent of Man* in 1875, and
the French naturalistic novelists, with Zola at their head, had
hastened to exploit Darwin's thesis that man, like other animals, must adapt himself to the environment in which he
lives. Ibsen, however, greatly disliked being compared with
Zola, for whose works he had a low regard.[4] "Zola," he once
said, "descends into the sewer to bathe in it; I to cleanse it."

Ibsen never liked admitting that any of his plays owed a
debt to any other writer; he said that in any age writers
tended to find similar themes. Half a century earlier, however, a *conte* by a Norwegian author named Mauritz Hansen
had been published entitled *The Daughter*, and the similarities between it and *Ghosts* are so striking that it is difficult
not to believe that, consciously or unconsciously, the former

---

[4] If indeed he had read any of them. When, six months after
the publication of *Ghosts*, a Swedish painter asked him what he
thought of Zola, Ibsen replied: "I don't read books. I leave that to
my wife and son." But he read newspapers in most minute detail,
including advertisements.

must have provided a starting-point for the latter. *The Daughter* tells how a dissipated lieutenant-colonel, formidably named Hannibal Hedebrandt, has in his youth had an affair with his maid, Else. Then he weds a lady of his own station but, on discovering that Else is with child, marries her off to a caretaker named Oeken. Else goes mad, and dies, but her daughter Henriette grows up in the Hedebrandt household; she is repelled by her supposed father, the caretaker, who has a wooden leg. It is of course perfectly possible, and I think likely, that Ibsen had read this story in his youth and had forgotten it, and that certain details had forced themselves up out of his unconscious—possibly influenced by the fact that he himself, at the age of eighteen[5], when a chemist's assistant in Grimstad, had had an illegitimate child by a servant girl, also named Else. Ibsen had, moreover, from a very early age, been repelled by the fact of his father having gone bankrupt, and Engstrand's club foot may possibly represent his father's inability to stand on both feet in the world. (He was to paint a more detailed portrait of his father two plays later, as Old Ekdal in *The Wild Duck*.)

Manders, as has been noted, was immediately motivated by Ibsen's indignation at the Norwegian Ecclesiastical Department's treatment of his son. But his contempt for priests was of long standing, and he had already portrayed unsympathetic specimens in *Love's Comedy* (Pastor Straamand), *Brand* (the Provost), and *The Pillars of Society*, in which Dr. Roerlund the schoolmaster, though not in fact a priest, is referred to contemptuously as "Pastor" by Lona Hessel. Regina was based on a maid whom the Ibsens had in Munich. She was of Bavarian birth but had spent some while in Paris, and incorporated various French expressions in the high German she used when speaking to Ibsen and his wife, though among her friends she talked in the Bavarian dialect.

Mrs. Alving is, so to speak, Nora as a mother, and one wonders whether her creation may not partly have been inspired by that "happy ending" which Ibsen had found himself com-

[5] Not sixteen, as erroneously stated in my introduction to *The Wild Duck*.

pelled to write for *A Doll's House* in order to prevent German adaptors from doing the same thing less competently.[6] In that version, Nora returns to her husband and children; and Mrs. Alving is not unlike a picture of what Nora might well have become in twenty years if she had done that. Like Nora, Mrs. Alving is strangled by convention and a misplaced sense of duty. "After Nora, I *had* to create Mrs. Alving." Viewed in this context, Oswald's inherited syphilis may be regarded as a symbol of the dead customs and traditions which we inherit, and which stunt and cripple us and lay waste our life.

If there is to be a last word on *Ghosts*, it belongs to C. E. Montague, even though he wrote it over fifty years ago. "It is strange;" he remarked in *Dramatic Values*. "There were people once who called *Ghosts* immoral. Was this, you ask now when you see it, the play that launched a thousand ships of critical fury? Why, it is rendingly, scaringly moral. When it is before you, you feel that some truths about conduct, which you had thought you knew pretty well, can only have been known as one knows a beast safely caged in a zoo, since now they are going about glaring at you with fanged mouths open; they have turned terrifyingly real. It is fairly arguable that—as Mr. Archer seems to feel—the fierceness of moral intention in *Ghosts* prevents it from ranking with Ibsen's best work. It has a kind of aghast grimness, a bald, austere hardness of conception and dry, level tensity in the working out that seem more expressive of the strong man rightly angered by preventable wrong than of the artist excited and even, in a sense, delighted by everything in the world, good and bad. Perhaps it was some sense of this that made Brandes say, when the play first came out and the foolish people were howling, that it might or might not be Ibsen's greatest work, but it was certainly his noblest deed. Immoral!"

M. M.

6 See page 10.

CHARACTERS

MRS. HELEN ALVING, widow of Captain Alving, late Chamber-
   lain to the King.
OSWALD ALVING, her son, a painter.
PASTOR MANDERS.
ENGSTRAND, a carpenter.
REGINA ENGSTRAND, Mrs. Alving's maid.

The action takes place on MRS. ALVING'S *country estate by a
large fjord in Western Norway.*

This translation of GHOSTS *was first performed on 6 April 1965 at the Theatre Royal, Stratford East, London, in a presentation by Stage Sixty, with the following cast:*

MRS. ALVING	Catherine Lacey
OSWALD	Barry Warren
PASTOR MANDERS	Leonard Rossiter
ENGSTRAND	Daniel Thorndike
REGINA	Patricia England

Directed by Adrian Rendle

ACT ONE

A spacious garden-room, with a door in the left-hand wall and two doors in the right-hand wall. In the centre of the room is a round table with chairs around it; on the table are books, magazines and newspapers. Downstage left is a window, in front of which is a small sofa with a sewing-table by it. Backstage the room opens out into a slightly narrower conservatory, with walls of large panes of glass. In the right-hand wall of the conservatory is a door leading down to the garden. Through the glass wall a gloomy fjord landscape is discernible, veiled by steady rain.

ENGSTRAND, *a carpenter, is standing at the garden door. His left leg is slightly crooked; under the sole of his boot is fixed a block of wood.* REGINA, *with an empty garden syringe in her hand, bars his entry.*

REGINA (*keeping her voice low*). What do you want? Stay where you are! You're dripping wet!

ENGSTRAND. It is God's blessed rain, my child.

REGINA. The Devil's damned rain, more like.

ENGSTRAND. Why, Regina, the way you talk! (*Limps a few steps into the room.*) What I wanted to say is—

REGINA. Here, you! Don't make such a noise with that foot. The young master's asleep upstairs.

ENGSTRAND. In bed—at this hour? Why, the day's half gone.

REGINA. That's none of your business.

ENGSTRAND. I was out drinking last night—

REGINA. I'm sure.

ENGSTRAND. We are but flesh and blood, my child—

REGINA (*drily*). Quite.

ENGSTRAND. And the temptations of this world are manifold. But God is my witness; I was at my bench by half past five this morning.

REGINA. Yes, yes. Come on now, clear off. I don't want to be caught having a rendezvous with you.

ENGSTRAND. You don't what?

REGINA. I don't want anyone to see you here. Come on, go away, get out.

ENGSTRAND (*comes a few steps nearer*). Not before I've had a word with you. This afternoon I'll be through with the job down at the school house, and tonight I'm catching the steamer back to town.

REGINA (*mutters*). *Bon voyage.*

ENGSTRAND. Thank you, my child. They're dedicating the new Orphanage here tomorrow, and there'll be celebrations, with intoxicating liquor. And no one shall say of Jacob Engstrand that he can't turn his back on temptation. (RE-GINA *laughs scornfully.*) Yes, well, there'll be a lot of tip-top people coming here tomorrow. Pastor Manders is expected from town.

REGINA. He's arriving today.

ENGSTRAND. Well, there you are. And I'm damned if I'm going to risk getting into his bad books.

REGINA. Oh, so that's it.

ENGSTRAND. What do you mean?

REGINA (*looks knowingly at him*). What are you trying to fool the Pastor into this time?

ENGSTRAND. Hush! Are you mad? Me try to fool Pastor Manders? Oh no, Pastor Manders is much too good a friend to me for that. Now what I wanted to talk to you about is this. I'm going back home tonight.

REGINA. The sooner you go the better.

ENGSTRAND. Yes, but I want to take you with me, Regina.

REGINA (*her jaw drops*). You want to take *me*—? What are you talking about?

ENGSTRAND. I want to take you with me, I say.

REGINA (*scornfully*). Home with you? Not likely I won't!

ENGSTRAND. Oh, we'll see, we'll see.

REGINA. You bet your life we'll see. You expect me to go
back and live with you? In that house? After Mrs. Alving's
brought me up in her own home, treats me as though I
was one of the family? Get out!

ENGSTRAND. What the hell's this? Are you setting yourself up
against your father, my girl?

REGINA (*mutters without looking at him*). You've said often
enough that I'm no concern of yours.

ENGSTRAND. Oh—you don't want to take any notice of that—

REGINA. What about all the times you've sworn at me and
called me a— oh, *mon dieu!*

ENGSTRAND. May God strike me dead if I ever used such a
vile word!

REGINA. Oh, I know what word you used.

ENGSTRAND. Yes, but that was only when I wasn't myself.
Hm. The temptations of this world are manifold, Regina.

REGINA. Ugh!

ENGSTRAND. And when your mother was being difficult. I had
to think up some way to nark her. She was always acting
the fine lady. (*Mimics.*) "Let me go, Engstrand! Stop it!
I've been in service for three years with Chamberlain Alving at Rosenvold, and don't you forget it!" (*Laughs.*)
She never could forget the Captain had been made a
Chamberlain when she was working for him.

REGINA. Poor Mother! You killed her soon enough with your
bullying.

ENGSTRAND (*uncomfortably*). That's right, blame me for everything.

REGINA (*turns away and mutters beneath her breath*). Ugh!
And that leg!

ENGSTRAND. What's that you said, my child?

REGINA. *Pied de mouton!*

ENGSTRAND. What's that, English?

REGINA. Yes.

ENGSTRAND. Ah, well. They've made a scholar of you out here
anyway, and that'll come in handy now, Regina.

REGINA (*after a short silence*). And—what was it you wanted
me for in town?

ENGSTRAND. Fancy asking such a question! What should a
father want from his only child? Aren't I a lonely, forsaken
widower?

REGINA. Oh, don't try to fool me with that rubbish. What do
you want me up there for?

ENGSTRAND. Well, it's like this. I'm thinking of starting out on
something new.

REGINA (*sniffs*). You've tried that often enough. And you've
always made a mess of it.

ENGSTRAND. Yes, but this time, you'll see, Regina! God rot
me if I don't—!

REGINA (*stamps her foot*). Stop swearing!

ENGSTRAND. Ssh, ssh! How right you are, my child! Now
what I wanted to say was this. I've put quite a bit of money
aside out of the work I've been doing at this new Orphanage.

REGINA. Have you? Good for you.

ENGSTRAND. Well, there ain't much for a man to spend his
money on out here in the country, is there?

REGINA. Well? Go on.

ENGSTRAND. Yes, well you see, so I thought I'd put the money
into something that might bring me in a bit. A kind of
home for sailors—

REGINA (*disgusted*). Oh, my God!

ENGSTRAND. A real smart place, you understand—not one of
those low waterfront joints. No, damn it, this is going to be
for captains and officers and—tip-top people, you understand.

REGINA. And I'm to—?

ENGSTRAND. You're going to help me. Just for appearance's
sake, of course. You won't have to work hard, my child.
You can fix your own hours.

REGINA. I see!

ENGSTRAND. Well, we've got to have a bit of skirt on show, I
mean that's obvious. Got to give them a little fun in the
evenings—dancing and singing and so forth. You must remember these men are wandering mariners lost on the
ocean of life. (*Comes closer.*) Now don't be stupid and

make things difficult for yourself, Regina. What can you make of yourself out here? What good is it going to do you, all this fine education Mrs. Alving's given you? I hear you're going to look after the orphans down the road. Is that what you want to do? Are you so anxious to ruin your health for those filthy brats?

REGINA. No, if things work out the way I— Ah well, they might. They might.

ENGSTRAND. What are you talking about?

REGINA. Never you mind. This money you've managed to save out here—is it a lot?

ENGSTRAND. All told I'd say it comes to between thirty-five and forty pounds.

REGINA. Not bad.

ENGSTRAND. Enough to make a start with, my child.

REGINA. Aren't you going to give me any of it?

ENGSTRAND. Not damn likely I'm not.

REGINA. Aren't you even going to send me a new dress?

ENGSTRAND. You just come back to town and set up with me, and you'll get dresses enough.

REGINA (laughs scornfully). I could do that on my own, if I wanted to.

ENGSTRAND. No, Regina, you need a father's hand to guide you. There's a nice house I can get in Little Harbour Street. They don't want much cash on the nail; and we could turn it into a sort of—well—sailors' mission.

REGINA. But I don't want to live with you! I don't want anything to do with you. Come on, get out.

ENGSTRAND. You wouldn't need to stay with me for long, my child. More's the pity. If you play your cards properly. The way you've blossomed out these last few years, you—

REGINA. Yes?

ENGSTRAND. You wouldn't have to wait long before some nice officer—perhaps even a captain—

REGINA. I don't want to marry any of them. Sailors haven't any *savoir vivre*.

ENGSTRAND. Haven't any what?

REGINA. I know sailors. There's no future in marrying them.

ENGSTRAND. All right then, don't marry them. You can do just as well without. (*Lowers his voice.*) The Englishman —him with the yacht—fifty pounds he paid out—and she wasn't any prettier than you.

REGINA (*goes towards him*). Get out!

ENGSTRAND (*shrinks*). Now, now, you wouldn't hit your own father!

REGINA. Wouldn't I? You say another word about mother, and you'll see! Get out, I tell you! (*Pushes him towards the garden door.*) And don't slam the door. Young Mr. Alving's—

ENGSTRAND. Yes, I know. He's asleep. Why do you fuss so much about him? (*More quietly.*) Ah-ha! You wouldn't be thinking of *him*, would you?

REGINA. Out, and be quick about it! You're out of your mind. No, not that way. Here's Pastor Manders. Go out through the kitchen.

ENGSTRAND (*goes right*). All right, I'll go. But you ask *him*— his Reverence. He'll tell you what a child's duty is to its father. I am your father, you know, whatever you say. I can prove it from the parish register.

He goes out through the second door, which REGINA *has opened and closed behind him. She looks quickly at herself in the mirror, dusts herself with her handkerchief, and straightens her collar; then she begins to water the flowers.* PASTOR MANDERS, *in an overcoat and carrying an umbrella, and with a small travelling bag on a strap from his shoulder, enters through the garden door into the conservatory.*

MANDERS. Good morning, Miss Engstrand.

REGINA (*turns in surprise and delight*). Why, Pastor Manders! Has the boat come already?

MANDERS. It arrived a few minutes ago. (*Enters the garden room.*) Very tiresome this rain we're having.

REGINA (*follows him*). A blessing for the farmers, though, sir.

MANDERS. Yes, you are right. We city people tend to forget that. (*Begins to take off his overcoat.*)

REGINA. Oh, please let me help you! There. Oh, it's soaking! I'll hang it up in the hall. Oh, and the umbrella! I'll open it out to let it dry.

She takes the coat and umbrella out through the other door, right. MANDERS *takes his bag from his shoulder and puts it and his hat on a chair. Meanwhile* REGINA *comes back.*

MANDERS. Ah, it's good to be under a dry roof again. Well, I trust all is well here?

REGINA. Yes, thank you, sir.

MANDERS. Everyone very busy, I suppose, getting ready for tomorrow?

REGINA. Oh, yes, there are one or two things to be done.

MANDERS. Mrs. Alving is at home, I hope?

REGINA. Oh, dear me, yes, she's just gone upstairs to make a cup of chocolate for the young master.

MANDERS. Ah, yes. I heard when I got off the boat that Oswald had returned.

REGINA. Yes, he arrived the day before yesterday. We hadn't expected him until today.

MANDERS. In good health and spirits, I trust?

REGINA. Oh yes, thank you, I think so. He felt dreadfully tired after his journey, though. He came all the way from Paris in one go—*par rapide*. I think he's having a little sleep just now, so we'd better talk just a tiny bit quietly.

MANDERS. Ssh! We'll be like mice!

REGINA (*moves an armchair near the table*). Now sit down and make yourself comfortable, sir. (*He sits. She puts a footstool under his feet.*) There now. Are you quite comfortable?

MANDERS. Thank you, thank you; yes, very comfortable. (*Looks at her.*) Do you know, Miss Engstrand, I really believe you've grown since I last saw you.

REGINA. Do you think so? Madam says I've rounded out a bit too.

MANDERS. Rounded out? Well, yes, a little perhaps. Not too much.

Short pause.

REGINA. Shall I tell madam you've come?

MANDERS. Thank you, there's no hurry, my dear child. Er—tell me now, Regina, how is your father getting on out here?

REGINA. Thank you, Pastor, he's doing very well.

MANDERS. He came to see me when he was last in town.

REGINA. No, did he really? He's always so happy when he gets a chance to speak to you, sir.

MANDERS. And you go down and see him quite often?

REGINA. I? Oh yes, of course—whenever I get the chance—

MANDERS. Your father hasn't a very strong character, Miss Engstrand. He badly needs a hand to guide him.

REGINA. Oh—yes, I dare say you're right there.

MANDERS. He needs to have someone near him whom he is fond of, and whose judgment he respects. He admitted it quite openly the last time he visited me.

REGINA. Yes, he said something of the sort to me too. But I don't know whether Mrs. Alving will want to lose me, especially now we've the new Orphanage to look after. Besides, I'd hate to leave Mrs. Alving. She's always been so kind to me.

MANDERS. But my dear girl, a daughter's duty! Naturally we would have to obtain your mistress's permission first.

REGINA. But I don't know that it'd be right and proper for me to keep house for an unmarried man at my age.

MANDERS. What! But my dear Miss Engstrand, this is your own father we're talking about!

REGINA. Yes—but all the same— Oh yes, if it was a nice house, with a real gentleman—

MANDERS. But my dear Regina—!

REGINA. Someone I could feel affection for and look up to as a father—

MANDERS. But my dear good child—!

REGINA. Oh, I'd so love to go and live in the city. Out here it's so dreadfully lonely—and you know, don't you, sir, what it means to be all alone in the world? And I'm quick and willing—I think I can say that. Oh, Pastor Manders, don't you know of a place I could go to?

MANDERS. I? No, I'm afraid I don't know of anyone at all.

REGINA. Oh, but do please think of me if ever you should, dear, dear Pastor Manders.

MANDERS (*gets up*). Yes, yes, Miss Engstrand, I certainly will.

REGINA. You see, if only I—

MANDERS. Will you be so good as to call Mrs. Alving for me?

REGINA. Yes, sir. I'll call her at once.

She goes out left. PASTOR MANDERS *walks up and down the room a couple of times, stands for a moment upstage with his hands behind his back and looks out into the garden. Then he comes back to the part of the room where the table is, picks up a book and glances at its title page, starts and looks at some of the others.*

MANDERS. Hm! I see!

MRS. ALVING *enters through the door left. She is followed by* REGINA, *who at once goes out through the door downstage right.*

MRS. ALVING (*holds out her hand*). Welcome to Rosenvold, Pastor.

MANDERS. Good morning, Mrs. Alving. Well, I've kept my promise.

MRS. ALVING. Punctual as always.

MANDERS. But you know it wasn't easy for me to get away. All these blessed boards and committees I sit on—

MRS. ALVING. All the kinder of you to arrive in such good time. Now we can get our business settled before lunch. But where's your luggage?

MANDERS (*quickly*). My portmanteau is down at the village store. I shall be sleeping there.

MRS. ALVING (*represses a smile*). I can't persuade you to spend a night in my house even now?

MANDERS. No, no, Mrs. Alving—it's very kind of you, but I'll sleep down there as usual. It's so convenient for when I go on board again.

MRS. ALVING. As you please. Though I really think two old people like you and me could—

MANDERS. Bless me, you're joking. But of course you must be very happy. The great day tomorrow—and you have Oswald home again.

MRS. ALVING. Yes, you can imagine how happy that makes me. It's over two years since he was home last. And now he's promised to stay with me the whole winter.

MANDERS. No, has he really? Well, that's nice of him. He knows his filial duty. I fancy life in Paris and Rome must offer altogether different attractions.

MRS. ALVING. Yes, but his home is here; and his mother. Ah, my dear boy; he loves his mother, God bless him.

MANDERS. It would be sad indeed if distance and dabbling in art and such things should blunt his natural affections.

MRS. ALVING. It certainly would. But luckily there's nothing wrong with him. I'll be amused to see whether you recognize him again. He'll be down later; he's upstairs now taking a little rest on the sofa. But please sit down, my dear Pastor.

MANDERS. Thank you. Er—you're sure this is a convenient moment—?

MRS. ALVING. Certainly.

She sits down at the table.

MANDERS. Good. Well, then— (*Goes over to the chair on which his bag is lying, takes out a sheaf of papers, sits down on the opposite side of the table and looks for a space to put down the papers.*) Well, to begin with, here are the— (*Breaks off.*) Tell me, Mrs. Alving, how do *these* books come to be here?

MRS. ALVING. Those books? I'm reading them.

MANDERS. You read writings of this kind?

MRS. ALVING. Certainly I do.

MANDERS. And does this kind of reading make you feel better or happier?

MRS. ALVING. I think they make me feel more secure.

MANDERS. How extraordinary! In what way?

MRS. ALVING. Well, they sort of explain and confirm many things that puzzle me. Yes, that's what's so strange, Pastor Manders—there isn't really anything new in these books—there's nothing in them that most people haven't already thought for themselves. It's only that most people either haven't fully realized it, or they won't admit it.

MANDERS. Well, dear God! Do you seriously believe that most people—?

MRS. ALVING. Yes, I do.

MANDERS. But surely not in this country? Not people like us?

MRS. ALVING. Oh, yes. People like us too.

MANDERS. Well, really! I must say—!

MRS. ALVING. But what do you object to in these books?

MANDERS. Object to? You surely don't imagine I spend my time studying such publications?

MRS. ALVING. In other words, you've no idea what you're condemning?

MANDERS. I've read quite enough about these writings to disapprove of them.

MRS. ALVING. Don't you think you ought to form your own opinion—?

MANDERS. My dear Mrs. Alving, there are many occasions in life when one must rely on the judgment of others. That is the way things are and it is good that it should be so. If it were not so, what would become of society?

MRS. ALVING. Yes, yes. You may be right.

MANDERS. Of course I don't deny there may be quite a lot that is attractive about these writings. And I cannot exactly blame you for wishing to keep informed of these intellectual movements in the great world outside about which one hears so much. After all, you have allowed your son to wander there for a number of years. But—

MRS. ALVING. But—?

MANDERS (*lowers his voice*). But one does not have to talk about it, Mrs. Alving. One really does not need to account to all and sundry for what one reads and thinks within one's own four walls.

MRS. ALVING. No, of course not. I quite agree with you.

MANDERS. Remember the duty you owe to this Orphanage which you decided to found at a time when your attitude towards spiritual matters was quite different from what it is now—as far as *I* can judge.

MRS. ALVING. Yes, yes, that's perfectly true. But it was the Orphanage we were going to—

MANDERS. It was the Orphanage we were going to discuss, yes. But—be discreet, dear Mrs. Alving! And now let us turn to our business. (*Opens the packet and takes out some of the papers.*) You see these?

MRS. ALVING. Are those the deeds?

MANDERS. All of them. Ready and completed. As you can imagine, it's been no easy task to get them all through in time. I really had to get out my whip. The authorities are almost painfully conscientious when you want a decision from them. But here we have them nevertheless. (*Leafs through them.*) Here is the executed conveyance of the farmstead named Solvik in the Manor of Rosenvold, with its newly constructed buildings, schoolrooms, staff accommodation and chapel. And here is the settlement of the endowment and the trust deed of the institution. Look. (*Reads.*) Deed of trust for the Captain Alving Memorial Home.

MRS. ALVING (*stares for a long while at the paper*). So there it is.

MANDERS. I thought I'd say Captain rather than Chamberlain. Captain looks less ostentatious.

MRS. ALVING. Yes, yes, as you think best.

MANDERS. And here is the bankbook for the capital which has been placed on deposit to cover the running expenses of the Orphanage.

MRS. ALVING. Thank you; but I think it would be more convenient if you kept that, if you don't mind.

MANDERS. Certainly, certainly. I think we may as well leave the money on deposit to begin with. Admittedly the interest isn't very attractive—four per cent with six months notice of withdrawal. If we could obtain a good mortgage later—of course it would have to be a first mortgage and of unimpeachable security—we might reconsider the matter.

MRS. ALVING. Yes, well, dear Pastor Manders, you know best about all that.

MANDERS. Anyway, I'll keep my eyes open. But now there's another matter I've several times been meaning to ask you about.

MRS. ALVING. And what is that?

MANDERS. Should the buildings of the Orphanage be insured or not.

MRS. ALVING. Yes, of course they must be insured.

MANDERS. Ah, but wait a minute, Mrs. Alving. Let us consider this question a little more closely.

MRS. ALVING. Everything I have is insured—buildings, furniture, crops, livestock.

MANDERS. Naturally. On your own estate. I do the same, of course. But you see, this is quite a different matter. The Orphanage is, so to speak, to be consecrated to a higher purpose.

MRS. ALVING. Yes, but—

MANDERS. As far as I personally am concerned, I see nothing offensive in securing ourselves against all eventualities—

MRS. ALVING. Well, I certainly don't.

MANDERS. But what is the feeling among the local people out here? You can judge that better than I can.

MRS. ALVING. The feeling?

MANDERS. Are there many people with a right to an opinion —I mean, people who really have the right to hold an opinion—who might take offence?

MRS. ALVING. Well, what do you mean by people who have the right to hold an opinion?

MANDERS. Oh, I am thinking chiefly of people sufficiently independent and influential to make it impossible for one to ignore their opinions altogether.

MRS. ALVING. There are quite a few people like that who I suppose might take offence—

MANDERS. You see! In town, we have a great many such

people. Followers of other denominations. People might
very easily come to the conclusion that neither you nor I
have sufficient trust in the ordinance of a Higher Power.

MRS. ALVING. But my dear Pastor, as long as you yourself—

MANDERS. I know, I know—my conscience is clear, that is
true. But all the same, we couldn't prevent a false and
unfavourable interpretation being placed on our action.
And that might well adversely influence the purpose for
which the Orphanage has been dedicated.

MRS. ALVING. If that were so I—

MANDERS. And I can't altogether close my eyes to the difficult
—I might even say deeply embarrassing—position in which
I might find myself. Among influential circles in town there
is a great interest in the cause of the Orphanage. After all,
it is to serve the town as well, and it is hoped that it may
considerably ease the burden of the ratepayers in respect
to the poor. But since I have acted as your adviser and
been in charge of the business side I must admit I fear
certain over-zealous persons might in the first place direct
their attacks against me—

MRS. ALVING. Well, you mustn't lay yourself open to that.

MANDERS. Not to speak of the attacks which would un-
doubtedly be launched against me in certain newspapers
and periodicals, and which—

MRS. ALVING. Enough, dear Pastor Manders. That settles it.

MANDERS. Then you do not wish the Orphanage to be insured?

MRS. ALVING. No. We will forget about it.

MANDERS (leans back in his chair). But suppose an accident
should occur—you never can tell—would you be able to
make good the damage?

MRS. ALVING. No, quite frankly I couldn't.

MANDERS. Well, but you know, Mrs. Alving, this is really
rather a serious responsibility we are taking on our shoulders.

MRS. ALVING. But do you think we have any alternative?

MANDERS. No, that's just it. I don't think there is any real
alternative. We must not lay ourselves open to misinter-

pretation. And we have no right to antagonize public opinion.

MRS. ALVING. At any rate you, as a clergyman, must not.

MANDERS. And I really think we must believe that such an institution will have luck on its side—nay, that it stands under special protection.

MRS. ALVING. Let us hope so, Pastor Manders.

MANDERS. Shall we take the risk, then?

MRS. ALVING. Yes, let us.

MANDERS. Good. As you wish. (*Makes a note.*) No insurance, then.

MRS. ALVING. It's strange you happened to mention this to-day—

MANDERS. I've often thought of raising the matter with you—

MRS. ALVING. Because yesterday we almost had a fire down there.

MANDERS. What!

MRS. ALVING. Well, it was nothing much really. Some shavings caught fire in the carpentry shop.

MANDERS. Where Engstrand works?

MRS. ALVING. Yes. They say he's very careless with matches.

MANDERS. He's got so many things to think about, poor man —so many temptations. Thank heaven I hear he has now resolved to lead a virtuous life.

MRS. ALVING. Oh? Who says so?

MANDERS. He has assured me so himself. And he's a good worker.

MRS. ALVING. Oh, yes—as long as he keeps sober—

MANDERS. Yes, that is a grievous weakness! But he is often compelled to yield to it because of his bad leg, he says. The last time he was in town I was quite touched. He came to see me and thanked me so sincerely because I had got him this job here, so that he could be near Regina.

MRS. ALVING. I don't think he sees her very often.

MANDERS. Oh yes, he told me himself. He talks to her every day.

MRS. ALVING. Oh, well. Possibly.

MANDERS. He is so conscious of his need to have someone

who can restrain him when temptation presents itself. That is what is so lovable about Jacob Engstrand, that he comes to one like a child and accuses himself and admits his weakness. The last time he came up and talked to me— Tell me, Mrs. Alving, if it were absolutely vital for the poor man to have Regina back to live with him again—

MRS. ALVING (*rises swiftly*). Regina!

MANDERS. You must not oppose it.

MRS. ALVING. I certainly shall. Anyway, Regina is going to work at the Orphanage.

MANDERS. But don't forget, he is her father—

MRS. ALVING. Oh, I know very well the kind of father he's been to her. No, I shall never consent to her going back to him.

MANDERS (*rises*). But my dear Mrs. Alving, you mustn't get so emotional about it. You seem quite frightened. It's very sad the way you misjudge this man Engstrand.

MRS. ALVING (*more quietly*). Never mind that. I have taken Regina into my house, and here she shall stay. (*Listens*) Hush now, dear Pastor Manders, let's not say anything more about it. (*Happily.*) Listen! There's Oswald coming downstairs. Now we will think of nothing but him.

OSWALD ALVING, *in a light overcoat, with his hat in his hand and smoking a big meerschaum pipe, enters through the door left.*

OSWALD (*stops in the doorway*). Oh, I'm sorry—I thought you were in the study. (*Comes closer.*) Good morning, Pastor.

MANDERS (*stares*). Why—! Most extraordinary!

MRS. ALVING. Well, Pastor Manders, what do you think of him?

MANDERS. I think—I think—! But is this really—?

OSWALD. Yes, this is the Prodigal Son, Pastor.

MANDERS. Oh, but my dear young friend—!

OSWALD. Well, the son, anyway.

MRS. ALVING. Oswald is thinking of the time when you used to be so strongly opposed to his becoming a painter.

MANDERS. Many a step which to human eyes seems dubious often turns out— (*Shakes his hand.*) Anyway, welcome, welcome! My dear Oswald—! I trust you will allow me to call you by your Christian name?

OSWALD. What else?

MANDERS. Excellent. Now, my dear Oswald, what I was going to say was this. You mustn't think I condemn the artistic profession out of hand. I presume there are many who succeed in keeping the inner man untarnished in that profession too.

OSWALD. Let us hope so.

MRS. ALVING (*happily*). I know one person who has remained pure both inwardly and outwardly. Just look at him, Pastor Manders.

OSWALD (*wanders across the room*). Yes, yes, Mother dear, please.

MANDERS. Unquestionably—there's no denying that. Besides, you have begun to acquire a name now. The newspapers often speak of you, and in most flattering terms. Well— that is to say, I don't seem to have read about you quite so much lately.

OSWALD (*by the flowers upstage*). I haven't done so much painting lately.

MRS. ALVING. Even painters have to rest now and then.

MANDERS. I suppose so. To prepare themselves and conserve their energies for some great work.

OSWALD. Yes. Mother, shall we be eating soon?

MRS. ALVING. In about half an hour. He still enjoys his food, thank heaven.

MANDERS. And his tobacco, I see.

OSWALD. I found Father's pipe upstairs in the bedroom, so I—

MANDERS. Of course!

MRS. ALVING. What do you mean?

MANDERS. When Oswald appeared in that doorway with that pipe in his mouth, it was just as though I saw his father alive again.

OSWALD. Oh? Really?

MRS. ALVING. Oh, how can you say that? Oswald takes after me.

MANDERS. Yes; but there's an expression at the corner of his mouth, something about his lips, that reminds me so vividly of Alving—at any rate now when he's smoking.

MRS. ALVING. How can you say that? Oswald has much more the mouth of a clergyman, I think.

MANDERS. True, true. Some of my colleagues have a similar expression.

MRS. ALVING. But put away that pipe, my dear boy. I don't want any smoke in here.

OSWALD (obeys). I'm sorry. I only wanted to try it. You see, I smoked it once when I was a child.

MRS. ALVING. What?

OSWALD. Yes. I was quite small at the time. I remember, I went upstairs to see Father in his room one evening. He was so happy and cheerful.

MRS. ALVING. Oh, you don't remember anything from that time.

OSWALD. Oh, yes, I remember very clearly, he picked me up and sat me on his knee and let me smoke his pipe. "Puff away, boy," he said, "puff hard." And I puffed as hard as I could. I felt myself go pale and the sweat broke out on my forehead in great drops. And that made him roar with laughter—

MANDERS. How very strange.

MRS. ALVING. My dear, it's just something Oswald has dreamed.

OSWALD. No, Mother, I didn't dream it. Surely you must remember—you came in and carried me back into the nursery. Then I was sick and I saw you crying. Did Father often play jokes like that?

MANDERS. In his youth he was an extremely gay young man—

OSWALD. And yet he managed to achieve so much. So much that was good and useful; although he died so young.

MANDERS. Yes, you have inherited the name of an industrious and worthy man, my dear Oswald Alving. Well, I hope this will spur you on.

OSWALD. Yes, it ought to, oughtn't it?

MANDERS. In any case it was good of you to come home and join us in honouring him.

OSWALD. It was the least I could do for Father.

MRS. ALVING. And the best thing of all is that I'm going to have him here for so long.

MANDERS. Yes, I hear you're staying the winter.

OSWALD. I am here for an indefinite period, Pastor. Oh, but it's good to be home!

MRS. ALVING (*warmly*). Yes, Oswald. It is, isn't it?

MANDERS (*looks at him sympathetically*). Yes, you went out into the world early, my dear Oswald.

OSWALD. I did. Sometimes I wonder if it wasn't too early.

MRS. ALVING. Oh, nonsense. It's good for a healthy lad; especially if he's an only child. It's bad for them to stay at home with their mother and father and be pampered.

MANDERS. That is a very debatable point, Mrs. Alving. When all is said and done, the parental home is where a child belongs.

OSWALD. I agree with you there, Pastor.

MANDERS. Take your own son. Well, it will do no harm to talk about it in his presence. What has been the consequence for him? Here he is, twenty-six or twenty-seven years old, and he's never had the opportunity to know what a real home is like.

OSWALD. I beg your pardon, sir, but there you're quite mistaken.

MANDERS. Oh? I thought you had spent practically all your time in artistic circles.

OSWALD. I have.

MANDERS. Mostly among young artists.

OSWALD. Yes.

MANDERS. But I thought most of those people lacked the means to support a family and make a home for themselves.

OSWALD. Some of them can't afford to get married, sir.

MANDERS. Yes, that's what I'm saying.

OSWALD. But that doesn't mean they can't have a home. Several of them have; and very good and comfortable homes at that.

MRS. ALVING *listens intently and nods, but says nothing.*

MANDERS. But I'm not speaking about bachelor establishments. By a home I mean a family establishment, where a man lives with his wife and children.

OSWALD. Quite. Or with his children and their mother.

MANDERS (*starts and claps his hands together*). Merciful heavens! You don't—?

OSWALD. Yes?

MANDERS. Lives with—with the mother of his children?

OSWALD. Yes, would you rather he disowned the mother of his children?

MANDERS. So you are speaking of unlegalized relationships! These so-called free marriages!

OSWALD. I've never noticed anything particularly free about the way such people live.

MANDERS. But how is it possible that—that any reasonably well brought up man or young woman can bring themselves to live like that—openly, for everyone to see?

OSWALD. But what else can they do? A poor young artist— a poor young girl— It costs a lot of money to get married. What can they do?

MANDERS. What can they do? I'll tell you, Mr. Alving, what they can do. They should have kept away from each other in the first place—that's what they should have done.

OSWALD. That argument won't get you far with young people who are in love and have red blood in their veins.

MRS. ALVING. No, that won't get you very far.

MANDERS (*takes no notice*). And to think that the authorities tolerate such behaviour! That it is allowed to happen openly! (*Turns to* MRS. ALVING.) Wasn't I right to be so concerned about your son? In circles where immorality is practised openly and is, one might almost say, accepted—

OSWALD. Let me tell you something, sir, I have been a regular Sunday guest in one or two of these irregular households—

MANDERS. On Sundays!

OSWALD. Yes, that's the day when one's meant to enjoy oneself. But I have never heard an offensive word there, far less ever witnessed anything which could be called immoral. No; do you know when and where I have encountered immorality in artistic circles?

MANDERS. No, I don't, thank heaven.

OSWALD. Well, I shall tell you. I have encountered it when one or another of our model husbands and fathers came down there to look around a little on their own—and did the artists the honour of visiting them in their humble bistros. Then we learned a few things. Those gentlemen were able to tell us about places and things of which we had never dreamed.

MANDERS. What! Are you suggesting that honourable men from this country—!

OSWALD. Have you never, when these honourable men returned home, have you never heard them hold forth on the rampancy of immorality in foreign countries?

MANDERS. Yes, of course—

MRS. ALVING. I've heard that, too.

OSWALD. Well, you can take their word for it. Some of them are experts. (*Clasps his head.*) Oh, that beautiful life of freedom—that it should be so soiled!

MRS. ALVING. You mustn't get over-excited, Oswald. It isn't good for you.

OSWALD. No you're right, Mother. It isn't good for my health. It's that damned tiredness, you know. Well, I'll take a little walk before dinner. I'm sorry, Pastor. I know you can't see it from my point of view. But I had to say what I felt.

He goes out through the second door on the right.

MRS. ALVING. My poor boy—!

MANDERS. Yes, you may well say that. So it's come to this.

MRS. ALVING *looks at him but remains silent.*

MANDERS (*walks up and down*). He called himself the prodigal son. Alas, alas!

MRS. ALVING *still looks at him.*

MANDERS. And what do you say to all this?

MRS. ALVING. I say that Oswald was right in every word he said.

MANDERS (*stops dead*). Right? Right! In expressing those principles!

MRS. ALVING. Here in my loneliness I have come to think like him, Pastor Manders. But I have never dared to bring up the subject. Now my son shall speak for me.

MANDERS. I feel deeply sorry for you, Mrs. Alving. But now I will have to speak to you in earnest. I am not addressing you now as your business manager and adviser, nor as your and your late husband's old friend. I stand before you now as your priest, as I did at the moment when you had strayed so far.

MRS. ALVING. And what has the priest to say to me?

MANDERS. First I wish to refresh your memory, Mrs. Alving. The occasion is appropriate. Tomorrow will be the tenth anniversary of your husband's death. Tomorrow the memorial to him who is no longer with us is to be unveiled. Tomorrow I shall address the whole assembled flock. But today I wish to speak to you alone.

MRS. ALVING. Very well, Pastor. Speak.

MANDERS. Have you forgotten that after barely a year of marriage you stood on the very brink of the abyss? That you abandoned your house and home—that you deserted your husband—yes, Mrs. Alving, deserted, deserted—and refused to return to him, although he begged and entreated you to do so?

MRS. ALVING. Have you forgotten how desperately unhappy I was during that first year?

MANDERS. Yes, that is the sign of the rebellious spirit, to demand happiness from this earthly life. What right have we to happiness? No, Mrs. Alving, we must do our duty! And your duty was to remain with the man you had chosen, and to whom you were bound by a sacred bond.

MRS. ALVING. You know quite well the kind of life Alving led at that time; the depravities he indulged in.

MANDERS. I am only too aware of the rumours that were circulating about him; and I least of anyone approve his conduct during his youthful years, if those rumours contained the truth. But a wife is not appointed to be her husband's judge. It was your duty humbly to bear that cross which a higher will had seen fit to assign to you. But instead you rebelliously fling down that cross, abandon the erring soul you should have supported, hazard your good name, and very nearly ruin the reputations of others.

MRS. ALVING. Others? Another's, you mean?

MANDERS. It was extremely inconsiderate of you to seek refuge with me.

MRS. ALVING. With our priest? With an old friend?

MANDERS. Exactly. Well, you may thank God that I possessed the necessary firmness—that I was able to dissuade you from your frenzied intentions and that it was granted to me to lead you back on to the path of duty and home to your lawful husband.

MRS. ALVING. Yes, Pastor Manders, that was certainly your doing.

MANDERS. I was merely a humble tool in the hand of a higher purpose. And that I persuaded you to bow to the call of duty and obedience, has not that proved a blessing which will surely enrich the remainder of your days? Did I not foretell all this? Did not Alving turn from his aberrations, like a man? Did he not afterwards live a loving and blameless life with you for the remainder of his days? Did he not become a public benefactor, did he not inspire you so that in time you became his right hand in all his enterprises? And a very capable right hand—oh, yes, I know that, Mrs. Alving, I give you credit for that. But now I come to the next great error of your life.

MRS. ALVING. And what do you mean by that?

MANDERS. Once you disowned your duties as a wife. Since then, you have disowned your duties as a mother.

MRS. ALVING. Ah—!

MANDERS. All your days you have been ruled by a fatal spirit
of wilfulness. You have always longed for a life uncon-
strained by duties and principles. You have never been
willing to suffer the curb of discipline. Everything that has
been troublesome in your life you have cast off ruthlessly
and callously, as if it were a burden which you had the
right to reject. It was no longer convenient to you to be a
wife, so you left your husband. You found it tiresome to
be a mother, so you put your child out to live among
strangers.

MRS. ALVING. Yes, that is true. I did.

MANDERS. And in consequence you have become a stranger
to him.

MRS. ALVING. No, no! That's not true!

MANDERS. It is. It must be. And how have you got him back?
Think well, Mrs. Alving! You have sinned greatly against
your husband. You admit that by raising the monument to
him down there. Confess too, now, how you have sinned
against your son. There may still be time to bring him
back from the paths of wantonness. Turn; and save what
may still be saved in him. (*With raised forefinger.*) For
verily, Mrs. Alving, as a mother you carry a heavy burden
of guilt. This I have regarded it as my duty to say to you.

Silence.

MRS. ALVING (*slow and controlled*). You have had your say,
Pastor; and tomorrow you will speak publicly at my husband's ceremony. I shall not speak tomorrow. But now I
shall say a few words to you, just as you have said a few
words to me.

MANDERS. Of course. You wish to excuse your conduct—

MRS. ALVING. No. I simply want to tell you what happened.

MANDERS. Oh?

MRS. ALVING. Everything that you have just said about me
and my husband and our life together after you, as you put
it, had led me back on to the path of duty—all that is
something of which you have no knowledge from your

own observations. From that moment you, who used to visit us every day, never once set foot in our house.

MANDERS. You and your husband moved from town shortly afterwards.

MRS. ALVING. Yes. And you never came out here to see us while my husband was alive. It was only the business connected with the Orphanage that compelled you to visit me.

MANDERS (*quietly and uncertainly*). Helen—if this is intended as a reproach, I must beg you to consider the—

MRS. ALVING. The duty you owed to your position, yes. And then I was a wife who had run away from her husband. One can never be too careful with such unprincipled women.

MANDERS. My dear . . . Mrs. Alving, you exaggerate grotesquely.

MRS. ALVING. Yes, yes, well, let us forget it. What I wanted to say was that when you judge my conduct as a wife, you are content to base your judgment on common opinion.

MANDERS. Yes, well; what of it?

MRS. ALVING. But now, Manders, now I shall tell the truth. I have sworn to myself that one day you should know it. Only you.

MANDERS. And what is the truth?

MRS. ALVING. The truth is that my husband died just as dissolute as he had always lived.

MANDERS (*gropes for a chair*). What did you say?

MRS. ALVING. Just as dissolute, at any rate in his desires, after nineteen years of marriage, as he was before you wedded us.

MANDERS. You call these youthful escapades—these irregularities—excesses, if you like—evidence of a dissolute life!

MRS. ALVING. That is the expression our doctor used.

MANDERS. I don't understand you.

MRS. ALVING. It doesn't matter.

MANDERS. I cannot believe my ears. You mean your whole married life—all those years you shared with your husband —were nothing but a façade!

MRS. ALVING. Yes. Now you know.

MANDERS. But—but this I cannot accept! I don't understand —I cannot credit it! But how on earth is it possible—how could such a thing be kept secret?

MRS. ALVING. I had to fight, day after day, to keep it secret. After Oswald was born I thought things became a little better with Alving. But it didn't last long. And now I had to fight a double battle, fight with all my strength to prevent anyone knowing what kind of a man my child's father was. And you know what a winning personality Alving had. No one could believe anything but good of him. He was one of those people whose reputations remain untarnished by the way they live. But then, Manders—you must know this too—then came the most loathsome thing of all.

MANDERS. More loathsome than this!

MRS. ALVING. I had put up with him, although I knew well what went on secretly outside the house. But when he offended within our four walls—

MANDERS. What are you saying? Here!

MRS. ALVING. Yes, here in our own home. In there—(*Points to the first door on the right.*)—it was in the dining-room I first found out about it. I had something to do in there and the door was standing ajar. Then I heard our maid come up from the garden to water the flowers in there.

MANDERS. Oh, yes?

MRS. ALVING. A few moments later I heard Alving enter the room. He said something to her. And then I heard—(*Gives a short laugh.*)—I still don't know whether to laugh or cry —I heard my own servant whisper: "Stop it, Mr. Alving! Let me go!"

MANDERS. What an unseemly frivolity! But it was nothing more than a frivolity, Mrs. Alving. Believe me.

MRS. ALVING. I soon found out what to believe. My husband had his way with the girl. And that relationship had consequences, Pastor Manders.

MANDERS (*petrified*). And all this took place in this house! In this house!

MRS. ALVING. I had endured much in this house. To keep him

at home in the evenings—and at night—I had to make myself his companion in his secret dissipations up in his room. There I had to sit alone with him, had to clink my glass with his and drink with him, listen to his obscene and senseless drivelling, had to fight him with my fists to haul him into bed—

MANDERS (*shocked*). I don't know how you managed to endure it.

MRS. ALVING. I had to, for my little son's sake. But when the final humiliation came—when my own servant—then I swore to myself: "This must stop!" And so I took over the reins of this house; both as regards him and everything else. For now, you see, I had a weapon against him; he dared not murmur. It was then that I sent Oswald away. He was nearly seven and was beginning to notice things and ask questions, the way children do. I couldn't bear that, Manders. I thought the child could not help but be poisoned merely by breathing in this tainted home. That was why I sent him away. And so now you know why he was never allowed to set foot in his home while his father was alive. No one knows what it cost me.

MANDERS. You have indeed been sorely tried.

MRS. ALVING. I could never have borne it if I had not had my work. Yes, for I think I can say that I have worked! All the additions to the estate, all the improvements, all the useful innovations for which Alving was praised—do you imagine he had the energy to initiate any of them? He, who spent the whole day lying on the sofa reading old court circulars? No; let me tell you this too; I drove him forward when he was in his happier moods; and I had to bear the whole burden when he started again on his dissipations or collapsed in snivelling helplessness.

MANDERS. And it is to this man that you raise a memorial.

MRS. ALVING. There you see the power of a guilty conscience.

MANDERS. A guilty—? What do you mean?

MRS. ALVING. I always believed that some time, inevitably, the truth would have to come out, and that it would be

believed. The Orphanage would destroy all rumours and
banish all doubt.

MANDERS. You certainly made no mistake there, Mrs. Alving.

MRS. ALVING. And then I had another motive. I wanted to
make sure that my own son, Oswald, should not inherit
anything whatever from his father.

MANDERS. You mean it was Alving's money that—?

MRS. ALVING. Yes. The annual donations that I have made
to this Orphanage add up to the sum—I have calculated it
carefully—the sum which made Lieutenant Alving, in his
day, "a good match."

MANDERS. I understand—

MRS. ALVING. It was the sum with which he bought me. I do
not wish that money to come into Oswald's hands. My son
shall inherit everything from me.

OSWALD ALVING *enters through the second door on the right;
he has removed his hat and overcoat outside.*

MRS. ALVING (*goes towards him*). Are you back already?
My dear, dear boy!

OSWALD. Yes; what's one to do outside in this eternal rain?
But I hear we're about to have dinner. How splendid.

REGINA (*enters from the kitchen with a parcel*). A parcel
has just come for you, madam. (*Hands it to her.*)

MRS. ALVING (*with a glance at* PASTOR MANDERS). Copies of
the songs for tomorrow's ceremony, I suppose.

MANDERS. Hm—

REGINA. Dinner is served, madam.

MRS. ALVING. Good. We'll come presently. I just want to—
(*Begins to open the parcel.*)

REGINA (*to* OSWALD). Shall it be white port or red port, Mr.
Oswald?

OSWALD. Both, Miss Engstrand.

REGINA. *Bien*—very good, Mr. Oswald.

She goes into the dining-room.

OSWALD. I'd better help her open the bottles—(*Follows her into the dining-room. The door swings half open behind him.*)

MRS. ALVING (*who has opened the parcel*). Yes, that's right. It's the copies of the songs, Pastor Manders.

MANDERS (*with folded hands*). How I am to make my address tomorrow with a clear conscience, I—!

MRS. ALVING. Oh, you'll find a way—

MANDERS (*quietly, so as not to be heard in the dining-room*). Yes, there mustn't be any scandal.

MRS. ALVING (*firmly, in a low voice*). No. But now this long, loathsome comedy is over. From the day after tomorrow, it will be as if the dead had never lived in this house. There will be no one here but my boy and his mother.

From the dining-room is heard the crash of a chair being knocked over. At the same time REGINA *says sharply, but keeping her voice low:*

REGINA. Oswald! Are you mad? Let me go!

MRS. ALVING (*starts in fear*). Ah!

She stares distraught at the half open door. OSWALD *coughs and begins to hum. A bottle is uncorked.*

MANDERS (*indignantly*). What is going on, Mrs. Alving? What was that?

MRS. ALVING (*hoarsely*). Ghosts. The couple in the conservatory—walk.

MANDERS. What are you saying! Regina—? Is she the child you—?

MRS. ALVING. Yes. Come. Not a word.

She grips PASTOR MANDERS' *arms and walks falteringly towards the door of the dining-room.*

ACT TWO

The same room. The mist still lies heavily over the landscape. PASTOR MANDERS *and* MRS. ALVING *enter from the dining-room.*

MRS. ALVING (*still in the doorway*). I'm glad you enjoyed it, Pastor Manders. (*Speaks into the dining-room.*) Aren't you joining us, Oswald?

OSWALD (*offstage*). No, thank you. I think I'll go out and take a walk.

MRS. ALVING. Yes, do. It's stopped raining now. (*Closes the door of the dining-room, goes over to the hall door and calls.*) Regina!

REGINA (*offstage*). Yes, madam.

MRS. ALVING. Go down to the wash-house and give them a hand with the garlands.

REGINA. Very good, madam.

MRS. ALVING *makes sure that* REGINA *has gone, then closes the door.*

MANDERS. He can't hear anything from in there, can he?

MRS. ALVING. Not when the door is shut. Anyway, he's going out.

MANDERS. I am still stunned. I don't understand how I managed to swallow a mouthful of that excellent meal.

MRS. ALVING (*restless but controlled, walks up and down*). Neither do I. But what is to be done?

MANDERS. Yes, what is to be done? Upon my word, I don't know. I'm so sadly inexperienced in matters of this kind.

MRS. ALVING. I am convinced that no harm has been done yet.

MANDERS. No, heaven forbid! Nevertheless, it's a most improper situation.

MRS. ALVING. It's only a casual whim of Oswald's. You can be certain of that.

MANDERS. Well, as I said, I don't know about these things; but I'm sure—

MRS. ALVING. She must leave the house. And at once. That's obvious—

MANDERS. Yes, naturally.

MRS. ALVING. But where to? We can't just—

MANDERS. Where to? Home to her father, of course.

MRS. ALVING. To whom, did you say?

MANDERS. To her—oh, no, Engstrand isn't her—! But, dear God, Mrs. Alving, how can this be possible? Surely you must be mistaken.

MRS. ALVING. Unfortunately I know I'm not mistaken. In the end Johanna had to confess to me; and Alving couldn't deny it. So there was nothing to be done but hush the matter up.

MANDERS. Yes, I suppose that was the only thing to do.

MRS. ALVING. The girl left my service at once, and was given a considerable sum of money to keep her mouth shut. The remaining difficulties she solved for herself when she got to town. She renewed an old acquaintance with Engstrand, let it be known, I dare say, how much money she had, and spun him a story about some foreigner or other who'd been here with a yacht that summer. Then she and Engstrand got themselves married in a hurry. Well, you married them yourself.

MANDERS. But how can that be true? I remember clearly how Engstrand came to me to arrange the wedding. He was completely abject, and accused himself most bitterly of having indulged with his betrothed in a moment of weakness.

MRS. ALVING. Well, he had to take the blame on himself.

MANDERS. But to be so dishonest! And to me! I certainly would never have believed that of Jacob Engstrand. I'll speak to him seriously about this. He can be sure of that.

And the immorality of it! For money! How much was it
you gave the girl?

MRS. ALVING. Fifty pounds.

MANDERS. Just imagine! To go and marry a fallen woman for
a paltry fifty pounds!

MRS. ALVING. What about me? I went and married a fallen
man.

MANDERS. Good God Almighty, what are you saying? A fallen man!

MRS. ALVING. Do you think Alving was any purer when I
accompanied him to the altar than Johanna was when Engstrand married her?

MANDERS. But the two things are utterly different—

MRS. ALVING. Not so different. Oh, yes, there was a big difference in the price. A paltry fifty pounds against an entire
fortune.

MANDERS. But how can you compare two such different situ-
ations? After all, you were obeying the counsels of your
heart, and of your family.

MRS. ALVING (does not look at him). I thought you understood the direction in which what you call my heart had
strayed at that time.

MANDERS (distantly). If I had understood anything of the
kind, I should not have been a daily guest in your husband's house.

MRS. ALVING. Anyway, I didn't follow my own counsel. That
is certain.

MANDERS. Well then, you obeyed your nearest relatives. Your
mother and your two aunts. As was your duty.

MRS. ALVING. Yes, that is true. The three of them worked out
a balance-sheet for me. Oh, it's incredible how patly they
proved that it would be utter madness for me to turn down
such an offer. If my mother could look down now and see
what all that promise of splendour has led to.

MANDERS. No one can be held responsible for the outcome.
And this much at least is sure, that your marriage was cele-
brated in an orderly fashion and in full accordance with
the law.

MRS. ALVING (*by the window*). All this talk about law and order. I often think that is what causes all the unhappiness in the world.

MANDERS. Mrs. Alving, now you are being sinful.

MRS. ALVING. Yes, perhaps I am. But I can't stand being bound by all these obligations and petty considerations. I can't! I must find my own way to freedom.

MANDERS. What do you mean by that?

MRS. ALVING (*taps on the window frame*). I should never have concealed the truth about Alving's life. But I dared not do otherwise—and it wasn't only for Oswald's sake. I was such a coward.

MANDERS. Coward?

MRS. ALVING. If people had known, they would have said: "Poor man, it isn't surprising he strays now and then. After all, his wife ran away from him."

MANDERS. Perhaps they would not have been altogether unjustified.

MRS. ALVING (*looks hard at him*). If I were a real mother, I would take Oswald and say to him: "Listen, my boy. Your father was a degenerate—"

MANDERS. But great heavens above—!

MRS. ALVING. And I would tell him everything I have told you. The whole story.

MANDERS. You scandalize me, Mrs. Alving.

MRS. ALVING. Yes, I know. I know! I scandalize myself. (*Comes away from the window.*) That's how cowardly I am.

MANDERS. You call it cowardice to do your simple duty! Have you forgotten that a child shall love and honour its father and mother?

MRS. ALVING. Let us not generalize so. Let us ask: "Shall Oswald love and honour Captain Alving?"

MANDERS. Is there not a voice in your mother's heart which forbids you to destroy your son's ideals?

MRS. ALVING. Yes, but what about the truth?

MANDERS. Yes, but what about the ideals?

MRS. ALVING. Oh, ideals, ideals! If only I weren't such a coward!

MANDERS. Don't despise our ideals, Mrs. Alving. Retribution will surely follow. Take Oswald in particular. He hasn't many ideals, I'm afraid. But this much I have discovered, that his father is to him an ideal.

MRS. ALVING. You are right there.

MANDERS. And you yourself have awakened and fostered these ideas of his, by your letters.

MRS. ALVING. Yes. I was bound by these obligations and considerations, so I lied to my son, year out and year in. Oh, what a coward, what a coward I have been!

MANDERS. You have established a happy illusion in your son, Mrs. Alving—and you should certainly not regard that as being of little value.

MRS. ALVING. Hm. I wonder. But I shan't allow him to use Regina as a plaything. He is not going to make that poor girl unhappy.

MANDERS. Good heavens, no! That would be dreadful.

MRS. ALVING. If I knew that he meant it seriously, and that it would make him happy—

MANDERS. Yes? What then?

MRS. ALVING. But that's impossible. Unfortunately Regina isn't that type.

MANDERS. How do you mean?

MRS. ALVING. If only I weren't such an abject coward, I'd say to him: "Marry her, or make what arrangements you please. As long as you're honest and open about it—"

MANDERS. Merciful God! You mean a legal marriage! What a terrible idea! It's absolutely unheard of—!

MRS. ALVING. Unheard of, did you say? Put your hand on your heart, Pastor Manders, and tell me—do you really believe there aren't married couples like that to be found in this country—as closely related as these two?

MANDERS. I simply don't understand you.

MRS. ALVING. Oh, yes you do.

MANDERS. You're thinking that by chance possibly—? Yes, alas, family life is indeed not always as pure as it should be. But in that kind of case, one can never be sure—at any rate, not absolutely— But in this case—! That you, a mother, could want to allow your own—

MRS. ALVING. But I don't *want* to. I wouldn't allow it for any price in the world. That's just what I'm saying.

MANDERS. No, because you are a coward, as you put it. But if you weren't a coward—! Great God in heaven, what a shocking relationship!

MRS. ALVING. Well, we all stem from a relationship of that kind, so we are told. And who was it who arranged things like that in the world, Pastor Manders?

MANDERS. I shall not discuss such questions with you, Mrs. Alving. You are not in the right spiritual frame of mind for that. But that you dare to say that it is cowardly of you—!

MRS. ALVING. I shall tell you what I mean. I am frightened, because there is in me something ghostlike from which I can never free myself.

MANDERS. What did you call it?

MRS. ALVING. Ghostlike. When I heard Regina and Oswald in there, it was as if I saw ghosts. I almost think we are all ghosts—all of us, Pastor Manders. It isn't just what we have inherited from our father and mother that walks in us. It is all kinds of dead ideas and all sorts of old and obsolete beliefs. They are not alive in us; but they remain in us none the less, and we can never rid ourselves of them. I only have to take a newspaper and read it, and I see ghosts between the lines. There must be ghosts all over the country. They lie as thick as grains of sand. And we're all so horribly afraid of the light.

MANDERS. Aha—so there we have the fruits of your reading. Fine fruits indeed! Oh, these loathsome, rebellious, free-thinking books!

MRS. ALVING. You are wrong, my dear Pastor. It was you yourself who first spurred me to think; and I thank and bless you for it.

MANDERS. I?

MRS. ALVING. Yes, when you forced me into what you called duty; when you praised as right and proper what my whole spirit rebelled against as something abominable. It was then that I began to examine the seams of your learning. I only wanted to pick at a single knot; but when I had worked it loose, the whole fabric fell apart. And then I saw that it was machine-sewn.

MANDERS (*quiet, shaken*). Is this the reward of my life's hardest struggle?

MRS. ALVING. Call it rather your life's most pitiful defeat.

MANDERS. It was my life's greatest victory, Helen. The victory over myself.

MRS. ALVING. It was a crime against us both.

MANDERS. That I besought you, saying: "Woman, go home to your lawful husband," when you came to me distraught and cried: "I am here! Take me!" Was that a crime?

MRS. ALVING. Yes, I think so.

MANDERS. We two do not understand each other.

MRS. ALVING. No; not any longer.

MANDERS. Never—never even in my most secret moments have I thought of you except as another man's wedded wife.

MRS. ALVING. Oh? I wonder.

MANDERS. Helen—

MRS. ALVING. One forgets so easily what one was like.

MANDERS. I do not. I am the same as I always was.

MRS. ALVING (*changes the subject*). Well, well, well—let's not talk any more about the past. Now you're up to your ears in commissions and committees; and I sit here fighting with ghosts, both in me and around me.

MANDERS. I will help you to bring to heel the ghosts around you. After all the dreadful things you have told me today, my conscience will not permit me to allow a young and unprotected girl to remain in your house.

MRS. ALVING. Don't you think it would be best if we could get her taken care of? I mean—well, decently married.

MANDERS. Indubitably. I think it would be desirable for her in every respect. Regina is just now at the age when—well, I don't really understand these things, but—

MRS. ALVING. Regina matured early.

MANDERS. Yes, didn't she? I seem to remember that she was noticeably well developed from a physical point of view when I prepared her for confirmation. But for the present at any rate she must go home. To her father's care—no, but of course, Engstrand isn't—! That he—that *he* could conceal the truth from me like that!

There is a knock on the door leading to the hall.

MRS. ALVING. Who can that be? Come in.

ENGSTRAND *(appears in the doorway in his Sunday suit)*. Begging your pardon, madam, but—

MANDERS. Aha! Hm!

MRS. ALVING. Oh, is it you, Engstrand?

ENGSTRAND. There weren't any of the servants about, so I took the liberty of giving a little knock.

MRS. ALVING. Yes, yes. Well, come in. Do you want to speak to me about something?

ENGSTRAND *(enters)*. No, thank you, ma'am. It's the Pastor I really wanted to have a word with.

MANDERS *(walks up and down)*. Hm; really? You want to speak to me? Do you indeed?

ENGSTRAND. Yes, I'd be so terribly grateful if—

MANDERS *(stops in front of him)*. Well! May I ask what is the nature of your question?

ENGSTRAND. Well, it's like this, Pastor. We've been paid off down there now—a thousand thanks, Mrs. Alving—and now we're ready with everything—and so I thought it'd only be right and proper if we who have worked so well together all this time—I thought we might conclude with a few prayers this evening.

MANDERS. Prayers? Down at the Orphanage?

ENGSTRAND. Well, of course, sir, if you don't think it's the right thing to do—

MANDERS. Oh yes, yes, indeed I do, but—hm—

ENGSTRAND. I've been in the habit of holding a little service myself down there of an evening—

MANDERS. Have you?

ENGSTRAND. Yes, now and then. Just a little edification, as you

might say. But I'm only a poor humble man and haven't
the proper gifts, God forgive me—and so I thought, seeing
as Pastor Manders happens to be out here—

MANDERS. Now look here, Engstrand, first I must ask you a
question. Are you in the correct frame of mind for such a
meeting? Do you feel your conscience is clear and free?

ENGSTRAND. Oh, God forgive us, let's not talk about conscience, Pastor.

MANDERS. Yes, that's just what we are going to talk about.
Well? What is your answer?

ENGSTRAND. Well—a man's conscience can be a bit of a beggar now and then—

MANDERS. Well, at least you admit it. But now, will you tell
me the truth! What's all this about Regina?

MRS. ALVING (quickly). Pastor Manders!

MANDERS (soothingly). Leave this to me—

ENGSTRAND. Regina? Good heavens, how you frighten me!
(Looks at MRS. ALVING.) Surely nothing's happened to
Regina?

MANDERS. Let us hope not. But what I meant was, what's all
this about you and Regina? You call yourself her father,
don't you? Hm?

ENGSTRAND (uncertainly). Well—hm—you know all about me
and poor Johanna.

MANDERS. Now I want no more prevarication. Your late wife
told the whole truth to Mrs. Alving before she left her
service.

ENGSTRAND. Well, may the—! No, did she really?

MANDERS. So now you are unmasked, Engstrand.

ENGSTRAND. And she promised and swore on the Bible that
she—

MANDERS. Swore on the Bible—!

ENGSTRAND. No, she only promised, but so sincerely.

MANDERS. And all these years you have concealed the truth
from me. Concealed it from me, who trusted you so implicitly.

ENGSTRAND. Yes, I'm afraid I have, I suppose.

MANDERS. Have I deserved this from you, Engstrand? Haven't

I always been ready to assist you with help, both spiritual
and material, as far as lay within my power? Answer!
Haven't I?

ENGSTRAND. Things would often have looked black for me if
it hadn't been for your Reverence.

MANDERS. And this is how you reward me! You cause me to
enter false statements in the parish register, and withhold
from me over a period of years the information which you
owed both to me and to the cause of truth! Your conduct
has been completely indefensible, Engstrand. From now
on, I wash my hands of you.

ENGSTRAND (*with a sigh*). Yes, of course, sir. I appreciate
that.

MANDERS. I mean, how could you possibly justify yourself?

ENGSTRAND. But wouldn't it have made things even worse for
poor Johanna if the truth had been allowed to come out?
Now just imagine if your Reverence had been in the same
situation as her—

MANDERS. I!

ENGSTRAND. Oh, for heaven's sake, I don't mean exactly the
same. But I mean, suppose your Reverence had something
to be ashamed of in the eyes of the world, as the saying
goes. We men mustn't judge a poor woman too harshly,
your Reverence.

MANDERS. But I'm not. It's you I'm reproaching.

ENGSTRAND. May I ask your Reverence a tiny question?

MANDERS. Yes, yes, what is it?

ENGSTRAND. Isn't it right and proper for a man to raise up the
fallen?

MANDERS. Of course it is.

ENGSTRAND. And isn't it a man's duty to stand by his word?

MANDERS. Certainly it is: but—

ENGSTRAND. That time when Johanna fell into misfortune
through that Englishman—or maybe he was an American,
or a Russian, as they call them—well, she came up to town.
Poor creature, she'd turned up her nose at me once or
twice; for she only looked at what was handsome and fine,
poor thing; and of course I had this thing wrong with my

leg. Well, your Reverence will remember how I'd ventured into a dancing-hall where foreign sailors were indulging in drunkenness and excess, as the saying goes.
And when I tried to exhort them to start leading a better
life—

MRS. ALVING (by the window). Hm—

MANDERS. I know, Engstrand. The ruffians threw you down
the stairs. You've told me about it before. Your injury is
something to be proud of.

ENGSTRAND. Oh, I take no pride in it, your Reverence. But
what I was going to say was, so she came along and poured
out all her troubles to me amid weeping and gnashing of
teeth. I'll be frank, your Reverence; it nearly broke my
heart to listen to her.

MANDERS. Did it really, Engstrand? Well, go on.

ENGSTRAND. Yes, well, so I said to her: "This American is a
vagrant on the sea of life," I said. "And you, Johanna,
you've committed a sin and are a fallen creature. But
Jacob Engstrand," I said, "he's got both feet firmly on the
ground"—speaking figuratively, you understand—

MANDERS. I understand you perfectly. Go on.

ENGSTRAND. Well, that's how I raised her up and made an
honest woman of her so that people shouldn't get to know
the wanton way she'd behaved with foreigners.

MANDERS. You acted very handsomely. The only thing I can't
understand is how you could bring yourself to accept
money—

ENGSTRAND. Money? I? Not a penny!

MANDERS (glances questioningly at MRS. ALVING). But—!

ENGSTRAND. Oh yes, wait a moment—now I remember. Johanna did have a few shillings with her. But I wouldn't
have any of it. "Fie!" I said, "that's Mammon, that's the
wages of sin. We'll throw that wretched gold—or notes, or
whatever it was—back in the American's face," I said. But
he'd taken his hook and disappeared across the wild sea,
your Reverence.

MANDERS. Had he, my dear Engstrand?

ENGSTRAND. Oh yes. And so Johanna and I agreed that the

money was to be used to bring up the child, and that's
what happened; and I can account for every shilling of it.

MANDERS. But this puts quite a different face on things.

ENGSTRAND. That's the way it was, your Reverence. And I
think I can say I've been a real father to Regina—as far as
stood within my power—for unfortunately I'm an ailing
man.

MANDERS. Now, now, my dear Engstrand—

ENGSTRAND. But this I can say, that I've brought up the child
tenderly and been a loving husband to poor Johanna and
ordered my household the way the good book says. But it
would never have entered my head to go along to your
Reverence in sinful pride and boast that for once I too had
done a good deed. No, when anything of that kind happens to Jacob Engstrand, he keeps quiet about it. I don't
suppose that's always the way, more's the pity. And when
I do go to see Pastor Manders I've always more than
enough of wickedness and weakness to talk to him about.
For I said it just now and I say it again—a man's conscience
can be a real beggar now and then.

MANDERS. Give me your hand, Jacob Engstrand.

ENGSTRAND. Why, good heavens, Pastor—!

MANDERS. No argument, now. (*Presses his hand.*) There!

ENGSTRAND. And if I was to go down on my bended knees
and humbly to beg your Reverence's forgiveness—?

MANDERS. You? No, on the contrary. It is I who must ask
your pardon—

ENGSTRAND. Oh no, really—

MANDERS. Indeed, yes. And I do so with all my heart. Forgive me that I could ever have misjudged you so. And if
there is any way in which I can show the sincerity of my
regrets and of my good-will towards you—

ENGSTRAND. Would your Reverence really do that?

MANDERS. Most gladly.

ENGSTRAND. Well, in that case there's a real opportunity just
now. With the money I've managed to put aside through
the blessed work here, I'm thinking of starting a kind of
home for sailors in the city.

MANDERS. *You* are?

ENGSTRAND. Yes, a kind of refuge like the one here, in a manner of speaking. The temptations for a sailor wandering on shore are so manifold. But in this house, with me there, it'd be like them having a father to take care of them, I thought.

MANDERS. What have you to say to that, Mrs. Alving!

ENGSTRAND. My means are rather limited, God knows. But if only someone would stretch out a helping hand—

MANDERS. Yes, well, let us consider the matter more closely. Your project interests me very deeply. But go along now and get everything in order and light candles so as to make the place cheerful, and we'll have a little edification together, my dear Engstrand. For now I think you're in the right frame of mind.

ENGSTRAND. Yes, I think I am. Well, goodbye, Mrs. Alving, and thank you for everything. And take good care of Regina for me. (*Wipes a tear from his eye.*) Poor Johanna's child! Hm—it's strange, but—it's just as though she'd grown to be a part of me. It is really, yes. (*Touches his forehead and goes out through the door.*)

MANDERS. Well, what have you to say about that man now, Mrs. Alving? That was quite a different explanation we were given there.

MRS. ALVING. It was indeed.

MANDERS. You see how terribly careful one must be about condemning one's fellows. But then, again, it is a deep joy to discover that one has been mistaken. Or what do you say?

MRS. ALVING. I say: you are a great baby, Manders. And you always will be.

MANDERS. I?

MRS. ALVING (*places both her hands on his shoulders*). And I say: I'd like to throw both my arms round your neck.

MANDERS (*frees himself quickly*). No, no, bless you! Such impulses—!

MRS. ALVING (*with a smile*). Oh, you needn't be frightened of me.

MANDERS (*by the table*). You have such an extravagant way
of expressing yourself sometimes. Now let me just gather
these documents together and put them in my case. (*Does
so.*) There! And now, *au revoir*. Keep your eyes open
when Oswald comes back. I'll be with you again presently.
(*Takes his hat and goes out through the hall.*)

MRS. ALVING (*sighs, looks out of the window for a moment,
tidies the room a little and is about to go into the dining-
room, but stops in the doorway and calls softly*). Oswald,
are you still at table?

OSWALD (*offstage*). I'm just finishing my cigar.

MRS. ALVING. I thought you'd gone for a little walk.

OSWALD. In this weather?

There is the clink of a glass. MRS. ALVING *leaves the door
open and sits down with her sewing on the sofa by the window.*

OSWALD (*still offstage*). Wasn't that Pastor Manders who left
just now?

MRS. ALVING. Yes, he's gone down to the Orphanage.

OSWALD. Hm. (*Clink of decanter and glass again.*)

MRS. ALVING (*with a worried glance*). Oswald dear, you
ought to be careful with that liqueur. It's strong.

OSWALD. It keeps out the damp.

MRS. ALVING. Won't you come in and talk to me?

OSWALD. I can't smoke in there.

MRS. ALVING. You know I don't mind cigars.

OSWALD. All right, I'll come, then. Just one tiny drop more.
There. (*He enters with his cigar and closes the door behind him. Short silence.*)

OSWALD. Where's the Pastor gone?

MRS. ALVING. I told you, he went down to the Orphanage.

OSWALD. Oh yes, so you did.

MRS. ALVING. You oughtn't to sit at table so long, Oswald.

OSWALD (*holding his cigar behind his back*). But I think it's
so nice, Mother. (*Strokes and pats her.*) To come home,
and sit at my mother's own table, in my mother's dining-
room, and eat my mother's beautiful food.

MRS. ALVING. My dear, dear boy.

OSWALD (*walks and smokes a trifle impatiently*). And what else is there for me to do here? I can't work—

MRS. ALVING. Can't you?

OSWALD. In this weather? Not a glimmer of sunlight all day. (*Walks across the room.*) That's the worst thing about it— not to be able to work—

MRS. ALVING. Perhaps you shouldn't have come home.

OSWALD. Yes, Mother, I had to.

MRS. ALVING. I'd ten times rather sacrifice the happiness of having you with me than that you should—

OSWALD (*stops by the table*). Tell me, Mother. Does it really make you so happy to have me home?

MRS. ALVING. Does it make me happy?

OSWALD (*crumples a newspaper*). I think it must be almost the same for you whether I'm alive or not.

MRS. ALVING. How can you have the heart to say that to your mother, Oswald?

OSWALD. But you managed so well to live without me before.

MRS. ALVING. Yes. I have lived without you. That is true.

Silence. Dusk begins to gather slowly. OSWALD *paces up and down the room. He has put down his cigar.*

OSWALD (*stops beside* MRS. ALVING). Mother, may I sit down on the sofa with you?

MRS. ALVING (*makes room for him*). Yes, of course, my dear boy.

OSWALD (*sits*). There's something I have to tell you, Mother.

MRS. ALVING (*tensely*). Yes?

OSWALD (*stares vacantly ahead of him*). I can't keep it to myself any longer.

MRS. ALVING. What? What do you mean?

OSWALD (*as before*). I couldn't bring myself to write to you about it; and since I came home I—

MRS. ALVING (*grips his arm*). Oswald, what is this?

OSWALD. Yesterday and today I've been trying to forget. To escape. But it's no good.

MRS. ALVING (*rises*). Tell me the truth, Oswald.

OSWALD (*pulls her down on to the sofa again*). Sit still and I'll try to tell you about it. I've complained so much about how tired I felt after the journey—

MRS. ALVING. Yes. Well?

OSWALD. But it isn't that that's wrong with me. It isn't any ordinary tiredness—

MRS. ALVING (*tries to rise*). You're not ill, Oswald!

OSWALD (*pulls her down again*). Sit still, Mother. Just keep calm. No, I'm not really ill; not what people usually call ill. (*Clasps his hands to his head.*) Mother, I'm spiritually broken—my will's gone—I shall never be able to work any more!

He throws himself into her lap, with his hands over his face, and sobs.

MRS. ALVING (*pale and trembling*). Oswald! Look at me! No, no, it isn't true!

OSWALD (*looks up at her despairingly*). Never to be able to work again! Never. Never. To be dead while I'm still alive. Mother, can you imagine anything so dreadful?

MRS. ALVING. My poor boy. How did this frightful thing happen to you?

OSWALD (*sits upright again*). Yes, that's just what I can't understand. I've never lived intemperately. Not in any way. You mustn't believe that of me, Mother. I've never done that.

MRS. ALVING. Of course I don't believe it, Oswald.

OSWALD. And yet it's happened to me. This dreadful thing.

MRS. ALVING. Oh, but my dear, dear boy, it'll be all right. You've just overworked. You take my word for it.

OSWALD (*heavily*). That's what I thought at first. But it isn't that.

MRS. ALVING. Tell me the whole story.

OSWALD. I shall, yes.

MRS. ALVING. When did you first notice it?

OSWALD. It was soon after the last time I'd been home, and had gone back again to Paris. I began to feel the most violent pains in my head—mostly at the back of my head, it seemed. It was as though a tight iron ring had been screwed round my neck and just above it.

MRS. ALVING. Yes?

OSWALD. At first I thought it was just the usual headaches I used to have so often while I was a child.

MRS. ALVING. Yes, yes—

OSWALD. But it wasn't. I soon realized that. I couldn't work any more. I wanted to begin on a new painting, but it was as though my powers had failed me. It was as though I was paralysed—I couldn't see anything clearly—everything went misty and began to swim in front of my eyes. Oh, it was dreadful! In the end I sent for the doctor. And he told me the truth.

MRS. ALVING. How do you mean?

OSWALD. He was one of the leading doctors down there. I had to tell him how I felt. And then he began to ask me a lot of questions, which seemed to me to have absolutely nothing to do with it. I didn't understand what the man was driving at—

MRS. ALVING. Yes!

OSWALD. In the end he said: "You've been worm-eaten from birth." That was the word he used: *vermoulu.*

MRS. ALVING (*tensely*). What did he mean by that?

OSWALD. I didn't understand either, and asked him to explain more clearly. And then the old cynic said—(*Clenches his fist.*) Oh—!

MRS. ALVING. What did he say?

OSWALD. He said: "The sins of the fathers shall be visited on the children."

MRS. ALVING (*rises slowly*). The sins of the fathers—!

OSWALD. I nearly hit him in the face—

MRS. ALVING (*walks across the room*). The sins of the fathers—

OSWALD (*smiles sadly*). Yes, what do you think of that? Of course I assured him it was quite out of the question. But do you think he gave in? No, he stuck to his opinion; and it was only when I brought out your letters and translated to him all the passages that dealt with Father—

MRS. ALVING. But then he—?

OSWALD. Yes, then of course he had to admit he was on the wrong track. And then I learned the truth. The incredible truth! This wonderfully happy life with my comrades, I should have abstained from. It had been too much for my strength. In other words, I have only myself to blame.

MRS. ALVING. Oswald! Oh, no, you mustn't think that!

OSWALD. There was no other explanation possible, he said. That's the dreadful thing. Beyond cure—ruined for life—because of my own folly. Everything I wanted to accomplish in the world—not even to dare to think of it—not to be *able* to think of it. Oh, if only I could start my life over again, and undo it all!

Throws himself face down on the sofa. MRS. ALVING *wrings her hands and walks to and fro, fighting silently with herself.*

OSWALD (*after a while, looks up and remains half-leaning on his elbow*). If it had been something I'd inherited. Something I wasn't myself to blame for. But this! To have thrown away in this shameful, thoughtless, light-hearted way one's whole happiness and health, everything in the world—one's future, one's life—

MRS. ALVING. No, no, my dear, blessed boy—this is impossible! (*Leans over him.*) Things are not as desperate as you think.

OSWALD. Oh, you don't know—! (*Jumps up.*) And then, Mother, that I should cause you all this grief! I've often almost wished and hoped that you didn't care very much about me.

MRS. ALVING. I, Oswald! My only son! The only possession I have in the world—the only thing I care about!

OSWALD (*seizes both her hands and kisses them*). Yes, yes, I know. When I am at home, of course I know it. And that's one of the hardest things to bear. But now you know. And now we won't talk about it any more today. I can't bear to think about it for long. (*Walks across the room.*) Get me something to drink, Mother.

MRS. ALVING. Drink? What do you want to drink now?

OSWALD. Oh, anything. You have some cold punch in the house, haven't you?

MRS. ALVING. Yes, but, my dear Oswald—

OSWALD. Oh, Mother, don't be difficult. Be nice now! I *must* have something to help me forget these worries. (*Goes into the conservatory.*) Oh, how—how dark it is in here! (MRS. ALVING *pulls a bell-rope, right.*) And this incessant rain. It goes on week after week; sometimes for months. Never to see the sun! In all the years I've been at home I don't remember ever having seen the sun shine.

MRS. ALVING. Oswald! You are thinking of leaving me!

OSWALD. Hm—(*Sighs deeply.*) I'm not thinking about anything. I *can't* think about anything. (*Softly.*) I take good care not to.

REGINA (*enters from the dining-room*). Did you ring, madam?

MRS. ALVING. Yes, bring in the lamp.

REGINA. Yes, madam, at once. I've already lit it. (*Goes.*)

MRS. ALVING (*goes over to* OSWALD). Oswald, don't hide anything from me.

OSWALD. I'm not, Mother. (*Goes over to the table.*) Haven't I told you enough?

REGINA *enters with the lamp and puts it on the table.*

MRS. ALVING. Oh, Regina, you might bring us half a bottle of champagne.

REGINA. Very good, madam. (*Goes.*)

OSWALD (*takes* MRS. ALVING'S *head in his hands*). That's the way. I knew my Mother wouldn't let her boy go thirsty.

MRS. ALVING. My poor, dear Oswald! How could I deny you anything now?

OSWALD (*eagerly*). Is that true, Mother? Do you mean it?

MRS. ALVING. Mean what?

OSWALD. That you wouldn't deny me anything?

MRS. ALVING. But, my dear Oswald—

OSWALD. Ssh!

REGINA (*brings a tray with a half-bottle of champagne and two glasses, and puts it down on the table*). Shall I open—?

OSWALD. No, thank you, I'll do it myself.

REGINA *goes.*

MRS. ALVING (*sits down at the table*). What did you mean just now, when you said I mustn't deny you anything?

OSWALD (*busy trying to open the bottle*). Let's taste this first.

The cork jumps out. He fills one glass and is about to do likewise with the other.

MRS. ALVING (*puts her hand over it*). Thank you, not for me.

OSWALD. Well, for me, then. (*Empties the glass, refills it and empties it again. Then he sits down at the table.*)

MRS. ALVING (*tensely*). Well?

OSWALD (*not looking at her*). Tell me, Mother—I thought you and Pastor Manders looked so strange—hm—quiet—at dinner.

MRS. ALVING. Did you notice?

OSWALD. Yes—hm. (*Short silence.*) Tell me—what do you think of Regina?

MRS. ALVING. What do I think?

OSWALD. Yes, isn't she splendid?

MRS. ALVING. Oswald dear, you don't know her as well as I do—

OSWALD. Oh?

MRS. ALVING. Regina spent too much time at home, I'm afraid. I ought to have brought her here to live with me sooner.

OSWALD. Yes, but isn't she splendid to look at, Mother? (*Fills his glass.*)

MRS. ALVING. Regina has many great faults—

OSWALD. Oh, what does that matter? (*Drinks again.*)

MRS. ALVING. But I'm fond of her all the same. And I am responsible for her. I'd rather anything in the world happened than that she should come to any harm.

OSWALD (*jumps up*). Mother, Regina's my only hope!

MRS. ALVING (*rises*). What do you mean by that?

OSWALD. I can't bear all this misery alone.

MRS. ALVING. But you have your mother to bear it with you.

OSWALD. Yes, that's what I thought. And that's why I came

home to you. But it won't work. I can see it; it won't work. I can't bear this life here.

MRS. ALVING. Oswald!

OSWALD. Oh, I must live differently, Mother. That's why I have to leave you. I don't want you to see.

MRS. ALVING. My poor, sick boy! Oh, but Oswald, as long as you're not well—

OSWALD. If it was just the illness, I'd stay with you, Mother. You're the best friend I have in the world.

MRS. ALVING. Yes, I am, Oswald, aren't I?

OSWALD (*walks around restlessly*). But it's all the remorse, the gnawing, the self-reproach. And then the fear! Oh—this dreadful fear!

MRS. ALVING (*follows him*). Fear? What fear? What do you mean?

OSWALD. Oh, don't ask me any more about it. I don't know. I can't describe it.

MRS. ALVING *crosses right and pulls the bell-rope.*

OSWALD. What do you want?

MRS. ALVING. I want my boy to be happy. He shan't sit here and brood. (*To* REGINA *who appears in the doorway.*) More champagne. A whole bottle.

REGINA *goes.*

OSWALD. Mother!

MRS. ALVING. Do you think we don't know how to live here, too?

OSWALD. Isn't she splendid to look at? The way she's made! And so healthy and strong!

MRS. ALVING (*sits at the table*). Sit down, Oswald, and let's talk calmly together.

OSWALD (*sits*). You don't know this, Mother, but I have done Regina a wrong. And I've got to put it right.

MRS. ALVING. A wrong?

OSWALD. Well, a little thoughtlessness—whatever you care to call it. Quite innocently, really. When I was home last—

MRS. ALVING. Yes?

OSWALD. She asked me so often about Paris, and I told her this and that about the life down there. And I remember, one day I happened to say: "Wouldn't you like to come there yourself?"

MRS. ALVING. Oh?

OSWALD. Well, she blushed violently, and then she said: "Yes, I'd like to very much." "Well, well," I replied, "that might be arranged"—or something of the sort.

MRS. ALVING. Yes?

OSWALD. Well, of course I forgot the whole thing. But the day before yesterday, when I asked her if she was glad that I was going to stay at home so long—

MRS. ALVING. Yes?

OSWALD. She gave me such a strange look and then she asked: "But then, what's going to become of my trip to Paris?"

MRS. ALVING. Her trip!

OSWALD. And then I got it out of her that she'd taken the whole thing seriously, that she'd been going around here thinking about me the whole time, and that she'd begun to learn French—

MRS. ALVING. I see—

OSWALD. Mother—when I saw that splendid, handsome, healthy girl standing there in front of me—well, I'd never really noticed her before—but now, when she stood there, so to speak, with open arms ready to receive me—

MRS. ALVING. Oswald!

OSWALD. Then I realized that in her I could find salvation; for I saw that she was full of the joy of life.

MRS. ALVING (*starts*). The joy of life! But how could that help?

REGINA (*enters from the dining-room with a bottle of champagne*). I'm sorry I was so long. I had to go down to the cellar—(*Puts the bottle on the table.*)

OSWALD. And fetch another glass.

REGINA (*looks at him, surprised*). There is Mrs. Alving's glass.

OSWALD. But fetch one for yourself, Regina.

REGINA *starts and throws a quick glance at* MRS. ALVING.

OSWALD. Well?

REGINA (*quietly, hesitantly*). Do you wish me to, madam?

MRS. ALVING. Fetch the glass, Regina.

REGINA *goes into the dining-room.*

OSWALD (*watches her go*). Do you see how she walks? With
   such purpose and gaiety!

MRS. ALVING. This must not happen, Oswald.

OSWALD. It's already decided. Surely you can see. It's no use
   trying to stop it.

REGINA *enters with an empty glass, which she keeps in her
hand.*

OSWALD. Sit down, Regina. (*She glances questioningly at*
   MRS. ALVING.)

MRS. ALVING. Sit down.

REGINA *sits on a chair by the dining-room door, with the
empty glass still in her hand.*

MRS. ALVING. Oswald, what was it you were saying about the
   joy of life?

OSWALD. Oh, yes—the joy of life, Mother—you don't know
   much about that here. I never feel it here.

MRS. ALVING. Not when you are with me?

OSWALD. Not when I'm at home. But you don't understand
   that.

MRS. ALVING. Oh, yes—I think I do now—almost.

OSWALD. The joy of life and the love of one's work. They're
   practically the same thing. But that you don't know anything about, either.

MRS. ALVING. No, I don't suppose we do. Oswald, tell me
   more about this.

OSWALD. Well, all I mean is that here people are taught to
   believe that work is a curse and a punishment, and that life
   is a misery which we do best to get out of as quickly as
   possible.

MRS. ALVING. A vale of tears, yes. And we do our best to make it one.

OSWALD. But out there, people don't feel like that. No one there believes in that kind of teaching any longer. They feel it's wonderful and glorious just to be alive. Mother, have you noticed how everything I've painted is concerned with the joy of life? Always, always, the joy of life. Light and sunshine and holiday—and shining, contented faces. That's what makes me afraid to be here at home with you.

MRS. ALVING. Afraid? What are you afraid of here with me?

OSWALD. I'm afraid that everything in me will degenerate into ugliness here.

MRS. ALVING (*looks hard at him*). You think that would happen?

OSWALD. I know it. Live the same life here as down there, and it wouldn't be the same life.

MRS. ALVING (*who has listened intently, rises, her eyes large and thoughtful*). Now I see.

OSWALD. What do you see?

MRS. ALVING. Now I understand for the first time. And now I can speak.

OSWALD (*rises*). Mother, I don't follow you.

REGINA (*who has also risen*). Shall I go?

MRS. ALVING. No, stay. Now I can speak. Now, my boy, you shall know everything. And then you can choose. Oswald! Regina!

OSWALD. Ssh! The Pastor—!

MANDERS (*enters from the hall*). Well, we've had a most splendid and profitable hour down there.

OSWALD. So have we.

MANDERS. We must assist Engstrand with this sailors' home. Regina must go and help him—

REGINA. No thank you, Pastor.

MANDERS (*notices her for the first time*). What! You here! And with a glass in your hand!

REGINA (*puts the glass down quickly*). Oh, *pardon*—

OSWALD. Regina is leaving with me, sir.

MANDERS. Leaving! With you!

OSWALD. Yes. As my wife. If she so wishes.

MANDERS. But, good heavens—!

REGINA. It isn't my doing, sir.

OSWALD. Or she will stay here, if I stay.

REGINA (*involuntarily*). Here?

MANDERS. I am petrified at you, Mrs. Alving.

MRS. ALVING. She will neither leave with you nor stay with you. Now I can speak the truth.

MANDERS. But you mustn't! No, no, no!

MRS. ALVING. I can and I will. And I shan't destroy any ideals, either.

OSWALD. Mother, what have you been hiding from me?

REGINA (*listens*). Madam! Listen! People are shouting outside!

She goes into the conservatory and looks out.

OSWALD (*at the window, left*). What's going on? Where's that light coming from?

REGINA (*cries*). The Orphanage is on fire!

MRS. ALVING (*at the window*). On fire!

MANDERS. On fire? Impossible! I've only just left it.

OSWALD. Where's my hat? Oh, never mind! Father's Orphanage—! (*Runs out through the garden door.*)

MRS. ALVING. My shawl, Regina! The whole building's alight!

MANDERS. Terrible! Mrs. Alving, there blazes the judgment of God upon this sinful house!

MRS. ALVING. Perhaps you are right. Come, Regina. (*She and REGINA hurry out through the hall.*)

MANDERS (*clasps his hands*). And not insured either! (*He follows them.*)

ACT THREE

The same. All the doors are standing open. The lamp is still burning on the table. Outside it is dark, with only a faint glow from the fire in the background, left. MRS. ALVING, *with a big shawl over her head, is standing in the conservatory, looking out.* REGINA, *also with a shawl round her, stands a little behind her.*

MRS. ALVING. All burnt. Burnt to the ground.

REGINA. It's still burning in the basement.

MRS. ALVING. Why doesn't Oswald come back? There's nothing to save.

REGINA. Would you like me to go down and take him his hat?

MRS. ALVING. Hasn't he even got his hat?

REGINA (*points to the hall*). No, it's hanging there.

MRS. ALVING. Let it hang. He must come up now. I'll go and look for him myself. (*Goes out through the garden door.*)

MANDERS (*enters from hall*). Isn't Mrs. Alving here?

REGINA. She's just this minute gone into the garden.

MANDERS. This is the most terrible night I have ever experienced.

REGINA. Yes, sir, isn't it a dreadful tragedy?

MANDERS. Oh, don't talk about it! I hardly dare even to think about it.

REGINA. But how can it have happened—?

MANDERS. Don't ask me, Miss Engstrand. How can I know? Are you, too, going to—? Isn't it enough that your father—?

REGINA. What's he done?

MANDERS. Oh, he's completely confused me.

ENGSTRAND (*enters from the hall*). Your Reverence—

MANDERS (*turns, alarmed*). Are you still pursuing me?

ENGSTRAND. Yes, well, God rot me if—oh, good heavens! But this is a terrible business, your Reverence.

MANDERS (*walks up and down*). It is indeed, it is indeed.

REGINA. What is?

ENGSTRAND. Well, you see, it all began with this prayer service. (*Aside.*) Now we've got him, my girl! (*Aloud.*) Fancy me being to blame for Pastor Manders being to blame for something like this.

MANDERS. But I assure you, Engstrand—

ENGSTRAND. But there was no one except your Reverence mucking around with the candles down there.

MANDERS (*stops*). Yes, so you keep on saying. But I'm sure I don't remember ever having had a candle in my hand.

ENGSTRAND. And I saw as plain as plain could be your Reverence take the candle and snuff it with your fingers and throw the wick right down among the shavings.

MANDERS. And you saw this?

ENGSTRAND. Yes, with these eyes.

MANDERS. That I cannot understand. It's not usually my habit to snuff out candles with my fingers.

ENGSTRAND. Yes, it looked a bit careless, I thought. But it can't really be as bad as you say, can it, your Reverence?

MANDERS (*paces uneasily up and down*). Oh, don't ask me.

ENGSTRAND (*walks with him*). And of course you haven't insured it, either?

MANDERS (*still walking*). No, no, no. I've told you.

ENGSTRAND (*still with him*). Not insured. And then to go straight over and set fire to it all. Oh, good heavens, what a tragedy.

MANDERS (*wipes the sweat from his forehead*). Yes, Engstrand, you may well say that.

ENGSTRAND. And that such a thing should happen to a charitable institution which was to have served the city as well as the countryside. The newspapers won't be too gentle with your Reverence, I'm afraid.

MANDERS. No, that's just what I'm thinking. That's almost the worst part of it. All these hateful attacks and accusations—! Oh, it's frightful to think about.

MRS. ALVING (*enters from the garden*). I can't persuade him to come away from the fire.

MANDERS. Ah, it's you, Mrs. Alving.

MRS. ALVING. Well, now you won't have to make that speech after all, Pastor Manders.

MANDERS. Oh, I'd have been only too happy to—

MRS. ALVING (*in a subdued voice*). It was all for the best. Nothing good would have come of this Orphanage.

MANDERS. You think not?

MRS. ALVING. What do you think?

MANDERS. Nevertheless, it was a terrible tragedy.

MRS. ALVING. We'll discuss it simply as a business matter. Are you waiting for the Pastor, Engstrand?

ENGSTRAND (*in the doorway to the hall*). That's right, madam.

MRS. ALVING. Well, sit down, then.

ENGSTRAND. Thank you, I'm happy standing.

MRS. ALVING (*to* MANDERS). I suppose you'll be leaving with the steamer?

MANDERS. Yes. In an hour.

MRS. ALVING. Would you be kind enough to take all the papers along with you? I don't want to hear another word about this. Now I have other things to think about—

MANDERS. Mrs. Alving—

MRS. ALVING. I'll send you a power of attorney so that you can take any measures you think fit.

MANDERS. I shall be only too happy to shoulder that responsibility. I fear the original purpose of the endowment will now have to be completely changed.

MRS. ALVING. I appreciate that.

MANDERS. Yes, I'm provisionally thinking of arranging for the Solvik property to be handed over to the parish. The freehold cannot by any means be said to be without value. It can always be put to some purpose or other. And the interest from the capital in the savings bank I could perhaps most suitably employ in supporting some enterprise or other which could be said to be of benefit to the town.

MRS. ALVING. As you please. It's a matter of complete in-
difference to me.

ENGSTRAND. Remember my home for sailors, your Reverence.

MANDERS. Yes, indeed, you have a point there. We shall have
to consider that possibility carefully.

ENGSTRAND. Consider? To hell with—oh, good heavens!

MANDERS (*with a sigh*). And I'm afraid I don't know how
long these matters will remain in my hands. Public opinion may force me to withdraw. It all depends on the outcome of the enquiry into the cause of the fire.

MRS. ALVING. What are you saying?

MANDERS. And one cannot possibly predict the outcome.

ENGSTRAND (*comes closer*). Oh, yes one can. Don't I stand
here, and isn't my name Jacob Engstrand?

MANDERS. Yes, yes, but—

ENGSTRAND (*more quietly*). And Jacob Engstrand isn't the
man to fail his blessed benefactor in his time of need, as
the saying goes.

MANDERS. But, my dear man, how—?

ENGSTRAND. Jacob Engstrand can be likened to an angel of
deliverance, as you might say, your Reverence.

MANDERS. No, no, I really cannot accept this.

ENGSTRAND. Oh, that's the way it's going to be. I know
someone who's taken the blame for another man's wickedness once before.

MANDERS. Jacob! (*Presses his hand.*) You are indeed a rare
person. Well, you too shall receive a helping hand. For
your seamen's home. That you can rely upon.

ENGSTRAND *wants to thank him, but is too moved to speak.*

MANDERS (*hangs his travelling bag on his shoulder*). Well,
let's be off. We two shall go together.

ENGSTRAND (*at the dining-room door, says quietly to*
REGINA). You come with me, my girl. You'll live as tight
as the yolk in an egg.

REGINA (*tosses her head*). *Merci!* (*Goes into the hall and
fetches* MANDERS' *overcoat.*)

MANDERS. Farewell, Mrs. Alving. And may the spirit of law and order soon enter into this house.

MRS. ALVING. Goodbye, Manders.

She goes towards the conservatory, as she sees OSWALD *come in through the garden door.*

ENGSTRAND (*while he and* REGINA *help* MANDERS *on with his overcoat*). Goodbye, my child. And if ever you find yourself in any trouble, you know where Jacob Engstrand is to be found. (*Quietly.*) Little Harbour Street—hm—! (*To* MRS. ALVING *and* OSWALD.) And the house for wandering sailors is going to be called Captain Alving's Home. And if I am allowed to run it according to my ideas, I think I can promise you it'll be a worthy memorial to him, God rest his soul.

MANDERS (*in the doorway*). Hm—hm! Come along, my dear Engstrand. Goodbye, goodbye. (*He and* ENGSTRAND *go out through the hall.*)

OSWALD (*goes over towards the table*). What was that he was talking about?

MRS. ALVING. Some kind of home that he and Pastor Manders are going to found.

OSWALD. It'll burn down just like this one.

MRS. ALVING. Why do you say that?

OSWALD. Everything will burn. There will be nothing left to remind people of Father. I, too, am burning.

REGINA *starts and stares at him.*

MRS. ALVING. Oswald! You ought not to have stayed down there so long, my poor boy.

OSWALD (*sits down at the table*). I think you're right.

MRS. ALVING. Let me wipe your face, Oswald. It's soaking wet. (*She dries him with her handkerchief.*)

OSWALD (*stares indifferently ahead of him*). Thank you, Mother.

MRS. ALVING. Aren't you tired, Oswald? Wouldn't you like to go upstairs and sleep?

OSWALD (*frightened*). No, no, I won't sleep. I never sleep. I
only pretend to. (*Heavily.*) It'll come soon enough.

MRS. ALVING (*looks worried at him*). My dear boy, you really
are ill.

REGINA (*tensely*). Is Mr. Alving ill?

OSWALD (*impatiently*). And shut all the doors! Oh, this fear
that haunts me—!

MRS. ALVING. Close them, Regina.

REGINA *closes the doors and remains standing by the hall
door.* MRS. ALVING *takes off her shawl.* REGINA *does likewise.*

MRS. ALVING (*brings a chair over to* OSWALD's *and sits down
beside him*). There now. I'll sit beside you—

OSWALD. Yes, do. And Regina must stay here too. Regina
must always be near me. You'll save me, Regina. Won't
you?

REGINA. I don't understand—

MRS. ALVING. Save you—?

OSWALD. Yes. When the time comes.

MRS. ALVING. But Oswald, you have your mother.

OSWALD. You? (*Smiles.*) No, Mother, you wouldn't do this
for me. (*Laughs heavily.*) You? Ha, ha! (*Looks earnestly
at her.*) Though really you're the one who ought to.
(*Violently.*) Why don't you speak to me as though I was
your friend, Regina? Why don't you call me Oswald?

REGINA (*quietly*). I don't think Mrs. Alving would like it.

MRS. ALVING. You may do so presently. Come over and sit
down here with us. (REGINA *sits quietly and diffidently on
the other side of the table.*) And now, my poor, tormented
boy, now I shall remove the burden from your mind—

OSWALD. You, Mother?

MRS. ALVING (*continues*). All this remorse and self-reproach
you speak of—

OSWALD. You think you can do that?

MRS. ALVING. Yes, Oswald, now I can. You spoke of the joy
of life; and that seemed to throw a new light over everything that has happened to me in my life.

OSWALD (*shakes his head*). I don't understand.

MRS. ALVING. You should have known your father when he was a young lieutenant. He was full of the joy of life, Oswald.

OSWALD. Yes, I know.

MRS. ALVING. It was like a sunny morning just to see him. And the untamed power and the vitality he had!

OSWALD. Yes?

MRS. ALVING. And this happy, carefree child—for he was like a child, then—had to live here in a little town that had no joy to offer him, only diversions. He had to live here with no purpose in life; simply a position to keep up. He could find no work into which he could throw himself heart and soul—just keeping the wheels of business turning. He hadn't a single friend capable of knowing what the joy of life means; only idlers and drinking-companions—

OSWALD. Mother—!

MRS. ALVING. And in the end the inevitable happened.

OSWALD. The inevitable?

MRS. ALVING. You said yourself this evening what would happen to you if you stayed at home.

OSWALD. You mean that Father—?

MRS. ALVING. Your poor father never found any outlet for the excess of vitality in him. And I didn't bring any sunshine into his home.

OSWALD. You didn't?

MRS. ALVING. They had taught me about duty and things like that, and I sat here for too long believing in them. In the end everything became a matter of duty—*my* duty, and *his* duty, and—I'm afraid I made his home intolerable for your poor father, Oswald.

OSWALD. Why did you never write and tell me about this?

MRS. ALVING. Until now I never saw it as something that I could tell you, because you were his son.

OSWALD. And how did you see it?

MRS. ALVING (*slowly*). I only saw that your father was a depraved man before you were born.

OSWALD (*quietly*). Ah—! (*Gets up and goes over to the window.*)

MRS. ALVING. And day in and day out I thought of only one thing, that Regina really belonged here in this house—just as much as my own son.

OSWALD (*turns swiftly*). Regina—!

REGINA (*jumps up and asks softly*). I?

MRS. ALVING. Yes, now you both know.

OSWALD. Regina!

REGINA (*to herself*). So Mother was one of them.

MRS. ALVING. Your mother was in many ways a good woman, Regina.

REGINA. Yes, but still, she was one of them. Yes, I've sometimes wondered; but—! Well, madam, if you'll allow me I think I'd better leave. At once.

MRS. ALVING. Do you really want to, Regina?

REGINA. Yes, I certainly do.

MRS. ALVING. Of course you must do as you please, but—

OSWALD (*goes over to* REGINA). Go now? But you belong here.

REGINA. *Merci*, Mr. Alving—yes, I suppose I'm allowed to say Oswald now. But it certainly isn't the way I'd hoped.

MRS. ALVING. Regina, I haven't been open with you—

REGINA. I should say not. If I'd known that Oswald was ill like this, I— Now that there can never be anything serious between us— No, I'm not going to stay out here in the country and wear myself out looking after invalids.

OSWALD. Not even for someone who is so close to you?

REGINA. I should say not. A poor girl has got to make the best of her life while she's young. Otherwise she'll be left high and dry before she knows where she is. And I've got the joy of life in me too, Mrs. Alving.

MRS. ALVING. Yes, I'm afraid you have. But don't throw yourself away, Regina.

REGINA. Oh, what will be will be. If Oswald takes after his father, I shouldn't be surprised but what I'll take after my mother. May I ask, madam, does Pastor Manders know this about me?

MRS. ALVING. Pastor Manders knows everything.

REGINA (*begins to put on her shawl*). Well then, I'd better get down to the steamer as quick as I can. The Pastor's such a nice man to get along with. And I'm sure I've as much a right to a little of that money as he has—that awful carpenter.

MRS. ALVING. I'm sure you're very welcome to it, Regina.

REGINA (*looks spitefully at her*). You might have brought me up like the daughter of a gentleman. It'd have been more appropriate considering. (*Tosses her head.*) Oh, what the hell does it matter? (*With a bitter glance at the bottle, still unopened.*) I can still drink champagne with gentlemen.

MRS. ALVING. And if ever you need a home, Regina, come to me.

REGINA. No thank you, madam. Pastor Manders will take care of me. And if things go really wrong, I know a house where I belong.

MRS. ALVING. Where is that?

REGINA. In Captain Alving's home for sailors.

MRS. ALVING. Regina—I can see it. You will destroy yourself.

REGINA. Oh, rubbish. *Adieu!* (*Curtseys and goes out through the hall.*)

OSWALD (*stands by the window, looking out*). Has she gone?

MRS. ALVING. Yes.

OSWALD (*mumbles to himself*). I think it was wrong, all this.

MRS. ALVING (*goes over behind him and places her hands on his shoulders*). Oswald, my dear boy, has this news upset you very much?

OSWALD (*turns his face towards her*). All this about Father, you mean?

MRS. ALVING. Yes, about your poor father. I'm so afraid it may have been too much for you.

OSWALD. What on earth makes you think that? Of course it came as a great surprise to me. But I can't really feel it makes any difference.

MRS. ALVING (*takes her hands away*). No difference! That your father was so miserably unhappy!

OSWALD. I feel sorry for him of course, as I would for anyone, but—

MRS. ALVING. Nothing else? For your own father!

OSWALD (*impatiently*). Oh, Father, Father! I never knew anything about Father. I don't remember anything about him, except that once he made me sick.

MRS. ALVING. This is terrible! Surely a child ought to love its father whatever may happen?

OSWALD. Even when a child has nothing to thank its father for? Has never known him? Do you really cling to that old superstition—you, who are otherwise so enlightened?

MRS. ALVING. Do you really think it's only a superstition—?

OSWALD. Yes, Mother, surely you realize that. It's one of those truisms people hand down to their children—

MRS. ALVING (*shudders*). Ghosts!

OSWALD (*walks across the room*). Yes, that's not a bad word for them. Ghosts.

MRS. ALVING (*emotionally*). Oswald! Then you don't love me either!

OSWALD. At least I know you—

MRS. ALVING. Know me, yes. But is that all?

OSWALD. And of course I know how fond you are of me; and for that I must be grateful to you. And you can do so much for me now that I'm ill.

MRS. ALVING. Yes, Oswald, I can, can't I? Oh, I could almost bless your sickness for bringing you home to me. I realize it now. You aren't mine. I must win you.

OSWALD (*impatiently*). Yes, yes, yes. These are just empty phrases. You must remember I'm sick, Mother. I can't be expected to bother about others. I've enough worry thinking about myself.

MRS. ALVING (*quietly*). I shall be patient and undemanding.

OSWALD. And cheerful, Mother!

MRS. ALVING. Yes, my dear boy—I know. (*Goes over to him.*) Have I freed you from all your anxiety and self-reproach now?

OSWALD. Yes, you have. But who will take away the fear?

MRS. ALVING. The fear?

OSWALD (*walks across the room*). Regina would have done it for the asking.

MRS. ALVING. I don't understand you. What's all this about fear—and Regina?

OSWALD. Is it very late, Mother?

MRS. ALVING. It's early morning. (*Looks out into the conservatory.*) The dawn's beginning to show upon the mountains. It's going to be a fine day, Oswald. In a little while you'll be able to see the sun.

OSWALD. I'll look forward to that. Oh, there's still so much for me to look forward to and live for—

MRS. ALVING. Of course there is!

OSWALD. Even if I can't work, there's—

MRS. ALVING. Oh, you'll soon be able to work again, my dear boy. You haven't all these gnawing and oppressing thoughts to brood over any longer now.

OSWALD. No, it was a good thing you managed to rid me of all those ideas. Once I've got over this one thing—! (*Sits on the sofa.*) Let's sit down and talk, Mother.

MRS. ALVING. Yes, let's. (*Moves an armchair over to the sofa, and sits close to him.*)

OSWALD. And while we talk the sun will rise. And then you'll know. And then I won't have this fear any longer.

MRS. ALVING. What will I know?

OSWALD (*not listening to her*). Mother, didn't you say earlier tonight that there wasn't anything in the world you wouldn't do for me if I asked you?

MRS. ALVING. Certainly I did.

OSWALD. And you'll keep your promise, Mother?

MRS. ALVING. Of course I will, my dearest, my only boy. I've nothing else to live for. Only you.

OSWALD. Yes, well, listen then. Mother, you're brave and strong, I know that. Now you must sit quite still while I tell you.

MRS. ALVING. But what is this dreadful thing you—?

OSWALD. You mustn't scream. You hear? Promise me that. We'll sit and talk about it quite calmly. Do you promise me that, Mother?

MRS. ALVING. Yes, yes, I promise. Only tell me.

OSWALD. Well then, all that business about being tired—and

not being able to think about work—that isn't the real illness—

MRS. ALVING. What is the real illness?

OSWALD. The illness which is my inheritance—(*Points to his
forehead and says quite quietly.*) That's in here.

MRS. ALVING (*almost speechless*). Oswald! No! No!

OSWALD. Don't scream. I can't bear it. Yes, Mother, it sits in
here, watching and waiting. And it may break out any
time; any hour.

MRS. ALVING. Oh, how horrible—!

OSWALD. Now keep calm. That's the way it is—

MRS. ALVING (*jumps up*). It isn't true, Oswald! It's impossible! It can't be true!

OSWALD. I had one attack down there. It soon passed. But
when I found out what I had been like, this raging fear
began to hunt me; and that's why I came back home to
you as quickly as I could.

MRS. ALVING. So that's the fear—

OSWALD. Yes—it's so unspeakably repulsive, you see. Oh, if
only it had been an ordinary illness that would have killed
me—! Because I'm not so frightened of dying; though I'd
like to live as long as I can.

MRS. ALVING. Yes, yes, Oswald, you must!

OSWALD. But this is so revolting. To be turned back into a
slobbering baby; to have to be fed, to have to be—! Oh—!
I can't think about it—!

MRS. ALVING. The child has its mother to nurse it.

OSWALD (*jumps up*). No, never! That's just what I won't
allow! I can't bear to think that I might stay like that for
years, growing old and grey. And perhaps you might die
and leave me. (*Sits in* MRS. ALVING's *chair.*) It might
not mean that I'd die at once, the doctor said. He called it
a softening of the brain or something. (*Smiles sadly.*) I
think that sounds so beautiful. I shall always think of
cherry-coloured velvet curtains—something delicious to
stroke.

MRS. ALVING (*screams*). Oswald!

OSWALD (*jumps up again and walks across the room*). And

now you've taken Regina from me. If only I had her! She would have saved me. I know.

MRS. ALVING (*goes over to him*). What do you mean by that, my beloved boy? Is there anything I wouldn't do to save you?

OSWALD. When I had recovered from the attack down there, the doctor told me that when it comes again—and it will come again—then there's no more hope.

MRS. ALVING. How could he be so heartless as to—?

OSWALD. I made him tell me. I told him I had arrangements to make. (*Smiles cunningly.*) And so I had. (*Takes a small box from his inside breast pocket.*) Mother, do you see this?

MRS. ALVING. What's that?

OSWALD. Morphine powders.

MRS. ALVING (*looks at him in horror*). Oswald—my boy—!

OSWALD. I've managed to collect twelve capsules—

MRS. ALVING (*tries to take it*). Give that box to me, Oswald.

OSWALD. Not, yet, Mother. (*Puts it back in his pocket.*)

MRS. ALVING. I can't bear this!

OSWALD. You must bear it. If Regina had been here now, I'd have told her how things were with me—and asked her to do me this last service. I'm sure she would have helped me.

MRS. ALVING. Never!

OSWALD. When the horror was on me and she saw me lying there like a new-born baby, helpless, lost—beyond all hope—

MRS. ALVING. Regina would never have done it.

OSWALD. She would have. Regina was so splendidly carefree. And she would soon have got bored with looking after an invalid like me.

MRS. ALVING. Then thank God that Regina is not here!

OSWALD. Yes, well, so now you will have to do this last service for me, Mother.

MRS. ALVING (*screams aloud*). I?

OSWALD. Who else?

MRS. ALVING. I! Your mother!

OSWALD. Exactly.

MRS. ALVING. I, who gave you life!

OSWALD. I didn't ask you for life. And what kind of a life have you given me? I don't want it. Take it back.

MRS. ALVING. Help! Help! (*Runs out into the hall.*)

OSWALD (*goes after her*). Don't leave me! Where are you going?

MRS. ALVING (*in the hall*). To fetch the doctor, Oswald. Let me go!

OSWALD (*also offstage*). You're not going anywhere. And no one's coming here. (*A key is turned.*)

MRS. ALVING (*comes back*). Oswald! Oswald—my child!

OSWALD (*follows her*). If you have a mother's love for me, how can you see me suffer like this?

MRS. ALVING (*after a moment's silence, says in a controlled voice*). Very well. (*Takes his hand.*) I give you my word.

OSWALD. You promise?

MRS. ALVING. If it becomes necessary. But it won't be. No, no, it's impossible.

OSWALD. Yes, let us hope so. And let us live together as long as we can. Thank you, Mother.

He sits in the armchair, which MRS. ALVING *has moved over to the sofa. The day breaks. The lamp continues to burn on the table.*

MRS. ALVING (*approaches him cautiously*). Do you feel calm now?

OSWALD. Yes.

MRS. ALVING (*leans over him*). You've just imagined these dreadful things, Oswald. You've imagined it all. All this suffering has been too much for you. But now you shall rest. At home with your own mother, my own dear, blessed boy. Point at anything you want and you shall have it, just like when you were a little child. There, there. Now the attack is over. You see how easily it passed! Oh, I knew it! And, Oswald, do you see what a beautiful day we're going to have? Bright sunshine. Now you can really see your home.

She goes over to the table and puts out the lamp. The sun rises. The glacier and the snow-capped peaks in the background glitter in the morning light.

OSWALD (*sits in the armchair facing downstage, motionless. Suddenly he says*). Mother, give me the sun.

MRS. ALVING (*by the table, starts and looks at him*). What did you say?

OSWALD (*repeats dully and tonelessly*). The sun. The sun.

MRS. ALVING (*goes over to him*). Oswald, how are you feeling?

OSWALD *seems to shrink small in his chair. All his muscles go slack. His face is expressionless. His eyes stare emptily.*

MRS. ALVING (*trembles with fear*). What's this? (*Screams loudly.*) Oswald! What is it? (*Throws herself on her knees beside him and shakes him.*) Oswald! Oswald! Look at me! Don't you know me?

OSWALD (*tonelessly as before*). The sun. The sun.

MRS. ALVING (*jumps to her feet in despair, tears her hair with both hands and screams*). I can't bear this! (*Whispers as though numbed.*) I can't bear it! No! (*Suddenly.*) Where did he put them? (*Fumbles quickly across his breast.*) Here! (*Shrinks a few steps backwards and screams.*) No; no; no! Yes! No; no! (*She stands a few steps away from him with her hands twisted in her hair, speechless, and stares at him in horror.*)

OSWALD (*still motionless*). The sun. The sun.

AN ENEMY OF THE PEOPLE

INTRODUCTION

Ibsen wrote *An Enemy of the People* in Rome between March and June 1882, less than six months after completing *Ghosts*. He had probably begun to plan it as early as 1880; on 26 November of that year he wrote to Edmund Gosse that he was "busy pondering a new play which I hope to complete during the summer," and both Lorenz Dietrichson and Kristofer Janson report conversations they had had with Ibsen around this time in which he expressed many of the opinions which he was later to put into Dr. Stockmann's mouth. But he had put this project aside in order to write *Ghosts*.

The extremely hostile reception that *Ghosts* received in Scandinavia on its appearance in December 1881[1] drove Ibsen into a fury. "What is one to say of the attitude taken by the so-called liberal press?" he wrote to Georg Brandes on 3 January 1882. "These leaders who talk and write of freedom and progressiveness and at the same time allow themselves to be the slaves of the supposed opinions of their subscribers! I become more and more convinced that there is something demoralizing about involving oneself in politics and attaching oneself to a party. Under no circumstances will I ever link myself with any party that has the majority behind it. Bjoernson says: 'The majority is always right.' As a practising politician I suppose he has to say that. But I say: 'The minority is always right.' I am of course not thinking of the minority of reactionaries who have been left astern by the big central party which we call liberal; I mean the minority which forges ahead in territory which the majority has not yet reached. I believe that he is right who is most closely

[1] See pages 107 ff.

attuned to the future. . . . For me liberty is the first condition of life, and the highest. At home people don't bother much about liberty but only about liberties—a few more or a few less, according to the party standpoint. I feel most painfully affected by this vulgarity, this plebeianism in our public discussion. In the course of their undeniably worthy efforts to turn our country into a democratic community, people have unwittingly gone a good way towards turning us into a mob community. The aristocracy of the intellect seems to be in short supply in Norway."

Later the same month (24 January 1882) he wrote to Olaf Skavlan: "I myself am responsible for what I write, and I alone. I cannot possibly embarrass any party, for I belong to none. I want to act as a lone *franc-tireur* in the outposts and operate on my own. . . . Is it only in the political field that men are to be allowed to work for freedom in Norway? Is it not first and foremost man's spirit that needs to be set free? Such spiritual slaves as we are cannot even use the freedoms we already have. Norway is a free country inhabited by serfs."

Normally, Ibsen allowed eighteen months to elapse between completing one play and beginning another[2]; but on 16 March he surprised Hegel by writing: "I am able to tell you that I am now fully occupied with preparations for my new play. This time it will be a peaceful work which can be read by cabinet ministers and wholesale merchants and their ladies, and from which the theatres will not need to shrink. I should have no difficulty in polishing it off, and I will try to have it ready quite early in the autumn." For once he found himself ahead of schedule, for on 21 June he was able to write to Hegel, still from Rome: "Yesterday I completed my new play. It is entitled An Enemy of the People, and is

---

[2] Between 1877, when he finished *The Pillars of Society*, and 1896, when he wrote *John Gabriel Borkman*, *An Enemy of the People* provides the only exception to this rule. *When We Dead Awaken*, Ibsen's last play, came three years after *John Gabriel Borkman*, but this was largely because 1898 was much taken up with preparations for the celebration of Ibsen's seventieth birthday.

in five acts. I am still a little uncertain whether to call it a
comedy or simply a play; it has much of the character of a
comedy, but there is also a serious basic theme. . . . In
a few days I shall start on the fair copy, which should be
ready at the latest by the end of July. I will send you the
manuscript in stages, as usual."

Unfortunately no working notes or preliminary draft of *An
Enemy of the People* have survived, so that we do not know,
as we do with most of his other plays, exactly how long he
took to write each act and what alterations he made from
his original conception.

At the beginning of August he left Rome for Gossensass
in the Tyrol, and from there, on 28 August, he sent Hegel
the fair copy of the first four acts. "The fifth," he explained,
"will follow in a few days, as I have already done half of it.
The reason the manuscript is arriving somewhat later than I
implied in my previous letter is that I have fair-copied the
whole play twice in order to achieve the maximum perfection
in the dialogue." On 9 September he posted the final act. "It
has been fun," he wrote, "working on this play, and I feel a
sense of deprivation and emptiness at being parted from it.
Dr. Stockmann and I got on most excellently; we are so alike
in many ways; but the Doctor has a more muddled head on
his shoulders than I have, and he has besides certain characteristics which will permit people to tolerate certain things
from his lips which they might not accept so readily if they
had issued from mine. If you have begun to read the manuscript, I think you will share this opinion."

An Enemy of the People was published by Gyldendals of
Copenhagen on 28 November 1882. The Christiania Theatre
and the Royal Theatres of Copenhagen and Stockholm, all of
which had rejected *Ghosts* as unfit for public presentation,
immediately acquired the production rights of *An Enemy of
the People*, apparently insensitive to the fact that the theme
of the latter play was the unworthiness of those who "do not
dare," and its conclusion: "The strongest man is he who
stands most alone." It was performed at the Christiania
Theatre on 13 January 1883; at Bergen on 24 January; at

Gothenburg in February, and in Copenhagen and Stockholm in March. In all three countries it was cordially, but not over-enthusiastically received. In 1884 it was staged in Rotterdam; but—strangely enough, in view of the popularity there of *The Pillars of Society* and *A Doll's House,* and the sensation caused by the publication of *Ghosts*—it was not performed in Germany until 5 March 1887, when it was produced at a charity matinée at the Ostend Theatre, Berlin. Its success was such that it was immediately placed in the regular bill, and was played twenty times. The same year it was produced in Helsinki; and, in 1888, at the Court Theatre in Meiningen, "where," William Archer noted, "the fourth act was naturally found to offer a superb opportunity for the Meiningen methods of stage-management." During the next few years it was widely performed in Germany, as well as in Berne, Vienna, and Prague. In 1890 Archer saw a production at the Residenz Theater, Munich. "It was vilely staged," he commented. "If they'd let me direct a couple of rehearsals, I'd have made a different play of it—but it was fairly played, and went like wildfire with the house."

In 1892 *An Enemy of the People* was acted in New York, in German[3]; and the following year Lugné-Poe staged it in Paris at the Théâtre de L'Oeuvre. "On the first night," writes Archer, "it was preceded by a lecture by M. Laurent Tail-hade, which consisted not so much of an exposition of the play, as of a violent attack upon all the "leading men" in French literature and politics. Beside it, Dr. Stockmann's harangue in the fourth act seems moderate and almost mealy-mouthed. . . . The audience listened, not without protest, to M. Tailhade's diatribe, until he thought fit to describe the recent Franco-Russian fêtes as an act of collective insanity. At this point a storm of indignation burst forth, which lasted without pause for a quarter of an hour, and was not allayed

[3] Several of the first American performances of Ibsen were in a language other than English, owing to the high proportion, in those days, of first-generation European immigrants. The world premiere of *Ghosts* took place in Chicago in Norwegian (or in a mixture of Norwegian and Danish).

by an attempt at intervention on the part of M. Lugné-Poe. The lecture closed amid wild confusion, and altogether the preliminary scene in the auditorium was like a spirited rehearsal of the meeting at Captain Horster's."

In 1893 *An Enemy of the People* was produced in England, by Herbert Beerbohm Tree at the Haymarket Theatre—the first Ibsen play to attract the attention of a fashionable actor-manager and receive the full West End treatment. Opinions as to the merits of the production, and of Tree's performance, varied; Ludwig Josephson, the Swedish director, was full of admiration, but William Archer and Bernard Shaw were not. "He is too emphatic, too pontifical, above all too *slow*," wrote Archer in the *World*. "He has not *le diable au corps*. He is too apt to rely for his effects upon solemn pauses, and to import into the vivid, ebullient Stockmann the aristocratic languor of Lord Illingworth and the dreaminess of Hamlet." Shaw commented similarly that Tree's performance "though humorous and entertaining in its way, was, as a character creation, the polar opposite of Ibsen's Stockmann." In 1895 Tree took his production to America, where it had a great success. The same year Ermete Novelli staged the play in Italy; and the following year it was produced in Spain.

Two of the most notable early interpretations of Dr. Stockmann were seen in Manchester. In 1894 Louis Calvert played it at the Gentlemen's Concert Hall, the dull-sounding venue of many interesting productions during the nineties. An anonymous staff reporter on the *Manchester Guardian* (possibly C. E. Montague, but the *Guardian* has no record of its authorship) wrote: "Mr. Calvert . . . gave us a living picture of the loose-limbed, broad-shouldered, untidy man, with his odd mixture of naivety and shrewdness, his genial friendliness, the largeness of his humanity, and yet, with all that, his fiery temper, his capacity for scorn and his indomitable stubbornness. An excellent touch was the half-assenting, half-impatient manner in which he received the virtuous platitudes—with which he agreed, but which were not alive enough to interest him—of his friends before they became his enemies." Fifteen years later, in 1909, Henry Austin played

the role at Miss Horniman's recently-founded Manchester
Gaiety Theatre, and C. E. Montague commemorated the performance in one of his most splendid critical passages:

> He is the best Stockmann we have seen. His turbid
> spate of speech is the very thing—a kind of short-winded
> fluency, copious and breathless at the same time, a
> shambling volubility, a stumbling gallop of the tongue;
> in his talk the emphases and the pauses are often fear-
> fully and wonderfully, but most significantly distributed,
> neither musically nor according to the sense, but with
> traceable periodic pulsations, suggesting some large, la-
> bouring engine of good-will throbbing half-frustratedly
> in the capacious bosom; to eye and ear he presents the
> perfect fusion of moral grandeur and mental woolliness
> into one great muddled soul, a noble goose or heroic
> owl; you get the full interplay of clear long sight to the
> things that are more excellent and mere peery, blear-
> eyed fumblings at the trifles that are clear to everyone
> else, the ordinary working meannesses and cowardices
> of existence; and another nice touch is the good soul's
> lack, or even inversion, of the instinct for pose—Mr. Aus-
> tin is capital at the points where Stockmann, when most
> sublime in essentials, dabs a sudden touch of grotesque-
> ness into the picture of exaltation with some little fit of
> child's crossness—mere mad waste of effect as it must
> seem to all amateurs of the *beau role*. . . . Mrs. Theo-
> dore Wright, as Mrs. Stockmann, acts with an energy of
> sincerity that makes her a regular running fountain of
> stage illusion for two whole stage scenes. She not only
> makes her part real but sheds reality all around it, on
> other characters, on the scenery, on everything within
> range; vividness radiates from her like heat from a stove.

In 1905 *An Enemy of the People* was the instance of a
demonstration even more remarkable than the one it had
caused in Paris in 1893. The place was Petrograd, the company that of the Moscow Arts Theatre, and Constantin
Stanislavsky, who was playing Dr. Stockmann, has described
the occasion vividly in his autobiography, *My Life and Art:*

In that time of political unrest—it was but a little while before the first revolution—the feeling of protest was very strong in all spheres of society. They waited for the hero who could tell the truth strongly and bravely in the very teeth of the government. It is not to be wondered at that the image of Dr. Stockmann became popular at once in Moscow, and especially so in Petrograd. *An Enemy of the People* became the favourite play of the revolutionists, notwithstanding the fact that Stockmann himself despised the solid majority and believed in individuals to whom he would entrust the conduct of life. But Stockmann protested, Stockmann told the truth, and that was considered enough.

On the day of the well-known massacre in Kazansky Square, *An Enemy of the People* was on the boards of our theatre. The average run of spectators that night was from the intelligentsia, the professors and learned men of Petrograd. I remember that the orchestra was filled almost entirely with grey heads. Thanks to the sad events of the day, the auditorium was very excited and answered even the slightest hints about liberty in every word of Stockmann's protest. In the most unexpected places in the play the thunder of applause would break in on the performance. . . . The atmosphere in the theatre was such that we expected arrests at any minute and a stop to the performance. Censors, who sat at all the performances of *An Enemy of the People* and saw to it that I, who played Dr. Stockmann, should use only the censored text, and raised trouble over every syllable that was not admitted by the censorship, were on this evening even more watchful than on other occasions. I had to be doubly careful. When the text of a role is cut and re-cut many times it is not hard to make a mistake and say too much or too little. In the last act of the play, Dr. Stockmann, putting into order his room which has been stoned by the crowd, finds in the general chaos his black coat,[4] in which he appeared at the meeting the day before. Seeing a rent in the cloth, Stockmann says to his wife: "One must never put on a new coat when one goes to fight for freedom and truth."

[4] More accurately, his trousers.

The spectators in the theatre connected this sentence with the massacre in Kazansky Square, where more than one new coat must have been torn in the name of freedom and truth. Unexpectedly, my words aroused such a pandemonium that it was necessary to stop the performance, into which a real mob scene was interpolated by impromptu. There had taken place the unification of the actor and the spectators, who took on themselves the role of chief actor in the theatre, that same mob action of which so much is said by the theoreticians of art. The entire audience rose from its seats and threw itself towards the footlights. Thanks to the fact that the stage was very low and there was no orchestra before it, I saw hundreds of hands stretched toward me, all of which I was forced to shake. The younger people in the audience jumped on to the stage and embraced Dr. Stockmann. It was not easy to establish order and to continue with the play. That evening I found out through my own experience what power the theatre could exercise.

Although the public reception of *Ghosts* was the immediate inspiration of *An Enemy of the People,* the opinions to which Ibsen gave expression in it were not new to him; we find them continually cropping up in his earlier correspondence, especially in his letters to the Danish critic Georg Brandes. As early as 1871, eleven years before he began *An Enemy of the People,* he had declared to Brandes: "I shall never be able to regard liberty as synonymous with political liberty. What you call liberty I call liberties, and what I call the fight for freedom is nothing but the eternal and living quest for the idea of freedom. He who possesses freedom otherwise than as an object to be sought possesses something dead and soulless. For the quintessence of freedom is the fact that as one acquires it, it grows, so that if anyone stops during his quest and says: 'Now I have it!', he reveals, by this very action, that he has lost it."

On 21 March 1872 he asserted to Frederik Gjertsen his "fundamental principle, in every context and situation, namely, that the minority is always right." And the following month he wrote to Brandes: "My dear friend, the liberals are

the worst enemies of freedom. Spiritual and intellectual freedom flourish best under absolutism; that has been proved in
France, and later in Germany, and it is now being proved in
Russia. . . . As regards this agitation which is being worked
up against you, with its lies and back-biting and so forth,
let me give you a piece of advice which from my own experience I know to be sovereign. Be an aristocrat! Aristocracy
is the only weapon against this kind of thing. Appear indif-
ferent; never write a word of reply in the newspapers; if you
polemicize in your writings, never direct your polemic against
this or that specific attack; never write a single word which
could make it seem that your enemies have found their mark;
in short, act as though you had no idea that anyone was
opposed to you."

On 19 December 1879, a fortnight after the publication of
A Doll's House, he wrote to Lorenz Dietrichson: "It seems to
me doubtful whether it is practicable to obtain better artistic
conditions in our country before the intellectual soil has been
thoroughly turned up and cleansed and drained of all its
swamp-like filth." This was a metaphor to which he was to
return in *An Enemy of the People.* And Kristofer Janson, the
poet who was a part-original of Hjalmar Ekdal in *The Wild
Duck,* reports a conversation he had with Ibsen on New
Year's Eve 1880, when Ibsen is thought to have been making his first plans for *An Enemy of the People.* "Ibsen flared
up. 'The majority? What is the majority? The ignorant mass!
The intelligence is always in the minority. How many of the
majority do you think are qualified to hold an opinion? Most
of them are just sheepdogs!' "[5]

"When my new play reaches you," Ibsen wrote to Brandes
on 21 September 1882, shortly after he had finished *An
Enemy of the People,* "you will perhaps be able to under-

[5] He also once remarked to Janson: "The only people with
whom I really have any sympathy are the nihilists and the social-
ists. They want something whole-heartedly, and they are consis-
tent." Ibsen did not object when, in 1890, Bernard Shaw identified
"Ibsenism" with socialism—indeed, he protested when some newspapers asserted that he had nothing to do with socialism.

stand what interest and, I may add, fun it has given me to
recall the many scattered and casual remarks I have made
in my letters to you." Nine months later, to the same cor-
respondent, he added a provocative postscript to the play.
"An intellectual pioneer," he declared, "can never gather a
majority about him. In ten years the majority may have
reached the point where Dr. Stockmann stood when the people held their meeting. But during those ten years the Doctor
has not remained stationary; he is still at least ten years ahead
of the others. The majority, the masses, the mob, will never
catch him up; he can never rally them behind him. I myself
feel a similarly unrelenting compulsion to keep pressing forward. A crowd now stands where I stood when I wrote my
earlier books. But I myself am there no longer. I am somewhere else—far ahead of them—or so I hope. At present I am
struggling with the draft of a new play in four acts. . . ."
This new play, the successor to *An Enemy of the People*, was
to be *The Wild Duck*.

The plot of *An Enemy of the People* had its origin in two
actual incidents to which Ibsen's attention had been drawn.
Alfred Meissner, a young German poet whom he knew in
Munich, told him how, when his father had been medical
officer at the spa of Teiplitz in the eighteen-thirties, there
had occurred an outbreak of cholera which the latter felt it
his duty to make public. As a result, the season was ruined,
and the citizens of Teiplitz became so enraged that they
stoned the Doctor's house and forced him to flee the town.
Then there had been the case in Norway of a chemist
named Harald Thaulow. For nearly ten years Thaulow had
furiously attacked the Christiania Steam Kitchens for neglect-
ing their duty towards the city's poor. He had delivered a
violent speech on the subject in 1874, when Ibsen was re-
visiting Norway; and on 23 February 1881, only a fortnight
before he died, Thaulow had attempted to read a prepared
speech at the annual general meeting of the Steam Kitchens.
The chairman of the meeting tried to prevent him from
speaking, and eventually the audience forced him, amid com-

motion, to remain silent. Ibsen read a report of this meeting in *Aftenposten* just at the time when his indignation at the reception of *Ghosts* was reaching its climax, and he must have recognized in the eccentric old chemist a spirit very kindred to his own. The newspaper account is worth quoting:

THAULOW. I will not be silenced. (*Continues reading.*)
CONSUL HEFTYE. Make him stop.

THAULOW *continues to read*. . . . *Several persons express their indignation by ostentatiously walking about in the hall. The* CHAIRMAN *asks the meeting whether they recognize his right to withdraw from* MR. THAULOW *the privilege of the floor. Unanimous cries of assent. The* CHAIRMAN *again asks* MR. THAULOW *to stop.*

THAULOW. I will not be gagged.
CHAIRMAN. In that case I shall proceed to—
THAULOW. I'll keep it short. (*Continues to read.*)
CONSUL HEFTYE. Is he to be allowed to go on?
THAULOW (*continues*). The glorious achievements of the Christiania Soup Kitchen . . . I'll be through in a minute.
CONSUL HEFTYE. At this rate the meeting'll be broken up.
CHAIRMAN. I regret to have to interrupt Herr Thaulow. Your observations—

THAULOW *goes on reading.*

CONSUL HEFTYE. Be quiet or leave the room!
THAULOW. Oh, very well. (*Sits down exhausted.*)

The CHAIRMAN *thereupon resumes the reading of the official report.* THAULOW *accompanies the reading with grunts and tries several times to obtain another hearing. At length, the opposition proving too much for him, he gives up the battle and leaves the hall saying:* Now I'll have no more to do with you. I'm tired of casting pearls before swine. This is a damned abuse being inflicted on free people in a free country. Goodbye! . . .

Stockmann himself, however, was primarily based on two old acquaintances of Ibsen, both distinguished writers—Jonas

Lie and Bjoernsterne Bjoernson. Ibsen had re-encountered Lie in Berchtesgaden in the summer of 1880 and had found him as confused, warm-hearted, inconsistent, and impatient as ever. Bjoernson shared the same warm-heartedness and impatience, plus eloquence, a strong family feeling, and an infinite capacity for moral indignation. But one must not forget, when considering the origins of Stockmann, that Ibsen himself had, as a younger man, been a fiery and eloquent speaker on causes that touched him. Lorenz Dietrichson has described him addressing a gathering of the Scandinavian community in Rome in 1864, on the subject of the Danish-German war. "All the bitterness which had for so long been stored up within him, all the fiery indignation and passion for the Scandinavian cause which he had bottled up for so long, found an outlet. His voice began to ring, and in the evening dusk one saw only his burning eyes. When he had finished, no one cried 'Bravo!' or raised his glass, but I think we all felt that that evening the Marseillaise of the North had rung out into the Roman night air." That is not very far from the Dr. Stockmann of Act Four; and it is worth remembering that the house in Skien in which Ibsen had been born was called Stockmannsgaarden.

One of the characters in *An Enemy of the People*, Aslaksen the printer, had already appeared in *The League of Youth*, completed in 1869. There he had been a sad little drunk; in the later play he has become a pillar of respectability and moderation. Morten Kiil, "the Badger," had been planned as a character for *The Pillars of Society*. He appears in the rough notes for that play, but never got into the final draft. Ibsen, like the Button Moulder's description of The Master in *Peer Gynt*, was

> a thrifty man . . .
> He never rejects as worthless anything
> Which he can use again as raw material.

As recently as October 1964 a number of previously unpublished letters of Ibsen were privately printed in a limited edition,[6] and among them are three of particular interest in which Ibsen discusses in detail the characters of *An Enemy of the People*. Hans Schroeder, the director of the Christiania Theatre who had rejected *Ghosts*—a memory which the unfortunate man was to carry with him for the rest of his days —had telegraphed Ibsen in Rome for permission to give the first public performance of *An Enemy of the People*. Ibsen agreed, stinging them for a lump payment of 4000 crowns (he had let them have *A Doll's House* for 2500), and a week later, on 14 December 1882, he wrote to Schroeder from Rome:

> Permit me to address to you a few lines concerning the forthcoming production of *An Enemy of the People*. It is not my intention or wish to attempt to influence *in absentio* either the staging or the casting; but the expression of certain feelings which I hold regarding various aspects of the play can do no harm. I trust I may assume that Mrs. Wolf will play Mrs. Stockmann. . . . If for the role of Hovstad you have an otherwise suitable actor of not too heroic build, that is the kind of man you should choose. Hovstad is the son of poor people, has grown up in a dirty home on wretched and inadequate food, has frozen and toiled horribly throughout his childhood, and subsequently, as a poverty-stricken young man, has continued to undergo considerable privation. Such living conditions leave their mark not only on a man's spirit but also on his outward appearance. Men of heroic exterior are an exception among the plebs. Whatever the circumstances Hovstad must always wear a depressed appearance, somewhat shrunken and stooping, and uncertain in his movements; all, of course, portrayed with complete naturalism. Billing's lines are so worded that they require an east-coast and not e.g. a Bergen dialect. He is, essentially, an east-coast character. Captain Horster has been ridiculously misunderstood by a Danish critic. He characterises Horster as an old man, Dr. Stockmann's old friend, etc. This is, of course, utterly

[6] *Henrik Ibsens Brevveksling med Christiania Theater 1878–1899*, edited with a commentary by Oeyvind Anker (Gyldendal Norsk Forlag, Oslo, 1964).

wrong. Horster is a young man, one of the young people whose healthy appetite delights the Doctor, though he is an infrequent visitor at the house because he dislikes the company of Hovstad and Billing. Already in Act One, Horster's interest in Petra must subtly and delicately be indicated, and during the brief exchanges between him and her in Act Five we must sense that they now stand at the threshold of a deep and passionate relationship.

Both the boys must be carefully instructed so that the difference in their characters is clearly established. And I must beg that in Act Four every possible actor at your disposal be used. The stage director must here enjoin the greatest possible naturalism and strictly forbid any caricaturing or exaggeration. The more realistic characters you can work into the crowd the better.

Throughout the play the stage director must inexorably insist that none of the players alter his or her lines. They must be spoken exactly as they stand in the text. A lively tempo is desirable. When I was last at the Christiania Theatre the speech seemed to me very slow. But above all, truthfulness to nature—the illusion that everything is real and that one is sitting and watching something that is actually taking place in real life. *An Enemy of the People* is not easy to stage. It demands exceptionally well-drilled ensemble playing, i.e., protracted and meticulously supervised rehearsals. But I rely upon the good will of all concerned. . . ."

Ten days later, on Christmas Eve, Ibsen had occasion to write again to Schroeder: "*Morgenbladet* has published an announcement about the casting for *An Enemy of the People*, in consequence of which I must further inconvenience you with a few lines. I see that Gundersen is to play the Mayor. This actor's appearance hardly suggests a man who cannot bear to eat hot food in the evening, has a bad stomach and an uncertain digestion, and lives on weak tea. Nor is it well suited to a man who is characterised as neat, refined, and fastidious. But these shortcomings can partly be countered by the right clothes and make-up. Mr. Gundersen must therefore pay careful attention to these two points. Nor does Mr. Reimers's physique fit such a temperament as Dr. Stockmann's; hot-headed people are in general more slightly built. The same advice accordingly applies to Mr. Reimers as that which I have suggested for Mr. Gundersen. He must make himself as thin and small as possible."

On 31 December 1882, Ibsen wrote again: "I fear I must once again trouble you with a few lines. From your kind letter which reached me yesterday I gather it is intended to have both the boys in my play acted by girls. This has somewhat disturbed me, since it seems to imply that sufficient attention has not been paid to the spirit in which this play was written and in which it requires to be staged. To allow boys' parts to be taken by women may sometimes be excusable in operetta, vaudeville, or the so-called romantic drama; for in these the prime requirement is unqualified illusion; every member of the audience is fully conscious throughout the evening that he is merely sitting in a theatre and watching a theatrical performance. But this should not be the case when *An Enemy of the People* is being acted. The spectator must feel as though he were invisibly present in Dr. Stockmann's living-room; everything here must seem real; the two boys included. Consequently they cannot be played by actresses dressed up in wigs and stays; their feminine figures will not be able to be concealed by their costume of shirt and trousers, and they will never make any spectator believe that he is looking at two real schoolboys from some small town. How in any case can a grown woman make herself look like a ten-year-old child? Both parts must therefore be played by children, at worst by a couple of small girls whose figures are not yet fully developed; and then damn the corsets and let them have big boys' boots on their legs. They must also, of course, be taught the way boys behave.

"It is stated in the play that at the public meeting Dr. Stockmann is to be dressed in black; but his clothes must not be new or elegant, and his white cravat should sit a little crooked."

Of all the roles, by any author, that Constantin Stanislavsky played, Dr. Stockmann was his favourite. "I felt myself more at home in the role of Stockmann," he confessed in *My Life and Art,* "than in any other role of my repertoire. . . . For me Stockmann was not a politician, not an orator at meetings, not a *raisonneur,* but a man of ideals, the true friend of his country and his people. He was the best and purest citizen of his motherland." Stanislavsky goes on to speak of "the inner image with all its peculiarities and details; the short-sighted eyes which spoke so eloquently of his inner blindness to human faults, the childlike and youthful manner of movement, the friendly relations with his children and family, the happiness, the love of joking and play, the gregariousness and attractiveness which forced all who came in touch with him to become purer and better, and to show the best sides of their natures in his presence. . . . I had only to think of the thoughts and cares of Stockmann and the signs of short sight would come of themselves, together with the forward stoop of the body, the quick step, the eyes that looked trustfully into the soul of the man or object on the stage with me, the index and middle fingers of the hand stretched forward of themselves for the sake of greater persuasiveness, as if to push my own thoughts, feelings, and words into the soul of my listener."[7]

An Enemy of the People has never received its full due in England, largely because, despite Calvert's and Austin's admirable performances in Manchester, the great role of Stockmann has never really been adequately portrayed in London. The Baths, too, have put managements off; and the kind of academic critic that dismisses *Emperor and Galilean* as "undramatic," *Brand* as "ambiguous," and *Little Eyolf* as "a falling-off" (to quote from a recent and embarrassing book intended as a vindication of Ibsen) has tended to reject *An Enemy of the People* as "thin." It lacks, perhaps, the extreme density of his later works, but there are precious few other plays outside the Greeks, Shakespeare, and Chekhov with which it need fear comparison. Nor can it glibly be dismissed

[7] Stanislavsky based his physical appearance in the role on that of Rimsky-Korsakov, and borrowed several gestures and characteristics from Gorki.

as a *jeu d'esprit*. Even adequately performed, it is one of the most compulsive of Ibsen's plays. The truths it expresses have not dated, and are not likely to as long as there are town councils and politicians. There will always, somewhere, in men's hearts if not in reality, be a Kazansky Square.

M. M.

CHARACTERS

DR. THOMAS STOCKMANN, medical officer at the Baths

MRS. STOCKMANN, his wife

PETRA, their daughter, a schoolteacher

EILIF
MORTEN } their sons, aged thirteen and ten

PETER STOCKMANN, the DOCTOR's elder brother, Mayor and Chief Constable, Chairman of the Baths Committee, etc.

MORTEN KIIL, master tanner, foster father to MRS. STOCKMANN

HOVSTAD, editor of the *People's Tribune*

BILLING, an employee on the newspaper

HORSTER, a sea captain

ASLAKSEN, a printer

People at a public meeting——men of all classes, a few women and a bunch of schoolboys.

The action takes place in a coastal town in Southern Norway.

This translation of An Enemy of the People *was commissioned by the Nottingham Theatre Trust, Ltd., and was first performed on 3 April 1962 at the Nottingham Playhouse with the following cast:*

DR. STOCKMANN	John Stratton
MRS. STOCKMANN	Dorothy Primrose
PETRA	Anne Stallybrass
EILIF	Terry Smith
MORTEN	Paul Nugent
MAYOR	Alan MacNaughtan
MORTEN KIIL	Stafford Byrne
HOVSTAD	Roland Curram
BILLING	Roger Jerome
HORSTER	Ronald Magill
ASLAKSEN	Bartlett Mullins

Directed by Allan Davis

ACT ONE

Evening in DR. STOCKMANN's *living-room. It is humbly but neatly furnished and decorated. In the wall to the right are two doors, of which the further leads out to the hall and the nearer to the* DOCTOR's *study. In the opposite wall, facing the hall door, is a door that leads to the other rooms occupied by the family. In the middle of this wall stands a tiled stove; further downstage is a sofa with a mirror above it. In front of the sofa is an oval table with a cloth on it. Upon this table stands a lighted lamp with a shade. Upstage, an open door to the dining-room, in which can be seen a table laid for the evening meal, with a lamp on it.*

At this table BILLING *is seated, a napkin tucked beneath his chin.* MRS. STOCKMANN *is standing by the table, offering him a plate with a large joint of beef on it. The other places around the table are empty, and the table is in the disorder of a meal that has been finished.*

MRS. STOCKMANN. There, Mr. Billing! But if you will come an hour late, you'll have to put up with cold.

BILLING (*eating*). Oh, but this is capital. Absolutely capital!

MRS. STOCKMANN. Well, you know how punctually my husband always likes to eat.

BILLING. It doesn't bother me. I enjoy eating alone, without having to talk to anyone.

MRS. STOCKMANN. Oh. Well, as long as you're *enjoying* it, that's— (*Listens towards the hall.*) Ah, this must be Mr. Hovstad.

BILLING. Very likely.

PETER STOCKMANN *enters wearing an overcoat and his mayoral hat, and carrying a stick.*

MAYOR. Good evening to you, my dear sister-in-law.

MRS. STOCKMANN (*goes into the living-room*). Why, good evening! Fancy seeing you here! How nice of you to come and call on us!

MAYOR. I just happened to be passing, so— (*Glances towards the dining-room.*) But I hear you have company.

MRS. STOCKMANN (*a little embarrassed*). Oh, no, no, that's no one. (*Quickly.*) Won't you have something too?

MAYOR. I? No, thank you! A cooked meal at night! My digestion would never stand that!

MRS. STOCKMANN. Oh, but surely just for once—

MAYOR. No, no! It's very kind of you, but I'll stick to my tea and sandwiches. It's healthier in the long run; and a little less expensive.

MRS. STOCKMANN (*smiles*). You speak as though Thomas and I were spendthrifts!

MAYOR. Not you, my dear sister-in-law. Such a thought was far from my mind. (*Points towards the* DOCTOR's *study.*) Isn't he at home?

MRS. STOCKMANN. No, he's gone for a little walk with the boys.

MAYOR. I wonder if that's wise so soon after a meal? (*Listens.*) Ah, this must be he.

MRS. STOCKMANN. No, I don't think it can be, yet. (*A knock on the door.*) Come in!

HOVSTAD, *the editor of the local newspaper, enters from the hall.*

MRS. STOCKMANN. Oh—Mr. Hovstad—?

HOVSTAD. Yes. Please excuse me, I was detained down at the printer's. Good evening, Your Worship.

MAYOR (*greets him somewhat stiffly*). Good evening. I suppose you are here on business?

HOVSTAD. Partly. About an article for my newspaper—

MAYOR. I guessed as much. I hear my brother is a regular contributor to the *People's Tribune*.

HOVSTAD. Yes, he usually drops us a line when he thinks the truth needs to be told about something.

MRS. STOCKMANN (*to* HOVSTAD, *pointing towards the dining-room*). Er—won't you—?

MAYOR. Great heavens, you mustn't think I blame him for writing for the kind of public he's most likely to find sympathetic to his ideas. Besides, I have no reason to bear your newspaper any ill will, Mr. Hovstad—

HOVSTAD. I should hope not.

MAYOR. On the whole I think I may say that an admirable spirit of tolerance reigns in our town. A fine communal spirit! And the reason for this is that we have this great common interest that binds us together—an interest which is the close concern of every right-minded citizen—

HOVSTAD. You mean the Baths?

MAYOR. Exactly! Our magnificent new Baths! Mark my words, sir! These Baths will prove the very heart and essence of our life! There can be no doubt about it.

MRS. STOCKMANN. Yes, that's just what Thomas says.

MAYOR. It's really astounding the strides this place has made during the past two or three years! The town is becoming prosperous. People are waking up and beginning to live. Buildings and ground rents are increasing in value every day.

HOVSTAD. And unemployment is going down.

MAYOR. Yes, there's that too. The burden upon the propertied classes of poor relief has been most gratifyingly reduced —and will be still more if only we have a really good summer this year, with plenty of visitors. What we want most is invalids. They'll give the Baths a good name.

HOVSTAD. And I hear the indications are promising.

MAYOR. They are indeed. Enquiries about accommodation are pouring in every day.

HOVSTAD. Well then, the Doctor's article will be most opportune.

MAYOR. Oh, has he written something new?

HOVSTAD. No, it's something he wrote last winter; a eulogy of the Baths and the excellent health facilities of the town. But I decided to hold it over.

MAYOR. Ah, there was a snag somewhere?

HOVSTAD. No, it wasn't that. I just thought it would be better to wait till the spring. Now people are thinking about where to spend their summer holidays—

MAYOR. Quite right! Quite right, Mr. Hovstad!

MRS. STOCKMANN. Thomas never stops thinking about those Baths.

MAYOR. Well, he is employed there.

HOVSTAD. Yes, and he was the one who really created it all, wasn't he?

MAYOR. Was he? Really? Yes, I have heard that certain people do hold that opinion. I must say I was labouring under the delusion that I had some modest share in promoting the enterprise.

MRS. STOCKMANN. That's what Thomas is always telling people.

HOVSTAD. No one denies that, Your Worship. You got it going and saw to all the practical details—we all know that. I only meant that the idea originated with the Doctor.

MAYOR. Yes, my brother's always been full of ideas—unfortunately. But when things have to be done, another kind of man is needed, Mr. Hovstad. And I should have thought that least of all in this house would—

MRS. STOCKMANN. But my dear brother-in-law—!

HOVSTAD. Surely Your Worship doesn't—?

MRS. STOCKMANN. Do go inside and get yourself something to eat, Mr. Hovstad. My husband will be here any moment.

HOVSTAD. Thank you—just a bite, perhaps. (*Goes into the dining-room.*)

MAYOR (*lowers his voice slightly*). It's extraordinary about people of peasant stock. They never learn the meaning of tact.

MRS. STOCKMANN. But is it really anything to bother about? Can't you and Thomas share the honour as brothers?

MAYOR. Well, I should have thought so; but it seems not everyone is content to share.

MRS. STOCKMANN. Oh, nonsense! You and Thomas always get on so well together. Ah, this sounds like him.

Goes over and opens the door leading to the hall.

DR. STOCKMANN (*laughing and boisterous*). Hullo, Catherine! I've another guest for you here! The more the merrier, what? Come in, Captain Horster! Hang your overcoat up there on the hook. No, of course, you don't wear an overcoat, do you? Fancy, Catherine, I bumped into him in the street! Had the devil of a job persuading him to come back with me!

CAPTAIN HORSTER *enters and shakes hands with* MRS. STOCK-MANN.

DR. STOCKMANN (*in the doorway*). Run along in now, lads. (*To* MRS. STOCKMANN.) They're hungry again already! This way, Captain Horster, you're going to have the finest roast beef you ever—!

Drives HORSTER *into the dining-room.* EILIF *and* MORTEN *go in too.*

MRS. STOCKMANN. Thomas! Don't you see who's—?

DR. STOCKMANN (*turns in the doorway*). Oh, hullo, Peter! (*Goes over and shakes his hand.*) Well, it's good to see you!

MAYOR. I'm afraid I can only spare a few minutes—

DR. STOCKMANN. Rubbish, we'll be having some hot toddy soon. You haven't forgotten the toddy, Catherine?

MRS. STOCKMANN. No, of course not. I've got the kettle on— (*Goes into the dining-room.*)

MAYOR. Hot toddy too—!

DR. STOCKMANN. Yes. Now sit down, and we'll have a good time.

MAYOR. Thank you. I never partake in drinking parties.

DR. STOCKMANN. But this isn't a party.

MAYOR. Well, but—! (*Glances towards the dining-room.*) It's really extraordinary the amount they eat!

DR. STOCKMANN (*rubs his hands*). Yes, there's nothing better than to see young people tuck in, is there? Always hungry! That's the way it should be! They've got to have food! Gives them strength! They're the ones who've got to ginger up the future, Peter.

MAYOR. May one ask what it is that needs to be "gingered up," as you put it?

DR. STOCKMANN. You must ask the young ones that—when the time comes. We can't see it, of course. Obviously—a couple of old fogeys like you and me—

MAYOR. Well, really! That's a most extraordinary way to describe us—

DR. STOCKMANN. Oh, you mustn't take me too seriously, Peter. I feel so happy and exhilarated, you see! It's so wonderful to be alive at a time like this, with everything germinating and bursting all around us! Oh, it's a glorious age we live in! It's as though a whole new world were coming to birth before our eyes!

MAYOR. Do you really feel that?

DR. STOCKMANN. Yes. Of course, you can't see it as clearly as I do. You've spent your life in this background, so it doesn't make the same impression on you as it does on me. But I've had to spend all these years sitting up there in that damned northern backwater, hardly ever seeing a new face that had a stimulating word to say to me. To me it's as though I had moved into the heart of some pulsing metropolis—

MAYOR. Hm; metropolis—!

DR. STOCKMANN. Oh, I know it must seem small in comparison with lots of other cities. But there's life here—promise—so many things to work and fight for! And that's what matters. (*Shouts.*) Catherine, hasn't the post come yet?

MRS. STOCKMANN (*from the dining-room*). No, not yet.

DR. STOCKMANN. And to be making a decent living, Peter! That's something one learns to appreciate when one's been living on the edge of starvation, as we have—

MAYOR. Oh, surely!

DR. STOCKMANN. Oh yes, I can tell you we were often pretty hard pressed up there. But now, we can live like lords! Today, for instance, we had roast beef for dinner; *and* there was enough left over for supper! Won't you have a bit? Let me show it to you anyway. Come on, have a look—

MAYOR. No, really—

DR. STOCKMANN. Well, look at this, then! Do you see? We've got a tablecloth!

MAYOR. Yes, I've noticed it.

DR. STOCKMANN. And a lampshade too! See? All from what Catherine's managed to save! It makes the room so cosy, don't you think? Come and stand here—no, no, no, not there! There, now! Look! See how the light sort of concentrates downwards? I really think it looks very elegant, don't you?

MAYOR. Well, if one can indulge in that kind of luxury—

DR. STOCKMANN. Oh, I think I can permit myself that now. Catherine says I earn almost as much as we spend.

MAYOR. Almost!

DR. STOCKMANN. Well, a man of science ought to live in a little style. I'm sure any magistrate spends far more in a year than I do.

MAYOR. Yes, I should think so! After all, a magistrate is an important public official—

DR. STOCKMANN. Well, a wholesale merchant, then. A man like that spends much more—

MAYOR. His circumstances are different.

DR. STOCKMANN. Oh, it isn't that I'm wasteful, Peter. I just can't deny myself the pleasure of having people around me! I need that, you know. I've been living outside the world for so long, and for me it's a necessity to be with people who are young, bold, and cheerful, and have lively, liberal minds—and that's what they are, all the men who are sitting in there enjoying a good meal! I wish you knew Hovstad a little better—

MAYOR. That reminds me, Hovstad told me he's going to print another article by you.

DR. STOCKMANN. An article by me?

MAYOR. Yes, about the Baths. Something you wrote last winter.

DR. STOCKMANN. Oh, that. No, I don't want them to print that now.

MAYOR. No? But I should have thought now would be the most suitable time.

DR. STOCKMANN. I dare say it would under ordinary circumstances. (*Walks across the room.*)

MAYOR (*watches him*). And what is extraordinary about the circumstances now?

DR. STOCKMANN (*stops*). I'm sorry, Peter, I can't tell you that yet. Not this evening, anyway. There may be a great deal that's extraordinary; or there may be nothing at all. It may be my imagination—

MAYOR. I must say you're making it all sound very mysterious. Is there something the matter? Something I mustn't be told about? I should have thought that I, as Chairman of the Baths Committee—

DR. STOCKMANN. And I should have thought that I, as—well, let's not start flying off the handle.

MAYOR. Heaven forbid. I'm not in the habit of flying off the handle, as you phrase it. But I must absolutely insist that all arrangements be made and executed through the proper channels and through the authorities legally appointed for that purpose. I cannot permit any underhand or backdoor methods.

DR. STOCKMANN. Have I ever used underhand or backdoor methods?

MAYOR. You will always insist on going your own way. And that's almost equally inadmissible in a well-ordered community. The individual must learn to fall in line with the general will, or, to be more accurate, with that of the authorities whose business it is to watch over the common good.

DR. STOCKMANN. I dare say. But what the hell has that to do with me?

MAYOR. Because that, my dear Thomas, is what you seem

never to be willing to learn. But take care. You'll pay for it some time. Well, I've warned you. Goodbye.

DR. STOCKMANN. Are you raving mad? You're barking completely up the wrong tree—

MAYOR. I'm not in the habit of doing that. Well, if you'll excuse me— (*Bows towards the dining-room.*) Goodbye, sister-in-law. Good day, gentlemen. (*Goes.*)

MRS. STOCKMANN (*comes back into the living-room*). Has he gone?

DR. STOCKMANN. Yes, Catherine, and in a damned bad temper.

MRS. STOCKMANN. Oh, Thomas, what have you done to him now?

DR. STOCKMANN. Absolutely nothing. He can't expect me to account to him until the time comes.

MRS. STOCKMANN. Account to him? For what?

DR. STOCKMANN. Hm; never mind, Catherine. Why the devil doesn't the post come?

HOVSTAD, BILLING, *and* HORSTER *have got up from the dining table and come into the living-room.* EILIF *and* MORTEN *follow a few moments later.*

BILLING (*stretches his arms*). Ah, a meal like that makes one feel like a new man! By jingo, yes!

HOVSTAD. His Worship wasn't in a very cheerful mood tonight.

DR. STOCKMANN. Oh, that's his stomach. He's got a bad digestion.

HOVSTAD. I expect we radical journalists stuck in his gullet.

MRS. STOCKMANN. I thought you were getting on rather well with him.

HOVSTAD. Oh, it's only an armistice.

BILLING. That's it! The word epitomises the situation in a nutshell.

DR. STOCKMANN. Peter's a lonely man, poor fellow; we must remember that. He has no home where he can relax; only business, business. And all that damned tea he pours into himself! Well, lads, pull up your chairs! Catherine, where's that toddy?

MRS. STOCKMANN (*goes into the dining-room*). It's just coming.

DR. STOCKMANN. You sit down here on the sofa with me, Captain Horster. You're too rare a guest in this house! Sit, sit, gentlemen!

The GENTLEMEN *sit at the table.* MRS. STOCKMANN *brings a tray with a kettle, decanters, glasses, etc.*

MRS. STOCKMANN. Here you are. This is arrack, and this is rum; and there's the brandy. Now everyone must help himself.

DR. STOCKMANN (*takes a glass*). Don't you worry about that! (*As the toddy is mixed.*) But where are the cigars? Eilif, you know where the box is. Morten, you can bring me my pipe. (*The* BOYS *go into the room on the right.*) I've a suspicion Eilif pinches a cigar once in a while, but I pretend I don't know! (*Shouts.*) And my smoking cap, Morten! Catherine, can't you tell him where I've put it? Oh, good, he's found it. (*The* BOYS *return with the things he asked for.*) Help yourself, my friends! I stick to my pipe, you know; this old friend's been my companion on many a stormy round up there in the north. (Clinks his glass with *theirs.*) Skol! Ah, I must say it's better to be sitting here, warm and relaxed!

MRS. STOCKMANN (*who is sitting, knitting*). Will you be sailing soon, Captain Horster?

HORSTER. I expect to be off next week.

MRS. STOCKMANN. It's America this time, isn't it?

HORSTER. That's the idea.

BILLING. But then you won't be able to vote in the next council elections!

HORSTER. Is there going to be a new election?

BILLING. Didn't you know?

HORSTER. No, such things don't interest me.

BILLING. But you must care about public affairs?

HORSTER. No, I don't understand these matters.

BILLING. All the same, one ought at least to vote.

HORSTER. Even if one doesn't understand what it's about?

BILLING. Understand? What's that got to do with it? Society's like a ship; everyone's got to lend a hand at the rudder.

HORSTER. Not in my ship!

HOVSTAD. It's curious how little sailors bother about what goes on in their own country.

BILLING. Most abnormal.

DR. STOCKMANN. Sailors are like birds of passage; wherever they happen to be, they regard that as home. Which means the rest of us must be all the more active, Mr. Hovstad. Have you anything salutary to offer us in the *People's Tribune* tomorrow?

HOVSTAD. Nothing of local interest. But the day after, I thought of printing your article—

DR. STOCKMANN. Oh God, yes, that article! No, look, you'll have to sit on that.

HOVSTAD. Oh? We've plenty of space just now; and I thought this would be the most suitable time—

DR. STOCKMANN. Yes, yes, I dare say you're right, but you'll have to wait all the same. I'll explain later—

PETRA, in hat and cloak, with a pile of exercise books under her arm, enters from the hall.

PETRA. Good evening.

DR. STOCKMANN. Hullo, Petra, is that you?

The others greet her, and she them. She puts down her cloak, hat and books on a chair by the door.

PETRA. And you're all sitting here having a party while I've been out working!

DR. STOCKMANN. Well, come and have a party too.

BILLING. May I mix you a tiny glass?

PETRA (*comes over to the table*). Thanks, I'll do it myself; you always make it too strong. Oh, by the way, Father, I've a letter for you.

Goes over to the chair on which her things are lying.

DR. STOCKMANN. A letter? Who from?

PETRA (*looks in her coat pocket*). The postman gave it to me just as I was going out—

DR. STOCKMANN (*gets up and goes over to her*). Why on earth didn't you let me have it before?

PETRA. I really didn't have time to run up again. Here it is.

DR. STOCKMANN (*seizes the letter*). Let me see it, child, let me see it! (*Looks at the envelope.*) Yes, this is it!

MRS. STOCKMANN. Is this what you've been waiting for so anxiously, Thomas?

DR. STOCKMANN. It is indeed. I must go and read it at once. Where can I find a light, Catherine? Is there no lamp in my room again?

MRS. STOCKMANN. Yes, there's one burning on your desk.

DR. STOCKMANN. Good, good. Excuse me a moment—

Goes into the room on the right.

PETRA. What on earth can that be, Mother?

MRS. STOCKMANN. I don't know. These last few days he's done nothing but ask about the post.

BILLING. Probably some patient out of town—

PETRA. Poor Father! He'll soon find he's bitten off more than he can chew. (*Mixes herself a glass.*) Ah, that tastes good!

HOVSTAD. Have you been at evening classes tonight, too?

PETRA (*sips her drink*). Two hours.

BILLING. And four hours this morning at the technical college—

PETRA (*sits at the table*). Five hours.

MRS. STOCKMANN. And you've got exercises to correct tonight, I see.

PETRA. Yes, lots.

HORSTER. You seem to have bitten off more than you can chew too, by the sound of it.

PETRA. Yes, but I like it. One feels so wonderfully tired afterwards.

BILLING. Wonderfully?

PETRA. Yes. One sleeps so soundly, afterwards.

MORTEN. You must be very wicked, Petra.

PETRA. Wicked?

MORTEN. Yes, if you work so much. Dr. Roerlund says work is a punishment for our sins.

EILIF (*sniffs*). Silly! Fancy believing stuff like that!

MRS. STOCKMANN. Now, now, Eilif!

BILLING (*laughs*). Ha! Very good!

HOVSTAD. Don't you want to work hard too, Morten?

MORTEN. No! Not me!

HOVSTAD. But surely you want to become something?

MORTEN. I want to be a Viking!

EILIF. But then you'll have to be a heathen.

MORTEN. All right, I'll be a heathen!

BILLING. I'm with you there, Morten! That's just the way I feel!

MRS. STOCKMANN (*makes a sign*). I'm sure you don't really, Mr. Billing.

BILLING. By jingo, I do! I *am* a heathen, and I'm proud of it! Before long we'll all be heathens. Just you wait and see.

MORTEN. Shall we be able to do anything we like then?

BILLING. Yes, Morten! You see—!

MRS. STOCKMANN. Hurry off now, boys. I'm sure you've some homework to do.

EILIF. I can stay a few minutes longer—

MRS. STOCKMANN. No, you can't. Be off, the pair of you!

The BOYS *say good night and go into the room on the left.*

HOVSTAD. Do you really think it can do the boys any harm to hear this kind of thing?

MRS. STOCKMANN. Well, I don't know. I just don't like it.

PETRA. Oh, really, Mother! I think you're being very stupid.

MRS. STOCKMANN. Perhaps I am; but I don't like it. Not here in the home.

PETRA. Oh, there's so much fear of the truth everywhere! At home and at school. Here we've got to keep our mouths shut, and at school we have to stand up and tell lies to the children.

HORSTER. Lie to them?

PETRA. Yes, surely you realise we have to teach them all kinds of things we don't believe in ourselves.

BILLING. I fear that is all too true!

PETRA. If only I had the money, I'd start a school of my own. And there things would be different.

BILLING. Ah! Money!

HORSTER. If you mean that seriously, Miss Stockmann, I could gladly let you have a room at my place. My father's old house is almost empty; there's a great big dining-room downstairs—

PETRA (laughs). Thank you! But I don't suppose it'll ever come to anything.

HOVSTAD. No, I think Miss Petra will probably turn to journalism. By the way, have you found time to look at that English novel you promised to translate for us?

PETRA. Not yet. But I'll see you get it in time.

DR. STOCKMANN *enters from his room with the letter open in his hand.*

DR. STOCKMANN (*waves the letter*). Here's news that's going to set this town by the ears, believe you me!

BILLING. News?

MRS. STOCKMANN. Why, what's happened?

DR. STOCKMANN. A great discovery has been made, Catherine!

HOVSTAD. Really?

MRS. STOCKMANN. By you?

DR. STOCKMANN. Precisely! By me! (*Walks up and down.*) Now let them come as usual and say it's all madman's talk and I'm imagining things! But they'll have to watch their step this time! (*Laughs.*) Yes, I fancy they'll have to watch their step!

PETRA. Father, for Heaven's sake tell us what it is!

DR. STOCKMANN. Yes, yes, just give me time and you'll hear everything. Oh, if only I had Peter here now! Well, it only goes to show how blindly we mortals can form our judgments—

HOVSTAD. What do you mean by that, Doctor?

DR. STOCKMANN (*stops by the table*). Is it not popularly supposed that our town is a healthy place?

HOVSTAD. Yes, of course.

DR. STOCKMANN. A quite unusually healthy place? A place which deserves to be recommended in the warmest possible terms both for the sick and for their more fortunate brethren?

MRS. STOCKMANN. Yes, but my dear Thomas—!

DR. STOCKMANN. And we ourselves have praised and recommended it, have we not? I have written thousands of words of eulogy both in the *People's Tribune,* and in pamphlets—

HOVSTAD. Yes, well, what of it?

DR. STOCKMANN. These Baths, which have been called the artery of the town, and its central nerve and—and God knows what else—

BILLING. "The pulsing heart of our city" is a phrase I once, in a festive moment, ventured to—

DR. STOCKMANN. No doubt. But do you know what they really are, these beloved Baths of ours which have been so puffed up and which have cost so much money? Do you know what they are?

HOVSTAD. No, what are they?

DR. STOCKMANN. Nothing but a damned cesspit!

PETRA. The Baths, Father?

MRS. STOCKMANN (*simultaneously*). Our Baths!

HOVSTAD (*simultaneously*). But, Doctor—!

BILLING. Absolutely incredible!

DR. STOCKMANN. These Baths are a whited sepulchre—and a poisoned one at that. Dangerous to health in the highest degree! All that filth up at Moellerdal—you know, that stinking refuse from the tanneries—has infected the water in the pipes that feed the Pump Room. And that's not all. This damnable muck has even seeped out onto the beach—

HORSTER. Where the sea baths are?

DR. STOCKMANN. Exactly!

HOVSTAD. But how can you be so sure about all this, Doctor?

DR. STOCKMANN. I've investigated the whole thing most thoroughly. Oh, I've long suspected something of the kind. Last year there were a lot of curious complaints among visitors who'd come for the bathing—typhoid, and gastric troubles—

MRS. STOCKMANN. Yes, so there were.

DR. STOCKMANN. At the time we thought these people had brought the disease with them. But later, during the winter, I began to have other thoughts. So I set to work to analyse the water as closely as I was able.

MRS. STOCKMANN. So that's what you've been toiling so hard at!

DR. STOCKMANN. Yes, you may well say I have toiled, Catherine. But of course I lacked the proper scientific facilities. So I sent specimens of both the drinking water and the sea water to the University to have them analysed by a chemist.

HOVSTAD. And now you have that analysis?

DR. STOCKMANN (shows the letter). Here is it! It establishes conclusively that the water here contains putrid organic matter—millions of bacteria! It is definitely noxious to the health even for external use.

MRS. STOCKMANN. What a miracle you found this out in time!

DR. STOCKMANN. You may well say that, Catherine.

HOVSTAD. And what do you intend to do now, Doctor?

DR. STOCKMANN. Put the matter right, of course.

HOVSTAD. Can that be done?

DR. STOCKMANN. It must be done! Otherwise the Baths are unusable—and all our work has been wasted. But don't worry. I'm pretty sure I know what needs to be done.

MRS. STOCKMANN. But, my dear Thomas, why have you kept all this so secret?

DR. STOCKMANN. Did you expect me to go round the town talking about it before I was certain? No, thank you, I'm not that mad.

PETRA. You might have told us—

DR. STOCKMANN. I wasn't going to tell anyone. But tomorrow you can run along to the Badger and—

MRS. STOCKMANN. Thomas, really!

DR. STOCKMANN. Sorry; I mean your grandfather. It'll shock the old boy out of his skin. He thinks I'm a bit gone in the head anyway—oh, and there are plenty of others who think the same! I know! But now these good people shall see! Now they shall see! (*Walks around and rubs his hands.*) There's going to be such a to-do in this town, Catherine! You've no idea! The whole water system will have to be relaid.

HOVSTAD (*gets up*). The whole of the water system—?

DR. STOCKMANN. Of course. The intake is too low. It'll have to be raised much higher up.

PETRA. Then you were right after all!

DR. STOCKMANN. Yes, Petra, do you remember? I wrote protesting against the plans when they were about to start laying it. But no one would listen to me then. Well, now I'll give them a real broadside. Of course, I've written a full report to the Baths Committee; it's been ready for a whole week, I've only been waiting to receive this. (*Shows the letter.*) But now I shall send it to them at once! (*Goes into his room and returns with a sheaf of papers.*) Look at this! Ten foolscap pages—closely written! I'm sending the analysis with it. A newspaper, Catherine! Get me something to wrap these up in. Good! There, now! Give it to—to—! (*Stamps his foot.*) What the devil's her name? You know, the maid! Tell her to take it straight down to the Mayor.

MRS. STOCKMANN *goes out through the dining-room with the parcel.*

PETRA. What do you think Uncle Peter will say, Father?

DR. STOCKMANN. What can he say? He must be grateful that so important a fact has been brought to light.

HOVSTAD. May I have your permission to print a short piece about your discovery in the *People's Tribune?*

DR. STOCKMANN. I'd be very grateful if you would.

HOVSTAD. I think it's desirable that the community should be informed as quickly as possible.

DR. STOCKMANN. Yes, yes, of course.

MRS. STOCKMANN (*comes back*). She's gone with it now.

BILLING. You'll be the first citizen in the town, Doctor, by jingo, you will!

DR. STOCKMANN (*walks round contentedly*). Oh, nonsense. I've really done nothing except my duty. I dug for treasure and struck lucky, that's all. All the same—!

BILLING. Hovstad, don't you think the town ought to organize a torchlight procession in honour of Dr. Stockmann?

HOVSTAD. I'll suggest it, certainly.

BILLING. And I'll have a word with Aslaksen.

DR. STOCKMANN. No, my dear friends, please don't bother with that nonsense. I don't want any fuss made. And if the Baths Committee should decide to raise my salary, I won't accept it! It's no good, Catherine, I won't accept it!

MRS. STOCKMANN. Quite right, Thomas.

PETRA (*raises her glass*). Skol, Father!

HOVSTAD ⎫ (*together*). Skol, skol, Doctor!
BILLING ⎭

HORSTER (*clinks his glass with the* DOCTOR'S). Here's hoping your discovery will bring you nothing but joy!

DR. STOCKMANN. Thank you, my dear friends, thank you! I'm so deeply happy! Oh, it's good to know that one has the respect of one's fellow-citizens! Hurrah, Catherine!

Seizes her round the neck with both hands and whirls round with her. MRS. STOCKMANN *screams and struggles. Laughter, applause, and cheers for the* DOCTOR. *The* BOYS *stick their heads in through the door.*

ACT TWO

The DOCTOR'S *living-room. The door to the dining-room is shut. Morning.*

MRS. STOCKMANN (*enters from the dining-room with a sealed letter in her hand, goes over to the door downstage right and peeps in*). Are you at home, Thomas?

DR. STOCKMANN (*offstage*). Yes, I've just come in. (*Enters.*) What is it?

MRS. STOCKMANN. A letter from your brother. (*Hands it to him.*)

DR. STOCKMANN. Aha, let's see what he says. (*Opens the envelope and reads.*) "I return herewith the manuscript you sent me—" (*Reads on, mumbling.*) Hm—!

MRS. STOCKMANN. Well, what does he say?

DR. STOCKMANN (*puts the papers in his pocket*). No, he just writes that he'll be coming up here to see me towards noon.

MRS. STOCKMANN. You must remember to stay at home, then.

DR. STOCKMANN. Oh, that'll be all right. I've finished my round for today.

MRS. STOCKMANN. I'm very curious to know how he's taken it.

DR. STOCKMANN. You'll see. He won't like the fact that I made this discovery and not he.

MRS. STOCKMANN. Doesn't it worry you? It does me.

DR. STOCKMANN. Well, he'll be happy at heart, of course. The trouble is, Peter gets so damned angry at the idea of anyone but himself doing anything for the good of the town.

MRS. STOCKMANN. You know, Thomas, I really think you

ought to share the honour with him. Couldn't you say it was he who started you thinking along these lines—?

DR. STOCKMANN. Gladly, as far as I'm concerned. As long as I get the matter put right, I—

OLD MORTEN KIIL (*puts his head in through the door leading from the hall, looks around enquiringly, chuckles to himself and asks slyly*). Is it—is it true?

MRS. STOCKMANN. Why, Father!

DR. STOCKMANN. Hullo, Father-in-law! Good morning, good morning!

MRS. STOCKMANN. Well, aren't you going to come in?

MORTEN KIIL. I will if it's true. If not, I'll be off—

DR. STOCKMANN. If what's true?

MORTEN KIIL. This nonsense about the water system. Is it true, eh?

DR. STOCKMANN. Of course it's true. But how did you hear about it?

MORTEN KIIL (*comes in*). Petra looked in on her way to school—

DR. STOCKMANN. Oh, did she?

MORTEN KIIL. Mm. And she told me. I thought she was just pulling my leg. But that's not like Petra.

DR. STOCKMANN. How could you think she'd do a thing like that?

MORTEN KIIL. Never trust anyone. That's my motto. You get made a fool of before you know where you are. So it is true, then?

DR. STOCKMANN. Absolutely true. Sit down now, Father. (*Coaxes him down onto the sofa.*) Isn't it a stroke of luck for the town?

MORTEN KIIL (*stifles a laugh*). Stroke of luck for the town?

DR. STOCKMANN. That I made this discovery in time—

MORTEN KIIL (*as before*). Oh, yes, yes, yes! But I never thought you'd start playing monkey tricks with your own flesh and blood!

DR. STOCKMANN. Monkey tricks?

MRS. STOCKMANN. Father dear—?

MORTEN KIIL (*rests his hands and chin on the handle of his stick and winks slyly at the* DOCTOR). What was it, now? Didn't you say some animals had got into the water pipes?

DR. STOCKMANN. Yes, bacteria.

MORTEN KIIL. Quite a number of them, so Petra told me. Regular army!

DR. STOCKMANN. Millions, probably.

MORTEN KIIL. But no one can see them. Isn't that right?

DR. STOCKMANN. Of course one can't *see* them.

MORTEN KIIL (*chuckles silently*). Devil take me if this isn't the best I've heard from you yet!

DR. STOCKMANN. What do you mean?

MORTEN KIIL. But you'll never get the Mayor to believe a tale like that.

DR. STOCKMANN. We'll see.

MORTEN KIIL. Do you think he's that daft?

DR. STOCKMANN. I hope the whole town will be that daft.

MORTEN KIIL. The whole town! That's perfectly possible! Serve them right, it'll teach them a lesson! They hounded me out of the Council—yes, that's what I call it, for they drove me out like a dog, they did! But now they're going to pay for it! You make fools of them, Stockmann!

DR. STOCKMANN. But, Father—

MORTEN KIIL. You make fools of them, my boy! (*Gets up.*) If you can put the Mayor and his friends out of countenance, I'll give a hundred crowns to the poor—immediately!

DR. STOCKMANN. That's very generous of you.

MORTEN KIIL. I'm not a rich man, mind! But if you do that, I'll remember the poor to the tune of fifty crowns; at Christmas.

HOVSTAD *enters from the hall.*

HOVSTAD. Good morning! (*Stops.*) Oh, am I intruding?

DR. STOCKMANN. No, come in, come in!

MORTEN KIIL (*chuckles again*). Him! Is he in with you on this?

HOVSTAD. What do you mean?

DR. STOCKMANN. Indeed he is.

MORTEN KIIL. I might have guessed it! So it's to be in the papers! Yes, you're a card all right, Stockmann! Well, you two put your heads together. I'm off.

DR. STOCKMANN. Oh, Father, stay a little longer.

MORTEN KIIL. No, I'm off. Pull out all the tricks you know! By God, I'll see you don't lose by it! (*Goes.* MRS. STOCKMANN *accompanies him out.*)

DR. STOCKMANN (*laughs*). Imagine, Hovstad, the old man doesn't believe a word I say about the water system!

HOVSTAD. Oh, so *that* was—?

DR. STOCKMANN. Yes, that's what we were talking about. I suppose that's why you've come too?

HOVSTAD. Yes. Can you spare me a moment or two, Doctor?

DR. STOCKMANN. As long as you want, my dear fellow.

HOVSTAD. Have you heard anything from the Mayor?

DR. STOCKMANN. Not yet. He'll be along shortly.

HOVSTAD. I've been thinking a lot about this since last night.

DR. STOCKMANN. Yes?

HOVSTAD. You're a doctor and a man of science, and to you this business of the water is something to be considered in isolation. I think you don't perhaps realise how it's tied up with a lot of other things.

DR. STOCKMANN. I don't quite understand you. Let's sit down, my dear chap. No, over there on the sofa.

HOVSTAD *sits on the sofa,* DR. STOCKMANN *in an armchair on the other side of the table.*

DR. STOCKMANN. Well?

HOVSTAD. You said yesterday that the pollution of the water was the result of impurities in the soil.

DR. STOCKMANN. Yes, we're pretty certain that filthy swamp up at Moellerdal is the cause of the evil.

HOVSTAD. Forgive me, Doctor, but I believe the real cause of all the evil is to be found in quite a different swamp.

DR. STOCKMANN. Which one?

HOVSTAD. The swamp in which our whole communal life is slowly rotting.

DR. STOCKMANN. Damn it, Mr. Hovstad, what kind of talk is this?

HOVSTAD. Little by little all the affairs of this town have fallen into the hands of a small clique of bureaucrats.

DR. STOCKMANN. Oh, come, you can't group them all under that description.

HOVSTAD. No, but the ones who don't belong to it are the friends and hangers-on of the ones who do. It's the rich men, the ones with names—they're the people who rule our life.

DR. STOCKMANN. They're shrewd and intelligent men.

HOVSTAD. Did they show shrewdness or intelligence when they laid the water pipes where they are now?

DR. STOCKMANN. No, that was very stupid, of course. But it's going to be put right now.

HOVSTAD. You think they'll enjoy doing that?

DR. STOCKMANN. Enjoy it or not, they'll be forced to do it.

HOVSTAD. If the press is allowed to use its influence.

DR. STOCKMANN. That won't be necessary, my dear fellow. I'm sure my brother will—

HOVSTAD. I'm sorry, Doctor, but I intend to take this matter up myself.

DR. STOCKMANN. In the newspaper?

HOVSTAD. When I took over the *People's Tribune* I did so with the fixed purpose of breaking up this ring of obstinate bigots who hold all the power in their hands.

DR. STOCKMANN. But you told me yourself what happened as a result. The paper almost had to close down.

HOVSTAD. We had to play it easy then, that's true. There was a risk that if these men fell, the Baths might not be built. But now we have them, and these fine gentlemen have become dispensable.

DR. STOCKMANN. Dispensable, perhaps. But we owe them a debt all the same.

HOVSTAD. Oh, that'll be handsomely acknowledged. But a radical writer like me can't let an opportunity like this pass unused. We must destroy the myth of these men's infalli-

bility. It must be rooted out like any other kind of superstition.

DR. STOCKMANN. Ah, I'm with you there. If it is a superstition,
then away with it!

HOVSTAD. I'd prefer not to attack the Mayor, since he's your
brother. But I know you feel as strongly as I do that truth
must precede all other considerations.

DR. STOCKMANN. Of course. (*Bursts out.*) But—! But—!

HOVSTAD. You mustn't think ill of me. I'm not more ambitious
or self-seeking than most men.

DR. STOCKMANN. But my dear fellow, who suggests you are?

HOVSTAD. I'm the son of poor people, as you know, and I've
had the chance to see what's needed most in the lower
strata of society. It's to have a share in the control of public
affairs. That's what develops ability, and knowledge, and
human dignity.

DR. STOCKMANN. I appreciate that.

HOVSTAD. And then I think a journalist has a lot to answer for
if he neglects an opportunity to achieve emancipation for
the masses—the small and the oppressed. Oh, I know—the
big boys will call me a demagogue and all that—but I
don't care. As long as my conscience is clear, I—

DR. STOCKMANN. That's the point, yes! That's exactly it, Mr.
Hovstad! All the same—damn it— (*A knock at the door.*)
Come in!

ASLAKSEN, *the printer, appears in the doorway leading from
the hall. He is humbly but decently dressed in black, with a
white and somewhat crumpled cravat, gloves, and a silk hat
in his hand.*

ASLAKSEN (*bows*). I trust you'll forgive me for being so bold,
Doctor—

DR. STOCKMANN (*gets up*). Why, hullo! Aren't you Aslaksen
the printer?

ASLAKSEN. I am indeed, Doctor.

HOVSTAD (*gets up*). Are you looking for me, Aslaksen?

ASLAKSEN. No, I had no idea I'd see you here. It was the Doctor himself I—

DR. STOCKMANN. Well, what can I do for you?

ASLAKSEN. Is it true what Mr. Billing tells me, that you're thinking of getting us a better water system?

DR. STOCKMANN. Yes, for the Baths.

ASLAKSEN. Ah, yes; I see. Well, I just came to say that I'm right behind you!

HOVSTAD (*to* DR. STOCKMANN). You see!

DR. STOCKMANN. I'm most grateful; but—

ASLAKSEN. You might find it useful to have us tradespeople behind you. We form a pretty solid majority in this town —when we choose to, mind! And it's always good to have the majority behind you, Doctor.

DR. STOCKMANN. True enough. But I don't see that any special effort is necessary here. Surely it's a perfectly straightforward matter—

ASLAKSEN. Yes, but you might be glad of us all the same. I know these local authorities. The boys in power don't like accepting suggestions from outside. So I thought it might not be out of place if we organized a little demonstration.

HOVSTAD. That's just what I feel.

DR. STOCKMANN. Demonstration? In what way will you demonstrate?

ASLAKSEN. Oh, with restraint, Doctor. I always insist on restraint. Restraint is the primary virtue of every citizen. That's my opinon, anyway.

DR. STOCKMANN. Yes, yes, Mr. Aslaksen. Your views are well known—

ASLAKSEN. Yes, I fancy they are. Now this business of the water system is very important to us tradespeople. It looks as though the Baths are going to prove as you might say a little goldmine for the town. We'll all be depending on the Baths for our livelihood, especially us property owners. That's why we want to give the project every support we can. And seeing as I'm Chairman of the Property Owners' Association—

DR. STOCKMANN. Yes?

ASLAKSEN. And seeing as I'm also on the Council of the Temperance Society— You do know I'm a temperance worker?

DR. STOCKMANN. Yes, yes.

ASLAKSEN. Well, so it stands to reason I come into contact with a lot of people. And seeing as I'm known to be a level-headed and law-abiding citizen, as you said yourself, it means I have a certain influence in the town—I wield a little power—though I say it myself.

DR. STOCKMANN. I'm well aware of that, Mr. Aslaksen.

ASLAKSEN. Yes, well—so it'd be an easy matter for me to arrange an address, if the occasion should arise.

DR. STOCKMANN. An address?

ASLAKSEN. Yes, a kind of vote of thanks from the citizens of this town to you for having carried this important matter to a successful conclusion. Of course, it stands to reason the wording's got to be restrained, so it won't offend the authorities and the other people as has the power. And so long as we're careful about that, I don't think anyone can take offence, can they?

HOVSTAD. Well, even if they don't particularly like it, they—

ASLAKSEN. No, no, no! We mustn't offend authority, Mr. Hovstad! We can't afford to defy the people on whom our lives depend. I've seen plenty of that in my time, and no good ever came out of it. But the sober expression of liberal sentiments can cause no affront.

DR. STOCKMANN (shakes his hand). My dear Mr. Aslaksen, I can't tell you how deeply happy I am to find all this support among my fellow-citizens. I am most moved, most moved. Well, now; what about a small glass of sherry?

ASLAKSEN. No, thank you! I never touch spirits.

DR. STOCKMANN. A glass of beer, then? What do you say to that?

ASLAKSEN. No, thank you, not that either, Doctor. I never touch anything so early in the day. And now I must be getting back to town to talk to some of the other property owners and prepare the atmosphere.

DR. STOCKMANN. It's really most kind of you, Mr. Aslaksen. But I simply cannot get it into my head that all this fuss is really necessary. I should have thought the matter would solve itself.

ASLAKSEN. The authorities move somewhat ponderously, Doctor. Heaven knows I don't intend any reflection on them—!

HOVSTAD. We'll give them a drubbing in print tomorrow, Mr. Aslaksen.

ASLAKSEN. But no violence, Mr. Hovstad! Proceed with restraint! Otherwise you'll get nowhere with them. You can rely on my judgment, for I have culled my knowledge in the school of life. Yes, well, I must say goodbye. You know now that we tradespeople stand behind you like a wall, Doctor. You have the solid majority on your side, whatever else may happen.

DR. STOCKMANN. Thank you, my dear Mr. Aslaksen. (*Shakes his hand.*) Goodbye, goodbye!

ASLAKSEN. Are you coming down to the press too, Mr. Hovstad?

HOVSTAD. I'll follow later. I've a few things to arrange first.

ASLAKSEN. Yes, yes.

Bows and goes out. DR. STOCKMANN *accompanies him out into the hall.*

HOVSTAD (*as the* DOCTOR *returns*). Well, what do you say to that, Doctor? Don't you think it's time this town was shaken out of its torpidity and its weak-kneed half-heartedness?

DR. STOCKMANN. You mean Aslaksen?

HOVSTAD. Yes, I do. Oh, he's honest enough in some respects, but he's stuck in the swamp. And most of the others are the same. They swing this way and that, and spend so much time looking at every side of the question that they never make a move in any direction.

DR. STOCKMANN. But Aslaksen seemed very well-meaning, I thought.

HOVSTAD. There's something I regard as more important than that. To know your own mind and have the courage of your convictions.

DR. STOCKMANN. Yes, you're right there.

HOVSTAD. That's why I'm so keen to seize this opportunity if

I can't get these well-meaning idiots to act like men for once. All this grovelling to authority has got to be stopped. This blunder they've made about the water system is quite indefensible, and that fact's got to be drummed into the ears of every citizen who's got the right to vote.

DR. STOCKMANN. Very well. If you think it's for the communal good, go ahead. But not till I've talked with my brother.

HOVSTAD. I'll get my editorial written anyway. And if the Mayor refuses to take action, then—

DR. STOCKMANN. Oh, but that's unthinkable.

HOVSTAD. It's a possibility. And if it should happen—?

DR. STOCKMANN. If it does, I promise you that—yes, you can print my report. Print the whole damned thing.

HOVSTAD. Is that a promise?

DR. STOCKMANN (*hands him the manuscript*). Here it is. Take it with you. It won't do any harm for you to read through it; and you can give it back to me afterwards.

HOVSTAD. Right, I'll do that. Well, goodbye, Doctor.

DR. STOCKMANN. Goodbye, goodbye! Don't you worry, Mr. Hovstad—everything's going to go quite smoothly. Quite smoothly!

HOVSTAD. Hm. We shall see.

Nods and goes out through the hall.

DR. STOCKMANN (*goes over to the dining-room and looks in*). Catherine—! Oh, hullo, Petra, are you here?

PETRA (*enters*). Yes, I've just got back from school.

MRS. STOCKMANN (*enters*). Hasn't he come yet?

DR. STOCKMANN. Peter? No. But I've been having a long talk with Hovstad. He's quite excited about this discovery of mine. It seems it has a much wider significance than I'd supposed. So he's placed his newspaper at my disposal, if I should need it.

MRS. STOCKMANN. But do you think you will?

DR. STOCKMANN. Oh no, I'm sure I won't. But it's good to know that one has the free press on one's side—the mouth-piece of liberal opinion. And what do you think? I've had a visit from the Chairman of the Property Owners' Association!

MRS. STOCKMANN. Oh? And what did he want?

DR. STOCKMANN. He's going to support me too. They're all going to support me, if there's any trouble. Catherine, do you know what I have behind me?

MRS. STOCKMANN. Behind you? No, what have you behind you?

DR. STOCKMANN. The solid majority.

MRS. STOCKMANN. I see. And that's a good thing, is it?

DR. STOCKMANN. Of course, it's a good thing! (*Rubs his hands and walks up and down.*) How splendid to feel that one stands shoulder to shoulder with one's fellow-citizens in brotherly concord!

PETRA. And that one's doing so much that's good and useful, Father.

DR. STOCKMANN. Yes, and for one's home town too!

MRS. STOCKMANN. There's the doorbell.

DR. STOCKMANN. Ah, this must be him! (*A knock on the inner door.*) Come in!

MAYOR (*enters from the hall*). Good morning.

DR. STOCKMANN (*warmly*). Hullo, Peter!

MRS. STOCKMANN. Good morning, Brother-in-law. How are you?

MAYOR. Oh, thank you; so-so. (*To the* DOCTOR.) Last night, after office hours, I received a thesis from you regarding the state of the water at the Baths.

DR. STOCKMANN. Yes. Have you read it?

MAYOR. I have.

DR. STOCKMANN. Well! What do you think?

MAYOR (*glances at the others*). Hm—

MRS. STOCKMANN. Come, Petra.

She and PETRA *go into the room on the left.*

MAYOR (*after a pause*). Was it necessary to conduct all these investigations behind my back?

DR. STOCKMANN. Well, until I was absolutely certain, I—

MAYOR. And now you are?

DR. STOCKMANN. Yes. Surely you must be convinced—?

MAYOR. Is it your intention to place this document before the Baths Committee as an official statement?

DR. STOCKMANN. Of course! Something must be done. And quickly.

MAYOR. I find your phraseology in this document, as usual, somewhat extravagant. Among other things, you say that all we have to offer our visitors at present is a permanent state of ill-health.

DR. STOCKMANN. Peter, how else can you describe it? Just think! That water's poisonous even if you bathe in it, let alone drink it! And we're offering this to unfortunate people who are ill and who have turned to us in good faith, and are paying us good money, in order to get their health back!

MAYOR. And your conclusion is that we must build a sewer to drain away these aforesaid impurities from the swamp at Moellerdal, and that the whole water system must be re-laid.

DR. STOCKMANN. Can you think of any other solution? I can't.

MAYOR. This morning I called upon the town engineer. In the course of our discussion I half jokingly mentioned these proposals as a thing we might possibly undertake some time in the future.

DR. STOCKMANN. Some time in the future?

MAYOR. He smiled at what he obviously regarded as my extravagance—as I knew he would. Have you ever troubled to consider what these alterations you suggest would cost? According to the information I received, the expense would probably run into several hundred thousand crowns.

DR. STOCKMANN. Would it be that much?

MAYOR. Yes. But that's not the worst. The work would take at least two years.

DR. STOCKMANN. Two years, did you say? Two whole years?

MAYOR. At least. And what do we do with the Baths in the meanwhile? Close them? Yes, we'd be forced to. You don't imagine anyone would come here once the rumour got around that the water was impure?

DR. STOCKMANN. But, Peter, it is!

MAYOR. And for this to happen just now, when the whole enterprise is coming to fruition! There are other towns around with qualifications to be regarded as health resorts. Do you think they won't start trying to attract the market? Of course they will! And there we shall be! We'll probably have to abandon the whole expensive scheme, and you will have ruined the town that gave you birth.

DR. STOCKMANN. I—ruined—!

MAYOR. It's only as a health resort—a spa—that this town has any future worth speaking of. Surely you realise that as well as I do.

DR. STOCKMANN. But what do you propose we do?

MAYOR. Your report has not completely convinced me that the situation is as dangerous as you imply.

DR. STOCKMANN. Oh, Peter, if anything it's worse! Or at least it will be in the summer, once the hot weather starts.

MAYOR. As I said, I believe that you are exaggerating the danger. A capable medical officer must be able to take measures— He must know how to forestall such unpleasantnesses, and how to remedy them if they should become obvious.

DR. STOCKMANN. Go on.

MAYOR. The existing water system at the Baths is a fact, and must be accepted as such. However, in due course I dare say the Committee might not be inflexibly opposed to considering whether without unreasonable pecuniary sacrifice it might not be possible to introduce certain improvements.

DR. STOCKMANN. And you think I'd lend my name to such chicanery?

MAYOR. Chicanery?

DR. STOCKMANN. That's what it would be! A fraud, a lie, a crime against the community, against the whole of society!

MAYOR. As I have already pointed out, I have not succeeded in convincing myself that any immediate or critical danger exists.

DR. STOCKMANN. Oh, yes you have! You must have! My arguments are irrefutable—I know they are! And you know that as well as I do, Peter! But you won't admit it, because it was you who forced through the proposal that the Baths and the water pipes should be sited where they are, and you refuse to admit that you made a gross blunder. Don't be such a fool, do you think I don't see through you?

MAYOR. And suppose you were right? If I do guard my reputation with a certain anxiety, it is because I have the welfare of our town at heart. Without moral authority I cannot guide and direct affairs as I deem most fit for the general good. For this, and diverse other reasons, it is vital to me that your report should not be placed before the Baths Committee. It must be suppressed for the general good. At a later date I shall bring the matter up for discussion, and we shall discreetly do the best we can. But nothing, not a single word, about this unfortunate matter must come to the public ear.

DR. STOCKMANN. Well, it can't be stopped now, my dear Peter.

MAYOR. It must and shall be stopped.

DR. STOCKMANN. It can't, I tell you. Too many people know.

MAYOR. Know? Who knows? You don't mean those fellows from the *People's Tribune*—?

DR. STOCKMANN. Oh, yes, they too. The free press of our country will see to it that you do your duty.

MAYOR (*after a short pause*). You're an exceedingly foolish man, Thomas. Haven't you considered what the consequence of this action may be for you?

DR. STOCKMANN. Consequence? Consequence for me?

MAYOR. Yes. For you and for your family.

DR. STOCKMANN. What the devil do you mean by that?

MAYOR. I think I have always shown myself a good brother to you, whenever you've needed help.

DR. STOCKMANN. You have, and I thank you for it.

MAYOR. I'm not asking for thanks. To a certain extent I've been forced to do it—for my own sake. I always hoped I might be able to curb you a little if I could help to improve your economic position.

DR. STOCKMANN. What! So it was only for your own sake that you—

MAYOR. Partly, I said. It's painful for a public servant to see his next of kin spend his entire time compromising himself.

DR. STOCKMANN. And you think I do that?

MAYOR. Unfortunately you do, without knowing it. You have a restless, combative, rebellious nature. And then you've this unfortunate passion for rushing into print upon every possible—and impossible—subject. The moment you get an idea you have to sit down and write a newspaper article or a whole pamphlet about it.

DR. STOCKMANN. Surely if a man gets hold of a new idea it's his duty as a citizen to tell it to the public?

MAYOR. People don't want new ideas. They're best served by the good old accepted ideas they have already.

DR. STOCKMANN. And you can say that to my face!

MAYOR. Yes, Thomas. I'm going to speak bluntly to you for once. Up to now I've tried to avoid it, because I know how hasty you are; but now I've got to tell you the truth. You've no idea how much harm you do yourself by this impulsiveness of yours. You abuse the authorities, and even the government—you throw mud at them, you claim you've been cold-shouldered and persecuted. But what else can you expect, when you're such a difficult person?

DR. STOCKMANN. Oh, so I'm difficult too, am I?

MAYOR. Oh, Thomas, you're impossible to work with. I've discovered that for myself. You never consider anyone else's feelings. You even seem to forget it's me you have to thank for getting you your job at the Baths—

DR. STOCKMANN. It was mine by right! I was the first person to see that this town could become a flourishing watering place! And I was the only person who did see it at that time! For years I fought alone for this idea! I wrote, and wrote—

MAYOR. No one denies that. But the time wasn't ripe then. Of course you weren't to know that, tucked away in your northern backwater. But as soon as the right moment arrived, I—and others—took the matter up—

DR. STOCKMANN. Yes, and made a mess of my wonderful plan! Oh yes, it's becoming very clear now what brilliant fellows you were!

MAYOR. As far as I can see, all you're looking for now is just another excuse for a fight. You've always got to pick a quarrel with your superiors—it's your old failing. You can't bear to have anyone in authority over you. You look askance at anyone who occupies a position higher than yours; you regard him as a personal enemy—and then, as far as you're concerned, one weapon of attack is as good as another. But now I've shown you what's at stake, for the whole town, and for myself too. And I'm not prepared to compromise.

DR. STOCKMANN. What do you mean?

MAYOR. Since you have been so indiscreet as to discuss this delicate matter, which you ought to have kept a professional secret, the affair obviously cannot be hushed up. All kinds of rumours will spread around, and the malicious elements among us will feed these rumours with details of their own invention. It is therefore necessary that you publicly deny these rumours.

DR. STOCKMANN. I don't understand you.

MAYOR. I feel sure that on further investigation you will convince yourself that the situation is not nearly as critical as you had at first supposed.

DR. STOCKMANN. Aha; you feel sure, do you?

MAYOR. I also feel sure you will publicly express your confidence that the Committee will painstakingly and conscientiously take all necessary measures to remedy any possible defects which may exist.

DR. STOCKMANN. But you can't remedy the defect by just patching things up! I'm telling you, Peter, unless you start again from scratch, it's my absolute conviction that—

MAYOR. As an employee you have no right to any independent conviction.

DR. STOCKMANN (starts). No right!

MAYOR. As an employee. As a private person—well, Heaven knows that's another matter. But as a subordinate official at the Baths you have no right to express any opinion which conflicts with that of your superiors.

DR. STOCKMANN. This is going too far! I, a doctor, a man of science, have no right—!

MAYOR. The question is not merely one of science. The problem is complex. The issues involved are both technical and economical.

DR. STOCKMANN. I don't care how you define the damned thing! I must be free to say what I think about anything!

MAYOR. Go ahead. As long as it isn't anything connected with the Baths. That we forbid you.

DR. STOCKMANN (shouts). You forbid—! You—! Why, you're just a—

MAYOR. I forbid you—I, your chief. And when I forbid you to do something, you must obey.

DR. STOCKMANN (controls himself). Peter—if you weren't my brother—!

PETRA (throws open the door). Father, don't put up with this!

MRS. STOCKMANN (follows her). Petra, Petra!

MAYOR. Ha! Eavesdroppers!

MRS. STOCKMANN. You were talking so loud—we couldn't help hearing—

PETRA. I was listening.

MAYOR. Well, I'm not altogether sorry—

DR. STOCKMANN (goes closer to him). You spoke to me of forbidding and obeying?

MAYOR. You forced me to use that tone.

DR. STOCKMANN. And you expect me to publicly swallow my own words?

MAYOR. We regard it as an unavoidable necessity that you issue a statement on the lines I have indicated.

DR. STOCKMANN. And if I don't—obey?

MAYOR. Then we shall be forced to issue an explanation, to calm the public.

DR. STOCKMANN. All right; but I shall write and refute you.

I stick to my view. I shall prove that I am right and you are wrong. And what will you do then?

MAYOR. Then I shall be unable to prevent your dismissal.

DR. STOCKMANN. What—!

PETRA. Father! Dismissal!

MRS. STOCKMANN. Dismissal!

MAYOR. Dismissal from your post as public medical officer. I shall feel compelled to apply for immediate notice to be served on you, barring you from any further connection with the Baths.

DR. STOCKMANN. You'd have the impudence to do that?

MAYOR. You're the one who's being impudent.

PETRA. Uncle, this is a disgraceful way to treat a man like Father!

MRS. STOCKMANN. Be quiet, Petra.

MAYOR (looks at PETRA). So we've opinions of our own already, have we? But of course! (To MRS. STOCKMANN.) Sister-in-law, you seem to be the most sensible person in this house. Use what influence you have over your husband. Make him realize the consequences this will have both for his family and—

DR. STOCKMANN. My family concerns no one but myself.

MAYOR. —both for his family, and for the town he lives in.

DR. STOCKMANN. I'm the one who has the town's real interests at heart! I want to expose the evils that sooner or later must come to light. I'm going to prove to people that I love this town where I was born.

MAYOR. Oh, you're blind! All you're trying to do is to stop up the source of the town's prosperity.

DR. STOCKMANN. That source is poisoned, man! Are you mad? We live by hawking filth and disease! And all this communal life you boast so much about is based upon a lie!

MAYOR. That's pure imagination—if nothing worse. The man who casts such foul aspersions against the town he lives in is an enemy of society.

DR. STOCKMANN (goes towards him). You dare to—!

MRS. STOCKMANN (throws herself between them). Thomas!

PETRA (grasps her father by the arm). Keep calm, Father!

MAYOR. I shall not expose myself to violence. You've been warned. Consider what is your duty to yourself and your family. Goodbye. (*Goes.*)

DR. STOCKMANN (*walks up and down*). And in my own house, too, Catherine!

MRS. STOCKMANN. Yes, Thomas. It's a shame and a scandal—

PETRA. I'd like to get my hands on him—!

DR. STOCKMANN. It's my own fault. I ought to have exposed them long ago; I should have bared my teeth; and used them! Calling me an enemy of society! By God, I'm not going to take that lying down!

MRS. STOCKMANN. But, Thomas dear, might is right—

DR. STOCKMANN. I'm the one who's right!

MRS. STOCKMANN. What's the good of being right if you don't have the might?

PETRA. Mother, how can you speak like that?

DR. STOCKMANN. So it's no use in a free society to have right on one's side? Don't be absurd, Catherine. Besides—don't I have the free press in front of me—and the solid majority behind me? That's might enough, I should have thought!

MRS. STOCKMANN. For Heaven's sake, Thomas, surely you're not thinking of setting yourself up against your brother?

DR. STOCKMANN. What the devil else do you expect me to do? Don't you want me to stand up for what I believe to be right?

PETRA. Yes, Father, you must!

MRS. STOCKMANN. It'll do you no good. If they won't, they won't.

DR. STOCKMANN (*laughs*). Oh, Catherine, just give me time. You'll see! I'm going to fight this war to the end.

MRS. STOCKMANN. Yes, and the end will be that you'll lose your job. You'll see.

DR. STOCKMANN. At least I shall have done my duty to the community; my duty to society. And they call me an enemy of society—!

MRS. STOCKMANN. What about your family, Thomas? And your home? Do you think you'll be doing your duty to the ones who depend on you?

PETRA. Oh, Mother, don't always think only of us.

MRS. STOCKMANN. It's easy for you to talk. You can stand on your own feet, if need be. But think of the boys, Thomas! And think of yourself too—and me—

DR. STOCKMANN. You must be mad, Catherine! If I give in like a coward to Peter and his wretched gang, do you think I'd ever have another moment of happiness in my life?

MRS. STOCKMANN. I don't know about that. But God preserve us from the happiness we're likely to enjoy if you go on digging your heels in. You'll have no means of livelihood, no regular income. Didn't we have enough of that in the old days? Remember that, Thomas. Think what it'll mean.

DR. STOCKMANN (*writhes, fighting with himself, and clenches his fists*). And these office lackeys can do this to a free and honourable man! Isn't it monstrous, Catherine?

MRS. STOCKMANN. Yes, they've behaved very wickedly to you, that's true. But Heaven knows, there's so much injustice one has to put up with in this world. There are the boys, Thomas. Look at them. What's to become of them? No, no, you can't have the heart.

EILIF *and* MORTEN *have meanwhile entered, carrying their schoolbooks.*

DR. STOCKMANN. My sons! (*Suddenly stands erect, his mind made up.*) Even if my whole world crashes about me, I shall never bow my head. (*Goes towards his room.*)

MRS. STOCKMANN. Thomas, what are you going to do?

DR. STOCKMANN (*in the doorway*). I want to have the right to look my sons in the eyes when they grow up into free men! (*Goes into his room.*)

MRS. STOCKMANN. Oh, God help us!

PETRA. Father's right, Mother! He'll never give in.

ACT THREE

The editorial office of the People's Tribune. *On the left in the background is the entrance door; to the right in the same wall is another door with glass panes through which the composing-room is visible. Another door is in the wall on the right. In the middle of the room is a big table covered with papers, newspapers, and books. Downstage left is a window; by it is a writing desk and a high chair. Two armchairs stand by the table, and there are other chairs along the walls. The room is gloomy and uncomfortable; the furniture is old, the armchairs dirty and torn. In the composing-room one or two* COMPOSITORS *are at work. Beyond them, a hand-press is being operated.*

HOVSTAD *sits writing at the desk. After a few moments* BILLING *enters right, with the* DOCTOR'S *manuscript in his hand.*

BILLING. I say, I say, I say!

HOVSTAD (*writing*). Have you read it?

BILLING (*puts the manuscript on the desk*). I should say I have!

HOVSTAD. Pretty forceful, isn't it?

BILLING. Forceful? He'll butcher them, by jingo! Every paragraph's a knock-out!

HOVSTAD. Those fellows won't give in at the first blow, though.

BILLING. That's true. But we'll go on bashing them, punch after punch, till their whole damned oligarchy falls to the ground! As I sat in there reading this, it was as though I saw the revolution dawning from afar!

HOVSTAD (*turns*). Hush, don't let Aslaksen hear.

BILLING (*lowers his voice*). Aslaksen's a coward, a jellyfish! He hasn't the guts of a man! But you'll have your way! You will publish the Doctor's article?

HOVSTAD. Yes, unless the Mayor backs down—

BILLING. That'd be a damned nuisance!

HOVSTAD. Whichever way it turns out we can exploit the situation. If the Mayor doesn't agree to the Doctor's proposal, he'll have all the tradespeople down on him—the Property Owners' Association, and the rest. And if he does agree to it he'll antagonise all the big shareholders in the Baths who up to now have been his chief supporters—

BILLING. Of course! They'll have to fork out a pile of money—

HOVSTAD. You bet they will. And then the clique will be broken, and day after day we'll drum it into the public that the Mayor's incompetent in more respects than one, and that all the responsible offices in the town, the whole municipal authority, ought to be handed over to people of liberal opinions.

BILLING. By jingo, that's the truth! I see it! I see it! We stand on the threshold of a revolution!

A knock on the door.

HOVSTAD. Quiet! (*Shouts.*) Come in.

DR. STOCKMANN *enters through the door upstage left.*

HOVSTAD (*goes to greet him*). Ah, here is the Doctor! Well?

DR. STOCKMANN. Print away, Mr. Hovstad!

HOVSTAD. So it's come to that?

BILLING. Hurrah!

DR. STOCKMANN. Print away, I say! Yes, it's come to that all right. Well, now they shall have it the way they want it. It's war now, Mr. Billing!

BILLING. War to the death, I hope! Give it to them, Doctor!

DR. STOCKMANN. This report is only the beginning. My head's already teeming with ideas for four or five other articles. Where's Aslaksen?

BILLING (*calls into the composing-room*). Aslaksen, come here a moment!

HOVSTAD. Four or five other articles, did you say? On the same theme?

DR. STOCKMANN. No—oh, good heavens no, my dear fellow! No, they'll be about quite different things. But it all stems from this business of the water system and the sewer. One thing leads to another, you know. It's like when you start to pull down an old building. Exactly like that.

BILLING. By jingo, that's true! You suddenly realize you'll never be finished till you've pulled down the whole rotten structure!

ASLAKSEN (*from the composing-room*). Pulled down! You're surely not thinking of pulling the Baths down, Doctor?

HOVSTAD. No, no, don't get frightened.

DR. STOCKMANN. No, we were talking about something else. Well, Mr. Hovstad, what do you think of my report?

HOVSTAD. I think it's an absolute masterpiece—

DR. STOCKMANN. Do you think so? That makes me very happy —very happy.

HOVSTAD. It's so clear and to the point; you don't have to be a specialist to follow the argument. I'm sure you'll have every enlightened person on your side.

ASLAKSEN. Every discriminating one too, I trust?

BILLING. Discriminating or not—you'll have the whole town behind you.

ASLAKSEN. Well then, I don't think we need be afraid to print it.

DR. STOCKMANN. I should damn well hope not.

HOVSTAD. It'll be in tomorrow morning.

DR. STOCKMANN. Good God yes, we can't afford to waste a single day. Oh, Mr. Aslaksen, there was one thing I wanted to ask you. You must take charge of this manuscript yourself.

ASLAKSEN. If you wish.

DR. STOCKMANN. Treat it as though it was gold. No misprints; every word is important. I'll drop back later; perhaps you'd let me look at a proof. I can't tell you how eager I am to see this thing in print—launched—!

BILLING. Launched, yes! Like a thunderbolt!

DR. STOCKMANN. —and submitted to the judgment of every intelligent citizen. Oh, you'd never guess what I've had to put up with today! I've been threatened with God knows what. They want to rob me of my elementary rights as a human being—

BILLING. Your rights as a human being!

DR. STOCKMANN. They want to degrade me, reduce me to the level of a beggar. They demand that I put my private interests above my most sacred and innermost convictions—

BILLING. By jingo, that's going too far!

HOVSTAD. You can expect anything from that lot.

DR. STOCKMANN. But they won't get far with me! I'll give it to them in black and white! I'll grapple with them every day in the *People's Tribune!* I'll sweep them with one broadside after another—!

ASLAKSEN. Yes, but remember—

BILLING. Hurrah! It's war, it's war!

DR. STOCKMANN. I'll beat them to the ground, I'll crush them, I'll flatten their defences for every honest man to see! By God I will!

ASLAKSEN. But do it soberly, Doctor. Act with restraint—

BILLING. No, no! Don't spare your powder!

DR. STOCKMANN (*continues imperturbably*). You see, it isn't just a question of the water system and the sewer. This whole community's got to be cleansed and decontaminated—

BILLING. That's the very word!

DR. STOCKMANN. All these skimpers and compromisers have got to be thrown out! There's got to be a clean sweep! Oh, such endless vistas have been opened up before my eyes today! I don't see my way quite clearly yet. But I will! We need fresh standard-bearers, my friends! Young men! Our advance posts must be manned by new captains!

BILLING. Hear, hear!

DR. STOCKMANN. As long as we stick together, it'll all happen so easily—so easily! The whole revolution will glide into existence like a ship from the stocks! Don't you agree?

HOVSTAD. I think we've every prospect now of getting the helm into the right hands.

ASLAKSEN. As long as we proceed with restraint, I don't think there can be any danger.

DR. STOCKMANN. Who the hell cares about danger? I'm doing this in the name of truth and of my conscience!

HOVSTAD. You're a man who deserves support, Doctor.

ASLAKSEN. Yes, the Doctor's a true friend of the town, that's certain. I'll go further; he's a friend of society!

BILLING. By jingo, Mr. Aslaksen, Dr. Stockmann is a friend of the people!

ASLAKSEN. I think the Property Owners' Association might be able to use that phrase.

DR. STOCKMANN (*moved, presses their hands*). Thank you, my dear, good friends—thank you! It's so refreshing for me to hear this. My brother described me in vastly different terms. By God, I'll give it back to him with interest! Now I must go and see a poor devil of a patient. But I'll be back! Take good care of that manuscript, Mr. Aslaksen. And for heaven's sake don't cut out any of the exclamation marks! If anything, put in a few more. Good, good. Well, good-bye! Goodbye, goodbye!

He shakes hands with them as they accompany him to the door and he goes out.

HOVSTAD. He's going to be damned useful to us.

ASLAKSEN. As long as he sticks to the Baths. But if he tries to go further, we'd be unwise to stay with him.

HOVSTAD. Hm; that all depends—

BILLING. You're such a damned coward, Aslaksen!

ASLAKSEN. Coward? Yes, when it's a question of fighting local authorities, I am a coward, Mr. Billing. That's a lesson I have learned in the school of life. But elevate me into the field of high politics, confront me with the Government, and then see if I am a coward!

BILLING. No, no, I'm sure you're not; but that's just where you're so inconsistent.

ASLAKSEN. Because I know my responsibilities as a citizen!

Throwing stones at the government can't harm society. It doesn't bother those fellows—they stay put. But local authorities can be overthrown, and then you may get inexperience at the helm, with disastrous results for property owners and the like.

HOVSTAD. But what about the education of people through self-government?

ASLAKSEN. When a man has interests to protect he can't think of everything, Mr. Hovstad.

HOVSTAD. Then I hope to God I never have any interests to protect.

BILLING. Hear, hear!

HOVSTAD. I'm not a trimmer, and I never will be.

ASLAKSEN. A politician should never commit himself, Mr. Hovstad. And you, Mr. Billing, you ought to put a reef or two in your sails if you want that job of clerk to the magistrates.

BILLING. I—?

HOVSTAD. *You*, Billing?

BILLING. Of course I only applied for it to put their backs up, you understand.

ASLAKSEN. Well, it's no business of mine. But since I'm being accused of cowardice and inconsistency, I'd like to make this clear—my political record is open for anyone to investigate. I've never changed my standpoint; apart from having learned more restraint. My heart still belongs with the people; but I don't deny that my head keeps one ear cocked towards the authorities. The local ones, anyway. (*Goes into the composing-room.*)

BILLING. Couldn't we change to some other printer, Hovstad?

HOVSTAD. Do you know anyone else who'd give us credit for printing and paper?

BILLING. It's a damned nuisance not having any *capital!*

HOVSTAD (*sits at the desk*). Yes, if we only had *that*—

BILLING. Ever thought of trying Dr. Stockmann?

HOVSTAD (*glancing through his papers*). What'd be the use of that? He hasn't a bean.

BILLING. No; but he's got a good man behind him. Old Morten Kiil—the fellow they call the Badger—

HOVSTAD (*writing*). Do you really think he's got much?

BILLING. By jingo, of course he has! And part of it must go to the Stockmanns—he's bound to provide for—well, the children, anyway.

HOVSTAD (*half turns*). Are you banking on that?

BILLING. Banking? I never bank on anything.

HOVSTAD. You'd better not. And don't bank on becoming clerk to the magistrates either, because I can promise you you won't.

BILLING. Do you think I don't know? *Not* to get it is just what I want! A snub like that puts you on your mettle. It gives you a fresh supply of gall, and you need that in a backwater like this, where hardly anything really infuriating ever happens.

HOVSTAD (*writing*). Yes, yes.

BILLING. Well, they'll soon hear from me! I'll go and write that appeal for funds to the Property Owners' Association. (*Goes into the room on the right.*)

HOVSTAD (*sitting at the desk, chews his pen and says slowly*). Hm! So that's the way the wind blows! (*There is a knock on the door.*) Come in!

PETRA *enters through the door upstage left.*

HOVSTAD (*gets up*). Why, hullo! Fancy seeing you here!

PETRA. Please forgive me—

HOVSTAD (*pushes forward an armchair*). Won't you sit down?

PETRA. No, thank you. I'm only staying a moment.

HOVSTAD. Is it something from your father—?

PETRA. No, something from me. (*Takes a book from her coat pocket.*) Here's that English novel.

HOVSTAD. Why are you giving it back to me?

PETRA. I don't want to translate it.

HOVSTAD. But you promised—

PETRA. I hadn't read it then. You can't have, either!

HOVSTAD. No—you know I don't understand English. But—

PETRA. Exactly. That's why I wanted to tell you—you'll

have to find something else to serialise. (*Puts the book on the table.*) You can't possibly print this in the *People's Tribune.*

HOVSTAD. Why not?

PETRA. Because it's diametrically opposed to what you believe.

HOVSTAD. Oh, that's the reason?

PETRA. I don't think you understand. Its theme is that there's a supernatural power which takes care of all the so-called good people in this world, and works things so that in the end everything turns out well for them and all the so-called bad people get punished.

HOVSTAD. Yes, well, that's all right. That's just what people want to read.

PETRA. But do you want to be the one who provides it for them? You don't believe a word of that! You know quite well it doesn't happen like that in real life.

HOVSTAD. Of course not. But an editor can't always do as he wishes. One often has to bow to people's feelings in minor matters. After all, politics are the most important things in life—for a newspaper, anyway. And if I want to win people over to my views about freedom and progress, I mustn't frighten them away. If they find a moral story like this in the back pages of the newspaper they're more likely to go along with what we print on the front page. It reassures them.

PETRA. Oh, really! You're not as crafty as that. I don't see you as a spider spinning webs to catch your readers!

HOVSTAD (*smiles*). Thank you for holding such a high opinion of me. No, actually, this was Billing's idea, not mine.

PETRA. Billing's!

HOVSTAD. Yes. He was talking on those lines here the other day. He's the one who's so keen that we should publish this novel. I'd never heard of the book.

PETRA. But Billing holds such progressive views—

HOVSTAD. Oh, there's more in Billing than meets the eye. I've just heard he's applied for the post of clerk to the magistrates.

PETRA. I don't believe that, Mr. Hovstad. How could he reconcile himself to doing a thing like that?

HOVSTAD. You'd better ask him.

PETRA. I'd never have thought that of Billing.

HOVSTAD. Wouldn't you? Does it so surprise you?

PETRA. Yes. Perhaps not, though. I don't really know—

HOVSTAD. We journalists aren't worth much, Miss Stockmann.

PETRA. How can you say that?

HOVSTAD. I sometimes think it.

PETRA. In the ordinary run of events, perhaps not—that I can understand. But now, when you've taken up such an important cause—now surely you must feel you're worth more than most men.

HOVSTAD. Yes, today I do feel a bit like that.

PETRA. It's true, isn't it! You do! Oh, it's a wonderful vocation you've chosen! To be able to pioneer neglected truths and brave new doctrines—the mere fact of standing fearlessly forth to defend a man who's been wronged—

HOVSTAD. Especially when this man who's been wronged is—hm—

PETRA. When he is a man of such honour and integrity?

HOVSTAD (more quietly). I was about to say: especially when he is your father.

PETRA (astounded). Mr. Hovstad!

HOVSTAD. Yes, Petra—Miss Petra—

PETRA. Is that what seems important to you? Not the issue itself. Not the truth—or the fact that this means everything to Father—

HOVSTAD. Yes—yes, of course—those things too—

PETRA. No, thank you. You let the cat out of the bag there, Mr. Hovstad. Now I shall never believe you again—about anything.

HOVSTAD. Does it make you so angry that I've done this for your sake?

PETRA. I'm angry because you haven't been honest with Father. You've been talking to him as though truth and the good of the people were what mattered most to you. You've been fooling both of us. You're not the man you've been pretending you are. And that I'll never forgive you—never!

HOVSTAD. You shouldn't speak so sharply to me, Miss Petra. Least of all just now.

PETRA. Why not now?

HOVSTAD. Because your father needs my help.

PETRA. So that's the sort of man you are!

HOVSTAD. No, no, I didn't mean that—please believe me—

PETRA. I know what to believe. Goodbye.

ASLAKSEN (*hurries in furtively from the composing-room*). For God's sake, Mr. Hovstad—! (*Sees* PETRA.) Oh, dear, that's unlucky—!

HOVSTAD (*goes after her*). But, Miss Petra—!

PETRA. Goodbye. (*Goes.*)

ASLAKSEN. Mr. Hovstad, listen, please!

HOVSTAD. Yes, yes, what is it?

ASLAKSEN. The Mayor's standing outside there in the composing-room!

HOVSTAD. The Mayor?

ASLAKSEN. Yes. He wants to talk to you. He came in the back way—didn't want to be seen, I suppose.

HOVSTAD. What can he want? No, wait, I'd better— (*Goes to the door of the composing-room, opens it, bows and invites the* MAYOR *to enter.*)

HOVSTAD. Keep a look out, Aslaksen, and make sure no one—

ASLAKSEN. Of course. (*Goes into the composing-room.*)

MAYOR. You weren't expecting to see me here.

HOVSTAD. No, frankly, I wasn't.

MAYOR (*looks round*). You've done this up quite nicely. Very pleasant.

HOVSTAD. Oh—

MAYOR. And here I am coming along and making demands on your time.

HOVSTAD. Not at all, sir. What can I do for you? Please allow me— (*Takes the* MAYOR's *hat and stick and puts them on a chair.*) Won't you sit down?

MAYOR (*sits at the table*). Thank you.

HOVSTAD *also sits at the table.*

MAYOR. Something—something extremely irritating has happened to me today, Mr. Hovstad.

HOVSTAD. Really? Of course, Your Worship has so many responsibilities—

MAYOR. This particular matter concerns the medical officer at the Baths.

HOVSTAD. Oh—the Doctor—?

MAYOR. He's written a sort of—report to the Baths Committee regarding some supposed defects in the Baths.

HOVSTAD. You amaze me.

MAYOR. Hasn't he told you? I thought he said—

HOVSTAD. Oh yes, that's true, he did say something—

ASLAKSEN (*from the composing-room*). I'd better have that manuscript—

HOVSTAD (*irritated*). Hm—it's there on the desk—

ASLAKSEN (*finds it*). Good.

MAYOR. Why, surely that's it!

ASLAKSEN. Yes, this is the Doctor's article, Your Worship.

HOVSTAD. Oh, is this what you were talking about?

MAYOR. The very thing. What do you think of it?

HOVSTAD. Of course I'm not a specialist, and I've only glanced through it—

MAYOR. But you're going to print it?

HOVSTAD. I can't very well refuse a signed contribution—

ASLAKSEN. I have no say in the contents of the paper, Your Worship—

MAYOR. Of course not.

ASLAKSEN. I only print what's put into my hands.

MAYOR. Absolutely.

ASLAKSEN. So if you'll excuse me— (*Goes towards the composing room.*)

MAYOR. No, wait a moment, Mr. Aslaksen. With your permission, Mr. Hovstad—

HOVSTAD. Of course, Your Worship.

MAYOR. You're an intelligent and discriminating man, Mr. Aslaksen.

ASLAKSEN. I'm glad Your Worship thinks so.

MAYOR. And a man of wide influence in more circles than one.

ASLAKSEN. Oh—mostly among humble people—

MAYOR. The small taxpayers are the most numerous, here as elsewhere.

ASLAKSEN. Yes, that's true.

MAYOR. And I've no doubt you know how most of them feel. Don't you?

ASLAKSEN. Yes, I think I may say I do, Your Worship.

MAYOR. Well then, since the less affluent of the citizens of this town are so laudably disposed to make this sacrifice, I—

ASLAKSEN. What!

HOVSTAD. Sacrifice—?

MAYOR. It's a fine token of public spirit; a remarkably fine token. I was about to confess I hadn't expected it. But you know the mood of the people better than I do.

ASLAKSEN. But, Your Worship—

MAYOR. And it will probably be no mean sacrifice that the ratepayers will be called upon to make.

HOVSTAD. The ratepayers?

ASLAKSEN. But I don't understand—surely the shareholders—?

MAYOR. According to a provisional estimate the alterations that the medical officer at the Baths regards as desirable will cost some two to three hundred thousand crowns.

ASLAKSEN. That's a lot of money; but—

MAYOR. We shall of course be forced to raise a municipal loan.

HOVSTAD (gets up). You surely don't mean that the ordinary citizens—?

ASLAKSEN. You mean you'd charge it on the rates! Empty the pockets of the tradespeople—?

MAYOR. Well, my dear Mr. Aslaksen, where else is the money to come from?

ASLAKSEN. That's the business of the gentlemen who own the Baths.

MAYOR. The Committee cannot see their way towards authorising any further expenditure.

ASLAKSEN. Is that quite definite, Your Worship?

MAYOR. I have gone into the matter very thoroughly. If the people want all these comprehensive alterations, then the people themselves will have to pay for them.

ASLAKSEN. But good God Almighty—oh, I beg Your Worship's pardon!—but this puts a completely different face on the situation, Mr. Hovstad.

HOVSTAD. It certainly does.

MAYOR. The worst of the matter is that we shall be compelled to close the Baths for two to three years.

HOVSTAD. Close them? You mean—close them completely?

ASLAKSEN. For two years?

MAYOR. That's how long the work will take, at the lowest calculation.

ASLAKSEN. But, good Heavens, we'll never be able to stand that, Your Worship! How are we property owners to live in the meantime?

MAYOR. I'm afraid that's a very difficult question to answer, Mr. Aslaksen. But what do you expect us to do? Do you imagine we shall get a single visitor here if we start spreading the idea that the water is contaminated, that we are living over a cesspit, that the whole town—?

ASLAKSEN. And all this is just pure speculation?

MAYOR. With the best will in the world I have been unable to convince myself that it is anything else.

ASLAKSEN. But if that's the case it's monstrous of Dr. Stockmann to have—I beg Your Worship's pardon, but—

MAYOR. I deplore your observation, Mr. Aslaksen, but I'm afraid it represents the truth. My brother has unfortunately always been an impulsive man.

ASLAKSEN. And you still want to support him in this action, Mr. Hovstad?

HOVSTAD. But who could have possibly guessed that—?

MAYOR. I have written a brief resumé of the situation as it appears to an impartial observer; and in it I have suggested how any possible flaws in the existing arrangements could safely be remedied by measures within the financial resources at present possessed by the Baths.

HOVSTAD. Have you that document with you, Your Worship?

MAYOR (*feels in his pocket*). Yes, I brought it with me just in case you—

ASLAKSEN (*quickly*). Oh, my goodness, there he is!

MAYOR. Who? My brother?

HOVSTAD. Where—where?

ASLAKSEN. He's just coming through the composing-room.

MAYOR. Most unfortunate! I don't want to meet him here, and I've something else I wanted to speak to you about.

HOVSTAD (*points towards the door, right*). Go in there till he's gone.

MAYOR. But—?

HOVSTAD. There's only Billing there.

ASLAKSEN. Quick, quick, Your Worship! He's coming now!

MAYOR. Very well. But get rid of him as soon as you can.

Goes out through the door on the right, which ASLAKSEN *opens and closes for him.*

HOVSTAD. Find something to do, Aslaksen.

He sits down and writes. ASLAKSEN *starts looking through a pile of newspapers on a chair to the right.*

DR. STOCKMANN (*enters from the composing-room*). Well, here I am again! (*Puts down his hat and stick.*)

HOVSTAD (*writing*). Already, Doctor? Aslaksen, hurry up with that thing we were talking about. We're badly behind-hand today.

DR. STOCKMANN (*to* ASLAKSEN). No proofs yet, by the sound of it?

ASLAKSEN (*without turning*). No, surely you didn't think they'd be ready yet.

DR. STOCKMANN. That's all right. I'm just impatient, as I know you'll appreciate. I can't rest till I've seen that thing in print.

HOVSTAD. Hm; it'll be a good time yet. Won't it, Aslaksen?

ASLAKSEN. I'm afraid so.

DR. STOCKMANN. Very well, my dear friends. I'll be back later.
I don't mind making the journey twice if need be! In such
a vital matter, with the welfare of the whole town at stake,
one mustn't grudge a little extra effort! (*Is about to go,
but stops and comes back*). Oh, by the way, there's one
more thing I must speak to you about.

HOVSTAD. I'm sorry, but couldn't it wait till another time—?

DR. STOCKMANN. I can tell you in two words. It's just this.
When people read my article in the paper tomorrow and
discover I've been racking my brains all winter working
silently for the welfare of the town—

HOVSTAD. But, Doctor—

DR. STOCKMANN. I know what you're going to say! You think
it was no more than my damned duty—my job as a citizen.
Yes, of course—I know that as well as you do. But my
fellow-citizens, you see—oh dear, those good people,
they're so fond of me—

ASLAKSEN. Yes, the people of this town have been very fond
of you, Doctor, up to today.

DR. STOCKMANN. Yes, and that's exactly why I'm frightened
that—what I mean is—when they read this—especially the
poorer people—as a clarion call bidding them take the
government of their town into their own hands—

HOVSTAD (*gets up*). Look, Doctor, I don't want to hide anything from you—

DR. STOCKMANN. Ah, something's already afoot! I might have
guessed! But I don't want it! If anything like that's being
organized, I—

HOVSTAD. Like what?

DR. STOCKMANN. Well, if anything like a torchlight procession or a banquet or—a subscription for some little token
of thanks is being organized, you must promise me
solemnly you'll squash the idea. And you too, Mr. Aslaksen! You hear!

HOVSTAD. I'm sorry, Doctor, but we might as well tell you
the truth now as later—

MRS. STOCKMANN, *in hat and cloak, enters through the door upstage left.*

MRS. STOCKMANN (*sees the* DOCTOR). I knew it!

HOVSTAD (*goes towards her*). You here too, Mrs. Stockmann?

DR. STOCKMANN. What the devil do you want here, Catherine?

MRS. STOCKMANN. Surely you can guess.

HOVSTAD. Won't you sit down? Or perhaps—?

MRS. STOCKMANN. Thank you, you needn't bother. And you mustn't take offence at my coming here to fetch my husband, for I'm the mother of three children, I'd have you realise.

DR. STOCKMANN. Oh really, Catherine, we know all this.

MRS. STOCKMANN. Well, it doesn't seem you've much thought for your wife and children today, or you wouldn't have come here to cause all of us misery.

DR. STOCKMANN. Are you quite mad, Catherine? Simply because a man has a wife and children, is he to be forbidden to proclaim the truth—to be a useful and active citizen—to serve the town he lives in?

MRS. STOCKMANN. Oh, Thomas, if only you'd use some restraint.

ASLAKSEN. That's exactly what I say. Restraint in all things.

MRS. STOCKMANN. And as for you, Mr. Hovstad, it's not right for you to persuade my husband to leave his house and home and trick him into involving himself in all this—

HOVSTAD. I haven't tricked anyone—

DR. STOCKMANN. Tricked! You think *I* allow myself to be tricked?

MRS. STOCKMANN. Yes, you do. Oh, I know you're the cleverest man in the town, but you're so dreadfully easy to fool, Thomas. (*To* HOVSTAD.) And don't forget he'll lose his job at the Baths if you print that thing he's written—

ASLAKSEN. What!

HOVSTAD. But Doctor—I—

DR. STOCKMANN (*laughs*). Just let them try! Oh no, Catherine—they'll watch their step! You see, I have the majority behind me!

MRS. STOCKMANN. Yes, that's just the trouble. They're an ugly thing to have behind you.

DR. STOCKMANN. Rubbish, Catherine! You go home now and take care of the house, and let me take care of society. How can you be frightened when I feel so calm and happy? (*Rubs his hands and walks up and down.*) Truth and the people will win this battle, never you fear! Oh, I can see every liberal-minded citizen in this town marching forward in an unconquerable army—! (*Stops by a chair.*) What—the devil is *this?*

ASLAKSEN (*looks at it*). Oh dear!

DR. STOCKMANN. The crown of authority! (*Takes the* MAYOR'S *hat carefully in his fingers and holds it in the air.*)

MRS. STOCKMANN. The Mayor's hat!

DR. STOCKMANN. And his marshal's baton too. How in the name of Hell—?

HOVSTAD. Well—

DR. STOCKMANN. Ah, I see! He's been here to talk you over! (*Laughs.*) He came to the wrong men! And then he saw me in the composing room— (*Roars with laughter.*) Did he run away, Mr. Aslaksen?

ASLAKSEN (*quickly*). Oh yes, Doctor, he ran away.

DR. STOCKMANN. Ran away leaving his stick and—? Rubbish! Peter never left anything behind in his life! But where the devil have you put him? Ah, yes, of course—in there! Now, Catherine, you watch!

MRS. STOCKMANN. Thomas, I beg you—!

ASLAKSEN. Don't do anything rash, Doctor!

DR. STOCKMANN *has put the* MAYOR'S *hat on his head and taken his stick. Then he goes across, throws the door open and brings his hand up to the hat in salute. The* MAYOR *enters, red with anger.* BILLING *follows him.*

MAYOR. What is the meaning of this disorderly scene?

DR. STOCKMANN. A little more respect if you please, my dear

Peter. I am the supreme authority in this town now. (*He walks up and down.*)

MRS. STOCKMANN (*almost in tears*). Thomas, please!

MAYOR (*follows him*). Give me my hat and stick!

DR. STOCKMANN (*as before*). You may be Chief of Police, but I'm the Mayor! I'm master of this whole town, I am!

MAYOR. Take off that hat, I tell you! Remember that that hat is an official emblem—

DR. STOCKMANN. Rubbish! Do you think the awakening lion of public opinion is going to let itself be frightened by a hat? We're starting a revolution tomorrow, I'd have you know! You threatened to sack me, but now I'm going to sack you—sack you from all your positions of responsibility! You think I can't? You're wrong, Peter! I have as my allies the conquering forces of social revolution! Hovstad and Billing will thunder in the *People's Tribune*, and Mr. Aslaksen will march forth at the head of the entire Property Owners' Association—

ASLAKSEN. No, I won't, Doctor.

DR. STOCKMANN. Indeed you will—!

MAYOR. Aha. But perhaps Mr. Hovstad will support this uprising?

HOVSTAD. No, Your Worship.

ASLAKSEN. Mr. Hovstad isn't so mad as to ruin himself and his newspaper for the sake of an hallucination.

DR. STOCKMANN (*looks around*). What the devil—?

HOVSTAD. You have presented your case in a false light, Doctor; and therefore I cannot support you.

BILLING. No, after what His Worship has had the grace to tell me in there, I shouldn't—

DR. STOCKMANN. Lies! I'll answer for the truth of my report! You just print it. I shan't be frightened to defend it.

HOVSTAD. I'm not printing it. I can't and I won't and I dare not print it.

DR. STOCKMANN. Dare not? What nonsense is this? You're the editor, and it's the editors who rule the press.

ASLAKSEN. No, Doctor. It's the subscribers.

MAYOR. Fortunately.

ASLAKSEN. It's public opinion, the educated reader, the property owners, and so forth—they're the ones who rule the press.

DR. STOCKMANN (*calmly*). And all these forces are ranged against me?

ASLAKSEN. They are. If your report got printed, it would mean ruin for the entire community.

DR. STOCKMANN. I see.

MAYOR. My hat and stick!

DR. STOCKMANN *takes off the hat and puts it on the table together with the stick.*

MAYOR (*takes them both*). Your little reign didn't last long.

DR. STOCKMANN. It isn't over yet. (*To* HOVSTAD.) You refuse absolutely, then, to print my report in the *People's Tribune?*

HOVSTAD. Absolutely. Out of consideration for your family, if for no other reason.

MRS. STOCKMANN. Never you mind his family, Mr. Hovstad.

MAYOR (*takes a paper from his pocket*). This will give the public full possession of the facts. It's an official statement. Mr. Hovstad—

HOVSTAD (*takes the paper*). Right. I'll see it's set up at once.

DR. STOCKMANN. But not mine! You think you can gag me and stifle the truth! But it won't be as easy as you think. Mr. Aslaksen, take this manuscript of mine and print it immediately as a pamphlet—at my own expense! I'll publish it myself! I want four hundred copies—five—no, make it six hundred copies!

ASLAKSEN. I wouldn't give you the use of my press if you offered me gold, Doctor. I daren't. Public opinion wouldn't allow me. You won't find a printer to take it anywhere in this town.

DR. STOCKMANN. Give it back to me then.

HOVSTAD *hands him the manuscript.*

DR. STOCKMANN (*takes his hat and stick*). I'll see the contents
are made known all the same. I'll summon a public meeting and read it! All my fellow-citizens shall know the
truth!

MAYOR. You won't find anyone in this town who'll lease you a
hall for such a purpose.

ASLAKSEN. Not one. I'm sure of that.

BILLING. By jingo, you won't.

MRS. STOCKMANN. This is too disgraceful! Why are they all
against you?

DR. STOCKMANN (*hotly*). I'll tell you why! It's because in this
town all the men are old women! Like you, they just think
of their families and not of the community.

MRS. STOCKMANN (*grasps his arm*). Then I'll show them that
an—an old woman can be a man—for once. I'm sticking
with you, Thomas.

DR. STOCKMANN. Well said, Catherine! The truth shall be
told—by God it will! If I can't lease a hall, I'll hire a drum-
mer to march through the town with me, and I'll read it
out at every street corner!

MAYOR. You can't be so crazy as to do that!

DR. STOCKMANN. I am!

ASLAKSEN. You won't find a single man in the whole town
who'll go with you.

BILLING. No, by jingo!

MRS. STOCKMANN. Don't you give in, Thomas! I'll ask the
boys to go with you.

DR. STOCKMANN. That's a splendid idea!

MRS. STOCKMANN. Morten will love to do it; and so will Eilif,
I'm sure.

DR. STOCKMANN. Yes, and Petra too! And you, Catherine!

MRS. STOCKMANN. No, no, not me. But I'll stand at the window and watch you. I'll do that.

DR. STOCKMANN (*throws his arms around her and kisses her*).
Thank you! Well, my fine gentlemen, let the trumpets
sound! Let's see whether meanness and mediocrity have
the power to gag a man who wants to clean up society!

DR. *and* MRS. STOCKMANN *go out through the door upstage left.*

MAYOR (*shakes his head thoughtfully*). Now he's driven her mad, too!

ACT FOUR

A big, old-fashioned room in CAPTAIN HORSTER's *house. In the background an open double-leaved door leads to a lobby. In the left-hand wall are three windows. Against the middle of the opposite wall has been placed a dais, on which stands a small table with two candles, a water carafe, a glass, and a bell. The room is further illuminated by bracket lamps between the windows. Downstage left stands a table with a candle on it, and a chair. Downstage right is a door, with a few chairs by it.*

A large gathering of CITIZENS, *of all classes. Here and there,* WOMEN *can be seen among the crowd, and there are a few* SCHOOLBOYS. *More and more people gradually stream in from the back, filling the room.*

A CITIZEN (*to* ANOTHER, *as he bumps against him*). Hullo, Lamstad! You here too this evening?

2ND CITIZEN. I never miss a public meeting.

3RD CITIZEN (*standing near them*). Brought your whistle, I hope?

2ND CITIZEN. Course I have. Haven't you?

3RD CITIZEN. You bet! And Skipper Evensen said he'd bring a bloody great horn!

2ND CITIZEN. He's a card, old Evensen!

Laughter among THE CROWD.

4TH CITIZEN (*joins them*). I say, what's this meeting about?

2ND CITIZEN. Dr. Stockmann's going to deliver a lecture attacking the Mayor.

4TH CITIZEN. But the Mayor's his brother.

1ST CITIZEN. That don't matter. Dr. Stockmann ain't afraid of no one.

3RD CITIZEN. But he's in the wrong. It said so in the *People's Tribune*.

2ND CITIZEN. Yes, he must be in the wrong this time. The Property Owners wouldn't let him use their hall, nor the People's Club neither.

1ST CITIZEN. He couldn't even get the hall at the Baths.

2ND CITIZEN. Well, what do you expect?

1ST CITIZEN. Which one do you think we ought to support?

4TH CITIZEN. Just keep your eye on old Aslaksen, and do as he does.

BILLING (*with a portfolio under his arm, pushes his way through* THE CROWD). Excuse me please, gentlemen! Can I get through, please? I'm reporting the meeting for the *People's Tribune*. Thank you! (*Sits down at the table, left.*)

CAPTAIN HORSTER *escorts* MRS. STOCKMANN *and* PETRA *in through the door downstage right.* EILIF *and* MORTEN *are with them.*

HORSTER. I thought you might sit here. You can slip out easily if anything should happen.

MRS. STOCKMANN. Do you think there'll be trouble?

HORSTER. One never knows, with a crowd like this. But sit down, and don't worry.

MRS. STOCKMANN (*sits*). It was very kind of you to offer my husband this room.

HORSTER. Well, no one else would, so I—

PETRA (*who has sat down too*). It was brave of you, too, Captain Horster.

HORSTER. Oh, that didn't call for much courage.

HOVSTAD *and* ASLAKSEN *come through* THE CROWD, *at the same time but separately.*

ASLAKSEN (*goes over to* HORSTER). Hasn't the Doctor come yet?

HORSTER. He's waiting in there.

There is a stir among the CROWD *near the door backstage.*

HOVSTAD (*to* BILLING). There's the Mayor! See?

BILLING. Yes, by jingo! So he's come after all!

The MAYOR *gently pushes his way through the* CROWD, *greeting people politely, and stations himself against the wall on the left. A few moments later* DR. STOCKMANN *enters through the door downstage right. He is dressed in black, with a frock coat and a white cravat. A few people clap uncertainly, but are countered by subdued hissing. Silence falls.*

DR. STOCKMANN (*in a low voice*). How do you feel, Catherine?

MRS. STOCKMANN. I'm all right. (*More quietly.*) Now don't lose your temper, Thomas!

DR. STOCKMANN. Oh, I'll control myself, don't you worry. (*Looks at his watch, steps up onto the dais and bows.*) It's a quarter past, so I'll begin— (*Takes out his manuscript.*)

ASLAKSEN. Surely a Chairman ought to be elected first?

DR. STOCKMANN. No, no, there's no need for that.

SEVERAL MEN (*shout*). Yes, yes!

MAYOR. I really think we should have someone in the chair.

DR. STOCKMANN. But Peter, I've called this meeting to deliver a lecture!

MAYOR. The Doctor's lecture may possibly give rise to divergent expressions of opinion.

SEVERAL VOICES FROM THE CROWD. A Chairman! A Chairman!

HOVSTAD. Public opinion seems to demand a Chairman.

DR. STOCKMANN (*controlling himself*). Very well. Let public opinion have its way.

ASLAKSEN. Would His Worship the Mayor be willing to undertake that function?

THREE MEN (*clap*). Bravo! Hear, hear!

MAYOR. For reasons which I'm sure you will appreciate, I must decline that honour. But fortunately we have among us a man whom I think we can all accept. I refer to the

Chairman of the Property Owners' Association, Mr. Aslaksen.

MANY VOICES. Yes, yes! Good old Aslaksen! Hurrah for Aslaksen!

DR. STOCKMANN *picks up his manuscript and descends from the dais.*

ASLAKSEN. If my fellow-citizens want to express their trust in me, I won't refuse their call.

Applause and cheers. ASLAKSEN *steps up onto the dais.*

BILLING (*writes*). "Mr. Aslaksen was chosen amid acclamation . . ."

ASLAKSEN. Now that I stand here may I crave permission to say a few brief words? I'm a mild and peace-loving man who believes in sensible discretion, and in—and in discreet good sense. Everyone who knows me knows that.

MANY VOICES. Yes! That's right, Aslaksen!

ASLAKSEN. Experience in the school of life has taught me that the most valuable virtue for any citizen is restraint—

MAYOR. Hear, hear!

ASLAKSEN. And that discretion and restraint are the best servants of society. I would therefore suggest to our respected fellow-citizen who has summoned this meeting that he endeavour to keep himself within the bounds of temperance.

DRUNKEN MAN (*by the entrance door*). Three cheers for the Temperance Society! Jolly good health!

A VOICE. Shut your damned trap.

MANY VOICES. Hush, hush!

ASLAKSEN. No interruptions, gentlemen, please! Does anyone wish to say anything before I—?

MAYOR. Mr. Chairman!

ASLAKSEN. Your Worship!

MAYOR. As everyone here is doubtless aware, I have close ties of relationship with the present medical officer at the Baths, and would consequently have preferred not to speak this evening. But my official position on the Committee of that organization, and my anxiety for the best interests of the town, force me to table a resolution. I hope I may assume that no citizen here present would regard it as desirable that dubious and exaggerated allegations concerning the sanitary conditions at the Baths should circulate outside this town.

MANY VOICES. No, no, no! Certainly not! We protest!

MAYOR. I therefore move that this meeting refuse the aforesaid medical officer permission to read or dilate upon his theories concerning the matter in question.

DR. STOCKMANN (*explosively*). Refuse permission? What the devil—?

MRS. STOCKMANN *coughs.*

DR. STOCKMANN (*composes himself*). Very well. You refuse permission.

MAYOR. In my statement to the *People's Tribune* I have acquainted the public with the essential facts so that every intelligent citizen can form his own judgment. Among other things I pointed out that the medical officer's proposals— quite apart from the fact that they amount to a vote of no confidence in the leading citizens of this town—will burden the ratepayers with the unnecessary expenditure of at least a hundred thousand crowns.

Groans and a few whistles.

ASLAKSEN (*rings his bell*). Order please, gentlemen! I beg leave to second His Worship's motion. I would add that in my view the Doctor has had an ulterior motive, no doubt unconscious, in stirring up this agitation. He talks about the Baths. But what he's really aiming at is a revolution. He wants to transfer authority into other hands. No one doubts the honesty of the Doctor's intentions. Heaven knows, there can be no two opinions about that! I too believe in popular self-government, so long as it doesn't impose too heavy an expense upon the taxpayer. But that's just what would happen here; so I'm blowed, if you'll excuse the expression, if I can support Dr. Stockmann in this matter. One can pay too high a price for gold; that's my opinion.

Lively expressions of assent from all sides.

HOVSTAD. I too feel impelled to explain my position. Dr. Stockmann's agitation won considerable sympathy at first, and I myself supported it as impartially as I was able. But then we found we had allowed ourselves to be misled by a false picture of the facts—

DR. STOCKMANN. That's a lie!

HOVSTAD. A not completely reliable picture, then. His Worship's statement has proved that. I hope no one here doubts the liberality of my views. The *People's Tribune's* attitude on major political questions is well known to you all. But I have learned from men of discretion and experience that in local matters it is the duty of a newspaper to observe a certain caution.

ASLAKSEN. Exactly my feelings.

HOVSTAD. Now in the matter under discussion it's quite clear that Dr. Stockmann has popular opinion against him. Well, I ask you, gentlemen, what is the primary duty of an editor? Is it not to reflect the opinions of his readers? Has he not been entrusted with what might be described as an unspoken mandate to advance the cause of those who hold the same views as himself, with all the eloquence of which he is capable? Or am I mistaken?

MANY VOICES. No, no, no! Mr. Hovstad is right!

HOVSTAD. It has caused me much heart-searching to break with a man under whose roof I have lately been a not infrequent guest—a man who has until this day rejoiced in the undivided affection of his fellow-citizens—a man whose only, or anyway principal fault is that he follows his heart rather than his head.

SCATTERED VOICES. That's true. Hurrah for Dr. Stockmann!

HOVSTAD. But my duty towards society left me no alternative. And there's one further consideration which forces me to oppose him, in the hope of halting him on the inauspicious road he has now begun to tread—consideration for his family—

DR. STOCKMANN. Stick to the water system and the sewer!

HOVSTAD. —consideration for his wife and children he has abandoned.

MORTEN. Does he mean us, Mother?

MRS. STOCKMANN. Hush!

ASLAKSEN. I shall now put His Worship's resolution to the vote.

DR. STOCKMANN. Don't bother! I won't say a word about those damned Baths. No. I've something else to tell you tonight.

MAYOR (*in a low voice*). What the devil's this?

A DRUNK MAN (*near the entrance door*). I pay my taxes! So I'm entitled to express my opinion! And it's my absolute 'n unintelligible opinion that—

SEVERAL VOICES. Keep quiet there!

OTHERS. He's drunk! Throw him out!

The DRUNK MAN *is removed.*

DR. STOCKMANN. Have I the floor?

ASLAKSEN (*rings his bell*). Dr. Stockmann has the floor.

DR. STOCKMANN. A few days ago, if anyone had tried to gag me like this I'd have fought like a lion for my sacred human rights! But now that doesn't matter. Now I have more important things to talk about.

THE CROWD *moves closer around him.* MORTEN KIIL *can be seen among them.*

DR. STOCKMANN (*continues*). I've been thinking a great deal these past few days. I've brooded so deeply that in the end my head began to spin—

MAYOR (*coughs*). Hm—!

DR. STOCKMANN. But then everything began to fall into place. I saw the whole picture of things quite clearly. And that's why I'm standing here this evening. I'm going to make a mighty revelation to you, my friends! I'm going to tell you about a discovery that is infinitely more important than the

fiddling little fact that our water system is poisoned and
our health baths sited above a cesspit!

MANY VOICES (*shout*). Leave the Baths alone! Don't talk
about them! We won't listen!

DR. STOCKMANN. This great discovery that I have made during these last few days is that all our spiritual sources are
poisoned, and that the whole of our vaunted social system
is founded upon a cesspit of lies!

ASTONISHED VOICES (*mutter in low tones*). What's that? What
did he say?

MAYOR. These are ridiculous insinuations—

ASLAKSEN (*his hand on the bell*). I must request the speaker
to moderate his language.

DR. STOCKMANN. I was young when I left home, and distance,
hunger, and memory threw, as it were, a brighter lustre
over this place and the people who dwelt here.

Some applause and cheers are heard.

DR. STOCKMANN. For years I lived far up in the north. As I
wandered among those people who lived scattered over the
mountains, I often thought it would have been better for
those poor degraded creatures if they'd had a vet instead
of a man like me!

Murmurs.

BILLING (*puts down his pen*). By jingo, I've never heard the
like of that—!

HOVSTAD. That's a filthy slander against a worthy community!

DR. STOCKMANN. Wait a moment! I sat there brooding like a
duck on an egg; and the chick I hatched was—the plan
for these Baths.

Clapping, and murmurs of disapproval.

DR. STOCKMANN. Then at long last fate smiled upon me and
allowed me to return. And then, my fellow-citizens, then I
thought I had nothing left to wish for in this world. No—I
had one ambition left—a burning desire to work with all

my heart and soul for the welfare of my home and my community.

MAYOR (*gazing into space*). You've a strange way of showing it!

DR. STOCKMANN. I went around here revelling blindly in my new-found happiness. But yesterday morning—no, it was the previous night, actually—my eyes were opened, and the first thing that greeted them was the stupendous imbecility of the authorities—

Noise, shouting, and laughter. MRS. STOCKMANN *coughs loudly.*

MAYOR. Mr. Chairman!

ASLAKSEN (*rings his bell*). As Chairman of this meeting, I—

DR. STOCKMANN. Oh, let's not start quibbling about words, Mr. Aslaksen. I only mean that I suddenly realized how really revoltingly our politicians had behaved down there at the Baths. I can't stand politicians! They're like goats in a plantation of young trees; they destroy everything! They block the way for a free man, however much he may twist and turn—and I'd like to see them rooted out and exterminated, like other vermin—

Commotion in the hall.

MAYOR. Mr. Chairman, are such calumnies to be permitted?

ASLAKSEN (*his hand on the bell*). Dr. Stockmann—!

DR. STOCKMANN. I can't understand why I'd never had a proper look at these gentlemen before. I'd had a prime example right in front of my eyes all the time—my brother Peter—procrastinating and purblind—!

Laughter, confusion, and whistling. MRS. STOCKMANN *sits and coughs.* ASLAKSEN *rings his bell loudly.*

THE DRUNK MAN (*who has come back*). Are you referring to me? My name's Petersen, but don't you damned well—

ANGRY VOICES. Throw that drunk out! Get rid of him!

The DRUNK MAN *is thrown out again.*

MAYOR. Who was that person?

A BYSTANDER. I don't know, Your Worship.

ASLAKSEN. The man was obviously intoxicated with German beer. Continue, Doctor; but please try to use restraint!

DR. STOCKMANN. Well, my fellow-citizens, I won't say anything more about our politicians. If anyone imagines from what I've just said that I've come here this evening to immolate these gentlemen, he's wrong—quite wrong. For I cherish the comforting belief that these laggards, these survivors from a dying world, are studiously cutting their own throats; they need no doctor's help to hasten their demise. And anyway, it isn't they who are the chief danger to society! They aren't the ones who are most active in poisoning the sources of our spiritual life and contaminating the ground on which we tread! It isn't they who are the most dangerous enemies of truth and freedom in our society!

SHOUTS FROM ALL SIDES. Who, then? Who is? Name them!

DR. STOCKMANN. Don't worry, I'll name them! Because this is the great discovery I've made today! (*Raises his voice.*) The most dangerous enemies of truth and freedom are the majority! Yes, the solid, liberal, bloody majority—they're the ones we have to fear! Now you know!

Complete uproar. Nearly everyone is shouting, stamping, and whistling. Some of the older men exchange stolen glances and seem to be enjoying the situation. MRS. STOCKMANN *gets up anxiously.* EILIF *and* MORTEN *go threateningly over to the* SCHOOLBOYS, *who are making a commotion.* ASLAKSEN *rings his bell and calls for silence.* HOVSTAD *and* BILLING *are both talking, but neither can be heard. At last silence is restored.*

ASLAKSEN. As Chairman I call upon the speaker to withdraw those mischievous observations.

DR. STOCKMANN. Never, Mr. Aslaksen! It's the majority in this community that is depriving me of my freedom and trying to forbid me to proclaim the truth.

HOVSTAD. The majority is always right.

BILLING. And speaks the truth, by jingo!

DR. STOCKMANN. The majority is never right! Never, I tell you! That's one of those community lies that free, thinking men have got to rebel against! Who form the majority—in any country? The wise, or the fools? I think we'd all have to agree that the fools are in a terrifying, overwhelming majority all over the world! But in the name of God it can't be right that the fools should rule the wise! (*Uproar and shouting.*) Yes, yes, you can shout me down! But you can't say I'm wrong! The majority has the power—unfortunately—but the majority is not right! The ones who are right are a few isolated individuals like me! The minority is always right! (*Uproar again.*)

HOVSTAD. So Dr. Stockmann's turned aristocrat since the day before yesterday!

DR. STOCKMANN. I've already said I don't want to waste words on the little flock of short-winded sheep puffing along in the rear! Life has nothing exciting left to offer them. But I'm thinking of the few, the individuals among us, who have adopted the new, fresh, burgeoning truths as their watchword!

HOVSTAD. I see, so you've become a revolutionary!

DR. STOCKMANN. Yes, Mr. Hovstad, by God I have! I intend to start a revolution against the lie that truth is a monopoly of the majority! What are these truths to which the majority clings? They're the truths which are so old that they're on the way to becoming decrepit! But when a truth's as old as that, gentlemen, it's also well on the way to becoming a lie!

Laughter and jeers.

DR. STOCKMANN. All these majority truths are like last year's salt pork; they're hams that have gone sour and green and tainted. And they're the cause of all the moral scurvy that's rotting our society!

ASLAKSEN. It seems to me that the honourable speaker has strayed somewhat from his text.

MAYOR. I warmly endorse the Chairman's observation.

DR. STOCKMANN. Oh, really, Peter, I think you must be quite

mad! I'm sticking as close to my text as any man could! My whole point is precisely this, that it's the masses, the mob, this damned majority—they're the thing that's poisoning the sources of our spiritual life and contaminating the ground we walk on!

HOVSTAD. And the great progressive majority does this simply by being sensible enough to believe in those truths which are indisputable and generally acknowledged?

DR. STOCKMANN. Oh, my good Mr. Hovstad, don't talk to me about undisputed truths! There's only one indisputable truth. It is that no society can live a healthy life if it feeds on truths that are old and marrowless.

HOVSTAD. Instead of all this generalising why don't you give us a few examples of these old and marrowless truths on which we're living?

Murmurs of agreement from several quarters.

DR. STOCKMANN. Oh, I could reel you off a whole list of the beastly things; but to start with I'll limit myself to one "acknowledged" truth which is really a damned lie, but which Mr. Hovstad and the *People's Tribune* and all the hangers-on of the *People's Tribune* feed on all the same.

HOVSTAD. And that is—?

DR. STOCKMANN. That is the doctrine which you have inherited from your forefathers and which you continue thoughtlessly to proclaim far and wide—the doctrine that the plebs, the masses, the mob, are the living heart of the people—that they are the people—and that the common man, all those ignorant and incompetent millions, have the same right to sanction and condemn, to advise and to govern, as the few individuals who are intellectually aristocrats.

BILLING. Now, really, by jingo—!

HOVSTAD (*simultaneously, shouts*). Mark that, fellow-citizens!

FURIOUS VOICES. Oh-ho, so we're not the people, aren't we? So it's only the aristocrats who have the right to rule?

A WORKER. Throw him out if he talks like that!

OTHERS. Chuck him through the door!

A CITIZEN (*shouts*). Blow that horn, Evensen!

Loud horn-blasts are heard. Whistles and furious uproar in the hall.

DR. STOCKMANN (*when the noise has abated somewhat*). Can't you be reasonable? Can't you bear to hear the truth just for once? I'm not asking you all to agree with me immediately! But I did expect Mr. Hovstad would admit I was right once he'd given the matter a little thought. After all, Mr. Hovstad claims to be a freethinker—

SURPRISED VOICES (*murmur*). Freethinker, did he say? What? Is Mr. Hovstad a freethinker?

HOVSTAD (*shouts*). Prove that, Dr. Stockmann! When have I said so in print?

DR. STOCKMANN (*thinks*). No, by Jove, you're right! You've never had the guts to admit it publicly. Well, I won't corner you, Mr. Hovstad. Let me be the freethinker, then. I shall now prove to you that the masses are nothing but raw material which may, some day, be refined into individuals!

Growls, laughter, and disturbances in the hall.

DR. STOCKMANN. Well, isn't that the way life works with the rest of creation? Look at the enormous difference there is between a breed of animal that's cultivated and one that is uncultivated! Consider dogs, with which we human beings have so much in common! Think first of a simple mongrel—one of those filthy, ragged, common curs that lope along the streets and defile the walls of our houses. And then put that mongrel next to a greyhound with a distinguished pedigree, whose ancestors have been fed delicate meals for generations and have had the opportunity to listen to harmonious voices and music! Don't you think the brain of that greyhound is differently developed from that of the mongrel? You bet your life it is! It's the pups of these cultivated animals that trainers teach to perform the most amazing tricks. A common mongrel couldn't learn to do such things if you stood it on its head!

Noise and laughter.

A CITIZEN (*shouts*). So we're dogs too now, are we?

ANOTHER. We're not animals, Doctor!

DR. STOCKMANN. Yes, my friend, we are animals! But there aren't many aristocratic animals among us. There's a terrifying difference between men who are greyhounds and men who are mongrels. And that's what's so absurd, that Mr. Hovstad is quite at one with me as long as we're talking about four-legged animals—

HOVSTAD. Well, they're only beasts.

DR. STOCKMANN. All right! But as soon as I start to apply the law to the ones who are two-legged, Mr. Hovstad balks at the consequences; he turns his whole philosophy upside down, and proclaims in the *People's Tribune* that the street mongrel is the champion of the menagerie. But that's how it always is, as long as a man remains possessed by this blind worship of the mob and hasn't worked his way out of spiritual bondage into aristocracy.

HOVSTAD. I don't want any kind of aristocracy. I come of simple peasant stock; and I'm proud that I have my roots deep down in the mob, whom you deride.

MANY WORKERS. Hurrah for Hovstad! Hurrah, hurrah!

DR. STOCKMANN. The kind of mob I'm talking about isn't only to be found at the bottom of the barrel. It swarms and mills all around us, even among the high peaks of society. Just look at your own smug, sleek Mayor! My brother Peter's as good a mobster as ever walked in two shoes.

Laughter and hisses.

MAYOR. I protest against these personal remarks.

DR. STOCKMANN (*unperturbed*). And that isn't because he stems like me from a villainous old pirate from Pomerania or somewhere down there—for we do—!

MAYOR. It's absurd, it's a myth! I deny it!

DR. STOCKMANN. Because he thinks what his superiors think, and his opinions are the opinions he's heard them express. The men who do that are spiritually of the mob; and that's why my noble brother Peter is so frighteningly un-

aristocratic in all essentials—and consequently so terrified
of all things liberal.

MAYOR. Mr. Chairman—!

HOVSTAD. So it's the aristocrats who are the liberals in this
country? That really is a new discovery!

Laughter among the CROWD.

DR. STOCKMANN. Yes, that's part of my discovery too. And
the reason is that liberality is almost exactly the same as
morality. And I say it's quite indefensible of the *Tribune*
day after day to proclaim the false gospel that the masses,
the mob, the solid majority, have a monopoly on liberality
and morality, and that vice and corruption and every kind
of spiritual filth are a kind of pus that oozes out of culture,
just as all that beastly stuff in the Baths oozes down from
the tanneries at Moellerdal!

Confusion and interruptions.

DR. STOCKMANN (*unperturbed, laughs in his excitement*).
And yet this same *People's Tribune* can preach that
the masses and the mob must be elevated to a higher
standard of living! Good God Almighty, if what the *People's Tribune* teaches were true, then to elevate the
masses would simply be to start them on the road to ruin!
But luckily the idea that culture demoralises is an old
inherited fairy tale. No, it's stupidity, poverty, and foul
living conditions that do the devil's work! In a house where
the rooms aren't aired and the floors swept every day—
my wife Catherine says they ought to be scrubbed, too,
but there can be two opinions on that—in such a house, I
say, within two or three years people lose the capacity for
moral thought and moral action. Lack of oxygen debilitates
the conscience. And there's a shortage of oxygen in many,
many houses in this town, from the sound of things, if
the whole of this damned majority can be so devoid of
conscience as to want to build the prosperity of their town
on a quagmire of deceit and lies.

ASLAKSEN. You can't cast an accusation like that against a whole community!

A MAN. I appeal to the Chairman to order the speaker to stand down.

EXCITED VOICES. Yes, yes! That's right! Make him stand down!

DR. STOCKMANN (*explodes*). Then I'll shout the truth at every street corner! I'll write in the newspapers of other towns! The whole country shall be told what is happening here!

HOVSTAD. It sounds almost as though the Doctor wishes to destroy this town.

DR. STOCKMANN. Yes, I love this town where I was born so dearly that I would rather destroy it than see it flourish because of a lie!

ASLAKSEN. Those are strong words.

Shouts and whistling. MRS. STOCKMANN *coughs in vain; the* DOCTOR *no longer hears her.*

HOVSTAD (*shouts through the uproar*). The man who can want to destroy a whole community must be a public enemy!

DR. STOCKMANN (*with increasing excitement*). A community that lives on lies deserves to be destroyed! I say that the town that houses such a community should be levelled to the ground! All those who live by lies ought to be exterminated like vermin! You will end by contaminating the entire country! You will bring it to the pass where the whole land will deserve to be laid waste! And if things go that far, then I say with all my heart: "Let the whole land be laid waste! Let the whole people be exterminated!"

A MAN. That's talking like an enemy of the people!

BILLING. There speaks the voice of the people, by jingo!

THE WHOLE CROWD (*screams*). Yes, yes, yes! He's an enemy of the people! He hates his country! He hates the people!

ASLAKSEN. Both as a citizen and as a human being I am deeply shocked by what I have had to hear. Dr. Stockmann has shown himself in his true colours in a manner of which I should never have dreamed him capable. I fear I must support the view expressed a moment ago by re-

spected citizens; and I move that we embody this opinion
in a resolution. I suggest the following: "This meeting declares the medical officer at the Baths, Dr. Thomas Stockmann, an enemy of the people."

Deafening cheers and applause. Many of the CROWD *form a
circle around* DR. STOCKMANN *and whistle at him.* MRS.
STOCKMANN *and* PETRA *have got to their feet.* MORTEN *and*
EILIF *are fighting with the other* SCHOOLBOYS, *who have been
whistling too. Some* ADULTS *part them.*

DR. STOCKMANN (*to the people who have been whistling*).
You fools! I tell you—!

ASLAKSEN (*rings his bell*). The Doctor no longer has the floor.
A formal ballot will take place; but to protect personal
feelings the voting should be done in writing and anonymously. Have you any clean paper, Mr. Billing?

BILLING. I've both blue and white here—

ASLAKSEN (*descends from the dais*). Good, that'll save time.
Tear it into squares; like that, yes. (*To the* CROWD.) Blue
means no, white means yes. I'll collect the votes myself.

The MAYOR *leaves the hall.* ASLAKSEN *and a couple of other*
CITIZENS *go around the* CROWD *with the pieces of paper in
hats.*

1ST CITIZEN (*to* HOVSTAD). What's come over the Doctor?
What's one to think?

HOVSTAD. You know how impulsive he is.

2ND CITIZEN (*to* BILLING). I say, you're a regular visitor in
that house. Have you ever noticed—does the fellow drink?

BILLING. I don't know what to reply, by jingo! There's always toddy on the table when anyone comes.

3RD CITIZEN. I think he just goes off his head now and then.

1ST MAN. Yes, don't they say there's madness in the family?

BILLING. Could be.

4TH MAN. No, it's pure spite. Wants revenge for something
or other.

BILLING. He did say something the other day about a rise in
salary. But he didn't get it.

ALL THE MEN (*with one voice*). Ah, that explains it!

THE DRUNK MAN (*in the thick of the* CROWD). I want a blue one! And I want a white one too!

SHOUTS. There's the drunk man again! Throw him out!

MORTEN KIIL (*comes up to* DR. STOCKMANN). Well, Stockmann, you see now what happens once you start playing monkey tricks?

DR. STOCKMANN. I have done my duty.

MORTEN KIIL. What was that you were saying about the tanneries at Moellerdal?

DR. STOCKMANN. You heard. I said that that's where all the filth comes from.

MORTEN KIIL. From my tannery too?

DR. STOCKMANN. I'm afraid your tannery is the worst of all.

MORTEN KIIL. Are you going to print that in the papers?

DR. STOCKMANN. I shall hide nothing.

MORTEN KIIL. That'll cost you dear, Stockmann. (*Goes.*)

A FAT MAN (*goes across to* HORSTER, *without greeting the* LADIES). Well, Captain, so you lend your house to enemies of the people?

HORSTER. I reckon I can do what I like with my own property.

FAT MAN. Then you won't object if I do the same with mine?

HORSTER. What do you mean?

FAT MAN. You'll hear from me tomorrow. (*Turns and goes.*)

PETRA. Isn't that the man who owns your ship, Captain Horster?

HORSTER. Yes.

ASLAKSEN (*with the voting papers in his hand, steps up onto the dais and rings his bell*). Gentlemen, allow me to inform you of the result. With only a single dissentient vote—

A YOUNG MAN. That's the drunk man!

ASLAKSEN. With only one dissentient vote, and that of a man not sober, this gathering of citizens unanimously declares the medical officer of the Baths, Dr. Thomas Stockmann, an enemy of the people! (*Shouts and gestures of approval.*) Long live our ancient and noble community! (*More cheers.*) Long live our worthy and active Mayor, who has so loyally ignored the ties of blood! (*Cheers.*) The meeting is closed. (*He steps down.*)

BILLING. Three cheers for the Chairman!

WHOLE CROWD. Hurrah for Mr. Aslaksen! Hurrah! Hurrah!

DR. STOCKMANN. My hat and coat, Petra. Captain, have you room in your ship for passengers to the new world?

HORSTER. For you and yours, Doctor, I'll make room.

DR. STOCKMANN (*as* PETRA *helps him on with coat*). Good! Come, Catherine! Come, boys! (*He takes his wife by the arm.*)

MRS. STOCKMANN (*quietly*). Thomas dear, let's go out the back way.

DR. STOCKMANN. No back way for me, Catherine! (*Raises his voice.*) You'll hear from your enemy of the people before he shakes the dust of this town from his feet! I'm not so forgiving as a certain person. I don't say "I forgive ye, for ye know not what ye do!"

ASLAKSEN (*shouts*). That comparison's a blasphemy, Dr. Stockmann!

BILLING. I'll say it is, by Go—! What a dreadful thing for respectable people to hear!

A COARSE VOICE. He's threatening us now!

EXCITED SHOUTS. Let's break his windows! Throw him in the fjord!

A MAN (*in the* CROWD). Blow your horn, Evensen! (*He imitates the sound of the horn twice.*)

Blasts on the horn, whistles and wild cries. The DOCTOR *goes with his family towards the door.* HORSTER *clears a way for them.*

THE WHOLE CROWD (*howls after them as they go*). Enemy of the people! Enemy of the people! Enemy of the people!

BILLING (*as he puts his notes in order*). I'm damned if I'll drink toddy with them tonight, by jingo!

The CROWD *swarms towards the door. The shouting spreads outside. From the street can be heard the cry:* "Enemy of the people! Enemy of the people! Enemy of the people!"

ACT FIVE

DR. STOCKMANN's *study. Bookshelves and cupboards containing medicine bottles along the walls. In the background is the exit to the hall; downstage left is the door to the living-room. In the wall on the right are two windows, all the panes of which are smashed. In the middle of the room stands the* DOCTOR's *desk, covered with books and papers. The room is in disorder. It is morning.*

DR. STOCKMANN, *in dressing gown and slippers and with his smoking-cap on his head, is crouched down raking under one of the cupboards with an umbrella. At length he pulls out a stone.*

DR. STOCKMANN (*speaks through the open door into the living-room*). Catherine, I've found another!

MRS. STOCKMANN (*from the living-room*). Oh, you'll find a lot more yet.

DR. STOCKMANN (*puts the stone among a heap of others on the table*). I shall keep these stones as sacred relics. Eilif and Morten shall see them every day, and when they're grown up they shall inherit them from me. (*Rakes under a bookshelf.*) Hasn't—what the devil's her name?—you know, the maid—hasn't she gone for the glazier yet?

MRS. STOCKMANN (*enters*). He said he didn't know if he'd be able to come today.

DR. STOCKMANN. The truth is, he doesn't dare.

MRS. STOCKMANN. Yes, Randine says he daren't because of the neighbours. (*Speaks into the living-room.*) What is it, Randine? Very well. (*Goes inside and returns immediately.*) Here's a letter for you, Thomas.

DR. STOCKMANN. Give it to me. (*Opens it and reads.*) I see.

MRS. STOCKMANN. Who's it from?

DR. STOCKMANN. The landlord. He's giving us notice to quit.

MRS. STOCKMANN. Is he really? He seems such a decent man—

DR. STOCKMANN (*looks at the letter*). He daren't do otherwise, he says. He's very sorry, but he daren't do otherwise—his fellow-citizens—respect for public opinion—certain obligations—dare not offend certain persons of influence—

MRS. STOCKMANN. There, Thomas, you see.

DR. STOCKMANN. Yes, yes, I see. They're all cowards in this town; none of them dares do anything for fear of the others. (*Throws the letter on the table.*) But we don't have to worry, Catherine. We're off to the new world now—

MRS. STOCKMANN. Thomas, do you really think it's a good idea, this going away?

DR. STOCKMANN. Am I to stay here when they've pilloried me as an enemy of the people, branded me, broken my windows? And just look at this, Catherine! They've torn my trousers, too!

MRS. STOCKMANN. Oh, no! And they're your best!

DR. STOCKMANN. One should never wear one's best trousers when one goes out to fight for freedom and truth. Oh, I don't mind so much about the trousers—you can always patch them up for me. It's the fact that these riff-raff dare to threaten me as though they were my equals—that's the thing I can't damned well stomach!

MRS. STOCKMANN. Yes, Thomas, they've behaved shockingly to you in this town. But does that mean we have to leave the country?

DR. STOCKMANN. Do you think the rabble aren't just as insolent in other towns? Oh, yes, Catherine—there isn't twopence to choose between them. To hell with the curs, let them yelp—that's not the worst. The worst is that throughout this country all the people are just party slaves. Mind you, they're probably not much better in America; the majority's rampant there too, and liberal public opinion and all the rest of the rubbish. But the context is larger there, you see. They may kill you, but they won't torture you slowly; they don't pin a free man in a vice like they do here. And if you want to, you can stay independent outside it all. (*Walks across the room.*) If only I knew of some primaeval forest or a little South Sea island that was going cheap—

MRS. STOCKMANN. But what about the boys, Thomas?

DR. STOCKMANN (*stops*). How extraordinary you are, Catherine! Would you rather they grew up in a society like this? You saw for yourself last night that half the people are raving lunatics; and if the other half haven't lost their wits it's only because they're beasts that don't have any wits to lose.

MRS. STOCKMANN. But, Thomas dear, you're so careless about what you say.

DR. STOCKMANN. What! Don't I tell them the truth? Don't they turn every idea upside down? Don't they merge right and wrong so that they can't tell the difference? Don't they call everything a lie which I know to be true? But the maddest thing of all is that you get grown men of liberal inclinations getting together in groups and convincing themselves and other people that they're progressive thinkers! Did you ever hear the like, Catherine?

MRS. STOCKMANN. Yes, yes, it's all very stupid, but—

PETRA *enters from the living-room.*

MRS. STOCKMANN. Are you back from school already?

PETRA. I've got the sack.

MRS. STOCKMANN. The sack?

DR. STOCKMANN. You too!

PETRA. Mrs. Busk gave me notice. So I thought I'd better leave at once.

DR. STOCKMANN. Quite right, by Heaven!

MRS. STOCKMANN. Who'd have thought Mrs. Busk was such a nasty woman?

PETRA. Oh, Mother, she's not nasty. It was quite obvious she didn't like doing it. But she said she dared not do otherwise. So I got the sack.

DR. STOCKMANN (*laughs and rubs his hands*). Dared not do otherwise! She too! Oh, that's splendid!

MRS. STOCKMANN. Well, after those dreadful scenes last night, you can't—

PETRA. It wasn't only that. Listen to this, Father.

DR. STOCKMANN. Yes?

PETRA. Mrs. Busk showed me no less than three letters she'd received this morning—

DR. STOCKMANN. Anonymous, of course?

PETRA. Yes.

DR. STOCKMANN. They daren't even sign their names, Catherine.

PETRA. Two of them stated that a gentleman who frequents this house announced in the Club last night that I held excessively free views on various subjects—

DR. STOCKMANN. I hope you didn't deny that.

PETRA. Not on your life! Mrs. Busk expresses pretty free views herself when we're alone together; but now that this has come out about me, she didn't dare to keep me.

MRS. STOCKMANN. Fancy—"a gentleman who frequents this house"! You see what thanks you get for your hospitality, Thomas!

DR. STOCKMANN. We won't go on living in this jungle any longer. Pack the bags as quickly as you can, Catherine. The sooner we get away from here, the better.

MRS. STOCKMANN. Hush—I think there's someone in the hall. Go and look, Petra.

PETRA (*opens the door*). Oh, is it you, Captain Horster? Please come in.

HORSTER (*from the hall*). Good morning. I felt I had to come along and see how everything was.

DR. STOCKMANN (*shakes his hand*). Thank you. It's extremely good of you.

MRS. STOCKMANN. And thank you for seeing us safely back last night, Captain Horster.

PETRA. How did you manage to get home again?

HORSTER. Oh, I managed. I'm pretty strong; and those fellows bark worse than they bite.

DR. STOCKMANN. Yes, isn't it amazing what wretched cowards
they are! Come here, I'll show you something. Look, here
are all the stones they threw through our windows. Just
look at them! Upon my soul, there aren't more than two
decent rocks in the whole lot; the others are just pebbles
—mere gravel! And yet they stood out there howling, and
swearing they'd beat the life out of me—but action—action—no, you won't see much of that in this town.

HORSTER. Just as well for you on this occasion, Doctor.

DR. STOCKMANN. Of course! But it annoys me all the same;
for if it ever comes to a serious fight, in defence of our
country, you'll see, Captain Horster—public opinion'll be
for safety first, and this sacred majority'll run for their lives
like a flock of sheep. That's what's so sad—it really hurts
me to think of it—no, damn it, I'm just being stupid!
They've said I'm an enemy of the people, so let me be an
enemy of the people!

MRS. STOCKMANN. You'll never be that, Thomas.

DR. STOCKMANN. Don't be so sure, Catherine. An ugly word
can be like the scratch of a needle on the lung. And that
damned phrase—I can't forget it—it's got stuck down here
in the pit of my stomach, and it's lying there chafing and
corroding me like an acid. And there's no magnesia that
will neutralise that.

PETRA. You must just laugh at them, Father.

HORSTER. People will think differently of you in time, Doctor.

MRS. STOCKMANN. Yes, Thomas, that's as sure as you're standing here.

DR. STOCKMANN. Perhaps, when it's too late. Well, it's their
funeral! Let them live like beasts; they'll be sorry they
drove a patriot into exile. When do you sail, Captain
Horster?

HORSTER. Hm—that was what I came to talk to you about,
as a matter of fact—

DR. STOCKMANN. Why, has something happened to the ship?

HORSTER. No. It's just that I shan't be going with her.

PETRA. They surely haven't given you the sack?

HORSTER (smiles). Indeed they have!

PETRA. You too!

MRS. STOCKMANN. There, Thomas, you see!

DR. STOCKMANN. And just because I spoke the truth! Oh, if I'd ever dreamed that such a thing could happen—

HORSTER. Don't worry about me. I'll find a job with a company somewhere else.

DR. STOCKMANN. But that boss of yours is a rich man, he's completely independent! Oh, damn, damn!

HORSTER. He's fair enough in the ordinary way. He said himself, he'd have liked to have kept me, if only he'd dared—

DR. STOCKMANN (laughs). But he didn't dare! No, of course not!

HORSTER. It isn't so easy, he said, when you belong to a party—

DR. STOCKMANN. That's the truest word he ever uttered! A party is like a mincing machine; it grinds everyone's brains into a pulp, and all you're left with is human sausages, all identical!

MRS. STOCKMANN. Thomas, really!

PETRA (to HORSTER). If only you hadn't seen us home, this might never have happened.

HORSTER. I don't regret it.

PETRA (holds out her hand). Thank you!

HORSTER (to DR. STOCKMANN). What I wanted to say was, if you still want to go, I have thought of another way—

DR. STOCKMANN. Fine; as long as we can get away quickly—

MRS. STOCKMANN. Hush—wasn't that a knock at the door?

PETRA. I think it's Uncle.

DR. STOCKMANN. Aha! (Shouts.) Come in!

MRS. STOCKMANN. Now, Thomas dear, do promise me—

The MAYOR enters from the hall.

MAYOR (in the doorway). Oh, you're engaged. I'll come back later—

DR. STOCKMANN. No, no. Please come in.

MAYOR. I wanted to speak to you privately.

MRS. STOCKMANN. We'll go into the living-room.

HORSTER. And I'll come back later.

DR. STOCKMANN. No, you go in too. I want to know more about that—

HORSTER. Right, I'll wait, then.

He goes with MRS. STOCKMANN *and* PETRA *into the living-room.*

MAYOR (*says nothing but glances at the windows*).

DR. STOCKMANN. Do you find it draughty here today? Put your hat on.

MAYOR. Thank you, if I may. (*Does so.*) I think I caught a cold last night. I stood there shivering—

DR. STOCKMANN. Really? I found it warm enough.

MAYOR. I regret that it didn't lie within my power to prevent those nocturnal extravagances.

DR. STOCKMANN. Did you come out here to tell me that?

MAYOR (*takes out a large letter*). I have this document for you, from the Directors of the Baths.

DR. STOCKMANN. Am I dismissed?

MAYOR. From the date of writing. (*Puts the letter on the table.*) It distresses us; but, frankly, we had no choice. Public opinion being what it is, we didn't dare—

DR. STOCKMANN (*smiles*). Didn't dare? I've heard that word before today.

MAYOR. I beg you to realise your position. From now on you can't reckon on having any practice whatever in this town.

DR. STOCKMANN. To hell with the practice! But what makes you so sure?

MAYOR. The Property Owners' Association has drawn up a round robin which it is sending from house to house. All respectable citizens are being urged not to employ you; and I'll guarantee that not a single householder will dare refuse to sign it. They just won't dare.

DR. STOCKMANN. Yes, yes, I don't doubt that. But what then?

MAYOR. My advice would be that you should leave town for a while—

DR. STOCKMANN. Yes, I'm thinking of doing that.

MAYOR. Good. Then, when you've had six months to think the matter over, you might after mature consideration,

possibly reconcile yourself to issuing a short statement
admitting your error and expressing your regret—

DR. STOCKMANN. And then, you mean, I might get my job
back?

MAYOR. It's not unthinkable.

DR. STOCKMANN. But what about public opinion? You daren't
offend that.

MAYOR. Public opinion is very fickle. And, quite frankly, it's
important to us that you should publish some such admission.

DR. STOCKMANN. Yes, that'd make you smack your lips,
wouldn't it? But, damn it, haven't I told you already what
I think of that kind of chicanery?

MAYOR. Your position was somewhat stronger then. You had
reason to suppose that the whole town was behind you—

DR. STOCKMANN. And now they're rubbing my face in the dirt!
(*Flares up.*) I don't care if I've got the devil himself and
his great-grandmother on my back! Never, I tell you,
never!

MAYOR. A man with a family has no right to act as you're doing. You have no right, Thomas!

DR. STOCKMANN. No right! There's only one thing in the
world that a free man has no right to do! Do you know
what that is?

MAYOR. No.

DR. STOCKMANN. No, of course you don't. But I'll tell you. A
free man has no right to befoul himself like a beast. He has
no right to get himself into the position where he feels the
need to spit in his own face!

MAYOR. That all sounds very plausible—if only there didn't
happen to exist another explanation for your stubbornness
—But there does.

DR. STOCKMANN. What do you mean by that?

MAYOR. You know perfectly well. But as your brother, and as
a man of the world, I would advise you not to put too much
trust in expectations that might so easily not be fulfilled.

DR. STOCKMANN. What on earth are you talking about?

MAYOR. Do you seriously expect me to believe that you don't

know of the arrangements that Morten Kiil has made in his will?

DR. STOCKMANN. I know that what little he has is to go to a home for retired artisans. But what's that got to do with me?

MAYOR. To begin with, it's not so little. Morten Kiil is a pretty wealthy man.

DR. STOCKMANN. I had no idea—!

MAYOR. Hm—hadn't you really? Then I suppose you also have no idea that a considerable proportion of his money is earmarked for your children, and that you and your wife will be able to enjoy the interest for the rest of your lives. Hasn't he told you?

DR. STOCKMANN. Indeed he has not! On the contrary, he's done nothing but complain about how disgracefully over-taxed he is. But are you quite sure of this, Peter?

MAYOR. I have it from an impeccable source.

DR. STOCKMANN. But, good Heavens—that means Catherine's future is secured—and the children's too! I say, I must tell her! (*Shouts.*) Catherine, Catherine!

MAYOR (*holds him back*). Hush, don't say anything yet.

MRS. STOCKMANN (*opens the door*). What is it?

DR. STOCKMANN. Nothing, my dear. Go back in again.

MRS. STOCKMANN *closes the door.*

DR. STOCKMANN (*paces up and down the room*). Their future secured! I can't believe it! All of them—and for life! Oh, it's a wonderful feeling to know that one's future is se-cured. For ever!

MAYOR. But that's just what it isn't. Morten Kiil can revoke that will any day or hour that he chooses.

DR. STOCKMANN. But he won't, my dear Peter. The Badger's much too delighted at the embarrassment I've caused to you and your worthy friends.

MAYOR (*starts and looks searchingly at him*). Aha! So that's the explanation!

DR. STOCKMANN. What do you mean?

MAYOR. This whole thing's been a conspiracy. These violent

and unprincipled accusations which you've levelled against the authorities in the name of truth were simply your price for being remembered in that vindictive old idiot's will.

DR. STOCKMANN (*almost speechless*). Peter—you are the lowest bastard I have ever met in all my life!

MAYOR. Things are finished between us now. Your dismissal is final. Now we have a weapon against you. (*He goes.*)

DR. STOCKMANN. The filthy—damn, damn! (*Shouts.*) Catherine! Scrub the floors behind him! Tell her to bring in a bucket—that girl—what the devil's her name?—the one who's always got a dirty nose—!

MRS. STOCKMANN (*in the doorway to the living-room*). Hush, hush, Thomas, please!

PETRA (*also in the doorway*). Father, Grandfather's here and says can he speak to you privately?

DR. STOCKMANN. Yes, of course. (*At the door.*) Come in, Father.

MORTEN KIIL *comes in.* DR. STOCKMANN *closes the door behind him.*

DR. STOCKMANN. Well, what is it? Sit down.

MORTEN KIIL. No, I won't sit. (*Looks around.*) Nice and cosy it looks here today, Stockmann.

DR. STOCKMANN. Yes, doesn't it?

MORTEN KIIL. Very nice. And fresh air, too! You've got enough of that oxygen you were talking about last night! Your conscience feels pretty good today, I suppose?

DR. STOCKMANN. Yes, it does.

MORTEN KIIL. I thought it would. (*Thumps himself on the breast.*) But do you know what *I've* got here?

DR. STOCKMANN. A good conscience too, I hope.

MORTEN KIIL (*snorts*). No, something better than that.

Takes out a thick pocketbook, opens it and shows a wad of papers.

DR. STOCKMANN (*looks at him in amazement*). Shares in the Baths?

MORTEN KIIL. They weren't hard to come by today.

DR. STOCKMANN. You mean you've been out and bought—?

MORTEN KIIL. As many as I could afford.

DR. STOCKMANN. But, my dear Mr. Kiil—the state those Baths are in now, you—!

MORTEN KIIL. If you act like a sensible man, you'll soon have them on their feet again.

DR. STOCKMANN. You see for yourself I'm doing all I can, but—! The people of this town are quite mad!

MORTEN KIIL. You said last night that the worst of the filth comes from my tannery. But if that were true, then my grandfather and my father before me, and I myself, have been polluting this town for generations like three angels of death. Do you think I'm going to let an imputation like that hang over my head?

DR. STOCKMANN. I'm afraid it looks as though you'll have to.

MORTEN KIIL. No, thank you! I value my name and reputation. People call me the Badger, I'm told. A badger's a dirty beast, isn't it? Well, I'll prove them wrong. I intend to live and die clean.

DR. STOCKMANN. And how are you going to go about that?

MORTEN KIIL. You're going to make me clean, Stockmann.

DR. STOCKMANN. I!

MORTEN KIIL. Do you know what money I've used to buy these shares with? No, you can't; but I'll tell you. It's the money Catherine and Petra and the boys are going to inherit when I'm gone. I've managed to put a little aside, you see.

DR. STOCKMANN (*flares up*). You mean you've spent Catherine's money on this?

MORTEN KIIL. Yes, now it's all invested in the Baths. So now we'll see if you're really as daft as you pretend, Stockmann. Every time you say there's vermin coming out of my tannery, it'll be as though you were cutting a pound of flesh from your wife's body, and Petra's and the children. But no self-respecting husband and father would do such a thing—unless he really was mad.

DR. STOCKMANN (*walks up and down*). Yes, but I *am* mad! I *am* mad!

MORTEN KIIL. You can't be that mad when your wife and children are at stake.

DR. STOCKMANN (*stops in front of him*). Why couldn't you have come and spoken to me before you went and bought all this waste paper?

MORTEN KIIL. Actions speak louder than words.

DR. STOCKMANN (*wanders around restlessly*). If only I weren't so sure—! But I *know* I'm right!

MORTEN KIIL (*weighs the pocketbook in his hand*). If you persist in this lunacy, these shares won't be worth much, you know.

He puts the pocketbook back in his pocket.

DR. STOCKMANN. But, damn it, science must be able to find some way. A preventative; or a purifier or something—

MORTEN KIIL. You mean something to kill these vermin?

DR. STOCKMANN. Yes, or render them harmless.

MORTEN KIIL. Couldn't you try rat poison?

DR. STOCKMANN. Oh, no, no! But everyone keeps saying it's just a fancy of mine. All right, then, let them have it that way. Those ignorant, narrow-minded curs denounced me as an enemy of the people, didn't they? And all but tore the clothes off my back!

MORTEN KIIL. And smashed your windows.

DR. STOCKMANN. Yes. And then this question of my duty towards my family. I must talk to Catherine. She knows about these things.

MORTEN KIIL. That's a good idea. She's a sensible woman. Follow her advice.

DR. STOCKMANN (*turns on him*). Why did you have to do such a stupid thing? Hazarding Catherine's money, and putting me in this frightful predicament! When I look at you, I feel as though I was looking at the devil himself—

MORTEN KIIL. Then I'd best be off. But I want your answer by two o'clock. If it's no, I'm giving these shares to the Old Folks Home—and I'll do it today.

DR. STOCKMANN. And what will Catherine get then?
MORTEN KIIL. Not a farthing.

The door to the hall is opened. HOVSTAD *and* ASLAKSEN *are seen there.*

MORTEN KIIL. Well! Look whom we have here!
DR. STOCKMANN (*stares at them*). What the devil—? Do you two still dare to visit me?
HOVSTAD. Indeed we do.
ASLAKSEN. We've something we want to talk to you about.
MORTEN KIIL (*whispers*). Yes or no—by two o'clock!
ASLAKSEN (*glances at* HOVSTAD). Aha!

MORTEN KIIL *goes.*

DR. STOCKMANN. Well, what do you want? Make it short.
HOVSTAD. I dare say you don't feel too kindly towards us in view of the stand we took at last night's meeting—
DR. STOCKMANN. Stand, you call it! A fine stand indeed! You just lay down like a couple of old women! Damn the pair of you!
HOVSTAD. Call it what you like; we *couldn't* do otherwise.
DR. STOCKMANN. You *dared* not do otherwise? Isn't that what you mean?
HOVSTAD. If you wish.
ASLAKSEN. But why didn't you tip us off? You only needed to drop a hint to Mr. Hovstad or me.
DR. STOCKMANN. Hint? About what?
ASLAKSEN. Why you were doing it.
DR. STOCKMANN. I don't understand.
ASLAKSEN (*nods conspiratorially*). Oh, yes you do, Dr. Stockmann.
HOVSTAD. There's no need to keep it secret any longer.
DR. STOCKMANN (*looks from one to the other*). What the devil—?
ASLAKSEN. Forgive the question, but isn't your father-in-law going round the town buying up all the shares in the Baths?
DR. STOCKMANN. He has bought some today; but—

ASLAKSEN. You'd have done wiser to employ someone else. Someone not quite so close to you.

HOVSTAD. And you shouldn't have done all this under your own name. Nobody need have known that the attack on the Baths came from you. You ought to have taken me into your confidence, Dr. Stockmann.

DR. STOCKMANN (*stares straight in front of him. A light seems to dawn on him, and he says as though thunderstruck*). Is it conceivable? Could such a thing really be *done*?

ASLAKSEN (*smiles*). Apparently. But it ought to be done with a certain subtlety, you know.

HOVSTAD. And there ought to be more than one person in on it. A man doesn't have so much responsibility to bear if he's in partnership.

DR. STOCKMANN (*composedly*). In brief, gentlemen, what do you want?

ASLAKSEN. Mr. Hovstad can explain better than—

HOVSTAD. No, you tell him, Aslaksen.

ASLAKSEN. Well, it's just this really, that now we know how the land lies, we think we might venture to put the *People's Tribune* at your disposal.

DR. STOCKMANN. You think you dare risk it? But what about public opinion? Aren't you afraid we might cause a storm?

HOVSTAD. We shall have to ride that storm.

ASLAKSEN. But you'll have to be quick on the trigger, Doctor. As soon as your campaign has done its job—

DR. STOCKMANN. As soon as my father-in-law and I have got all the shares cheaply, you mean—?

HOVSTAD. It is of course principally in the cause of science that you are seeking to gain control of the Baths.

DR. STOCKMANN. Of course. It was in the cause of science that I got the old Badger to come in with me on this. And then we'll tinker a bit with the water system and do a little digging on the beach, and it won't cost the ratepayers half a crown. I think we'll get away with, don't you? Eh?

HOVSTAD. I think so—if you have the *People's Tribune* behind you.

ASLAKSEN. In a free society the press is a power to be feared, Doctor.

DR. STOCKMANN. Quite. And public opinion too. Mr. Aslaksen, you'll answer for the Property Owners' Association?

ASLAKSEN. The Property Owners' Association and the Temperance Society. Have no fear.

DR. STOCKMANN. But, gentlemen—I blush to mention the matter, but—what consideration—er—

HOVSTAD. Well, of course we'd like to help you absolutely gratis. But the *People's Tribune* is going through an awkward period just now; we're having an uphill struggle, and I'm very reluctant to wind things up just now, when there are such splendid causes that need our support.

DR. STOCKMANN. Of course. That'd be a bitter pill for a friend of the people like you to have to swallow. (*Flares up.*) But I—I am an enemy of the people! (*Strides around the room.*) Where's that stick of mine? Where the devil did I put my stick?

HOVSTAD. What do you mean?

ASLAKSEN. You surely aren't thinking of—?

DR. STOCKMANN (*stops*). And suppose I don't give you a penny of my shares? We rich men are pretty close with our money, you must remember.

HOVSTAD. And *you* must remember that this little business of the shares would bear more than one interpretation.

DR. STOCKMANN. Yes, that'd be right up your street, wouldn't it? If I don't come to the aid of the *People's Tribune*, you'll misrepresent my motives—you'll start a witch-hunt, drive me to ground, and throttle the life out of me as a hound throttles a hare!

HOVSTAD. That's the law of nature. Every animal has to fight for survival, you know.

ASLAKSEN. Bread doesn't grow on trees. You must take it where you can find it.

DR. STOCKMANN. Then see if you can find any in the gutter! (*Strides around the room.*) Now, by Heaven, we'll see which is the strongest animal of us three! (*Finds his umbrella.*) Aha! (*Swings it.*) Now—!

HOVSTAD. You wouldn't dare to assault us!

ASLAKSEN. Be careful with that umbrella!

DR. STOCKMANN. Out of the window with you, Mr. Hovstad!

HOVSTAD (*at the doorway to the hall*). Are you out of your mind?

DR. STOCKMANN. Get through that window, Mr. Aslaksen! Jump, I tell you! Don't dally!

ASLAKSEN (*runs round the desk*). Doctor, Doctor, restrain yourself! I'm a weak man—I can't stand excitement—! (*Screams.*) Help, help!

MRS. STOCKMANN, PETRA, *and* CAPTAIN HORSTER *enter from the living-room.*

MRS. STOCKMANN. In Heaven's name, Thomas, what's going on here?

DR. STOCKMANN (*brandishes the umbrella*). Jump out, I tell you! Down into the gutter!

HOVSTAD. An unprovoked assault—I call you to witness, Captain Horster! (*Runs out through the hall.*)

MRS. STOCKMANN (*holds the* DOCTOR). Thomas, for mercy's sake control yourself!

ASLAKSEN (*desperate*). Restraint, Doctor! Restr—oh, dear! (*Scampers out through the living-room.*)

DR. STOCKMANN (*throws away the umbrella*). Damn it, they got away after all!

MRS. STOCKMANN. But what did they want?

DR. STOCKMANN. I'll tell you later. I've other things to think about just now. (*Goes to the table and writes on a visiting card.*) Look at this, Catherine. What do you see here?

MRS. STOCKMANN. "No, no, no"—what does that mean?

DR. STOCKMANN. I'll explain that later too. (*Holds out the card.*) Here, Petra, tell that smutty-nosed girl to run up to the Badger with this as quickly as she can. Hurry!

PETRA *goes out with the card through the hall.*

DR. STOCKMANN. If I haven't had all the Devil's messengers after me today, I really don't know who's left! But now I'll sharpen my pen against them until it's like a dagger!

I'll dip it in gall and venom! I'll fling my inkstand against their stupid skulls!

MRS. STOCKMANN. But Thomas, we're leaving!

PETRA *returns.*

DR. STOCKMANN. Well?

PETRA. She's taken it.

DR. STOCKMANN. Good! Leaving, did you say? No, by God, we're not! We're staying here, Catherine!

PETRA. Staying?

MRS. STOCKMANN. In this town?

DR. STOCKMANN. Yes! This is the chosen battlefield, and it's here that the battle must be fought! And it's here that I shall win! As soon as you've sewn up those trousers of mine, I'll go into town and look for a house. We've got to have a roof over our heads when winter comes.

HORSTER. I can let you have my house.

DR. STOCKMANN. Would you?

HORSTER. Of course. I've plenty of rooms, and I'm hardly ever there.

MRS. STOCKMANN. Oh, Captain Horster, how kind of you!

PETRA. Thank you!

DR. STOCKMANN (*presses his hand*). Thank you, thank you! Well, that problem's behind us! I'll start my campaign this very day! Oh, Catherine, there's so much to be done! But luckily I'll be able to devote my whole time to it. Look at this. I've been sacked from the Baths—

MRS. STOCKMANN (*sighs*). Ah, well. I was expecting that.

DR. STOCKMANN. And they want to take away my practice too! All right, let them! At least I'll keep my poor patients —they're the ones who can't pay—well, Heaven knows they're the ones who need me most. But, by God, they'll have to listen to me! I'll preach to them morning, noon, and night.

MRS. STOCKMANN. Oh, Thomas, Thomas! Surely you've seen what good preaching does!

DR. STOCKMANN. You really are absurd, Catherine! Am I to allow myself to be chased from the field by public opinion, and the majority, and such fiddle-faddle? No, thank you! What I want is so simple and straightforward and easy! I only want to knock it into the heads of these curs that the Liberals are the most insidious enemies of freedom—that party programmes strangle every new truth that deserves to live—and that expediency and self-interest turn morality and justice upside down, so that in the end life here becomes intolerable. Well, Captain Horster, don't you think I ought to be able to get people to grasp that?

HORSTER. I dare say. I don't really understand these things.

DR. STOCKMANN. Well, you see, the real point is this! It's the party bosses—they're the ones who've got to be rooted out! A party boss is like a hungry wolf—he needs a certain number of baby lambs to devour every year if he is to survive. Look at Hovstad and Aslaksen! How many innocent and vital young idealists have they knocked on the head! Or else they mangle and maul them till they're fit for nothing but to be property owners or subscribers to the *People's Tribune!* (*Half sits on the table.*) Come here, Catherine! Look how beautifully the sun's shining in through the windows today! And smell this glorious, fresh spring air which is being wafted in to us.

MRS. STOCKMANN. Oh, my dear Thomas, if only we could live on sunshine and spring air!

DR. STOCKMANN. Well, you may have to pinch and scrape a little, but we'll manage. That's the least of my worries. No, the worst is that I don't know of anyone sufficiently free and unplebeian to carry on my work after me.

PETRA. Oh, never mind that, Father. You'll find someone in time. Look, here are the boys!

EILIF *and* MORTEN *enter from the living-room.*

MRS. STOCKMANN. Have you been given a holiday today?

MORTEN. No. But we had a fight with the other boys in the break, so—

EILIF. That's not true! It was the other boys who fought with us!

MORTEN. Yes. So I said to Dr. Roerlund I thought it would be better if we stayed at home for a few days.

DR. STOCKMANN (*snaps his fingers and jumps from the table*). I've got it! By Heaven, I've got it! Neither of you shall ever set foot in that school again!

THE BOYS. Not go to school!

MRS. STOCKMANN. But, Thomas—!

DR. STOCKMANN. Never, I say! I'll teach you myself! You won't learn a damned thing—

MORTEN. Hurray!

DR. STOCKMANN. But I'll make you free men—aristocrats! Petra, you'll have to help me.

PETRA. Yes, Father, of course.

DR. STOCKMANN. And we'll hold the school in the room where they branded me as an enemy of the people. But we need more pupils. I must have at least twelve to begin with.

MRS. STOCKMANN. You won't find them in this town.

DR. STOCKMANN. We shall see. (*To the* BOYS.) Do you know any street urchins—real guttersnipes—?

EILIF. Oh yes, Father, I know lots!

DR. STOCKMANN. That's fine! Get hold of a few for me. I'm going to experiment with mongrels for once. They have good heads on them sometimes.

EILIF. But what shall we do when we've become free men and aristocrats?

DR. STOCKMANN. Then, my boys, you'll chase all these damned politicians into the Atlantic Ocean!

EILIF *looks somewhat doubtful.* MORTEN *jumps and cheers.*

MRS. STOCKMANN. Let's hope it won't be the politicians who'll chase you out, Thomas.

DR. STOCKMANN. Are you quite mad, Catherine? Chase me out! Now, when I am the strongest man in town?

MRS. STOCKMANN. The strongest—now?

DR. STOCKMANN. Yes! I'll go further! I am now one of the strongest men in the whole world.

MORTEN. Hurrah!

DR. STOCKMANN (*lowers his voice*). Hush! You mustn't talk about it yet! But I've made a great discovery!

MRS. STOCKMANN. Not again!

DR. STOCKMANN. Yes—yes! (*Gathers them round him and whispers to them.*) The fact is, you see, that the strongest man in the world is he who stands most alone.

MRS. STOCKMANN (*smiles and shakes her head*). Oh, Thomas—!

PETRA (*warmly, clasps his hands*). Father!

ROSMERSHOLM

INTRODUCTION

Ibsen wrote *Rosmersholm* in Munich during the summer of 1886, at the age of fifty-eight.

Two years earlier, while he was finishing *The Wild Duck* in Gossensass, his wife and son had revisited Norway for the first time in eleven years. They had sailed right up to the North Cape, and she had written to him with an infectious enthusiasm about the splendour of the landscape. That September (1884) Bjoernson came to the Tyrol, and Ibsen met his old friend and rival for the first time in twenty years. They spent much time together, and Bjoernson tried to persuade Ibsen to return to Norway and take over the directorship of the Christiania Theatre. Ibsen refused, but only after a struggle. "Both times you threw out the suggestion," he wrote to Bjoernson on 29 September 1884, "a restlessness and longing filled my mind. But . . . my wife has just written to me from up there: 'I would never have believed that we were so much in the black books of the conservatives as has, by a multitude of signs, proved to be the case.' I do not for a moment doubt that her observation is correct. When ten years ago, after a ten years absence, I sailed up the fjord, I literally felt my chest tighten with a feeling of sickness and unease. I had the same sensation during the whole of my stay there; I was no longer myself with all those cold and uncomprehending Norwegian eyes staring at me from the windows and pavements." Nevertheless, Suzannah's letters, and the meetings with Bjoernson, had awakened a nostalgia in him.

During the winter of 1884–85 Ibsen began to lay plans for a new play. As was his custom, he pondered it for months

without putting pen to paper (though his first notes may
possibly date from this period). In April 1885 he wrote optimistically that he was hoping to complete it within a few
months, so that it could be published in time for the Christmas sales. But he had done nothing further about it by the
summer, when on an impulse he yielded to his nostalgia and
decided to go back to Norway. The decision was sudden, for
as late as 25 April he wrote from Rome to his publisher,
Frederik Hegel of Gyldendals, that he was probably going to
spend the summer in the Tyrol "where I hope to be able to
work in peace and get my new play ready by the autumn."
But six weeks later he was in Christiania. En route, in Copenhagen, he declared that he was thinking of spending the rest
of his life in Norway, perhaps purchasing a small house on a
fjord outside Christiania where he could "live in isolation,
occupied exclusively with my work." In the event, however, he stayed less than four months, from the beginning of
June until the end of September. His experiences in Norway
during this summer of 1885 form the background to *Rosmersholm*.

Ibsen spent only a few days in Christiania before proceed-
ing north to Trondheim, but what he saw and heard in that
time left a deep and disagreeable impression on him. The
previous year, 1884, there had been an important political
development in Norway; and an explanation of the events
that led up to this may be helpful to an understanding of
Rosmersholm. The King of Sweden, who was also King of
Norway, ruled the country through a Cabinet, which he
chose personally, and a Storthing, or Parliament; but the
members of the Cabinet had no seats in the Storthing, and
acknowledged no responsibility except to the King. He held
a veto over the Storthing; but this veto was suspensive, not
absolute, so that a bill passed by three successive Storthings
could become law despite the veto.

In the 1870s there arose the incongruous situation that the
Storthing was overwhelmingly Liberal, while the Cabinet
remained Conservative. In 1872, accordingly, the Storthing
passed a bill that Cabinet ministers should sit in the Storthing.

King Oscar vetoed this. It was passed twice more by successive Storthings, and so should have become law; but the King now declared that on matters affecting the Constitution his veto was absolute and permanent. Faced with this apparent impasse, the Storthing took the extreme measure of impeaching the members of the Cabinet before the Supreme Court, and one by one the ministers were dismissed and fined. The King selected a new and equally Conservative ministry; the Storthing dug in its heels; the King refused to yield, and it was rumoured that he was considering a *coup d'état;* but eventually, on 26 June 1884, he sent for the leading Liberal statesman, Johan Sverdrup,[1] and invited him to form a ministry. The conflict thus ended in a complete victory for the Liberals.[2]

Such was the situation that greeted Ibsen when he arrived in Christiania in June 1885. "Since he had last been home," noted Henrik Jaeger in his early biography (I quote Archer's fine translation), "the great political battle had been fought out, and had left behind it a fanaticism and bitterness of spirit which astounded him. He was struck by the brutality of the prevailing tone; he felt himself painfully affected by the rancorous and vulgar personalities which drowned all rational discussion of the principles at stake; and he observed with sorrow the many enmities to which the contest had given rise. Men who had hitherto been the closest friends were now the bitterest foes; and this although they had done each other no personal wrong, but had merely arrived at different views of life. On the whole, he received the impression —as he lately remarked in conversation—that Norway was inhabited not by two million human beings, but by two million cats and dogs. This impression has recorded itself in the picture of party divisions presented in *Rosmersholm*. The bitterness of the vanquished is admirably embodied in Rector Kroll; while the victors' reluctance to speak out their whole

[1] Caricatured by Ibsen as Stensgaard in *The League of Youth*.
[2] For a more detailed account of these happenings, see William Archer's article in the *Fortnightly Review* of September 1885.

hearts is excellently characterized in the freethinker and op-
portunist Mortensgaard."

Ibsen's disillusionment at this evidence of pettiness and
party strife is apparent from a statement he made at Trondheim on 14 June. The local Workers' Association had organized a procession with banners in his honour, and Ibsen
made a speech of thanks. In it, he declared: "There is still
much to be done in this country before we can be said to
have achieved full freedom. But our present democracy
scarcely has the power to accomplish that task. An element
of nobility must enter into our political life, our government,
our members of parliament and our press. I am of course not
thinking of nobility of wealth, of learning, or even of ability
or talent. I am thinking of nobility of character, of mind and
of will. That alone can make us free.[3] And this nobility,
which I hope may be granted to our people, will come to us
from two sources, the only two sections of society which have
not as yet been corrupted by party pressure. It will come to
us from our women and our working men. The reshaping of
social conditions which is now being undertaken in Europe is
principally concerned with the future status of the workers
and of women. That is what I am hoping and waiting for,
and what I shall work for, all I can."

These inter-party bitternesses affected Ibsen personally.
The right-wingers, as Suzannah had noted, regarded him as
an apostate; several of his former friends in Christiania held
aloof from him, or so he felt, and the respectable citizens of
Trondheim did not acclaim him as the workers did. Seventeen
months later, on 10 November 1886, shortly after he had
finished *Rosmersholm,* Ibsen summed up his feelings about
Norway in a letter to Georg Brandes. "The impressions, experiences, and observations which I brought back from my
trip to Norway in the summer of last year," he wrote, "had

---

[3] Ibsen had already adumbrated this idea in *An Enemy of the
People* (1882); and in his notes for *The Wild Duck* he had written: "A new aristocracy will arise. It will not be the aristocracy of
birth or of wealth, of talent or knowledge. The aristocracy of the
future will be the aristocracy of the mind and of the will."

for a long while a confusing effect on me. . . . Never have I felt so foreign to my Norwegian fellow-countrymen's *Thun und Treiben* as after the lessons which this past year has taught me. Never so repelled. Never so nauseated."

There had, however, been one compensation. From Trondheim he had, in June 1885, gone on to Molde, a pretty seaside town on the north-west coast, which so pleased him that he spent two months there.[4] In Molde he met a former acquaintance, the Swedish poet Count Carl Snoilsky. Snoilsky, at forty-four, was thirteen years younger than Ibsen, and had first met him in Rome over twenty years earlier in 1864. They had met again in Sweden in 1869 and 1877, when Ibsen had been disappointed at Snoilsky's apparent movement towards a more conservative outlook (he had taken a position in the Swedish Foreign Office), and at the withering of his creative talent.

In his youth Snoilsky had been a facile and successful poet; but after he had married, and become a civil servant, his creative springs dried up, and for ten years he found himself scarcely able to write a line. "I have wasted my life," he noted sadly in 1874, "and it is too late to change things now." But in 1879, at the age of thirty-eight, he left the Foreign Office, divorced his wife, married one of her relatives, and went abroad into voluntary exile. At once he found himself able to write again, and published one volume after another. But the kind of poetry he was writing now was very different from the charming lyrics that had made his name. He, the refined nobleman, had become absorbed by the class struggle and the spirit of revolution. He longed to enter into contact with the common people; but his own upbringing and aristocratic heritage inhibited him. In 1883, two years before he met Ibsen at Molde, Snoilsky wrote: "Certainly creative literature can have an enormous influence, as Ibsen has shown, in the debating of social problems. . . . [But] my powers do not suffice for so lofty a task, and so broad a public. I dare not aim so high. I am, moreover, conscious of my main handicap—that I have not, from childhood, lived the

[4] He was later to use it as the setting for *The Lady from the Sea*.

life of the *people*—my education and upbringing in the narrow classical tradition have unfitted me, in common with the vast majority of our *littérateurs*, to address the humbler strata of society in a language they understand. Unlike my colleagues, however, I am often painfully conscious of this barrier, this limitation, and do my best to transcend it."

Three years after their divorce, Snoilsky's first wife died of consumption, and many people blamed him for her death. But Ibsen, during the four days he spent with Snoilsky at Molde, took a great liking both to him and to his new wife; he thought her sensitivity and strength of character largely responsible for Snoilsky's regeneration as a person. He was deeply interested in Snoilsky's conviction that poetry should not deal merely with the "beautiful," but should be connected with contemporary thought and ideas (he had boldly and outspokenly defended *Ghosts*); and also in the temperamental difficulty which Snoilsky found in accepting this intellectual conviction. Snoilsky had expressed this difficulty in a poem, *The White Lady*, about the sixteenth-century Duke Charles of Sweden, later King Charles IX, the brother and co-deposer of Erik XIV. Snoilsky portrayed Duke Charles as a man nagged by an uneasy conscience, in contrast to his son, the great Gustav II Adolf, who had no fear of such ghosts. Ibsen had depicted a similar contrast in *The Pretenders*, between Earl Skule and Haakon Haakonsson; and Snoilsky found himself in the same predicament as Earl Skule and Duke Charles—he could not shake off his inherited instincts and identify himself with the people. Gradually Snoilsky had resigned himself to the idea that he really belonged among the mediaeval troubadours rather than among the socially-conscious poets of the eighteen-eighties.[5] Ibsen was

[5] On 4 April 1886 Snoilsky wrote to Ibsen that he was "written out" (*utsjungen*); that he had learned from Ibsen "the untenability of a purely aesthetic appreciation of life," and had come to look on "all poetry that failed to deal with major contemporary problems as something superfluous." He therefore regarded himself as superfluous, and had decided to "retire." Fortunately he did not; and one of his later poems, *Ibsen at Molde*, provides a memorable portrait of Ibsen.

to base the character of John Rosmer very recognizably on Snoilsky; and Rebecca bears certain resemblances, though she is not to be identified with her, to Snoilsky's second wife.

Ibsen left Norway towards the end of September 1885, and returned to Munich. He took some time to sort out his impressions of his visit. "Ever since my return here," he was later to write to Georg Brandes in the letter already quoted (10 November 1886), "I have been plagued by a new play which absolutely demanded to be written. But only when I had completely clarified my experiences, and drawn my conclusions from them, could I think about translating the fruit thereof into a creative work."

He pondered the play all winter and spring. On 4 December 1885 he wrote to Frederik Hegel: "I am now pretty well in the clear with my plan for my new play, and shall be starting to write it in a few days. It will be in four acts, and interests me greatly." Two and a half months later, on 14 February 1886, he wrote to Snoilsky that he was "fully occupied with a new play, which has long been in my thoughts and for which I made some close studies during my trip to Norway during the summer." But still it would not come, and on 20 February he informed Edvard Fallesen, the director of the Royal Theatre in Copenhagen, that it "cannot be expected before the autumn."

Some time during this period, we do not know when, he made some brief notes and began a draft, of which he completed less than an act. The notes contain the following:

WHITE HORSES

He, the refined, aristocratic character, who has changed to a liberal viewpoint and been ostracized by all his former friends and acquaintances. A widower; has been unhappily married to a half-mad melancholic, who ended by drowning herself.

She, the governess of his two daughters, emancipated, hot-blooded, somewhat ruthless beneath a refined exterior. Is regarded by their acquaintances as the evil spirit of the house; an object of suspicion and gossip.

Eldest (sic) *daughter;* is in danger of succumbing to inactivity and loneliness. She has rich talents which are lying unused.

Younger daughter; sharply observant; passions beginning to dawn.

The journalist; genius, tramp.

In the living room of the vicarage. S. and Miss B. in conversation. The student enters from a walk. Old retired apothecary on business; goes. The family assembled. The Captain. The magistrate with daughter on a visit and with an invitation; it is accepted; then the change of heart is to be revealed. The family alone; the talk turns to the white horses.[6]

The few pages which exist of the first draft open with a former priest, aristocratically named Boldt-Roemer, talking to his children's governess, Miss Radeck. Thanks to her, he has seen the light of liberalism and renounced the priesthood; it is hinted that his former wife was drowned in the mill-pool. The local schoolmaster, Hekman, enters, and tries to persuade Boldt-Roemer, whose name now changes to Rosenhjelm, to champion the Conservative cause against Mortensgaard. Rosenhjelm is protesting that he is unfitted for such a task when the fragment ends.

On 25 May 1886 Ibsen scrapped what he had written and began an entirely new draft. The title page shows that it was still to be called *The White Horses,* and that it was now to be in five acts. It progressed swiftly; Act One was ready by 1 June, and Act Two by 8 June. This draft opens similarly to the final version as we know it; the two principals are now named Rebecca and Rosmer; but Rebecca is Rosmer's second wife. Dr. Gylling (Kroll) enters; it is established that the Rosmers are newly married. Rosmer's first name is Eilert and his dead wife was Agate (later Agnete); they had a son, Alfred, who is also dead. We learn that the Rosmers have always, by tradition, been alternately soldiers and priests;

[6] This paragraph is separate to the rest, and may have been jotted down at an earlier date.

Rosmer's father, formidably named Eilert Hanibal (*sic*) Rosmer, was a soldier, so his son had to be a priest. "So it has been for more than two hundred years." The tutor, Ulrik Rosenhjelm, enters (Ibsen often, when he abandoned a name, transferred it to some other character), and makes the references to Rebecca as "the pastor's wife" which are effectively retained in the final version. After he has gone, Gylling wonders whether to get him to write ("anonymously, of course") for the new paper which he (Gylling) is founding as a counterblast to Mortensgaard. Rebecca tells Rosmer that she has given Rosenhjelm an introduction to Mortensgaard; Rosmer observes that Rosenhjelm will now be receiving invitations from both editors. It is established that Rosmer is to reveal his change of heart tomorrow. Rebecca refers to the white horses, and gets Mrs. Helset (*sic*) to tell the legend of them. The act ends with Rebecca saying: "All the free people I have known—all the ones who thought they were free —they've all had some kind of white horse that they never cease to believe in." ROSMER: "You mean that full freedom is to—?" REBECCA: "Is to get rid of one's white horses."

In Act Two, Rosmer reveals to Rebecca that he has shirked revealing his change of heart to his friends. She persuades him to go to Gylling and make a clean breast of it; but Gylling is now announced. Gylling tells of Sejerhjelm's (*sic*) bad behaviour in town. Now at last Rosmer reveals his change of heart, and abandonment of his religious beliefs. Gylling is shocked, and reveals that Beate (*sic*) told him before she killed herself that Rosmer and Rebecca loved each other (though she did not, in this draft, say that they "had" to marry). Rebecca has now become Miss Dankert.

On 10 June Ibsen began Act Three; it is set, as in the final version, in Rosmer's study, and Rebecca has now become Miss West. But five days later, in the middle of the Mortensgaard scene, he scrapped this draft completely, throwing out the title *White Horses* (which he may have thought too reminiscent of *Ghosts*[7]), and renaming it *Rosmersholm*. This

[7] Eight weeks before, on 14 April, he had seen *Ghosts* on the stage for the first time, at Augsburg. This may possibly account for

draft he completed in a day over seven weeks; Act One took from 15–28 June, Act Two from 1–12 July, Act Three from 15–24 July, and Act Four from 26 July to 4 August.

This draft is essentially the play as we know it, though Ibsen made an unusual number of small corrections when he came to fair-copy it, continuing, among other things, to alter the names of the supporting characters. It contains, however, one or two interesting variations. Rebecca tells Rosmer and Gylling that when she came to the district from Finnmark with Dr. West, aged a little over twenty, she was "not what people call an—an innocent woman." Rosmer asks who the man was; she replies: "Someone who had absolute power over me. He had taught me everything. Everything I knew about life then." This description, which may or may not be intended to refer to Dr. West (we do not know whether Ibsen had yet conceived the idea of making him Rebecca's lover) strongly foreshadows the Stranger in Ibsen's next play, *The Lady from the Sea,* into which he was also to put the two daughters of his first notes for *Rosmersholm.* (The Stranger, like Dr. West and Rebecca, came from Finnmark, the extreme north of Norway, a region associated by Norwegians with trolls and strange magic; Rebecca likens herself in the final version to a sea-troll hanging on to the ship of Rosmer's life to hold it back, and it is Rosmer's need to feel clean and pure, without which he cannot feel free, that leaves Rebecca powerless, as church bells take the power from trolls.) And in the last act of this draft, it is Hetman (Brendel), not Rosmer, who gives Rebecca the idea of killing herself to show her love:

HETMAN. Is she leaving?
ROSMER. Tonight.
REBECCA. In half an hour.

---

the obvious similarities between the two plays. Both have as their theme the influence of the dead over the living. In both, the action is dominated by a dead person, Captain Alving and Beata Rosmer. And Rosmer, like Oswald Alving, is the last, unhappy member of his line.

HETMAN. You don't understand how to keep your women. The first one left you too.

ROSMER. Yes, she did.

HETMAN. Brave woman. She went freely—to smooth your path. . . . That woman must have had some kind of wings, I reckon.

REBECCA. Wings? Why wings?

HETMAN. Didn't she raise herself so high that she was able to die for her love? . . . I could have sworn no living soul could do that.

ROSMER. To resort to death—to prove one's love?

REBECCA. I shall not leave tonight.

ROSMER (in anguish). Yes, go! Go!

HETMAN. Stay, my pretty lady. There's no danger for you. He won't tempt you down under the water. Farewell!

When Ibsen fair-copied the play, he altered this, and instead gave Brendel the speech about the necessity of a woman cutting off her finger and ear to show her love for a man. Dr. Arne Duve, in his book *Symbolikken i Henrik Ibsens Skuespill* (1945), points out what Ibsen cannot, of course, have known, that finger and ear are common symbols for the male and female sexual organs; though I have never heard this speech spoken in a way that suggested that either the Brendel or the Rebecca had the faintest idea what it implied. Dr. Duve also observes that Beata means "the happy one," and that the word "west" commonly suggests defeat and death; though I think that here it probably possesses its other symbolic significance of "the unknown," as in the idea, found in so many national mythologies, of mysterious "islands of the west."[8]

On 6 August, Ibsen began his fair copy but, as already noted, he made a great number of small revisions, and did not finish it until 27 September. "This play," he told Hegel in

[8] But a witch named Rebecca West had been burned in Worcestershire during the seventeenth century (the case is mentioned in Margaret Murray's *The God of the Witches*), and it is conceivable that Ibsen had read of this somewhere and, consciously or unconsciously, borrowed the name.

a letter on 2 October, "is to be regarded as the fruit of studies and observations which I had cause to make during my stay in Norway during the summer of last year. It cannot, as far as I can surmise, offer grounds for attack from any quarter. I hope, though, that it may provoke a lively debate. I especially anticipate one in Sweden."

Rosmersholm was published by Gyldendals of Copenhagen on 23 November 1886, in an edition of 8000 copies, and received its premiere at the National Theatre in Bergen on 17 January 1887. Even more than its predecessor, *The Wild Duck*, it baffled the critics and public, and, like *The Wild Duck*—and, for that matter, all the plays that Ibsen subsequently wrote—won nothing like the contemporary acclaim that had greeted *Brand*, *Peer Gynt*, *The Pillars of Society*, *A Doll's House*, and *An Enemy of the People*. It had a cool welcome when it was staged in Christiania on 12 April, and ran for only ten performances. No more than six further performances of it were given in Christiania during the next two years, and it was not produced there again before 1900. Its first performance in Germany, at Augsburg on 6 April 1887, with Ibsen present, was a disaster, and so was the first London production on 23 February 1891, with Florence Farr and F. R. Benson. William Archer collected some of the press reactions in his essay *The Mausoleum of Ibsen*:

A handful of disagreeable and somewhat enigmatical personages . . . Ibsen is a local and provincial dramatist.
                                                        (*The Times*)

Impossible people do wild things for no apparent reason . . . Those portions of the play which are comprehensible are utterly preposterous . . . Ibsen is neither dramatist, poet, philosopher, moralist, teacher, reformer —nothing but a compiler of rather disagreeable eccentricities.   (*Standard*)

Brain-sick extravagances.   (*Daily News*)

Not a play but a tiresome exposition of a fantastic theory that no healthy mind can accept.
                                                (*Morning Advertiser*)

Love, truth, religion and self-respect have still some hold upon us, and it is hardly likely that Ibsen's gloomy ideas will be generally accepted.   (*Morning Post*)

Must nauseate any properly-constituted person.
(*Mirror*)

Gruesome play . . . repulsive drama . . . greeted with the silence of contempt when the curtain finally fell.   (*The People*)

Studies in insanity best fitted for the lecture room in Bedlam . . . At the fall of the curtain there was loud applause and but the faintest attempt at hissing.
(*The Stage*)

The whole affair is provincial and quite contemptible.
(*Saturday Review*)

Mr. Ibsen does not call *Rosmersholm* a farce; but that is because of his modesty . . . To judge it seriously either as literature or as drama is impossible.
(*St. James's Gazette*)

These Ibsen creatures are "neither men nor women, they are ghouls," vile, unlovable, unnatural, morbid monsters, and it were well indeed for society if all such went and drowned themselves at once.   (*Gentlewoman*)

To descant upon such morbid, impracticable rubbish would be an insult to the understanding of every reader, except an Ibsenite . . . If Herr Ibsen were well smothered in mud with his two creations [i.e., *A Doll's House* and *Rosmersholm*], and with every copy of his plays, the world would be all the better for it.
(*Licensed Victuallers' Gazette*)

England was, of course, particularly backward in its appreciation of Ibsen; but the general reaction, even among Ibsen's admirers, was that the play was obscure, and that the characters were abstractions rather than credible human beings. One of the few people to appreciate it was Strindberg who, in the spring following the publication of *Rosmersholm*, wrote an appreciation of it in an essay entitled *Soul-murder*

(*Själamord*). In this, he declared that *Rosmersholm* was "unintelligible to the theatre public, mystical to the semi-educated, but crystal-clear to anyone with a knowledge of modern psychology"—one of the very few occasions on which he ever paid public tribute to Ibsen. One can understand the attraction that *Rosmersholm* held for Strindberg, for he too was deeply interested in "magnetism" and "hypnosis," the ability of one person to gain control over the mind of another. He had treated this theme himself in *The Father*, which he began only two months after *Rosmersholm* appeared, and was to do so again the following year in *Creditors;* while the degenerating effect of an aristocratic heritage was to be the theme, also the following year, of *Miss Julie.*

Gradually *Rosmersholm* came to be appreciated. Bernard Shaw, reviewing Lugné-Poe's Paris production when it visited London in 1895, described the play as "this most enthralling of all Ibsen's works." In Italy, Eleonora Duse made Rebecca one of her most famous roles; Edward Gordon Craig did the decor for her—"one scene only—a vast room of great beauty"—and composed an eloquent programme note. "There is the powerful impression of unseen forces closing in upon the place," he wrote; "we hear continually the long drawn out note of the horn of death." The first American production took place on 28 March 1904 at the Princess Theatre in New York, when Florence Kahn, later the wife of Max Beerbohm, played Rebecca to the Rosmer of William Morris. It was ill-received. "The presentation was in almost every respect a disappointment," commented the *Dramatic Mirror.* "Not only did the players murder the play; they buried its meaning so deep that many of the scenes were unintelligible." Three years later, however, Minnie Fiske presented *Rosmersholm* at New Haven, Connecticut, with herself as Rebecca, on, if we are to believe the records, Christmas Day 1907, bringing it to the Lyric Theatre in New York five days later. It ran there for four weeks, and was then toured for 199 consecutive performances, reaching as far west as San Francisco. The cast included Bruce McRae as Rosmer, George Arliss as Ulrik Brendel, and Florence Mont-

gomery as Mrs. Helseth. The best English Rebecca was probably the young Edith Evans in 1926, though the part was
also finely acted by Flora Robson in 1930 (at Cambridge,
with Robert Donat as Rosmer), and Jean Forbes-Robertson
in 1936. Peggy Ashcroft gave a performance in 1959 which
was widely praised, though I found it deeply disappointing;
admirably accomplished, it suggested none of the passionate
overtones of Rebecca's character. There was no earthly reason why this woman should have killed herself. But she was
handicapped by a horribly flattened and truncated text. To
date (1965), London has seen twelve professional productions of *Rosmersholm,* more than of any other Ibsen play except *Ghosts* (25), *A Doll's House* (20), *Hedda Gabler* (16),
and *The Master Builder* (15).

As stated above (in the introduction to *An Enemy of the
People,* p. 212), Ibsen's letters to the Christiania Theatre
(1878–1899) have recently been published, and several of
these make interesting reference to *Rosmersholm.* On 2 January 1887, replying to Hans Schroeder's suggestions for
casting the play, Ibsen delivered himself of some pungent
comments on the taste of the man who had rejected *Ghosts.*
"You think Mrs. Gundersen was born to play Rebecca. I don't
agree. Mrs. Gundersen's strength is for the big declamatory
line, and there are none of those in my play. How could she
manage these seemingly light but exceedingly pregnant dia-
logues? Dual personalities, complex characters, are not her
forte. Then you want Gundersen to play Rosmer. Permit me
to ask what the effect is likely to be when Rebecca tells how
she has been gripped by "a wild and sensual longing" for
him? Or when Brendel calls him "my boy," etc.? Or when Dr.
Kroll hectors and browbeats him? Is G's personality compati-
ble with this and much else? For Rosmer you must choose
the most delicate and sensitive personality that your theatre
can lay its hands on. . . . That the role of Dr. Kroll, that
pedagogic autocrat, should be entrusted to Mr. Bjoernson[9]
is, I trust, a joke on which I need waste no further ink. Is it,

[9] Bjoern Bjoernson, the son of Bjoernsterne Bjoernson.

though, conceivable that this monstrous idea is being seriously harboured? If the artistic direction of the theatre is so totally lacking in critical and self-critical ability, I fear that I can await the production only with the direst misgivings."

Schroeder yielded, with a fair grace, and the cast was altered in accordance with Ibsen's wishes. A month later, Ibsen addressed to him some further advice about the characters. "Dr. Kroll," he wrote from Munich on 5 February 1887, "is an authoritarian with a passion for domineering as is so often the case with headmasters. He is, of course, of good family; Major Rosmer's son married his sister. The Doctor's manner is therefore that of a well-born government official. Despite a certain asperity which now and then manifests itself, his behaviour in general is friendly and agreeable. He can be lovable when he pleases, or when he is with people he likes. But it is to be noted that he only likes those people who share his opinions. The rest irritate him, and with them he easily becomes ruthless and reveals a tendency towards malice. His appearance is distinguished; he is handsomely dressed, in black. Coat almost down to his knees, but no lower. He wears a white cravat, large and old-fashioned, which goes twice round his neck. I.e., no tie. His dress explains why Ulrik Brendel at first takes him for Pastor Rosmer and then for a 'brother of the cloth.' In Act One, Rosmer also wears a black coat, but grey trousers and a tie or cravat of the same colour. In Acts Three and Four, however, he is dressed entirely in black.[10]

"Rebecca's manner must on no account carry any hint of imperiousness or masculinity. She does not *force* Rosmer forward. She *tempts* him. A controlled power, a quiet determination, are of the essence of her character."

During rehearsals for the Christiania production, Constance Bruun, the young actress who had been chosen instead of Laura Gundersen to play Rebecca, was taken ill,

[10] Oeyvind Anker well observes that Ibsen's minute instructions regarding dress remind one of the meticulous costume drawings he had made during his employment at the Bergen Theatre from 1851 to 1857.

and the part was given to another young actress, Sophie Reimers. She wrote to Ibsen in Munich asking his advice; he gave it briefly (25 March 1887): "No declamation. No theatricalities. No grand mannerisms! Express every mood in a manner that will seem credible and natural. Never think of this or that actress whom you may have seen. Observe the life that is going on around you, and present a real and living human being."

Rosmersholm baffles readers and audiences, to say nothing of directors and actors, even today, and few Rebeccas indeed have ever made convincing either her refusal to marry Rosmer, when that has been her principal aim all along, or her ultimate suicide. By far the most penetrating analysis of the play, and of the secret motives which impel the characters, was made by Sigmund Freud in his essay *Character-Types*, which he wrote during the 1914 war. In the second section of this essay, sub-titled "Those wrecked by success," he deals with the common and disturbing psychological phenomenon of people who, when what they most want at last lies within their grasp, find themselves unable to seize hold of it. After an illuminating consideration of Lady Macbeth, Freud moves on to *Rosmersholm*, and makes an analysis of Rebecca which seems to me utterly convincing:

"Ibsen has made it clear," writes Freud, "by many little touches, worked in with masterly subtlety, that this Rebecca does not actually lie, but is never entirely straightforward. Just as, in spite of her freedom from prejudice, she has understated her age by a year, so is her confession to the two men [Rosmer and Kroll] not entirely complete, and through the persistence of Kroll it is supplemented on some important points. Hence it is open to us, too, to conjecture that the explanation of her refusal only exposes one motive in order to conceal another . . . The influence of Rosmer may even only be a cloak which conceals another influence that was operative, and a notable indication points in this new direction."

When, Freud continues, in the final scene, after her confession about herself and Beata, Rosmer again asks Rebecca to become his wife, by implication forgiving her, "she does not answer, as she might, that no forgiveness can rid her of the consciousness of guilt incurred by her malignant deception of poor Beata; but she charges herself with another reproach which affects us as coming strangely from this freethinking woman, and in no wise corresponds to the importance which Rebecca attaches to it . . . She has had sexual relations with another man; and we do not fail to observe that these relations, which occurred at a time when she was free and accountable to nobody, seem to her a greater hindrance to the union with Rosmer than her truly criminal behaviour to his wife. . . .

"After she has learned that she has been the mistress of her own father, she surrenders herself wholly to her now overmastering sense of guilt. She confesses to Rosmer and Kroll that she was a murderess; she rejects for ever the happiness to which she has paved the way by crime; and prepares for departure. But the true origin of her sense of guilt, which wrecks her at the moment of attainment, remains a secret. We have seen that it is something quite other than the atmosphere of Rosmersholm and the refining influence of Rosmer. . . . Rebecca's feeling of guilt finds its source in the shame of incest, even before Kroll with analytical insight has made her aware of it. When we fully reconstruct and supplement the past, we shall feel sure that she cannot have been without an inkling of the intimate relation between her mother and Dr. West. It must have made a strong impression on her when she became her mother's successor with this man; and she thus stood under the domination of the Oedipus-complex, even though she did not know that this universal phantasy had been a reality in her case. When she came to Rosmersholm, the inward force of this first experience drove her to bring about, by definite action, the same situation which had been realized in the original instance, though not by her doing—to get rid of the wife and mother, that she might take her place with the husband and father. She describes with a convincing insistence how against her will she was obliged to proceed, step by step, to the removal of Beata. . . . Everything that befell her at Rosmersholm, the passion for Rosmer and the enmity towards his wife, was from the first a consequence of the Oedipus-complex—a compulsive replica of her relations with her mother and Dr. West.

"And so the sense of guilt which first causes her to reject Rosmer's proposal is at bottom indistinguishable from the deeper one which drives her to her confession after Kroll has opened her eyes. But just as under the influence of Dr. West she had become a freethinker and contemner of religious morality, so she is transformed by her love for Rosmer into a being with a conscience and an ideal. This much of the mental process within her she does herself understand, and so she is justified in describing Rosmer's influence as the motive of the change in her—the only one of which she could be aware.

"The practising psychoanalytic physician knows how frequently, or how invariably, a girl who enters a household as servant, companion or governess, will consciously or unconsciously weave a day-dream, which derives from the Oedipus-complex, about the disappearance of the mistress of the house and the master taking the newcomer to wife in her stead. *Rosmersholm* is the greatest work of art among those that treat of this common girlish phantasy. What makes it a tragedy is the circumstance that the early history of the heroine in actual fact had completely anticipated her day-dream."

Rosmersholm marks Ibsen's final withdrawal as a playwright from the polemical field. The year after writing it, on 12 September 1887, he declared in a speech at Gothenburg that his political interests were waning and, with them, his eagerness for battle. He may have based the character of Rosmer principally on Snoilsky; but he put a good deal of himself into it too. Although he enjoyed writing and making speeches on controversial subjects, he disliked embroiling himself, and what he had seen of the results of party strife in Norway in 1885 determined him to withdraw still further from the battle. *Rosmersholm* is the last of his plays which introduces public or local politics as a decisive factor in shaping people's characters and destinies. In *The League of Youth, The Pillars of Society, Ghosts,* and *An Enemy of the People,* such politics had played an important part; the actions of Stensgaard, Bernick, Manders, and Peter Stockmann are, at critical moments, influenced by a fear of offending local political opinion. Gregers Werle in *The Wild Duck* is very much a political animal; and *A Doll's House,* though politics do not enter directly into it, struck at the heart of one of the most controversial issues of the day. But in the six plays which follow *Rosmersholm,* the battle is out of earshot. It is the trolls within, not the trolls without, that determine the destinies of Ellida and Hilde Wangel, Hedda Gabler, Halvard Solness, the Allmers, the Borkmans, and Arnold Rubek. They are conscious of strange, sick passions which direct their lives; and *Rosmersholm* provides a link between Ibsen's old method and his new. Rosmer is the last of his characters to be caught up in and undermined by local politics; and Rebecca is the first of those passionate but inhibited lovers who dominate the dark plays of his final period.

His disillusionment with politics, arising from his experiences in Norway in 1885, was complete. In a speech in Stockholm on 24 September 1887, he declared his belief that the present age was the end of an era, and that a new age was dawning, a third kingdom in which "current political and social conceptions will cease to exist." As Professor Francis Bull has put it, in Trondheim he had a programme, in Stockholm a dream vision. In 1885 he had identified himself with the age; in 1887 and afterwards, he cherished only a vague hope for an unguessable future.

M. M.

CHARACTERS

JOHN ROSMER, owner of Rosmersholm, a former parish priest
REBECCA WEST, living at Rosmersholm
DR. KROLL, a headmaster, brother-in-law to ROSMER
ULRIK BRENDEL
PETER MORTENSGAARD
MRS. HELSETH, housekeeper at Rosmersholm

The action takes place at Rosmersholm, an old country seat in the neighbourhood of a small town by a fjord in western Norway.

ACT ONE

The morning-room at Rosmersholm; spacious, old-fashioned and comfortable. Downstage on the right-hand wall is a tiled stove decorated with fresh birch branches and wild flowers. Upstage of this, a door. In the rear wall, folding doors to the hall. In the left-hand wall, a window. Downstage of this, a stand with flowers and plants. By the stove, a table with a sofa and easy chairs. Around the walls hang portraits, some old, some comparatively new, of priests, officers, and court officials in uniform. The window is open, as are the door to the hall and the front door beyond. Outside, an avenue of old trees is visible, leading to the estate. A summer evening. The sun has set.

REBECCA WEST *is seated in an armchair by the window, crocheting a large white woollen shawl, which is almost completed. Now and then she glances enquiringly out from behind the flowers. After a few moments* MRS. HELSETH *enters right.*

MRS. HELSETH. I'd better start laying the table soon, hadn't I, miss?

REBECCA. Yes, would you? I'm sure the Pastor will be back soon.

MRS. HELSETH. Isn't it draughty there, miss?

REBECCA. A little. Would you close it, please?

MRS. HELSETH *goes over and shuts the door leading to the hall. Then she crosses to the window.*

MRS. HELSETH (*about to close it, looks out*). Why, isn't that the Pastor coming now?

REBECCA (*quickly*). Where? (*Gets up.*) Yes, that's him. (*Behind the curtain.*) Get back. Don't let him see us.

MRS. HELSETH (*moves back into the room*). Oh, look, miss! Fancy that! He's beginning to use the mill-path again.

REBECCA. He did the day before yesterday, too. (*Peers out between the curtain and the window-frame.*) But now we'll see whether—

MRS. HELSETH. Will he dare take the footbridge?

REBECCA. That's what I want to find out. (*After a pause.*) No. He's turning. He's going round the top today, too. (*Leaves the window.*) The long way round.

MRS. HELSETH. Ah well, miss. It must be hard for the Pastor to cross that bridge. After what happened there—

REBECCA (*gathers her crocheting*). They cling to their dead here at Rosmersholm.

MRS. HELSETH. If you want my opinion, miss, it's the dead who cling to Rosmersholm.

REBECCA (*looks at her*). The dead?

MRS. HELSETH. Yes. It's almost as though they couldn't free themselves from the ones they left behind.

REBECCA. What makes you say that?

MRS. HELSETH. Well, otherwise this white horse wouldn't keep on appearing.

REBECCA. Mrs. Helseth, what exactly is all this about this white horse?

MRS. HELSETH. Oh, it's nothing. You wouldn't believe such things, anyway.

REBECCA. Do you believe in it, then?

MRS. HELSETH (*goes across and shuts the window*). Ah, you'd only laugh at me, miss. (*Looks out.*) Why—isn't that the Pastor on the mill-path again—?

REBECCA (*looks out*). That? (*Goes to the window.*) No, that's—why, that's Dr. Kroll!

MRS. HELSETH. Yes, so it is!

REBECCA. Well, that's a pleasant surprise. He must be coming to call on us.

MRS. HELSETH. He walks straight over the bridge, he does.

Though she was his sister, and his own flesh and blood. Well, I'll go in and lay then, miss.

She goes out right. REBECCA *stands for a moment at the window; then she waves, smiles and nods towards the new visitor. Dusk is beginning to fall.*

REBECCA (*walks over and speaks through the door, right*). Mrs. Helseth, do you think you could give us something a little extra tonight? I expect you know what the headmaster likes best.

MRS. HELSETH (*offstage*). Very good, miss. You leave it to me.

REBECCA (*opens the door to the hall*). Well, at last—! Dear Dr. Kroll, how good to see you!

DR. KROLL (*in the hall, puts down his stick*). Thank you. I trust I don't call at an inconvenient moment?

REBECCA. You? Don't be absurd.

KROLL (*enters*). Enchanting as ever! (*Looks around.*) Is Rosmer up in his study?

REBECCA. No, he's taking a walk. He's been a little longer than usual. But he'll be back any minute now. (*Indicates the sofa.*) Do please sit down until he comes.

KROLL (*puts down his hat*). Thank you, thank you. (*Sits and looks around.*) Well, how very attractive you've made this old room look! Flowers everywhere.

REBECCA. Mr. Rosmer loves to have fresh flowers around.

KROLL. So do you, I imagine.

REBECCA. Yes. I find them so beautifully soothing. In the old days we had to deny ourselves that pleasure.

KROLL (*nods sadly*). Poor Beata couldn't stand their perfume.

REBECCA. Nor their colours. They—confused her.

KROLL. Yes. I remember. (*More lightly.*) Well, how are things out here?

REBECCA. Oh, life goes on. Quiet and peaceful. One day very like another. And how are things with you? Your wife—?

KROLL. Ah, my dear Miss West, let's not talk about me. Every family has its troubles. Especially in such times as we live in now.

REBECCA (*after a moment, sits in an armchair by the sofa*).

Why haven't you come out to see us? You haven't been
once these holidays.

KROLL. Well, one doesn't like to bother people—

REBECCA. If you knew how we've missed you—

KROLL. —and anyway, I've been away—

REBECCA. So I've heard. I gather you've been addressing
public meetings.

KROLL (*nods*). Yes, what do you say to that? Never thought
I'd turn political agitator in my old age, did you?

REBECCA (*smiles*). You've always been a bit of an agitator,
Dr. Kroll.

KROLL. For my own amusement, yes. But now I'm taking it
seriously. Do you ever see these radical newspapers?

REBECCA. Well, yes, I can't deny—

KROLL. My dear Miss West, there's no earthly reason why
you shouldn't. A person such as yourself—

REBECCA. That's what I think. I have to keep up with things.
Keep informed about what's going on—

KROLL. Of course I suppose one can't expect you as a woman
to take active sides in this civil dispute—I nearly said civil
war—that's raging here. But then, you must have read all
this mud that's been thrown at me by these so-called rep-
resentatives of the people? It's really infamous the crudities
that they indulge in.

REBECCA. I thought you gave them a pretty good nip or two.

KROLL. I did! I say it myself. Yes, I've tasted blood now!
They'll learn I'm not the cheek-turning kind—! (*Breaks
off.*) But let's not discuss this distressing subject this
evening.

REBECCA. No, dear Dr. Kroll, I'd rather not.

KROLL. Tell me, how are you finding life at Rosmersholm
now that you're alone here? Since our poor Beata—?

REBECCA. Oh, thank you, I'm quite happy. Of course it seems
very empty without her. And sad—I miss her terribly. But
apart from that—

KROLL. Do you plan to stay? Permanently, I mean?

REBECCA. Dear Dr. Kroll, I don't really think about it one

way or the other. I've grown so used to the place now, I almost feel I belong here.

KROLL. But of course. So I should hope.

REBECCA. And as long as Mr. Rosmer feels I can be of any use and comfort to him—well, I think I'll stay.

KROLL (*looks at her, moved*). You know, it's a pretty noble thing for a woman to sacrifice her youth for other people.

REBECCA. What else would I have had to live for?

KROLL. First you had that foster-father of yours to look after —I know how unreasonable he was, once he got paralysed, and what a strain that must have been—

REBECCA. Oh, he wasn't so—unreasonable in the old days, when we were living up in the north. It was those dreadful sea voyages that broke him. But once we'd moved down here—yes, we did have one or two difficult years before his troubles ended.

KROLL. Weren't the years that followed even more difficult for you?

REBECCA. No, how can you say such a thing! I loved Beata— and she so needed care and affection, the poor darling.

KROLL. Bless you for remembering her so charitably.

REBECCA (*moves a little closer to him*). Dear Dr. Kroll, you say that so kindly and sincerely—I'm sure you have no bad feeling about this.

KROLL. Bad feeling? What do you mean?

REBECCA. Well, it wouldn't be so strange if you found it rather painful to see a stranger like me running Rosmersholm.

KROLL. Great heavens alive, how—?

REBECCA. But you don't. (*Gives him her hand.*) Thank you, dear Dr. Kroll! Thank you, thank you!

KROLL. But how in heaven's name could such an idea enter your head?

REBECCA. I began to worry a little because you so seldom visited us.

KROLL. Then you've been barking up the wrong tree, Miss West. And besides—nothing has really changed here. I mean, it was you, and you alone, who ran Rosmersholm during those last unhappy months of poor Beata's life.

REBECCA. I was only a substitute for Mrs. Rosmer.

KROLL. Yes, well— You know what, Miss West? For my own part, I shouldn't be at all sorry to see you—but one mustn't speak of such things yet.

REBECCA. What do you mean?

KROLL. If things should so turn out that you should fill the place left by—

REBECCA. I have the place I want, Dr. Kroll.

KROLL. Materially, perhaps; but not—

REBECCA (*interrupts earnestly*). Shame on you, Dr. Kroll! How can you sit here joking about such a subject?

KROLL. Ah well, our good John Rosmer probably feels he's had his share of matrimony. All the same—

REBECCA. No, please, this is really too ridiculous.

KROLL. All the same—! Tell me, Miss West—if it isn't an impertinent question—how old are you?

REBECCA. I'm ashamed to admit I am already twenty-nine, Dr. Kroll. Coming up to thirty.

KROLL. Really. And Rosmer—how old is he? Let me see. He's five years younger than I am—well then, he must be around forty-three. I think that would be highly suitable.

REBECCA (*rises*). Indeed, yes. Most suitable. Will you take tea with us this evening?

KROLL. Thank you—yes, I had thought of staying. There's something I want to discuss with our friend. And, by the way, Miss West—just in case you should start having any further foolish thoughts, I intend to visit you both regularly—just like in the old days.

REBECCA. Oh yes, please do! (*Presses his hands.*) Thank you, thank you! You're so good and kind!

KROLL (*a little growlishly*). Am I? That's more than I ever hear at home.

JOHN ROSMER *enters right.*

REBECCA. Mr. Rosmer—do you see who's sitting here?

ROSMER. Mrs. Helseth told me.

DR. KROLL *has got up.*

ROSMER (*softly, emotionally, clasps* KROLL'S *hands*). Welcome
back to Rosmersholm, my dear Kroll! (*Puts his hands on*
KROLL'S *shoulders and looks him in the eyes.*) My dear
old friend! I knew everything would be all right between
us again.

KROLL. But, my dear fellow—have you too had this idiotic
delusion that there was something wrong?

REBECCA (*to* ROSMER). What a blessing it was only an idiotic
delusion!

ROSMER. Was it really, Kroll? But then, why did you never
come to see us?

KROLL (*earnestly, softly*). Because I didn't want to be a living
reminder of your years of unhappiness—and of—of her who
ended in the mill-race.

ROSMER. That was very kind of you. You're always so con-
siderate. But I promise you it was quite unnecessary.
Come, Kroll—let's sit down on the sofa. (*They sit.*) No, I
don't find it painful to be reminded of Beata. We speak
about her every day.

KROLL. Do you really?

REBECCA (*lights the lamp*). Indeed we do.

ROSMER. But it stands to reason. We both loved her so dearly.
And Rebec—Miss West and I both know we did all we
could to help the poor darling. We have nothing with
which to reproach ourselves. Our memory of Beata is
purely a happy one.

KROLL. You dear, good people! From now on I shall come
and visit you every day.

REBECCA (*sits in an armchair*). Well, let's see if you keep
your word.

ROSMER (*somewhat hesitantly*). Kroll—I'm deeply grieved
that our friendship was ever interrupted. I've always
greatly valued your advice, all the years we've known each
other. Ever since I left school.

KROLL. Well, yes, and I'm proud of it. Is there something particular at the moment that—?

ROSMER. There's a lot I want to discuss with you. I'd very
much welcome a heart-to-heart talk.

REBECCA. Yes, do. I think it must be such a comfort to have an old friend one can—

KROLL. Oh, believe me, there's even more that I want to discuss with you. I suppose you know I've now become an active politician?

ROSMER. Yes, so you have. How did that happen?

KROLL. I had to, Rosmer. Couldn't help it—though I put up a pretty stiff fight against it! One can't just go on being an idle observer. Now that these dreadful radicals have come to power, I feel the moment has come. So I've persuaded our little circle of friends in town to close their ranks. The moment has come, I tell you!

REBECCA (*with a gentle smile*). Isn't it a little late, now?

KROLL. Well, I won't deny it would have been better if we could have stemmed the tide earlier. But who could have foreseen what was going to happen? Not I, at any rate. (*Gets up and walks round the room.*) But now my eyes have been opened. Would you believe it, the spirit of anarchy has forced its way into the school itself!

ROSMER. The school? Surely not your school?

KROLL. Indeed it has. My own school. What do you think of that! I have discovered that for over six months the boys in the Sixth Form—some of them, anyway—have been running a secret society! And they've taken out a subscription to that damned paper of Mortensgaard's!

REBECCA. The *Morning Star*?

KROLL. Yes—fine mental sustenance for the future leaders of our country, eh? But the worst of the matter is that it's all my best pupils who have banded together in this conspiracy against me. It's only the dunces and the idlers who've kept aloof.

REBECCA. Does this worry you so much, Dr. Kroll?

KROLL. Worry me! To see my whole life's work obstructed and threatened! But that's not the worst. There's something else. (*Looks round.*) There isn't anyone listening?

REBECCA. No, of course not.

KROLL. Well, then—you will hardly credit it, but this discord and subversion has penetrated into my own house—into the calm and peace of my very home! It has destroyed the tenor of my family life.

ROSMER (*rises*). What! Your own home—!

REBECCA (*goes over to* KROLL). But, my dear Dr. Kroll, what on earth has happened?

KROLL. Would you believe it—my own children—! Well, to cut a long story short, Lauritz is the ringleader of the conspiracy. And Hilda has embroidered a red cover to hide the *Morning Star* in.

ROSMER. That I'd never have imagined! In your own home—!

KROLL. Who'd have dreamed it was possible! In my home, where obedience and order have always reigned—where until now all voices have spoken as one—!

REBECCA. How does your wife take all this?

KROLL. That's the most incredible thing of all. All her life, in great things and small, she's shared my opinions and supported everything I've said—and now even she's started taking the children's side. And she blames *me* for what has happened. Says I've repressed them. As though it weren't necessary to give them an occasional—! Well, so I've had trouble at home, too. But of course I don't talk about it. Such things are best kept quiet. (*Walks across the room.*) Oh dear, oh dear, oh dear! (*Stops by the window with his hands behind his back and looks out.*)

REBECCA (*has gone over to* ROSMER *and, unnoticed by* KROLL, *whispers quickly*). Tell him!

ROSMER (*similarly*). Not tonight.

REBECCA (*as before*). Yes, now.

She goes over and attends to the lamp.

KROLL (*comes across the room*). Well, my dear Rosmer, so now you know how the spirit of the age has cast its shadow over my domestic as well as my official life. These decadent, cankerous, demoralizing heresies—must I not fight them with all the weapons I can muster? Yes, Rosmer, that is what I intend to do! Not only with my tongue, but with my pen!

ROSMER. Do you think you'll be able to achieve anything?

KROLL. I shall at any rate have performed my duty as a citizen. And I regard it as the duty of every right-minded and patriotic Norwegian to do the same. Actually, that's the chief reason I came out to see you this evening.

ROSMER. But, my dear fellow, what could I—?

KROLL. You must rally to our cause. Help your old friends, lend us all your strength.

REBECCA. But, Dr. Kroll, you know how Mr. Rosmer hates that kind of public activity.

KROLL. He must overcome his hatred. You're too passive, Rosmer. You sit here walled in by your books—oh, heaven knows I've every respect for research and scholarship. But this is no time for such indulgences, more's the pity. You don't seem to realize what the situation in our country is. Practically every single accepted idea has been turned topsy-turvy. It's going to be a battle to get these vicious heresies rooted out.

ROSMER. I agree. But that kind of work is hardly in my line.

REBECCA. And I think Mr. Rosmer has come to look at life from a more liberal viewpoint than before.

KROLL (starts). More liberal—!

REBECCA. More open-minded. Less prejudiced.

KROLL. What on earth do you mean? Rosmer—surely you couldn't be so feeble as to imagine that these demagogues have won anything more than a temporary victory?

ROSMER. My dear Kroll, you know how little I understand politics. But I believe that in recent years people have perhaps begun to think more independently.

KROLL. And you regard that as a good thing? Anyway, you're quite wrong, my friend. Just you find out for yourself the opinions that these radicals are propagating! It's hardly any different from the rubbish that's preached in the pages of the *Morning Star*.

REBECCA. Yes, Mortensgaard has a lot of influence over people around here.

KROLL. Isn't it incredible! A man with a past like that! Thrown out of his teaching job for an immoral relationship! A man like that setting himself up as a leader of the people! And he's succeeding! He's actually succeeding! I hear he's now planning to expand his newspaper. I'm told on good authority that he's looking for a partner.

REBECCA. Why don't you and your friends start a rival newspaper?

KROLL. That's exactly what we're doing. This very day we have bought the *County Telegraph*. The financial question presented no difficulties. But—(*Turns to* ROSMER.) Well, this is really what I came to speak to you about. It's the running of the paper—the editorial side—that is our problem, you see. Tell me, Rosmer—remembering the issues at stake, couldn't you see your way to helping us out?

ROSMER (*almost as though frightened*). I?

REBECCA. How could you imagine such a thing?

KROLL. I know you hate public meetings and don't want to expose yourself to the kind of rough stuff that goes on there. But the more secluded work of an editor, or what I might rather call the—

ROSMER. No, no, my dear chap, you mustn't ask me to do this.

KROLL. I'd gladly have a shot at it myself. But I couldn't possibly manage it. I'm already so overburdened with obligations. You, on the other hand, no longer have any professional commitments. Of course the rest of us will give you all the help we can—

ROSMER. I can't, Kroll. I'm not the right man for it.

KROLL. Not the right man? That's what you said when your father procured this living for you—

ROSMER. I was right. That was why I went my own way.

KROLL. Oh, if you're only as good an editor as you were a man of God, we shan't complain.

ROSMER. Look, Kroll, I'm telling you once and for all. I won't do it.

KROLL. Well, at least you'll let us use your name.

ROSMER. My name?

KROLL. Yes, the mere name of John Rosmer will be a great asset to our paper. The rest of us are known to be politically committed. I gather that I myself am already branded as a furious fanatic. So our names aren't likely to make any con-

verts among the misguided masses. But you—you've always
stood outside the battle. Your goodness and incorruptibility,
your sensitivity and intellect, your unimpeachable integrity,
are known and prized by everyone throughout the county.
To say nothing of the honour and respect which you com-
mand as a former man of God! And, last but by no means
least, there's the name of your family.

ROSMER. Oh, the name of my family—

KROLL (*points to the portraits*). The Rosmers of Rosmersholm. Men of God and men of war. Respected servants
of their country. Every one of them a man of honour who
knew his duty. A family that for nigh on two hundred
years has been venerated and looked up to as the first in
the county. (*Puts a hand on* ROSMER's *shoulder*.) Rosmer
—you owe it to yourself and to the traditions of your family to defend and protect everything that has hitherto been
held sacred in our society. (*Turns.*) Well, what do you
say, Miss West?

REBECCA (*with a soft, quiet laugh*). Dear Dr. Kroll! I find
all this unspeakably ludicrous.

KROLL. What! Ludicrous!

REBECCA. Yes. You might as well know—

ROSMER (*quickly*). No, no—please! Not now!

KROLL (*looks from one to the other*). My dear friends, what
on earth—? (*Breaks off.*) Hm!

MRS. HELSETH *enters through the door right.*

MRS. HELSETH (*to* ROSMER). There's a man at the servants'
entrance. He says he wants to speak with you, sir.

ROSMER (*relieved*). Is there? Well, tell him to come in.

MRS. HELSETH. Here? Into the drawing room?

ROSMER. Of course.

MRS. HELSETH. But he doesn't look the type to bring in here.

REBECCA. How does he look, Mrs. Helseth?

MRS. HELSETH. Oh, not at all respectable, miss.

ROSMER. Didn't he say who he was?

MRS. HELSETH. Yes, I think he said he was called Hekman or
something.

ROSMER. I don't know anyone of that name.

MRS. HELSETH. He said something about being called Ulrik, too.

ROSMER (*starts*). Ulrik Hetman! Was that it?

MRS. HELSETH. Hetman—yes, that was it.

KROLL. I'm sure I've heard that name before—

REBECCA. Wasn't that the name he used to write under—you remember, that strange old—?

ROSMER (*to* KROLL). It is Ulrik Brendel's pen-name, Kroll.

KROLL. Ulrik Brendel! That charlatan. Yes, I remember him.

REBECCA. So he's still alive.

ROSMER. The last I heard of him, he'd joined up with a troupe of strolling players.

KROLL. The last *I* heard of him, he was in the workhouse.

ROSMER. Please ask him to come in, Mrs. Helseth.

MRS. HELSETH. As you say, sir. (*She goes.*)

KROLL. Are you really going to allow that man into your drawing room?

ROSMER. Surely you remember? He used to be my tutor.

KROLL. I remember he used to come here and stuff your head full of radical nonsense, until your father chased him out of the door with a horsewhip.

ROSMER (*a little bitterly*). Father always acted the Major, even in his own house.

KROLL. Thank him in his grave for it, my dear Rosmer. Ha!

MRS. HELSETH *opens the door on the right for* ULRIK BRENDEL, *exits and closes it behind him. He is a handsome figure, somewhat emaciated, but brisk and lively, with grey hair and beard. He is dressed like a common tramp, in a worn frock coat and bad shoes; no shirt is visible. Old black gloves; a soft, dirty hat beneath his arm; and a walking stick in his hand.*

ULRIK BRENDEL (*hesitates at first, then walks briskly over to* KROLL *and holds out his hands*). Good evening, John!

KROLL. I beg your pardon—

BRENDEL. Didst think to see my face again Within these hated walls?

KROLL. I beg your pardon. (*Points.*) *That* is—

BRENDEL (*turns*). But of course! *Le voilà!* John—*mon garçon —ah, mon petit chéri—!*

ROSMER (*shakes his hand*). My dear old tutor!

BRENDEL. Certain memories notwithstanding, I was loth to pass this ancient seat without a fleeting visit.

ROSMER. You are most heartily welcome here. Never fear that.

BRENDEL. And this charming lady—? (*Bows.*) Your wife, of course.

ROSMER. Miss West.

BRENDEL. A close relative, no doubt. And yon stranger—? A brother of the cloth, I see.

KROLL. My name is Kroll, sir. I am the local headmaster.

BRENDEL. Kroll? Kroll? *Momento!* Had you, sir, in your salad days, pretensions towards philology?

KROLL. Naturally I read the subject.

BRENDEL. Why, *Donnerwetter*, then I used to know you!

KROLL (*deprecatingly*). Please!

BRENDEL. Weren't you—?

KROLL (*as before*). Please!

BRENDEL. —one of those crusading moralisers who got me expelled from the University Debating Society?

KROLL. Very possibly. But I must disclaim any closer relationship.

BRENDEL. Ah, well. *Nach Belieben*, Herr Doctor! What boots it? Ulrik Brendel remains the man he is.

REBECCA. Are you making for town, Mr. Brendel?

BRENDEL. A hit, madam—a palpable hit! At intervals in life I find myself impelled to strike a blow for existence. Against the grain; but, *enfin!—la necessité—!*

ROSMER. But, my dear Mr. Brendel, won't you let me help you? Somehow or other—?

BRENDEL. Ha? What a suggestion! Wouldst thou profane the bond that binds us? Never, John—never!

ROSMER. But what are you planning to do in town? Believe me, you won't find it easy to—

BRENDEL. Leave that to me, my boy. The die is cast. You see

me at the outset of a great campaign, that dwarfs my previous reconnoitrings. (*To* KROLL.) Dare I ask the Herr Professor if—*unter uns*—there chances to be a reasonably respectable and capacious lecture hall in your esteemed town?

KROLL. I suppose the largest is the Workers' Union—

BRENDEL. And has Your Honour any influence in this doubtless august body?

KROLL. I have nothing whatever to do with them.

REBECCA (*to* BRENDEL). You ought to get in touch with Peter Mortensgaard.

BRENDEL. *Pardon, madame!* What kind of a *fou* is that?

ROSMER. What makes you think he's a fool?

BRENDEL. The very name tells me that the bearer is a plebeian.

KROLL. I hadn't expected that answer.

BRENDEL. But I will conquer my nausea. I have no choice. When a man such as myself stands at a crossroads in his life—*enfin!* It is ordained. I shall contact this individual— enter into negotiations—

ROSMER. Are you seriously at a crossroads?

BRENDEL. My dear boy, don't you know that Ulrik Brendel is always serious? Yes, John! I intend to become a new man. To abandon the role of modest onlooker.

ROSMER. But how do you—?

BRENDEL. I now descend into the arena of life! We live in a storm-wracked and ecliptical age. I shall step forth to lay my humble mite upon the altar of emancipation!

KROLL. You too—?

BRENDEL (*to them all*). Is the company acquainted with my *obiter scripta?*

KROLL. No, to be frank, I—

REBECCA. I've read several. My guardian used to have them.

BRENDEL. Then, fair lady, you have wasted your time. It is all bunk. Take my word for it.

REBECCA. Oh?

BRENDEL. What you have read. My major works remain unknown. Save to myself.

REBECCA. Why is that?

BRENDEL. Because they are not yet written.

ROSMER. But, my dear Mr. Brendel—

BRENDEL. As you remember, *cher Jean*, I'm a bit of a sybarite. A gourmet. Always have been. I like to savour things in solitude. Then I enjoy them doubly—nay, tenfold! When golden dreams descended on me, enveloping me in mist —when new and dazzling ideas were born in me, and wafted me heavenwards on their swift pinions—I fashioned them into poems, visions, images! In draft, you understand—

ROSMER. Yes, yes.

BRENDEL. Ah, John! I have drunk deep of pleasure! The riddling mystery of creation—in draft, as I said—the applause, the eulogies, the fame, the laurels—I have garnered them all with hands that shook with joy. I have sated myself in secret dreams with a rapture—ah!—that drugged my senses—

KROLL. Hm!

ROSMER. But you never wrote any of it down?

BRENDEL. Not a word. The dull toil of the scribe has always repelled me. And why should I profane my own ideals when I can enjoy them undisturbed in their virgin purity? But now I offer them up. I feel like a mother about to deliver her unspotted daughters into the rough arms of their husbands. But I offer them, notwithstanding—a sacrifice upon the altar of emancipation. A sequence of inspiring lectures—throughout the country—!

REBECCA (*animatedly*). This is a noble gesture, Mr. Brendel! You are sacrificing the dearest thing you possess.

ROSMER. The only thing.

REBECCA (*looks meaningly at* ROSMER). How many other men would do this? Would have the courage to do it?

ROSMER (*returns her glance*). Who knows?

BRENDEL. My audience is moved. That quickens my heart— and strengthens my will. I shall proceed to action. One thing, though—(*To* KROLL.) Can Your Reverence tell me —is there a Temperance Association in this town? A Society of Total Abstinence? Doubtless there is.

KROLL. Indeed, yes. I myself am its president, at your service.

BRENDEL. I knew it by your face! Well, then, it is not impossible that I may look in on you and enrol for a week.

KROLL. I beg your pardon. We do not enrol members by the week.

BRENDEL. À la bonheur, Herr Pedagogue. Ulrik Brendel has never forced his presence on such institutions. (*Turns.*) But I must not tarry longer in this house, so rich in memories. I must press on to town, and select a suitable abode. There is, I trust, a respectable hotel?

REBECCA. Won't you have a drink to warm you before you go?

BRENDEL. In what way "warm" me, gracious lady?

REBECCA. A cup of tea, or—

BRENDEL. Thanks, bountiful hostess. I never presume on private hospitality. (*Makes a farewell gesture to them all with his hand*). Auf Wiedersehen, mein Herrschaft! (*Goes towards the door, but turns.*) Ah, true, I had forgotten. John —Pastor Rosmer—will you, for auld lang syne, do your old tutor a small service?

ROSMER. With all my heart.

BRENDEL. *Bien!* Then lend me—just for a day or two—a well-ironed evening shirt.

ROSMER. Is that all?

BRENDEL. For once I march on foot. My luggage is being sent after me.

ROSMER. Of course. But isn't there anything else—?

BRENDEL. Well—since you mention it—could you conceivably spare an old, used, summer overcoat?

ROSMER. Yes, yes, of course.

BRENDEL. And if you should chance to have a decent pair of boots to match the coat—

ROSMER. I'm sure that can be arranged. As soon as we know your address I'll have them all sent on.

BRENDEL. Under no circumstances! I wish no inconvenience to be caused. I'll take these trifles with me.

ROSMER. Very well. Come upstairs with me, then.

REBECCA. No, let me. Mrs. Helseth and I can see to it.

BRENDEL. Never could I permit this *belle madame*—

REBECCA. Oh, nonsense. Now just you come with me, Mr. Brendel. (*Goes out right.*)

ROSMER (*detains him*). Tell me—isn't there anything else I can do to help you?

BRENDEL. Other way? I really can't imagine—*oui, parbleu*, now I think of it—! John—you haven't by any chance five shillings on you?

ROSMER. We'll see. (*Opens his purse.*) I've a couple of ten shilling notes—

BRENDEL. Don't bother. I can always get them changed in town. You shall have the change shortly. Don't forget—two ten shilling notes. *Guten nacht*, my own, dear boy! Worshipful sir, good night. (*He goes right, where* ROSMER *takes leave of him and closes the door behind him.*)

KROLL. Merciful heaven! So that was the Ulrik Brendel who people once believed would reshape the world!

ROSMER (*quietly*). At least he has had the courage to live life the way he thought it should be lived. I don't think that's so small an achievement.

KROLL. What! A life like his! Don't tell me he's turning your head again.

ROSMER. Oh, no, Kroll. Now I see my way clearly.

KROLL. Let us hope so, my dear Rosmer. You're so impressionable.

ROSMER. Come and sit down. I want to talk to you.

KROLL. By all means. (*They sit on the sofa.*)

ROSMER (*after a few moments*). We've made it pleasant and comfortable here, don't you think?

KROLL. Yes. It is very pleasant and comfortable here now. And peaceful. Yes, you've found yourself a home, Rosmer. And I have lost mine.

ROSMER. Don't say that, Kroll. Things will come right.

KROLL. Never. Never. The memory will always rankle. Things will never be as they were.

ROSMER. Now listen, Kroll. We two have been very close for so many years. Do you think anything could happen that could ever make us cease to be friends?

KROLL. I can't imagine anything that could make us enemies. Why do you ask?

ROSMER. You mind so violently if people don't share your opinions.

KROLL. Well, possibly—but you and I agree on pretty well everything. In essentials, anyway.

ROSMER (*quietly*). No. Not any longer.

KROLL (*tries to jump up*). What do you mean?

ROSMER (*puts a hand to restrain him*). No, you must sit still. Please, Kroll. I beg you.

KROLL. What is this? I don't understand you.

ROSMER. A new spring has dawned in my mind. A new youth, a new way of thought. So that—now I stand—

KROLL. Where? Where do you stand?

ROSMER. Where your children stand.

KROLL. You? You! But that's impossible! Where do you say you stand?

ROSMER. On the same side as Lauritz and Hilda.

KROLL (*bows his head*). An apostate! John Rosmer an apostate!

ROSMER. I ought to have felt a sense of joy at what you call my apostasy. But it grieved me. Because I knew it would grieve you deeply.

KROLL. Rosmer—Rosmer! I shall never recover from this. (*Looks sadly at him.*) To think that you can ally yourself with the forces of evil that are seeking to destroy our unhappy country.

ROSMER. I want to ally myself with the forces of emancipation.

KROLL. Yes, I know. That is the name given to it by the seducers, and by the victims they lead astray. But do you really believe that there is any emancipation to be hoped for from this spirit that is doing its best to poison our whole communal life?

ROSMER. I am not identifying myself with that spirit. Nor with either of the contending parties. I want to bring together men from all sides in a spirit of unity. As many as possible, and as urgently as possible. I want to devote my life and all my strength to this one end, of creating a responsible public opinion in our country.

KROLL. Don't you think we've had enough of public opinions? Personally, I think we're all well on the way to being dragged down into the gutter where only the common people can thrive.

ROSMER. That is exactly where I feel the task of public opinion lies.

KROLL. Task? What task?

ROSMER. To make all the people in this country noblemen.

KROLL. All the people—?

ROSMER. As many as possible, anyway.

KROLL. How?

ROSMER. By emancipating their minds and purifying their wills.

KROLL. You're a dreamer, Rosmer. Will *you* emancipate them? Will *you* purify them?

ROSMER. No, my dear friend. I can only try to open their eyes to the need for it. They must do it themselves.

KROLL. And you think they can?

ROSMER. Yes.

KROLL. By their own strength?

ROSMER. Yes, by their own strength. There is no other.

KROLL (*gets up*). Is this proper language from a man of God?

ROSMER. I am no longer a man of God.

KROLL. Yes, but—the faith you were brought up in—?

ROSMER. I no longer have it.

KROLL. No longer—!

ROSMER (*gets up*). I have given it up. I *had* to give it up, Kroll.

KROLL (*controls his emotion*). I see. Yes, yes, yes. The one follows the other. Was that why you left the Church?

ROSMER. Yes. When I saw things clearly—when I knew for sure that it was not a passing temptation, but something that I never could nor would escape from—then I left.

KROLL. So it has been fermenting inside you all this time. And we—your friends—were told nothing about it. Rosmer,

Rosmer—how could you hide this dreadful truth from us?

ROSMER. Because I thought it was something that concerned only myself. Besides, I didn't want to cause you and my other friends unnecessary distress. I thought I could go on living here as before, quiet and peaceful and happy. I wanted to read, to bury myself in those fields of thought that had hitherto been closed to me. To find my way into the great world of truth and freedom to which my eyes have now been opened.

KROLL. Apostate! Every word proves it. But why are you confessing all this? And why just now?

ROSMER. You have forced me to, Kroll.

KROLL. I? I forced you—!

ROSMER. When I heard about your violent conduct at those meetings—when I read about all the cruel speeches you made there—those hateful outbursts against your opponents—your scornful condemnation of everything they stood for—! Oh, Kroll! That you, you, could become like that! Then I saw my duty plainly. This strife that is being waged makes people evil. Their hearts must be filled with peace and joy and understanding. That is why I now stand forth to declare myself openly. I, too, want to test my strength. Couldn't you—from your side—help me, Kroll?

KROLL. Never while I draw breath shall I compromise with the forces that are seeking to destroy our society.

ROSMER. Then if we must fight, at least let us fight with honourable weapons.

KROLL. Whoever is not with me in such issues, him I no longer know. And I owe him no consideration.

ROSMER. Does that apply to me too?

KROLL. It's you who have broken with me, Rosmer.

ROSMER. Is this a breach, then?

KROLL. Yes! It is a breach with all those who have hitherto been your friends. Now you must face the consequences.

REBECCA WEST *enters right, and throws the door wide open.*

REBECCA. There! Now he's off to his sacrificial orgy. And now we can go and eat. Dr. Kroll!

KROLL (*takes his hat*). Good night, Miss West. I have no further business in this house.

REBECCA (*tensely*). What is it? (*Shuts the door and comes closer.*) Have you told him—?

ROSMER. Yes, he knows now.

KROLL. We won't let you go, Rosmer. We'll force you to come back to us.

ROSMER. I shall never do that.

KROLL. We'll see. You are not the kind of man who can stand alone.

ROSMER. I shall not be alone. There are two of us to bear the solitude together.

KROLL. Ah—! (*A suspicion crosses his mind.*) That too! Beata's words—!

ROSMER. Beata—?

KROLL (*dismisses the thought*). No, no. That was vile. Forgive me.

ROSMER. What? What do you mean?

KROLL. Please forget it. No, it's unthinkable! Forgive me. Goodbye. (*Goes towards the door leading to the hall.*)

ROSMER (*goes after him*). Kroll! We can't part like this. I'll come and see you tomorrow.

KROLL (*in the hall, turns*). You shall not set foot in my house! (*Takes his stick and goes.*)

ROSMER *stands for a second in the open doorway. Then he closes the door and walks across to the table.*

ROSMER. It doesn't matter, Rebecca. We shall manage. We two loyal friends. You and I.

REBECCA. What do you think he meant when he said: "It's unthinkable"?

ROSMER. Oh, don't bother about that, my dear. Whatever it was, he didn't believe it. Tomorrow I'll go in and see him. Good night.

REBECCA. Are you going to bed so early again tonight? After this?

ROSMER. Tonight as always. I feel so at peace now that it's

over. You see—I am quite calm, Rebecca. You must take it calmly too, my dear. Good night.

REBECCA. Good night, dear friend. And sleep well.

ROSMER *goes out through the hall door. We hear him mount the stairs.* REBECCA *walks over and pulls a bellrope by the stove. After a few moments* MRS. HELSETH *enters right.*

REBECCA. You can clear the table again, Mrs. Helseth. The Pastor doesn't want anything. And the Doctor has gone home.

MRS. HELSETH. The Doctor gone? What's wrong with him?

REBECCA (*takes her crochet-work*). He thought a storm was blowing up—

MRS. HELSETH. That's strange. There isn't a cloud in the sky this evening.

REBECCA. As long as he doesn't see the white horse. I'm afraid we may soon be hearing from one of these ghosts of yours.

MRS. HELSETH. God forgive you, Miss West! Don't say such wicked things!

REBECCA. All right, all right—

MRS. HELSETH (*lowers her voice*). Do you really think someone's going to go soon, miss?

REBECCA. No, of course not. But there are so many kinds of white horses in this world, Mrs. Helseth. Well, good night. I'm going to my room.

MRS. HELSETH. Good night, miss.

REBECCA *goes out right with her crochet-work.*

MRS. HELSETH (*turns down the lamp, shakes her head and mumbles to herself*). Blessed Jesus! That Miss West. The way she talks sometimes.

ACT TWO

JOHN ROSMER's *study. In the left-hand wall is the entrance door. In the rear wall, a doorway with a curtain drawn aside from it, leading into his bedroom. Right, a window. In front of it, a desk, covered with books and papers. Bookshelves and bookcases around the walls. Frugally furnished. Downstage left, an old-fashioned couch with a table by it.*

JOHN ROSMER, *wearing a smoking jacket, is seated in a high-backed chair at the desk. He is cutting a pamphlet and glancing through it, pausing now and then to dwell.*

There is a knock on the door left.

ROSMER (*without turning*). Come in.

REBECCA WEST *enters in a dressing gown.*

REBECCA. Good morning.

ROSMER (*turning the pages*). Good morning, my dear. Is there something you want?

REBECCA. I only wanted to ask if you've slept well.

ROSMER. Oh, yes. So deeply and peacefully. No dreams— (*Turns.*) And you?

REBECCA. Oh—yes, thank you. Towards morning.

ROSMER. I don't know when I last felt as easy in my heart as I do now. Oh, I'm so thankful I got that off my chest.

REBECCA. Yes, you shouldn't have kept it to yourself for so long, John.

ROSMER. I can't understand how I could have been such a coward.

REBECCA. Oh, it isn't a question of cowardice—

ROSMER. Oh, yes it was. When I think about it honestly, there was a good deal of cowardice in it.

REBECCA. All the more credit to you, then, for managing to overcome it. (*Sits down beside him on a chair by the desk.*) But now I want to tell you about something I've done—you mustn't be angry with me—

ROSMER. Angry? My dear, how could you imagine—?

REBECCA. Well, it was perhaps a little high-handed of me, but—

ROSMER. Well, tell me what it was.

REBECCA. Last night, when that Ulrik Brendel was leaving, —I wrote him a few lines to take to Mortensgaard.

ROSMER (*a little doubtfully*). But, my dear Rebecca—! Well, what did you write?

REBECCA. I said he'd be doing you a service if he took care of that unfortunate man and gave him all the help he could.

ROSMER. My dear, you shouldn't have done that. That'll only have done Brendel harm. Besides, I'd much rather not have anything to do with Mortensgaard. You know the trouble I had with him once.

REBECCA. Don't you think it might be a good idea if you made things up with him?

ROSMER. I? With Mortensgaard? Why do you say that?

REBECCA. Well, you can't really feel safe now—now that you've quarrelled with your friends.

ROSMER (*looks at her and shakes his head*). Surely you don't imagine that Kroll or any of the others would want to be vindictive? That they might be thinking of—?

REBECCA. First reactions, you know—one can't be sure. I think possibly—after the way he took it—

ROSMER. Oh, you ought to know him better than that. Kroll's nothing if not a gentleman. I'll go along this evening and have a word with him. I'll talk to all of them. You'll see, everything'll be all right—

MRS. HELSETH *enters through the door left.*

REBECCA (*rises*). What is it, Mrs. Helseth?

MRS. HELSETH. Dr. Kroll's downstairs in the hall.

ROSMER (*gets up quickly*). Kroll!

REBECCA. Do you think he—?

MRS. HELSETH. He asks if he can come up and speak with you, sir.

ROSMER (*to* REBECCA). What did I tell you! Yes, of course he can. (*Goes to the door and calls down the stairs.*) Come up, my dear fellow. I'm delighted to see you.

ROSMER *stands holding the door open.* MRS. HELSETH *goes.* REBECCA *draws the curtain across the open doorway. Then she begins tidying here and there.* DR. KROLL *enters, hat in hand.*

ROSMER (*quiet, moved*). I knew it couldn't be the last time we'd—

KROLL. Today I see things in a different light from yesterday.

ROSMER. I knew you would. Now you've had time to think the matter over—

KROLL. You completely misunderstand me. (*Puts his hat on the table by the couch.*) It is imperative that I speak with you privately.

ROSMER. Surely Miss West—?

REBECCA. No, no, Mr. Rosmer. I'll go.

KROLL (*looks her up and down*). I must ask you to excuse me, Miss West, for calling so early, and catching you before you have had time to—

REBECCA (*surprised*). What do you mean? Do you find it improper that I should walk around at home in a dressing gown?

KROLL. Heaven forbid. I don't pretend to know what is regarded as proper nowadays at Rosmersholm.

ROSMER. Kroll—what on earth's come over you today?

REBECCA. Good morning, Dr. Kroll. (*She goes out left.*)

KROLL. By your leave— (*Sits on the couch.*)

ROSMER. Yes, my dear fellow, let's sit down and have a frank talk about this. (*Sits on a chair opposite* KROLL.)

KROLL. I haven't closed my eyes since I left this house. I lay awake all night, thinking and thinking.

ROSMER. And what have you come to tell me?

KROLL. It'll take a long time, Rosmer. Let me begin with a kind of—prologue. I can tell you a little about Ulrik Brendel.

ROSMER. Has he been to see you?

KROLL. No. He got himself settled in some low tavern. In the lowest possible company, naturally. He drank and stood drinks as long as his pockets were full. Then he started abusing them, called them scum and riff-raff. Which of course they were. Then they beat him up and threw him in the gutter.

ROSMER. I'm afraid he's quite incorrigible.

KROLL. He'd pawned your coat, too. But it seems he's managed to get that redeemed. Can you guess by whom?

ROSMER. You?

KROLL. No. The gallant Mr. Mortensgaard.

ROSMER. I see.

KROLL. I gather the first call Mr. Brendel made was upon that "idiot" and "plebeian."

ROSMER. It seems to have turned out well for him—

KROLL. Very. (*Leans over the table, a little closer to* ROSMER.) But that brings me to something about which—for the sake of our old—our former friendship—I feel it my duty to warn you.

ROSMER. What on earth do you mean, Kroll?

KROLL. I mean that there's some game being played in this house behind your back.

ROSMER. How can you say that? Are you referring to Reb— to Miss West?

KROLL. I am. I can well understand her point of view. She's been accustomed for so long to having her own way here. None the less—

ROSMER. My dear chap, you're completely mistaken. She and I have no secrets from each other. On any subject.

KROLL. Do her confessions to you include the fact that she's been corresponding with the editor of the *Morning Star*?

ROSMER. Oh, you mean that note she gave Ulrik Brendel.

KROLL. You know about it, then. And do you approve of her opening up a relationship with this scandalmonger who seeks every week to make a laughing-stock of me, both professionally and in my public life?

ROSMER. My dear Kroll, I'm sure that aspect of the matter hasn't even occurred to her. In any case, she is perfectly free to act as she chooses, just as I am.

KROLL. Indeed? Yes, I suppose that's all part of this new philosophy you've become so enamoured of. I assume Miss West shares your standpoint?

ROSMER. She does. The two of us have worked towards it together.

KROLL (looks at him and slowly shakes his head). Oh, you poor, blind dupe!

ROSMER. I? What makes you say that?

KROLL. Because I dare not—will not think the worst. No, no! Let me finish! You do value my friendship, Rosmer? And my respect? Or perhaps you don't?

ROSMER. I surely don't need to answer that question.

KROLL. Very well. But there are other questions that do demand an answer—a full explanation on your part. Will you allow me to submit you to a kind of—cross-examination?

ROSMER. Cross-examination?

KROLL. Yes. I want to question you on certain matters which you may find it painful to be reminded of. You see—this business of your apostasy—your emancipation, as you call it—ties up with much else about which, for your own sake, I want you to speak frankly to me.

ROSMER. My dear fellow, ask anything you like. I've nothing to hide.

KROLL. Tell me, then. What do you really think was the main reason Beata killed herself?

ROSMER. Have you any doubts? Or rather—can anyone ever hope to know why a poor, irresponsible mental invalid decides to end her misery?

KROLL. Are you so sure that Beata was insane? The doctors were by no means certain.

ROSMER. If the doctors had seen her as I so often saw her, they would have had no doubts.

KROLL. I had none—at the time.

ROSMER. How could one? Those uncontrollable, sick fits of sensuality—and the way she expected me to reciprocate them. She—frightened me. And then that illogical and remorseless way she reproached herself during those last years.

KROLL. Yes, when she learned she'd never be able to have any children.

ROSMER. Yes, well, I mean—! To feel such appalling and inescapable anguish about something that was in no way her fault! Is that sanity?

KROLL. Hm—! Do you happen to recall whether you had any books in the house that dealt with the—purpose of marriage —from the so-called "progressive," modern viewpoint?

ROSMER. I remember Miss West lent me a book about that. She'd inherited her guardian's library, as you know. But, my dear Kroll, you surely don't imagine we were so careless as to mention anything like that to poor Beata? I assure you on my honour, we are completely innocent in this matter. It was her own deranged imagination that gave her these wild ideas.

KROLL. I can tell you one thing, anyway. That poor, tormented, overstrung woman ended her life in order that you might be happy—and free to live—the life you wanted to.

ROSMER (half rises from his chair). What do you mean by that?

KROLL. You must listen calmly to me now, Rosmer, because now at last I can tell you this. During the year before she died, Beata twice visited me to tell me how desperate and frightened she was.

ROSMER. About this?

KROLL. No. The first time she came and said she feared you were in danger of becoming an apostate. That you were thinking of abandoning your ancestral faith.

ROSMER (*eagerly*). That's impossible, Kroll! Quite impossible! You must be mistaken about this.

KROLL. Why?

ROSMER. Because as long as Beata was alive, I was still in doubt—still battling with myself. And I fought that battle alone. I didn't speak of it to a soul. I don't think even Rebecca—

KROLL. Rebecca?

ROSMER. I mean—Miss West. I call her Rebecca for convenience.

KROLL. So I have noticed.

ROSMER. So I can't imagine how Beata could ever have got that idea. And why didn't she talk to me about it? She never did. She never said a word.

KROLL. Poor creature. She begged and prayed *me* to speak to you.

ROSMER. Then why didn't you?

KROLL. I naturally assumed she was distraught. Making an accusation like that against a man like you! Well, then she came again—about a month later. She seemed calmer then. But as she was leaving, she said: "Soon now they can expect to see the white horse at Rosmersholm."

ROSMER. Yes, yes. The white horse. She spoke so often about that.

KROLL. And when I tried to persuade her to stop having such morbid ideas, she simply replied: "I haven't much time left. John must marry Rebecca now—at once."

ROSMER (*almost speechless*). What did you say? *I* marry—?

KROLL. It was a Thursday afternoon. On the Saturday evening, she threw herself off the bridge into the mill-race.

ROSMER. And you never warned us—!

KROLL. You know yourself how often she used to say she hadn't long to live.

ROSMER. Yes, I know. All the same—you should have warned us!

KROLL. I thought of it. But by then it was too late.

ROSMER. But why haven't you mentioned it since? Why have you kept quiet about all this?

KROLL. What good would it have done to come here and cause you still further suffering? I naturally supposed it was just some crazy delusion. Until last night.

ROSMER. And now you don't?

KROLL. Was Beata deluded when she said you were going to abandon your childhood faith?

ROSMER (*stares unseeingly*). Yes. That I can't understand. That's the most incredible thing—

KROLL. Incredible or not, she proved right. And now I ask you, Rosmer—how much truth is there in her other accusation? Her final one, I mean?

ROSMER. Accusation? How was that an accusation?

KROLL. You don't seem to have noticed the way she phrased it. She had to go, she said. Why? Well?

ROSMER. So that I could marry Rebecca—

KROLL. Those weren't quite her words. Beata used a different expression. She said: "I haven't much time left. John *must* marry Rebecca now—at once."

ROSMER (*looks at him for a moment, then rises*). Now I understand you, Kroll.

KROLL. Well? What is your answer?

ROSMER (*quite calm and controlled the whole time*). To such a question—? The only proper answer would be to show you the door.

KROLL (*gets up*). As you wish.

ROSMER (*moves in front of him*). Now you listen to me. For over a year—ever since Beata died—Rebecca West and I have lived alone together here at Rosmersholm. All that time you have known of Beata's accusation against us. But never for a single moment have I noticed that you objected to Rebecca and me living here together.

KROLL. I didn't know until last night that this was an association between an apostate and a—an emancipated woman.

ROSMER. Ah—! Then you think there is no purity of spirit to be found in apostates and emancipated people? You don't believe they can have any sense of morality?

KROLL. I have little faith in any morality that is not rooted in Christian faith.

ROSMER. And you assume that this applies to Rebecca and me
too? To our relationship—!

KROLL. With all deference to both of you, I cannot shrug off
the opinion that there is no great gulf between free thought
and—hm!

ROSMER. And what?

KROLL. And free love—since you force me to use the words.

ROSMER (*quietly*). And you aren't ashamed to say that to
me! You, who have known me ever since I was a child.

KROLL. That is precisely the reason. I know how easily you
let yourself be influenced by the people you associate with.
And this Rebecca of yours—well, this Miss West—we don't
know so very much about her. In short, Rosmer—I am not
giving you up. And you—for God's sake try to save yourself
while there's still time.

ROSMER. Save myself? How—?

MRS. HELSETH *looks in through the door left.*

ROSMER. What is it?

MRS. HELSETH. I wanted to ask Miss West if she could come
down.

ROSMER. Miss West is not up here.

MRS. HELSETH. Oh? (*Looks round.*) That's strange. (*Goes.*)

ROSMER. You were saying—?

KROLL. Now listen. I'm not going to ask what went on here in
secret while Beata was alive—or what may still be going on
here now. I know you were deeply unhappy in your marriage. And that must to some degree excuse your conduct.

ROSMER. Oh, how little you really know me—!

KROLL. Don't interrupt me. What I wish to say is—that if this
association with Miss West is to continue, it is absolutely
essential that this change of heart, this dreadful apostasy
into which she has lured you, be hushed up. Let me speak!
Let me speak! I say that if you must be mad, then in God's
name think and believe anything you wish—one way or the
other. But keep your opinions to yourself. This is after all
a purely personal matter. You don't have to shout these
things from every street corner.

ROSMER. I do have to abandon a position which is both false and ambiguous.

KROLL. But you have a duty to your family traditions, Rosmer. Remember that! Since time immemorial Rosmersholm has been a stronghold of order and morality—of respect and reverence for everything that is accepted and upheld by the best elements in our society. The whole county has always taken its tone from Rosmersholm. Should the rumour become current that you yourself have broken with what I may call the Rosmer tradition, it will cause the most fatal and irreparable confusion.

ROSMER. My dear Kroll, I can't see it like that. I feel I have a bounden duty to create a little light and happiness in those places where for so many years the Rosmer family has created nothing but darkness and misery.

KROLL (*looks sternly at him*). A worthy ambition for a man who is to be the last of his line! Let sleeping dogs lie, Rosmer. That is no task for you. You were born to live peacefully among your books.

ROSMER. Possibly. But now I want to take part in the battle of life, at least once. I too!

KROLL. The battle of life! Do you know what that will mean for you? It will mean a battle to the death with all your friends.

ROSMER (*quietly*). They are not all as fanatical as you.

KROLL. You're an ingenuous fool, Rosmer. You've no experience of life. You don't realize what a storm is about to break over you.

MRS. HELSETH *peers in through the door.*

MRS. HELSETH. Miss West asked me to say—

ROSMER. What is it?

MRS. HELSETH. There's a man downstairs who wants a word with you, sir.

ROSMER. Is it the one who was here last night?

MRS. HELSETH. No, it's that Mortensgaard.

ROSMER. Mortensgaard!

KROLL. Aha! So it's come to that, has it? It's come to that already!

ROSMER. What does he want with me? Why didn't you tell him to go away?

MRS. HELSETH. Miss West said I was to ask if he might come up.

ROSMER. Tell him I'm engaged—

KROLL (*to* MRS. HELSETH). Ask him to come up, Mrs. Helseth.

MRS. HELSETH *goes.*

KROLL (*takes his hat*). I quit the field—for the moment. But the main battle has still to be fought.

ROSMER. As truly as I live, Kroll—I have nothing whatever to do with Mortensgaard.

KROLL. I no longer believe you. In anything. From now on I can never believe you. Now it is war to the knife. We'll see if we can't clip your wings.

ROSMER. Oh, Kroll! How can you sink so low?

KROLL. That comes well from you. Have you forgotten Beata?

ROSMER. Are you going to start all that again?

KROLL. No. The riddle of the mill-race I leave to you, and to your conscience. If you still have any.

PETER MORTENSGAARD *softly and quietly enters the room left. He is a slightly-built little man with thinning reddish hair and beard.*

KROLL (*throws a look of hatred at him*). So! The *Morning Star!* Standing sentinel over Rosmersholm! (*Buttons his coat.*) Well, that leaves me in no doubt which course I must steer.

MORTENSGAARD (*quietly, to* KROLL). The *Morning Star* will always shine to guide you on your path.

KROLL. Yes, you've long shown your goodwill towards me. I seem to remember a Commandment which says: "Thou shalt not bear false witness against thy neighbour."

MORTENSGAARD. You don't need to school me in the Commandments, Dr. Kroll.

KROLL. Not the Seventh?

ROSMER. Kroll—!

MORTENSGAARD. If I should need instruction, the Pastor is surely the most appropriate person.

KROLL (*with suppressed scorn*). The Pastor? Yes—Pastor Rosmer is unquestionably the best-informed authority on that subject. Well, gentlemen—I wish you a fruitful conversation. (*Goes, banging the door behind him.*)

ROSMER (*stands staring at the door, and says to himself*). Well, well—so be it, then. (*Turns.*) Tell me, Mr. Mortensgaard, what brings you out here to visit me?

MORTENSGAARD. It was actually Miss West I came to see. I felt I had to thank her for the kind letter she sent me yesterday.

ROSMER. I know she wrote to you. Have you spoken with her?

MORTENSGAARD. For a moment. (*With a slight smile.*) I hear there has been a change of heart regarding certain matters here at Rosmersholm.

ROSMER. My attitude has changed towards many things. I might almost say—everything.

MORTENSGAARD. So Miss West gave me to understand. She thought it might be a good idea if I came up and had a little chat with you about this.

ROSMER. About what, Mr. Mortensgaard?

MORTENSGAARD. May I have your permission to announce in the *Morning Star* that you have changed your views—and that you are devoting yourself to the cause of liberalism and progress?

ROSMER. Certainly you may. Indeed, I beg you to.

MORTENSGAARD. Then I shall publish it tomorrow morning. This will be a sensational item of news, that Pastor Rosmer of Rosmersholm now feels he can fight the good fight under our banner too.

ROSMER. I don't quite follow you.

MORTENSGAARD. Well, I mean, it gives our party a strong moral boost every time we win a devout Christian to our cause.

ROSMER (*somewhat surprised*). Then you don't know—? Didn't Miss West tell you about that too?

MORTENSGAARD. What, Pastor? Miss West seemed in rather a hurry. She said I should come upstairs and hear the rest from you.

ROSMER. Well then, I must tell you that I have emancipated myself in more senses than one. In every direction. I have completely renounced the teaching of the Church.

MORTENSGAARD (*looks at him amazed*). Well, strike me dumb! *You* renounce the—!

ROSMER. Yes, I now stand where you yourself have stood for so long. You can publish that in the *Morning Star* tomorrow too.

MORTENSGAARD. Publish that? No, my dear Pastor. I'm sorry, but I think we'd best turn a blind eye to that.

ROSMER. Turn a blind eye—?

MORTENSGAARD. To begin with, I mean.

ROSMER. But I don't understand—

MORTENSGAARD. Well, you see, Pastor—you probably don't know the ins and outs of things the way I do. But since you've come over to the liberal way of thinking—and since, as Miss West said, you want to lend a hand in the movement—then I take it you want to help us in every way you possibly can.

ROSMER. Indeed I do.

MORTENSGAARD. Well, I only want to let you know, Pastor, that if you come into the daylight about this business of your leaving the Church, you tie your hands from the start.

ROSMER. You think so?

MORTENSGAARD. Yes, don't you deceive yourself. There won't be much you'll be able to achieve then, not in this part of the country. Besides—we've enough freethinkers in the movement already, Pastor. I had it on the tip of my tongue to say "too many"! What the party needs is good Christians —that's something everyone has to respect. And that's what we're so short of. So it'd be best if you could keep mum about everything that the public don't need to know. That's only my opinion.

ROSMER. I see. In other words, you daren't associate yourself
with me if I openly declare my apostasy?

MORTENSGAARD (shakes his head). I couldn't risk it, Pastor.
I've made it a rule of late never to support anyone or anything that's anti-Church.

ROSMER. Have you, of late, yourself rejoined the Church?

MORTENSGAARD. That's another matter.

ROSMER. I see. Yes, I follow you.

MORTENSGAARD. Pastor—you must remember that my hands,
more than most people's, aren't completely free.

ROSMER. What binds them?

MORTENSGAARD. The fact that I am a marked man.

ROSMER. Ah—I see.

MORTENSGAARD. A marked man, Pastor. You of all people
ought to remember that. It was you who put the mark on
me.

ROSMER. If I had felt then as I do now, I would have dealt
less harshly with your misdemeanour.

MORTENSGAARD. I don't doubt it. But now it's too late. You've
branded me once and for all. Branded me for my whole
life. I don't suppose you fully realize what a thing like that
means. But now you may soon be feeling the pinch yourself, Pastor.

ROSMER. I?

MORTENSGAARD. Yes. Surely you don't suppose Dr. Kroll and
his cronies are going to forgive you for what you've done
to them? And the County Telegraph is going to be pretty
rough from now on, I hear. You may find yourself a marked
man too.

ROSMER. I don't think they'll be able to hurt me. My conscience is clean.

MORTENSGAARD (with a quiet smile). That's a bold claim to
make, Pastor.

ROSMER. Maybe. But I have the right to make it.

MORTENSGAARD. Even if you examine your own conduct as
closely as you once examined mine?

ROSMER. You say that very strangely. What are you driving
at? Have you something special in mind?

MORTENSGAARD. Yes, there is one thing. Only one. But it'd be enough, if any nasty-minded enemy of yours happened to hear about it.

ROSMER. Will you be good enough to let me know what this might be?

MORTENSGAARD. Can't you guess, Pastor?

ROSMER. No, I can't. I haven't the faintest idea.

MORTENSGAARD. Well, then, I'd better tell you. I have in my possession an odd letter that was once written here at Rosmersholm.

ROSMER. Miss West's letter, you mean? Is there anything odd about that?

MORTENSGAARD. No, not about that. But I did once get another letter from this house.

ROSMER. Also from Miss West?

MORTENSGAARD. No, Pastor.

ROSMER. Well, from whom, then? From whom?

MORTENSGAARD. From the late Mrs. Rosmer.

ROSMER. From my wife? *You* received a letter from my wife?

MORTENSGAARD. I did.

ROSMER. When?

MORTENSGAARD. Shortly before the poor lady's death. It'd be about eighteen months ago now. And it struck me as very odd.

ROSMER. You know that my wife was mentally ill at that time.

MORTENSGAARD. I know many people thought that. But I don't think you'd notice it from this letter. When I say it was odd, I mean in another way.

ROSMER. What in heaven's name did my poor wife find to write to you about?

MORTENSGAARD. I have the letter at home. She starts by saying that she is living in great fear and trembling. There are so many wicked people around here, she writes. And these people only think of causing you mischief and injury.

ROSMER. Me?

MORTENSGAARD. So she says. And then there comes the really odd thing. Shall I tell you, Pastor?

ROSMER. Yes! Tell me everything! Everything!

MORTENSGAARD. The poor lady begs and beseeches me to be magnanimous. She says she knows it was the Pastor that got me sacked from my school. But she begs me with all her heart not to take my revenge.

ROSMER. How did she think you could take revenge?

MORTENSGAARD. She says in the letter that if I should happen to hear any rumours about sinful goings-on at Rosmersholm, I mustn't pay any attention to them, because it was only bad people spreading such things around to make you unhappy.

ROSMER. Does it say that in the letter?

MORTENSGAARD. You can read it yourself, Pastor, any time that's convenient.

ROSMER. But I don't understand—! What did she think these wicked rumours referred to?

MORTENSGAARD. Firstly, that you'd abandoned the faith you'd been brought up in. Mrs. Rosmer said that was quite untrue. Secondly—hm—

ROSMER. Secondly?

MORTENSGAARD. Well, secondly she writes—it's a bit confused, this part—that she knows nothing whatever of any immoral relationship at Rosmersholm. That no wrong has ever been done to her as a wife—and if such rumours should come to my ears, she begs me not to mention them in the *Morning Star*.

ROSMER. Did she name anyone?

MORTENSGAARD. No.

ROSMER. Who brought you this letter?

MORTENSGAARD. I've promised not to tell. It was brought to me one evening, after dark.

ROSMER. If you had bothered to enquire, you would have learned that my poor unhappy wife was not completely in her right mind.

MORTENSGAARD. I did enquire, Pastor. But I must say that wasn't exactly the impression I received.

ROSMER. No? But why do you choose to warn me now about this old and confused letter?

MORTENSGAARD. To warn you to be very careful, Pastor Rosmer.

ROSMER. Personally, you mean?

MORTENSGAARD. Yes. You must remember that, from now on,
you are no longer sacrosanct.

ROSMER. You seem convinced I have something I ought to
hide.

MORTENSGAARD. I can't see myself why a man who's found
emancipation shouldn't be allowed to live his life to the
full. But, as I said, from now on you'd best be careful. If
any rumour should get about that might offend people's
sense of right and wrong, you can be sure the whole of
our progressive movement will suffer for it. Goodbye,
Pastor Rosmer.

ROSMER. Goodbye.

MORTENSGAARD. And I'll go straight down to the press and
print the great news in the *Morning Star*.

ROSMER. Print everything.

MORTENSGAARD. I'll print everything that our good readers
need to know.

He bows and leaves. ROSMER *remains standing in the doorway while* MORTENSGAARD *goes down the stairs. The front
door is heard to close.*

ROSMER (*in the doorway, calls softly*). Rebecca! Reb—! Hm.
(*Louder.*) Mrs. Helseth—isn't Miss West down there?

MRS. HELSETH (*from the hall*). No, Pastor. She's not here.

The curtain backstage is drawn aside, and REBECCA *is revealed in the doorway.*

REBECCA. John!

ROSMER (*turns*). What! Were you in my bedroom! My dear,
what were you doing there?

REBECCA (*goes over to him*). I was listening.

ROSMER. But Rebecca—how could you do such a thing?

REBECCA. Yes, I could. He said it so horribly, that thing about
the dressing gown—

ROSMER. Ah, so you were there already when Kroll—?

REBECCA. Yes. I wanted to know what he was up to.

ROSMER. I would have told you.

REBECCA. You wouldn't have told me everything. And certainly not in his words.

ROSMER. Did you hear everything, then?

REBECCA. Most of it. I had to go downstairs for a moment when Mortensgaard came.

ROSMER. And then you came back—

REBECCA. Please don't be angry with me, my dear.

ROSMER. You must do whatever you think right. You are a free woman. But what do you think about all this, Rebecca? I've never felt I needed you as I do now.

REBECCA. We both knew this would happen sometime.

ROSMER. No, no. Not this.

REBECCA. Not this?

ROSMER. I always feared that sooner or later our pure and beautiful friendship might be misinterpreted and reviled. Not by Kroll. I'd never imagined anything like this of him. But by all those others, with their foul minds and their ignoble eyes. Oh yes, Rebecca—I was right to keep our relationship so jealously to ourselves. It was a dangerous secret.

REBECCA. Oh, what does it matter what other people think? *We* know that we are guiltless.

ROSMER. I? Guiltless? Yes, I used to think that—until today. But now—now, Rebecca—

REBECCA. Well, now what?

ROSMER. How am I to explain that terrible accusation of Beata's?

REBECCA (*vehemently*). Oh, don't talk about Beata! Don't think about Beata any more! You've managed to free yourself from her at last. She's dead.

ROSMER. Since I learned this, she has become hideously alive again.

REBECCA. No, no! You mustn't, John! You mustn't!

ROSMER. Yes, I tell you. We must try to get to the bottom of this. How can she have got this mad idea into her head?

REBECCA. Surely you aren't beginning to doubt that she was —mad?

ROSMER. Yes, Rebecca—that's just what I can't be so sure of any longer. And besides—even if she was—

REBECCA. If she was—? Yes, what then?

ROSMER. I mean—what was it that drove her sick mind over the edge into madness?

REBECCA. Oh, what good can it do to go around brooding about it?

ROSMER. I can't help it, Rebecca. I can't stop these doubts nagging at me, even if I wanted to.

REBECCA. But it can be dangerous—to circle continuously around one morbid thought.

ROSMER (*paces around restlessly, pondering*). I must have betrayed my feelings somehow. She must have noticed how happy I began to feel after *you* came here.

REBECCA. But, my dear, even if this is true—

ROSMER. Think. . . . She must have noticed that we read the same books. That we loved to be together, and to talk about all these new ideas. But—I don't understand! I was so careful not to let her suspect anything. When I think back, why, it was almost as though my life depended on it, the way I kept her apart from us, and from everything that concerned us. Didn't I, Rebecca?

REBECCA. Yes, yes, of course you did.

ROSMER. And you did too. And yet—! Oh, it's too dreadful to think of! So she was going round here, in her sick love for me—always silent, silent—watching us—noting everything— and misinterpreting everything.

REBECCA (*clasps her hands*). Oh, I should never have come to Rosmersholm!

ROSMER. To think what she must have suffered in silence! All the dreadful fantasies her sick brain must have built up around us! Did she never say anything to you that led you to suspect anything?

REBECCA (*seems startled*). To me! Do you suppose I'd have stayed here a day longer?

ROSMER. No, no, of course not. Oh, what a struggle it must

have been for her! And she fought it alone, Rebecca. In despair, and quite alone. And then, in the end, that terrible accusing victory—in the mill-race.

He throws himself down in the chair at the desk, puts his elbows on it and covers his face with his hands.

REBECCA (*approaches him cautiously from behind*). Now, listen, John. If it lay in your power to call Beata back—to you—to Rosmersholm—would you do it?

ROSMER. Oh, how can I tell what I would or wouldn't do? I can think of nothing but this one thing—that can never be undone.

REBECCA. You were just beginning to live, John. You *had* already begun. You had made yourself free—free in every way. You felt so relieved and happy—

ROSMER. Oh, yes, Rebecca. I did, I did. And now this dreadful discovery—

REBECCA (*behind him, her arms on the back of his chair*). How beautiful it was when we used to sit downstairs in the drawing-room in the dusk. Helping each other to plan our lives anew. You were going to lay hold of life—the living life of today, you called it! You wanted to go like a liberating angel from home to home, winning people's hearts and souls. Creating nobility all around you—in wider and ever wider circles.

ROSMER. Happy, noble men.

REBECCA. Yes—happy.

ROSMER. Because it is happiness that makes men noble, Rebecca.

REBECCA. Don't you think—suffering too? Deep suffering?

ROSMER. Yes—if one manages to survive it. Overcome it. Conquer it.

REBECCA. That is what you must do.

ROSMER (*shakes his head sadly*). I shall never conquer this—not completely. There will always remain a doubt. A question. I shall never again be able to enjoy the one thing that makes life so wonderful to live.

REBECCA (*over the back of the chair, more quietly*). What is that, John?

ROSMER (*looks up at her*). The sense of calm and happy innocence.

REBECCA (*takes a step back*). Yes. Innocence.

Short pause.

ROSMER (*with his elbow on the desk, leans his head on his hand and looks straight ahead of him*). And the way she managed to work it all out. How systematically she must have pieced it all together! First she begins to doubt my faith. How could she have suspected that? But she did. And then her suspicion increased to certainty. And then— yes, of course, then it was easy for her to imagine all the rest. (*Sits up in his chair and runs his hands through his hair.*) Oh, all these dreadful speculations! I shall never be free from them. I feel it. I know it. They will always haunt me, and remind me of the dead.

REBECCA. Like the white horse of Rosmersholm.

ROSMER. Yes. Rushing out from the darkness. From the silence.

REBECCA. And for the sake of this accursed chimaera you are prepared to turn your back upon life—that burning life, which you had begun to awake to?

ROSMER. Yes, it is hard. Hard, Rebecca. But I have no choice. How could I possibly forget all this?

REBECCA (*behind the chair*). By creating a new relationship.

ROSMER (*starts and looks up*). A new relationship?

REBECCA. Yes. A new relationship to the world outside. Live, work, act. Don't sit here brooding over insoluble riddles.

ROSMER (*gets up*). A new relationship? (*Walks across the room, stops by the door, then comes back.*) One question occurs to me. Haven't you too asked yourself that question, Rebecca?

REBECCA (*catches her breath*). I don't—know—what you mean.

ROSMER. How do you suppose our relationship is going to shape itself after today?

REBECCA. I think our friendship will continue—whatever happens.

ROSMER. That's not quite what I meant. What first brought us together—and binds us so closely—our belief that man and woman can live together in pure comradeship—

REBECCA. Yes, yes—well?

ROSMER. I mean, such a relationship—like ours—doesn't it demand a life led in serenity and peace?

REBECCA. Go on.

ROSMER. But what I see lying ahead of me is a life of strife and unrest, and emotional disturbance. I want to live, Rebecca! I'm not going to let myself be beaten by fear. I'm not going to let my life be dictated, either by the living or by—anyone else.

REBECCA. No, no, you mustn't. Be free, John! You must be free!

ROSMER. Then can't you guess what I'm thinking? Don't you know? Can't you see that the only way I can free myself from all these nagging memories—from the horror of the past—?

REBECCA. Yes?

ROSMER. —is to confront it with something new, and living, and real?

REBECCA (catches at the back of the chair). What do you mean?

ROSMER (comes closer). Rebecca—if I were now to ask you —will you be my second wife?

REBECCA (is speeechless for a moment, then cries in joy). Your wife! Your—! I!

ROSMER. Yes. Let us try. We two shall be one. The place left here by the dead must not stand empty.

REBECCA. I—take Beata's place—?

ROSMER. Then her part in the saga of Rosmersholm will be finished. Completely finished. For ever and ever.

REBECCA (quietly, trembling). Do you believe that, John?

ROSMER. It must be so. It must! I can't—I will not go through life with a corpse on my back. Help me to throw it off, Rebecca. And then let us lay all memories to rest in freedom, and joy, and love. You shall be my wife—the only wife I have ever had.

REBECCA (*controlled*). Don't ever speak of this again. I shall never be your wife.

ROSMER. What! Never? But—don't you think you could come to love me? Isn't there already—something of love—in our friendship?

REBECCA (*puts her hands to her ears as though in terror*). Don't talk like that, John! Don't say such things!

ROSMER (*grasps her arm*). Yes, yes. It could happen. I can see from your face, you feel it too. Don't you, Rebecca?

REBECCA (*again calm and composed*). Listen, now. I tell you —if ever you speak of this again, I shall leave Rosmersholm.

ROSMER. Leave! You? You couldn't. It's impossible.

REBECCA. It is even more impossible that I should become your wife. That I can never be. Never in this world.

ROSMER (*looks surprised at her*). "Can't," you said? And you said it so strangely. Why can't you?

REBECCA (*clasps both his hands*). My dear—for both our sakes—don't ask me why. (*Lets go of him.*) No, John. (*She goes towards the door, left.*)

ROSMER. From now on, I can ask no other question but "Why?"

REBECCA (*turns and looks at him*). Then it is finished.

ROSMER. Between you and me?

REBECCA. Yes.

ROSMER. It will never be finished between us. You will never leave Rosmersholm.

REBECCA (*her hand on the door-knob*). No, perhaps I won't. But if you ever ask me that again—it will be finished none the less, John.

ROSMER. Finished none the less? How?

REBECCA. Because then I shall go the way Beata went. Now you know, John.

ROSMER. Rebecca!

REBECCA (*in the doorway, nods slowly*). Now you know. (*Goes.*)

ROSMER (*stares as though lost at the closed door*). Rebecca!

ACT THREE

The living room at Rosmersholm. The window and the hall door stand open. Morning sunshine outside.

REBECCA WEST, *dressed as in Act One, is standing at the window, watering and arranging the flowers. Her crochet-work is lying in the armchair.* MRS. HELSETH *is going around with a feather mop, dusting the furniture.*

REBECCA (*after a brief silence*). The Pastor's very late down this morning.

MRS. HELSETH. Oh, he's often like that. He'll be here soon.

REBECCA. Have you seen him at all?

MRS. HELSETH. Only for a moment. When I came up with the coffee, he went into his bedroom and started dressing.

REBECCA. I ask because yesterday he wasn't very well.

MRS. HELSETH. Yes, he looked poorly. I wonder if there isn't something the matter between him and his brother-in-law.

REBECCA. What could that be?

MRS. HELSETH. I wouldn't know. Perhaps that Mortensgaard's set them against each other.

REBECCA. That's quite possible. Do you know this Peter Mortensgaard?

MRS. HELSETH. I do not. The idea, miss! A man like that!

REBECCA. You mean, because he edits that nasty paper?

MRS. HELSETH. Oh, it isn't just that. Surely you heard, miss. He had a child with some married woman whose husband had left her.

REBECCA. Yes, I did hear that. But that must have been long before I came here.

MRS. HELSETH. Oh goodness, yes, miss. He was quite a young

man. I reckon she ought to have known better. He wanted
to marry her. But they put a stop to that. And they made
him suffer for it, all right. But since then, my word, he's
done all right for himself. There's plenty of people as
aren't ashamed to run after him now.

REBECCA. Yes, most of the poorer people turn to him when
they need help.

MRS. HELSETH. Oh, it isn't only the poor ones—

REBECCA (gives her a furtive glance). Oh?

MRS. HELSETH (by the sofa, dusting busily). The kind of people you'd least expect, so I've heard say, miss.

REBECCA (arranging the flowers). That's just an idea you've
got, Mrs. Helseth. You couldn't know about a thing like
that.

MRS. HELSETH. You think I couldn't know, miss? Oh yes, I
know all right. If you want the truth, I once took a letter
to Mortensgaard myself.

REBECCA (turns). No—did you?

MRS. HELSETH. Indeed I did. And that letter was written here
at Rosmersholm.

REBECCA. Really, Mrs. Helseth?

MRS. HELSETH. As I stand here. And written on fine paper it
was, too. With fine red wax on the envelope.

REBECCA. And it was entrusted to you? Well then, Mrs. Helseth, it isn't difficult to guess who sent it.

MRS. HELSETH. Oh?

REBECCA. Obviously poor Mrs. Rosmer, when she was ill—

MRS. HELSETH. It's you that say so, miss, not me.

REBECCA. But what was in the letter? No, of course—you
can't know.

MRS. HELSETH. Hm—maybe I do, for all that.

REBECCA. Did she tell you what she'd written?

MRS. HELSETH. No, she didn't do that. But when he, that
Mortensgaard, had read it, he started asking me all kinds
of questions, sly-like, so that I soon knew what was in it.

REBECCA. What do you think she said? Oh, dear Mrs. Helseth, do please tell me!

MRS. HELSETH. No, I won't, miss. Not for all the money in the world.

REBECCA. Oh, you can tell me. You and I are such good friends.

MRS. HELSETH. God forbid I should ever let on to you about that, miss. I can't say more than that it was some awful thing they'd gone and put into that poor woman's sick mind.

REBECCA. Who had?

MRS. HELSETH. Wicked people, Miss West. Wicked people.

REBECCA. Wicked—?

MRS. HELSETH. That's the word I used. Really wicked people, they must have been.

REBECCA. Who do you think it could have been?

MRS. HELSETH. Oh, I know what I think. But heaven forbid I should open *my* mouth. There's a certain lady in town— hm—!

REBECCA. I can see you mean Mrs. Kroll.

MRS. HELSETH. Yes, she's a fine one. Always been snooty to me, she has. And she's never had any liking for you.

REBECCA. Do you think Mrs. Rosmer was in her right mind when she wrote that letter to Mortensgaard?

MRS. HELSETH. Depends what you mean by right mind, miss. I wouldn't say she was out of it.

REBECCA. But she became so distressed when she learned she could never have any children. That was when the madness started.

MRS. HELSETH. Yes, she took that badly, poor woman.

REBECCA (*takes her crochet-work and sits in the chair by the window*). Actually—don't you think that was a good thing for the Pastor, Mrs. Helseth?

MRS. HELSETH. What, miss?

REBECCA. That there weren't any children. Hm?

MRS. HELSETH. Well, I don't know what I ought to answer to that.

REBECCA. Yes, believe you me. It was the best thing for him. Pastor Rosmer wasn't made to sit here listening to little children crying.

MRS. HELSETH. Little children don't cry at Rosmersholm, miss.

REBECCA (*looks at her*). Don't cry?

MRS. HELSETH. No. Little children have never cried in this house, not as long as anyone can remember.

REBECCA. That's strange.

MRS. HELSETH. Yes, isn't it, miss? But it's part of the Rosmers. And there's another strange thing. When they grow up, they never laugh. Never laugh until the day they die.

REBECCA. That's most extraordinary—

MRS. HELSETH. Have you ever heard or seen the Pastor laugh?

REBECCA. No—now I think of it, I almost believe you're right. But people in general don't laugh much around here, I think.

MRS. HELSETH. That they don't. It started at Rosmersholm, people say. And then it spread around like a kind of plague, I shouldn't be surprised.

REBECCA. You're a deep woman, Mrs. Helseth.

MRS. HELSETH. Ah, you mustn't sit there making fun of me, miss— (*Listens.*) Ssh, ssh! Here's the Pastor coming down. He doesn't like seeing dusters about.

She goes out through the door right. JOHN ROSMER, *stick and hat in hand, enters from the hall.*

ROSMER. Good morning, Rebecca.

REBECCA. Good morning, my dear. (*After a moment, crocheting.*) Are you going out?

ROSMER. Yes.

REBECCA. It's a lovely day.

ROSMER. You didn't come up to see me this morning.

REBECCA. No—I didn't. Not today.

ROSMER. Aren't you going to from now on?

REBECCA. Oh, I don't know yet.

ROSMER. Is there anything for me?

REBECCA. The *County Telegraph* has come.

ROSMER. The *County Telegraph*—!

REBECCA. It's lying there on the table.

ROSMER (*puts down his hat and stick*). Is there anything in it about—?

REBECCA. Yes.

ROSMER. And you didn't send it up—?

REBECCA. You'll read it soon enough.

ROSMER. I see. (*Takes the paper and reads it standing at the table*). What! ". . . cannot warn our readers sufficiently against irresponsible renegades . . ." (*Looks at her.*) They call me a renegade, Rebecca.

REBECCA. They mention no names.

ROSMER. What difference does that make? (*Reads on.*) "Secret traitors against justice and morality"—Judases who have the impertinence to blazon their apostasy as soon as they think that the most appropriate—and most profitable —moment has come." "Outrageous attacks on the posthumous reputations of our ancestors"—"in the hope that those temporarily in power will not omit suitably to reward. . . ." (*Puts the paper down on the table.*) And they write this about me. These people who have known me so long and so well. They don't believe it, they know there isn't a word of truth in it, but they write it, all the same.

REBECCA. There's more to come.

ROSMER (*takes up the paper again*). "Immaturity of judgment the only possible excuse . . . corrupting influence— possibly extending also to fields of personal conduct which we do not at present wish to make the subject of public discussion or complaint. . . ." (*Looks at her.*) What does that mean?

REBECCA. That's a reference to me.

ROSMER (*puts down the paper*). Rebecca—this is the action of dishonourable men.

REBECCA. Yes, I hardly think they're the ones to complain about Mortensgaard.

ROSMER (*walks up and down*). Something must be done. Everything that is good in men will be destroyed if this kind of thing is allowed to continue. But it shall not! Oh, how happy—how happy I would feel if I could bring a little light into all this gloom and ugliness!

REBECCA (*rises*). Yes, John, yes! That would be something great and noble to live for!

ROSMER. If only I could awake them to self-knowledge. Bring them to a feeling of shame and repentance. Teach them to approach one another in tolerance and love, Rebecca.

REBECCA. Yes! Only put all your energies into that, and you'll see. You will win!

ROSMER. I think it could be done. If I could succeed, what a joy it would be to be alive! No more hateful strife. Only emulation. Every eye directed towards the same goal. Every will, every mind, striving forwards—upwards—each by its own natural and predestined path. Happiness for all—created by all. (*Chances to look out through the window, starts and says sadly.*) Ah! Not through me.

REBECCA. Not—? Not through you?

ROSMER. And not *for* me, either.

REBECCA. Oh, John, you mustn't let such doubts get the better of you.

ROSMER. Happiness—my dear Rebecca—happiness consists above all else in a calm and happy sense of innocence. Freedom from guilt—

REBECCA (*stares straight ahead*). Oh, can't you ever stop thinking about guilt?

ROSMER. You don't know how it feels. But I—

REBECCA. You least of all.

ROSMER (*points out through the window*). The mill-race—

REBECCA. Oh, John—!

MRS. HELSETH *looks in through the door right.*

MRS. HELSETH. Miss!

REBECCA. Later, later. Not now.

MRS. HELSETH. Just a word, miss.

REBECCA *goes over to the door.* MRS. HELSETH *tells her something. They whisper together for a moment.* MRS. HELSETH *nods and goes.*

ROSMER (*uneasily*). Was it for me?

REBECCA. No, only something about the housekeeping. You ought to go out and get some fresh air, John. Take a good long walk.

ROSMER (*takes his hat*). Yes, come along. We'll go together.

REBECCA. No, my dear, I can't just now. You go on your own. But stop brooding about these things. Promise me that.

ROSMER. I'm afraid I shall never be able to forget them.

REBECCA. But how can you let anything so groundless have such power over you—?

ROSMER. Is it so groundless, Rebecca? I've been lying awake all night thinking about it. Wasn't Beata perhaps right after all?

REBECCA. What do you mean?

ROSMER. In believing that I was in love with you, Rebecca.

REBECCA. Wasn't—she—right?

ROSMER (*puts his hat on the table*). This is the question I keep asking myself. Have we two been deceiving ourselves in calling our relationship a friendship?

REBECCA. You mean we ought to have called it—?

ROSMER. Love. Yes, Rebecca, I mean that. Even when Beata was alive, I thought only of you. You were the one I yearned for. With you I found a happiness that was calm and joyful and not merely based on sensuality. When you really think about it, Rebecca—we were like two children falling sweetly and secretly in love. We made no demands, we dreamed no dreams. Wasn't that how you felt too? Tell me.

REBECCA (*torn within herself*). Oh—I don't know what to reply to that.

ROSMER. And this life we lived so passionately—with each other and for each other—we mistook for friendship. No, Rebecca—our relationship has been a spiritual marriage— perhaps from the first moment we knew each other. So that I am guilty. I had no right to do this—no right, for Beata's sake.

REBECCA. No right to live in happiness? Do you believe that, John?

ROSMER. She saw our relationship through the eyes of *her* love. Condemned it by the measure of *her* love. She had to. Beata couldn't have judged us in any other way than she did.

REBECCA. But then how can you blame yourself for what finally happened?

ROSMER. It was her love for me that threw her into the mill-race. That fact remains inescapable, Rebecca. And it is useless for me to try to escape from it.

REBECCA. Don't think about it! Think only of the great and noble task to which you have dedicated your life!

ROSMER (*shakes his head*). That can never be accomplished, Rebecca. Not by me. Not after what I know now.

REBECCA. Why not by you?

ROSMER. Because there can never be victory for a cause that is rooted in guilt.

REBECCA (*bursts out*). Oh, these doubts, these fears, these scruples—are all inherited! They talk at Rosmersholm about the dead haunting the living in the shape of white horses. I think this is just one of them.

ROSMER. Perhaps it is. But what help is that if I cannot escape from it? You must believe me, Rebecca. What I say is true. For a cause to win a lasting victory, it must be led by a man whose soul is joyful and free from guilt.

REBECCA. Is joy something that means so much to you, John?

ROSMER. Joy? Yes, Rebecca. It is.

REBECCA. You, who can never laugh?

ROSMER. Yes, in spite of that. Oh, Rebecca—believe me—I could be the most joyful man on earth.

REBECCA. You must go for your walk now, my dear. Take a good, long one. You hear? Look, here's your hat. And your stick.

ROSMER (*takes them*). Thank you. You won't come with me?

REBECCA. No, no, I can't just now.

ROSMER. Very well. I shall feel you're with me, though. As I always do.

He goes out through the hall. After a few moments REBECCA *glances out after him through the open door. Then she walks towards the door right.*

REBECCA (*opens it and calls softly*). All right, Mrs. Helseth.
  You can let him in now.

She goes over towards the window. Shortly afterwards DR.
KROLL *enters right. He bows silently and formally, and keeps
his hat in his hand.*

KROLL. Has he gone?

REBECCA. Yes.

KROLL. Does he usually stay out long?

REBECCA. Usually, yes. But today I wouldn't be sure. So if
  you don't want to meet him—

KROLL. No, no. I want to talk to you. Alone.

REBECCA. Then we'd better start. Please sit down.

She sits in an armchair by the window. DR. KROLL *sits in a
chair beside her.*

KROLL. Miss West—you can hardly imagine how deeply this
  hurts me—this change that has taken place in John Rosmer.

REBECCA. We expected it would—at first.

KROLL. Only at first?

REBECCA. Mr. Rosmer was sure that sooner or later you would
  come to feel as he does.

KROLL. I?

REBECCA. You and all his friends.

KROLL. Well, there you see what poor judgment he has where
  life and human nature are concerned.

REBECCA. In any case—since he now feels bound to free himself from all former ties—

KROLL. Ah but, you see, that's exactly what I don't believe.

REBECCA. What do you believe, then?

KROLL. I think you're the one who's behind all this.

REBECCA. Your wife gave you that idea, Dr. Kroll.

KROLL. Never mind where I got it from. The point is that I
  feel strong doubts—overwhelmingly strong doubts—when
  I consider the sum of your conduct since first you came
  here.

REBECCA (*looks at him*). I seem to remember there was a
  time when you felt an overwhelmingly strong belief in

me, dear Dr. Kroll. A passionate belief in me, I might almost have said.

KROLL (*lowers his voice*). Whom could you not bewitch—if you put your mind to it?

REBECCA. Are you suggesting that—?

KROLL. Yes, you did. I'm not any longer so foolish as to suppose that you felt anything for me. You merely wanted to gain admittance to Rosmersholm. Get a footing here. And you wanted me to help you. Yes, I see it all now.

REBECCA. You seem to have forgotten that it was Beata herself who begged and prayed me to come here.

KROLL. Yes, after you'd bewitched her too. Or would you call that friendship, what she came to feel for you? She began to worship you, to idolize you, and in the end it developed into a—what shall I call it?—into a kind of desperate infatuation. Yes, that's the word for it.

REBECCA. You must please remember your sister's state of mind. I don't really think I can be described as emotionally unstable.

KROLL. No, indeed you are not. But that makes you all the more dangerous to people you want to get into your clutches. You find it so easy to act remorselessly and ruthlessly, simply because you are so cold-blooded.

REBECCA. Cold-blooded? Are you so sure of that?

KROLL. Quite sure, now. Otherwise you couldn't have gone on here year after year pursuing your end so calculatedly. Yes, yes—you've got what you wanted. You have him in your power—and Rosmersholm too. But to achieve all this, you didn't shrink from sacrificing his personal happiness.

REBECCA. That's not true! It isn't I, it's you who have made him unhappy.

KROLL. I?

REBECCA. Yes, when you led him to believe that he was to blame for the dreadful thing that happened to Beata.

KROLL. So he feels deeply about that?

REBECCA. Of course he does. You know how sensitive he is—

KROLL. I thought these so-called emancipated men were able to set themselves above such scruples. But that's how it is, eh? Ah well—I knew it really. The descendant of these men who look down on us here can't find it so easy to tear himself free from something that's been handed down in his family from generation to generation.

REBECCA (*drops her eyes thoughtfully*). John Rosmer is deeply rooted in the traditions of his family. That is certainly true.

KROLL. Yes, and you ought to have remembered it if you'd had any real feeling for him. But of course you couldn't have that kind of feeling. Your background is so vastly different from his.

REBECCA. What do you mean, my background?

KROLL. I mean your family background. Your—origins, Miss West.

REBECCA. I see. Yes, that's quite true. My background is very humble. All the same—

KROLL. I don't mean socially. I was thinking of your moral background.

REBECCA. I don't understand.

KROLL. The circumstances of your birth.

REBECCA. I beg your pardon?

KROLL. I say this merely because it explains your whole conduct.

REBECCA. I don't follow you. Kindly explain what you mean.

KROLL. I assumed you knew. Otherwise one would hardly see why you were adopted by Dr. West—

REBECCA (*rises*). Ah. Now I understand.

KROLL. And took his name. Your mother's name was Gamvik.

REBECCA (*walks across the room*). My father's name was Gamvik, Dr. Kroll.

KROLL. Your mother's occupation must of course have brought her into frequent contact with the district physician.

REBECCA. It did.

KROLL. And as soon as your mother dies, he takes you into his own home. He treats you harshly. Yet you stay with him. You know he won't leave you a penny—all you got was a case of books. Yet you stay with him. Put up with his tantrums—look after him until the day he dies.

REBECCA (*over by the table, looks scornfully at him*). And all this you can only explain by the suggestion that there was something immoral—something criminal—about my birth?

KROLL. What you did for him I attribute to an unconscious filial instinct. Your whole conduct seems to me irrefutable evidence of your birth.

REBECCA (*vehemently*). There isn't a word of truth in anything you say! Dr. West hadn't even arrived in the district when I was born.

KROLL. I beg your pardon, Miss West. He came there the previous year. I have done a little research into the matter.

REBECCA. You're wrong, I tell you! Completely wrong!

KROLL. You said the day before yesterday that you were twenty-nine. Coming up to thirty.

REBECCA. Oh? Did I say that?

KROLL. You did. From which I calculate—

REBECCA. Stop. There's no need to calculate anything. I may as well tell you at once: I am a year older than I admitted.

KROLL (*smiles disbelievingly*). This is something new. What is the explanation?

REBECCA. When I reached twenty-five I thought I was a little old to be unmarried. So I subtracted a year.

KROLL. You? An emancipated woman? Do you have old-fashioned prejudices regarding the right age for marriage?

REBECCA. Yes. It was silly of me—laughable, even. But one always has some little prejudice clinging to one that one can't shake off. That's human nature.

KROLL. Possibly. But my calculation may be correct all the same. Because Dr. West paid your district a brief visit the year before he became employed there.

REBECCA (*cries*). That's a lie!

KROLL. Is it?

REBECCA. Yes. My mother never mentioned that.

KROLL. Didn't she?

REBECCA. No. Never. Nor Dr. West. Not a word.

KROLL. Might that not have been because they both had reason to forget a year? Just as you have done, Miss West. Perhaps it's a family trait.

REBECCA (*walks around, twisting and untwisting her hands*). It isn't possible. It's only something you're trying to make me imagine. It can't be true. It can't! Not possibly—!

KROLL (*gets up*). But my dear—why in heaven's name are you taking it so to heart? You quite frighten me. What am I to imagine—?

REBECCA. Nothing. You are to imagine nothing.

KROLL. Then you really must explain to me why this fact— this possibility, if you like—so alarms you?

REBECCA (*composes herself*). It's quite simple, Dr. Kroll. I just don't want people to think of me as illegitimate.

KROLL. I see. Well, let's settle for that explanation—for the moment. So you have retained a certain—prejudice on that issue too?

REBECCA. Yes, I have.

KROLL. Well, I suppose it's the same with most of this so-called emancipation of yours. You've read books that have given you a whole lot of new ideas and opinions. You've picked up a smattering of new-fangled theories about this and that—theories that seem to upset much of what has hitherto been regarded as gospel and unchallengeable. But you've only accepted all this intellectually, Miss West. You don't really feel it in your blood.

REBECCA (*thoughtfully*). You may be right about that.

KROLL. Yes, just ask yourself honestly, and you'll see! And if it's like that with you, then it's easy to guess how John Rosmer must feel about it. It's pure and absolute madness —it's—why, it's suicide for him even to think of standing forth publicly and claiming to be an apostate! We know what a shy and reticent man he is. Imagine him being repudiated and persecuted by his old associates! Exposed to the contempt and ridicule of all the best people in society! He's never the kind of man to endure that.

REBECCA. He must. It's too late for him to draw back now.

KROLL. It is certainly not too late. By no means. The whole matter can be hushed up—or at least explained away as a

temporary, if regrettable, aberration. But—one condition is
absolutely imperative.

REBECCA. And what is that?

KROLL. You must get him to legalise the relationship, Miss
West.

REBECCA. His relationship with me?

KROLL. Yes. You must make him do that.

REBECCA. You can't rid yourself of the conviction that our
relationship is of the kind that requires to be—legalised,
as you put it?

KROLL. I have no wish to get involved in the matter personally. But I have observed in the past that the prejudices,
as you would call them, which people find it easiest to
overcome—hm—!

REBECCA. Concern the relationship between man and woman?

KROLL. Yes—to speak frankly—that is my experience.

REBECCA (*wanders across the room and looks out through
the window*). It was on the tip of my tongue to say—I hope
you are right, Dr. Kroll.

KROLL. What do you mean by that? You said it so strangely.

REBECCA. Oh, nothing. Let's not talk any more about it. Ah
—here he is.

KROLL. Already! Then I'll be off.

REBECCA (*goes over to him*). No—wait. There's something
I'd like you to hear.

KROLL. Not now. I don't think I could bear to see him.

REBECCA. Please stay, I beg you. Do. Or you'll regret it later.
This is the last time I shall beg anything of you.

KROLL (*looks at her amazed, and puts down his hat*). Very
well, Miss West. So be it.

A moment's silence. Then JOHN ROSMER *enters from the
hall.*

ROSMER (*sees* KROLL *and stops in the doorway*). What! You
here?

REBECCA. He didn't want to meet you, John.

KROLL (*involuntarily*). John!

REBECCA. Yes, Dr. Kroll. Mr. Rosmer and I call each other

by our Christian names. Our relationship has led to that
excess.

KROLL. Was that what you wanted me to hear?

REBECCA. That—and other things too.

ROSMER (*comes closer*). Why have you come here?

KROLL. I wanted to make one last effort to stop you, and to
win you back.

ROSMER (*points to the newspaper*). After what I have read
here?

KROLL. I did not write that.

ROSMER. Did you do anything to stop it?

KROLL. That would have been a betrayal of the cause I stand
for. And anyway, it did not lie within my power.

REBECCA (*tears the newspaper into pieces, crumples them
and throws them behind the stove*). There. Now they're
out of sight. Let them be out of mind, too. There's going
to be nothing more like that, John.

KROLL. Yes, if you can persuade him to see sense—

REBECCA. Come, my dear, let's sit down—all three of us. I
want to tell you everything.

ROSMER (*sits unwillingly*). What's come over you, Rebecca?
You're so—dreadfully calm. What is it?

REBECCA. The calmness of decision. (*Sits.*) You sit down
too, Dr. Kroll.

KROLL *sits on the sofa.*

ROSMER. Of decision, you say. What decision?

REBECCA. I want to give you back what you need to be able
to live. You shall have your joyful innocence returned to
you, my dear.

ROSMER. What on earth is all this?

REBECCA. I just want to tell you something. That's all that's
necessary.

ROSMER. Well, tell me.

REBECCA. When I came down here from the north—with Dr.
West—I felt that a great new world was opening up for
me. The Doctor had taught me so many things. Everything

I knew about life—then. (*With difficulty, and scarcely audibly.*) But then—

KROLL. Yes?

ROSMER. But, Rebecca—I know all this.

REBECCA (*composes herself*). Yes, yes—you're right really. I suppose you do know all this.

KROLL (*looks closely at her*). I think perhaps I should go.

REBECCA. No, stay where you are, Dr. Kroll. (*To* ROSMER.) Yes, that was it, you see—I wanted to be part of this new age that was dawning. To share in all these new discoveries—! Dr. Kroll told me one day that Ulrik Brendel had had a great influence over you when you were young. I thought it must surely be possible for me to carry on what he had begun.

ROSMER. Did you come here with that purpose—?

REBECCA. I wanted us two to go forward together into freedom. Onward—always onward. But between you and full freedom there was always this dreadful and insuperable barrier.

ROSMER. What barrier?

REBECCA. I mean, John, that you could only blossom into freedom outside in the bright sunshine. But you stayed here, ailing and sickening in the darkness of that dreadful marriage.

ROSMER. You never spoke of my marriage like that before.

REBECCA. No, I didn't dare. I was afraid you might hate me for it.

KROLL (*nods to* ROSMER). You hear that!

REBECCA (*continues*). But I knew well where your salvation lay. Your only hope of salvation. So I took action.

ROSMER. What do you mean, took action?

KROLL. Are you saying that you—!

REBECCA. Yes, John. (*Rises.*) Please don't move. Nor you, Dr. Kroll. It wasn't you, John. You are innocent. It was I who lured—who ended by luring Beata into the labyrinth.

ROSMER (*jumps up*). Rebecca!

KROLL (*rises from the sofa*). The labyrinth!

REBECCA. The labyrinth—that led to the mill-race. Now you know, both of you.

ROSMER (*stunned*). But I don't understand—! What is she saying? I don't understand a word—!

KROLL. Oh, yes, Rosmer. I am beginning to understand.

ROSMER. But what did you do? What could you have said to her? There was nothing. Absolutely nothing.

REBECCA. She learned that you were emancipating yourself from your old-fashioned prejudices.

ROSMER. But I wasn't, not then.

REBECCA. I knew you soon would.

KROLL (*nods to* ROSMER). Aha!

ROSMER. Go on. What else? I want to know the rest, too.

REBECCA. Not long afterwards—I begged and prayed her to let me leave Rosmersholm.

ROSMER. Why did you want to leave then?

REBECCA. I didn't want to leave. I wanted to stay here. But I told her I felt it would be best for us all—if I went away for a while. I let her understand that if I stayed any longer —something might—something might happen—

ROSMER. You said that? You did that?

REBECCA. Yes, John.

ROSMER. And—that is what you meant when you said you "took action"?

REBECCA (*in a broken voice*). Yes.

ROSMER (*after a moment*). Have you confessed everything now, Rebecca?

REBECCA. Yes.

KROLL. Not everything.

REBECCA (*looks at him, frightened*). What else could there be?

KROLL. Didn't you, in the end, make Beata understand that it was necessary—not merely that it was best, but that it was necessary—for your sake and for Rosmer's—that you should go away somewhere—as quickly as possible? Well?

REBECCA (*softly and barely audibly*). I may perhaps have said something like that.

ROSMER (*sinks into the armchair by the window*). And she

—poor, sick creature—went around here believing in this web of lies and treachery! Believing in it implicitly! Unquestioningly! (*Looks up at* REBECCA.) And she never turned to me. Never said a word— Oh, Rebecca. I see it now. *You* dissuaded her!

REBECCA. She had got it into her head that because she was a barren wife she had no right to be here. And then she got it into her head that it was her duty to you to make room for someone else.

ROSMER. And you—you did nothing to put this idea out of her head?

REBECCA. No.

KROLL. Perhaps you even encouraged it? Answer! Did you?

REBECCA. She may have understood me so.

ROSMER. Yes, yes! She always bowed to you in everything. And so she made room. (*Jumps up.*) How could you— how could you play this ghastly game?

REBECCA. I thought it was a choice between two lives, John.

KROLL (*sternly and magisterially*). You had no right to make such a choice.

REBECCA (*vehemently*). But do you think I did all this calculatedly and in cold blood? No, I was different then from what I am now—standing here and talking about it. And besides—I think a person can have two wills. I wanted to be rid of Beata. Somehow or other. But I never thought it would happen. Every step that I ventured forward, I felt as though a voice cried within me: "No further! Not an inch further!" But I *couldn't* stop! I had to venture another inch. Just one. And then another—just one more. And then it happened. That's how such things do happen.

Short silence.

ROSMER (*to* REBECCA). And what do you suppose will happen to you now? When this becomes known?

REBECCA. I don't care what happens to me. It doesn't much matter.

KROLL. No word of remorse. Perhaps you feel none?

REBECCA (*coldly aloof*). I'm sorry, Dr. Kroll, but that is some-

thing which concerns no one but myself. I shall settle that
matter alone.

KROLL (*to* ROSMER). And this is the woman with whom you
share your roof. In an intimate relationship! (*Looks around
at the portraits.*) Oh, if those who are gone had eyes to
see you now!

ROSMER. Are you going back to town?

KROLL (*takes his hat*). Yes. As quickly as possible.

ROSMER (*takes his hat likewise*). Then I shall accompany you.

KROLL. You will! Yes, I knew we hadn't lost you for good.

ROSMER. Come then, Kroll. Come!

They go out through the hall without looking at REBECCA.
*After a few moments, she goes cautiously over to the window
and peers out through the flowers.*

REBECCA (*speaks half-aloud to herself*). Not over the bridge
today, either. Round. Never past the mill-race. Never.
(*Leaves the window.*) Ah, well. (*Goes over and pulls the
bellrope. After a few seconds* MRS. HELSETH *enters right.*)

MRS. HELSETH. What is it, miss?

REBECCA. Mrs. Helseth, will you be so kind as to have my
trunk brought down from the attic?

MRS. HELSETH. Trunk?

REBECCA. Yes, the brown sealskin trunk. You know.

MRS. HELSETH. Yes, I know. But good heavens, miss—surely
you're not going on a journey?

REBECCA. Yes, Mrs. Helseth. I am going on a journey.

MRS. HELSETH. Not at once?

REBECCA. As soon as I've packed.

MRS. HELSETH. Well, I never heard the like! But you'll soon
be back, of course, miss?

REBECCA. No, I shall never come back here again.

MRS. HELSETH. Never! But, blessed Jesus, what's to become of
Rosmersholm once you've left? Just when the poor Pastor
was beginning to be so happy and comfortable.

REBECCA. Yes. But today something frightened me, Mrs.
Helseth.

MRS. HELSETH. Frightened you? Mercy on us, what?

REBECCA. I thought I caught a glimpse of white horses.

MRS. HELSETH. White horses! In broad daylight?

REBECCA. Oh, they never sleep, the white horses of Rosmersholm. (*Changes her tone.*) Well—my trunk then, please,
   Mrs. Helseth.

MRS. HELSETH. Very good, Miss West. Your trunk.

They both go out right.

ACT FOUR

The living room at Rosmersholm. It is late evening. The lamp, beneath its shade, is burning on the table. REBECCA WEST *is standing by the table packing some small belongings in a valise. Her cloak, hat, and the white crocheted shawl are hanging over the back of the sofa.*

MRS. HELSETH *enters right.*

MRS. HELSETH (*speaks softly and seems uneasy*). All your things are down now, miss. They're inside the back door.

REBECCA. Good. You've ordered the coachman?

MRS. HELSETH. Yes. He asks what time you'll be requiring him.

REBECCA. I should think about eleven. The steamer leaves at midnight.

MRS. HELSETH (*hesitates a little*). But the Pastor? Suppose he isn't back by then.

REBECCA. I shall leave in any case. If I don't see him, you can tell him I'll write. A long letter. Tell him that.

MRS. HELSETH. Well, that's all very well, writing. But—poor Miss West—I think you ought to try and speak with him once more.

REBECCA. Perhaps. And perhaps not.

MRS. HELSETH. Dear oh dear, that I should live to see this day! I'd never have believed it.

REBECCA. Wouldn't have believed what, Mrs. Helseth?

MRS. HELSETH. Well, I really thought Pastor Rosmer had more in him than this.

REBECCA. More in him?

MRS. HELSETH. Indeed yes, miss.

REBECCA. But, my dear Mrs. Helseth, what do you mean by that?

MRS. HELSETH. I mean what's right and proper, miss. He oughtn't to run away from things like that.

REBECCA (*looks at her*). Now listen, Mrs. Helseth. Tell me honestly. Why do you think I'm going away?

MRS. HELSETH. Bless you, miss, you've no choice! Oh dear, oh dear, oh dear. But I don't think the Pastor's acted rightly. That Mortensgaard had some excuse—*she* still had her husband alive. So they couldn't have married, however much they wanted. But the Pastor—well!

REBECCA (*with a faint smile*). Could you have imagined anything like that between me and Pastor Rosmer?

MRS. HELSETH. Never. I mean—not until today.

REBECCA. But today—?

MRS. HELSETH. Well—after all those terrible things people say they've written about the Pastor in the newspapers—

REBECCA. Aha.

MRS. HELSETH. A man as can go over to Mortensgaard's way of thinking—well, he's capable of anything. That's my opinion.

REBECCA. Perhaps. But what about me, then? What do you say about me?

MRS. HELSETH. God bless you, miss—I don't see as how anyone can blame you. It isn't so easy for a single woman to hold out on her own. I mean, we're all human, Miss West.

REBECCA. That's very true, Mrs. Helseth. We are all human. What are you listening for?

MRS. HELSETH (*quietly*). Blessed Jesus, miss, I do believe that's him.

REBECCA (*starts*). Then he's—! (*Resolutely.*) Very well. So be it.

JOHN ROSMER *enters from the hall.*

ROSMER (*sees her clothes and valise, turns to* REBECCA *and asks*). What does this mean?

REBECCA. I am leaving.

ROSMER. Now?

REBECCA. Yes. (*To* MRS. HELSETH.) Eleven o'clock, then.

MRS. HELSETH. Very good, miss. (*Goes out right.*)

ROSMER (*after a short pause*). Where are you going, Rebecca?

REBECCA. North with the steamer.

ROSMER. North? Why there?

REBECCA. That's where I came from.

ROSMER. But you have nothing to do up there now.

REBECCA. I've nothing here either.

ROSMER. What do you intend to do?

REBECCA. I don't know. I just want to be finished with it all.

ROSMER. Be finished with it?

REBECCA. Rosmersholm has broken me.

ROSMER (*suddenly alert*). What?

REBECCA. Broken me completely. When I first came here, I was so alive and fearless. Now I am a slave to a strange and foreign law. After today I don't think I shall ever dare attempt anything again.

ROSMER. Why not? What is this law you say you—?

REBECCA. Oh, my dear, let's not talk about that now. What happened between you and Dr. Kroll?

ROSMER. We have settled our differences.

REBECCA. I see. So that's how it ended.

ROSMER. He gathered all our old friends together at his house. They made me realize that the task of making the world noble is not for me. And anyway, it's such a hopeless idea, Rebecca. I shall forget about it.

REBECCA. Ah, well. Perhaps it's best that way.

ROSMER. You say that now? Do you believe that?

REBECCA. I have come to believe it. During the past few days.

ROSMER. You are lying, Rebecca.

REBECCA. Lying—?

ROSMER. Yes, you are lying. You have never believed in me. You have never believed that I was the man to carry that cause to victory.

REBECCA. I believed we two might do it together.

ROSMER. That isn't true. You believed that *you* might be able to achieve something in life. And that you could use me to that end. That I could serve your purpose. That's what you believed.

REBECCA. Now listen, John—

ROSMER (*sits sadly on the sofa*). Oh, never mind. I see the whole thing clearly now. You've used me like a kind of glove.

REBECCA. Now listen, John. Let's talk about this. It will be for the last time. (*Sits in a chair by the sofa.*) I was going to write to you about it, when I had got back to the north. But perhaps you'd better hear it now.

ROSMER. Have you something more to confess?

REBECCA. Yes. The most important thing of all.

ROSMER. The most important thing?

REBECCA. The thing you've never guessed. The thing that both excuses and condemns all the rest.

ROSMER (*shakes his head*). I don't understand any of this.

REBECCA. It's quite true that I once intrigued to gain admittance to Rosmersholm. I thought I might manage to find success and happiness here. One way or another—you understand.

ROSMER. Then you achieved what you wanted.

REBECCA. I think I could have achieved anything—then. Because I feared nothing. I still had a free will. I had no inhibitions. I wasn't afraid of human relationships. But then there came—the thing that broke my will—and frightened me for ever.

ROSMER. What happened? Speak so that I can understand you.

REBECCA. It came over me—this blinding, uncontrollable passion—! Oh, John—!

ROSMER. Passion? You—! For what?

REBECCA. For you.

ROSMER (*tries to spring up*). What!

REBECCA (*restrains him*). Sit still, my dear. There's something else you have to hear.

ROSMER. Are you trying to say—that you've loved me—in that way!

REBECCA. I thought it was love—then. Yes, I thought it was love. But it wasn't. It was what I tell you. A blinding, uncontrollable passion.

ROSMER (*with difficulty*). Rebecca—is it really *you—you*—that you're talking about?

REBECCA. Yes, John. Whom else?

ROSMER. Then it was this that—it was this that made you "take action," as you call it.

REBECCA. It swept over me like a storm at sea. Like one of those storms we sometimes get in the winter, far up in the north. It seizes you—and carries you with it, John— whithersoever it will. It's useless even to try to resist it.

ROSMER. And it swept poor Beata into the mill-race.

REBECCA. Yes. It was a fight for survival. Between Beata and me.

ROSMER. You were always the strongest at Rosmersholm. Stronger than Beata and me together.

REBECCA. I knew you so well, John. I knew I could never reach you until you'd been set free. Physically and mentally.

ROSMER. But I don't understand you, Rebecca. You—you and everything you've done—it's all an insoluble riddle to me. Now I am free—physically and mentally. Now you stand at the goal you set yourself from the beginning. And yet—

REBECCA. I have never been further from my goal than now.

ROSMER. And yet—when I asked you yesterday—when I begged you: "Be my wife!"—you cried out in terror that it could never happen.

REBECCA. I was crying in despair, John.

ROSMER. Why?

REBECCA. Because Rosmersholm has drained my strength. It has broken my courage and paralysed my will. The time is past when I was afraid of nothing. I have lost the power to take action, John.

ROSMER. Tell me how this has happened.

REBECCA. It has happened through living with you.

ROSMER. But how? How?

REBECCA. When I found myself alone here with you—and you had found yourself—

ROSMER. Yes, yes?

REBECCA. —because you were never really yourself, as long as Beata was alive—

ROSMER. I'm afraid you're right there—

REBECCA. But then, when I began living here with you—alone in peace, just the two of us—when you shared all your thoughts with me, unreservedly—every mood and feeling, just as it came to you—then the great change happened. To me, I mean. Gradually, you understand. Almost imperceptibly—but irresistibly. To the very depths of my soul.

ROSMER. Rebecca!

REBECCA. All the rest—that blinding, sickening passion—faded away from me. All my tormenting furies fell silent and still. A calm came over me—the kind of calm you find on a bird-cliff up in the far north, under the midnight sun.

ROSMER. Go on. Tell me all you can.

REBECCA. There isn't much else, John. Only that—it was then that I began to love. The great and selfless love that asks for nothing more than companionship. The way it's been between us.

ROSMER. Oh, if only I'd had any inkling of all this—!

REBECCA. It's best the way it is. Yesterday—when you asked me if I would be your wife—my heart cried aloud with joy—

ROSMER. Yes, Rebecca. I sensed it.

REBECCA. Just for a moment, I was able to forget myself. My old spirit and will were crying out for their freedom. But now they no longer have any power or strength.

ROSMER. How do you explain what has happened to you?

REBECCA. It's the Rosmer view of life—or yours, anyway. It has infected my will.

ROSMER. Infected—?

REBECCA. And poisoned it. Enslaved it to a law which I had not previously recognized. You—being with you—has ennobled my soul—

ROSMER. Oh, if I could only believe that!

REBECCA. You can believe it all right. The Rosmer view of life ennobles. But—(shakes her head)—but—but—

ROSMER. But—? Well?

REBECCA. But it kills happiness, John.

ROSMER. How can you say that, Rebecca?

REBECCA. For me, anyway.

ROSMER. Can you be so sure of that? If I were to ask you again now—if I were to go on my knees and beg you—?

REBECCA. Oh, my dearest—please don't ever speak of that again. It's impossible—! You'd better know, John. Before I came to Rosmersholm—something happened to me—

ROSMER. More than you've told me?

REBECCA. Yes. Something else. Something more terrible—

ROSMER (*with a faint smile*). Isn't it strange, Rebecca? Do you know, once or twice I'd wondered about that.

REBECCA. Did you? And yet—? In spite of that—?

ROSMER. I never believed it. I just—played with the thought, you know.

REBECCA. If you want me to, I'll tell you about that too.

ROSMER. No, no! I don't want to hear a word about it. Whatever it may be—I can forget it.

REBECCA. But I can't.

ROSMER. Oh, Rebecca—

REBECCA. Yes, John. That's what's so dreadful—that now, when all life's happiness is offered to me with open hands —now I've become the kind of person whose conscience about the past makes it impossible for me to accept it.

ROSMER. Your past is dead, Rebecca. It no longer has any hold on you. It has nothing to do with you. All that happened to someone else.

REBECCA. Oh, my dearest, those are just words. What about that sense of innocence you spoke about? Where shall I find that?

ROSMER (*sadly*). Yes, yes. Innocence.

REBECCA. Yes, innocence. The secret of joy and happiness. Wasn't that the lesson you wanted to teach your new generation of happy, noble men?

ROSMER. Oh, don't remind me of that. That was only a hopeless dream, Rebecca. A wild delusion that I no longer believe in. People cannot be ennobled from without, Rebecca.

REBECCA (*quietly*). Not even by love, don't you think?

ROSMER (*thoughtfully*). Ah, that would be the thing! The greatest thing that life could have to offer. If it were true. (*Writhes in distress.*) But how can I find the answer to that question? The real answer?

REBECCA. Don't you believe me, John?

ROSMER. Oh, Rebecca—how can I believe you in anything now? You've hidden so much from me. Now you come forward with this new idea. If you've some hidden purpose behind all this, for God's sake tell me straight out what it is! If there's anything you want, I'll willingly do anything I can for you.

REBECCA (*twists her hands*). Oh, this killing doubt—! John, John!

ROSMER. Yes, isn't it terrible, Rebecca? But I can't help it. I shall never be able to free myself from this doubt. Never be sure that you really love me, purely and with all your heart.

REBECCA. But doesn't something deep inside you tell you that a change has taken place in me? And that this change has been caused by you, and by you alone?

ROSMER. Oh, Rebecca—I no longer believe in my ability to change people. I no longer have any faith in myself. Neither in myself nor in you.

REBECCA (*looks sadly at him*). How will you be able to live then, John?

ROSMER. I don't know. I don't know at all. I don't think I can live. In any case, I don't know anything worth living for.

REBECCA. Oh, life—life is its own renewer. Let us hold fast to it, John. We leave it soon enough.

ROSMER (*jumps up restlessly*). Then give me back my faith! My faith in you, Rebecca! My faith in your love! I want proof! Proof!

REBECCA. Proof? But how can I give you proof—?

ROSMER. You must. (*Walks across the room.*) I can't stand this desolation—this emptiness—this—this—

There is a loud knock on the door leading from the hall.

REBECCA (*jumps up from her chair*). Ah—did you hear that?

The door opens. ULRIK BRENDEL *enters. He is wearing a stiff shirt, a black coat, and good boots outside his trousers. Otherwise he is dressed as before. He looks confused.*

ROSMER. Oh, is it you, Mr. Brendel?

BRENDEL. John, my boy! *Ave—atque vale!*

ROSMER. Where are you going so late?

BRENDEL. Downhill.

ROSMER. What do you—?

BRENDEL. I am homeward bound, *mon cher élève!* My heart is homesick for the great void.

ROSMER. Something has happened to you, Mr. Brendel. What is it?

BRENDEL. You perceive the transformation? Ah—well you may. When I last set foot in this room, I stood before you as a man of substance, slapping my breast pocket.

ROSMER. Oh? I don't quite understand—

BRENDEL. But tonight you see a dethroned monarch kneeling on the ashes of his incinerated palace.

ROSMER. If there's any way I can help you—

BRENDEL. You have retained the heart of a child, my dear John. Can you spare me a loan?

ROSMER. Yes, yes, of course.

BRENDEL. Could you possibly stretch to an ideal or two?

ROSMER. What did you say?

BRENDEL. A few cast-off ideals. You'd be doing a good deed. I'm cleaned out, dear boy. Absolutely stripped.

REBECCA. Didn't you give your lecture?

BRENDEL. No, seductive lady. Would you believe it! As I raised my hand to empty the cornucopia of plenty, I made the distressing discovery that I was bankrupt.

REBECCA. But all those unwritten works you spoke about?

BRENDEL. For five and twenty years I have squatted like a miser on his padlocked money-bags. And then yesterday, when I opened them to bring my riches forth—there was nothing! The mills of time had ground everything into dust. *Nichts*—nothing!

ROSMER. But are you sure of this?

BRENDEL. No room for doubt, my duck. The President convinced me of that.

ROSMER. The President?

BRENDEL. His Excellency, if you prefer. *Ganz nach belieben.*

ROSMER. Whom do you mean?

BRENDEL. Peter Mortensgaard, of course.

ROSMER. What!

BRENDEL (*confidentially*). Ssh, ssh, ssh! Peter Mortensgaard is the lord and master of the future! Never have I encountered so sublime a presence. Peter Mortensgaard possesses the secret of omnipotence. He can do anything he sets his mind to.

ROSMER. Don't you believe that.

BRENDEL. Yes, my boy! Because Peter Mortensgaard never wants to do more than lies within his power. Peter Mortensgaard knows how to live life without ideals. And *that,* you see—*that* is precisely the secret of action and of victory. It is the sum of all the world's wisdom. *Basta!*

ROSMER (*softly*). Now I understand. Yes, you are leaving here poorer than you came.

BRENDEL. *Bien!* And now take a *Beispeil* of your old tutor. Blot out everything he ever imprinted on your mind. Build not thy citadel on shifting sand. And take care—proceed warily—before you build on this charming creature who now sweetens your existence.

REBECCA. Do you mean me?

BRENDEL. I do, bewitching lady from the sea.

REBECCA. Why should I be nothing for a man to build his life on?

BRENDEL (*takes a step closer*). I gather that my former pupil has a cause which he wishes to carry to victory.

REBECCA. Well?

BRENDEL. His victory is assured. But—mark this well—on one inescapable condition.

REBECCA. What is that?

BRENDEL (*takes her gently by the wrist*). That the woman who loves him shall, with a glad heart, go out into the

kitchen and chop off her delicate rosy-white finger—*here*
—just *here* at the middle joint. *Item*, that the aforesaid
adoring woman—equally gladly—shall snip off her incom-
parably formed left ear. (*Lets go of her and turns to*
ROSMER.) Farewell, Johannes! Forward to victory!

ROSMER. Are you going now? It's a dark night.

BRENDEL. Night and darkness are best. Peace be with you.
(*He goes.*)

There is a moment's silence in the room.

REBECCA (*takes a deep breath*). Oh, how close and suffocat-
ing it is in here!

She goes to the window, opens it, and remains standing there.

ROSMER (*sits in the armchair by the stove*). There's no other
way, Rebecca. I see it now. You *must* leave.

REBECCA. Yes. I see no choice.

ROSMER. Let us make the most of these last moments. Come
over here and sit beside me.

REBECCA (*goes over and sits on the sofa*). What is it, John?

ROSMER. First I want to tell you that you have no need to
worry about your future.

REBECCA (*smiles*). Hm. *My* future.

ROSMER. I prepared for all contingencies a long time ago.
Whatever may happen, you are provided for.

REBECCA. That too, my dear?

ROSMER. Surely you must have known—?

REBECCA. It's a long time since I thought of anything like
that.

ROSMER. Yes, yes—you must have imagined things could never
be different between us from the way they were.

REBECCA. Yes, I did feel that.

ROSMER. So did I. But if I were to go—

REBECCA. Oh, John. You will live longer than I.

ROSMER. This wretched life is my own to do what I wish with.

REBECCA. What do you mean? You aren't thinking of—?

ROSMER. Would it be so strange? After the humiliating defeat
I have suffered? I, who was to carry my cause to victory—!

And now I have fled the field—before the battle has even
begun!

REBECCA. Take up the fight again, John! Only try, and you'll
see! You will win! You will ennoble hundreds of souls—
thousands! Only try!

ROSMER. Oh, Rebecca! I no longer have any faith in that
cause.

REBECCA. But it has already stood the test. You have ennobled one human being at least. Me, for as long as I live.

ROSMER. If only I could believe you.

REBECCA (*clasps her hands*). Oh, John! Is there nothing—
nothing that could make you believe it?

ROSMER (*starts as though in fear*). Don't say that, Rebecca!
Please! Don't ever talk about that!

REBECCA. Yes, we must talk about it. Do you know of anything that could dispel your doubt? I can't think of a way.

ROSMER. Thank God that you can't. Thank God for us both.

REBECCA. No, no, no—I can't rest satisfied with that! If you
know of anything that can acquit me in your eyes, I demand it as my right that you name it.

ROSMER (*as though forced to speak against his will*). Let's
see, then. You say you have discovered the true meaning
of love. That through me your soul has been ennobled. Is
this true? Have you calculated correctly, Rebecca? Shall
we check your calculation?

REBECCA. I am ready.

ROSMER. When?

REBECCA. Anytime. The sooner the better.

ROSMER. Then show me, Rebecca—if you—for my sake—this
very night—! (*Breaks off.*) Oh, no, no, no!

REBECCA. Yes, John! Yes, yes! Tell me, and you'll see!

ROSMER. Have you the courage—and the will—with a glad
heart, as Ulrik Brendel said—for my sake, now, tonight—
freely and willingly—to go the way that Beata went?

REBECCA (*draws herself up from the sofa and says almost
speechlessly*). John!

ROSMER. Yes, Rebecca. This is the question I shall never be
able to escape from—after you are gone. Every hour of the

day it will haunt me. Oh—I seem to see you there before my eyes. You are standing on the bridge. In the middle of it. Now you are leaning out over the parapet. You sway as the rushing water draws you down. No. Then you shrink back. You have not the courage to do as she did.

REBECCA. But if I had the courage? And the will, to do it gladly? What then?

ROSMER. Then I would have to believe you. I would regain my faith in my life's work. Faith in my ability to ennoble humanity. Faith in the capacity of man to be ennobled.

REBECCA (*slowly takes her shawl, throws it over her head and says calmly*). You shall have your faith back.

ROSMER. Have you the courage—and the will—to do this, Rebecca?

REBECCA. That you will be able to judge tomorrow—or later —when they fish me up.

ROSMER (*clutches at his forehead*). There's a—demonic fascination—in this—!

REBECCA. I don't want to stay lying down there. Longer than necessary. You must see that they find me.

ROSMER (*jumps up*). But all this—is madness! Go—or stay. I will believe you—I will take your word for it. This time too.

REBECCA. Words, John! Let's have no more cowardice and running away. How can you take my word for anything after today?

ROSMER. But I don't want to see you defeated, Rebecca.

REBECCA. There will be no defeat.

ROSMER. There will be. You will never have the courage to go Beata's way.

REBECCA. You think not?

ROSMER. Never. You are not like Beata. You don't see life through distorted eyes.

REBECCA. But I see it through Rosmer eyes. The crime that I have committed—demands atonement.

ROSMER (*looks fixedly at her*). Is that what you believe in your heart?

REBECCA. Yes.

ROSMER (*with decision*). Very well. Then I kneel to our emancipated view of life, Rebecca. We acknowledge no judge over us. Therefore we must pass judgment upon ourselves.

REBECCA (*misunderstands him*). Yes, John, yes. If I go, it will save what is best in you.

ROSMER. There is nothing left in me to save.

REBECCA. There is. But I—after today I would be like a sea-troll, hanging on to the ship that is to carry you forward and holding it back. I must be cast overboard. Would you have me linger on up here in the world, dragging my life along like a cripple? I must retire from the game, John.

ROSMER. If you go—then I shall go with you.

REBECCA (*smiles almost imperceptibly, looks at him and says more quietly*). Yes, John. Come with me—and witness—

ROSMER. I shall go with you, I said.

REBECCA. To the bridge, yes. You will never dare to walk on it.

ROSMER. You have noticed that?

REBECCA (*sadly, broken*). Yes. That was what made my love hopeless.

ROSMER. Rebecca, now I place my hand on your head. (*He does as he says.*) And take you in marriage as my lawful wife.

REBECCA (*clasps both his hands and bows her head against his breast*). Thank you, John. (*Lets go of him.*) And now I go—gladly.

ROSMER. Man and wife should go together.

REBECCA. Only as far as the bridge, John.

ROSMER. And on to it. As far as you go, I shall go with you. Now I am no longer afraid.

REBECCA. Are you so completely sure—that this way is the best one for you?

ROSMER. I know that it is the only one.

REBECCA. Suppose you are wrong? Suppose it is only an illusion? One of those white horses of Rosmersholm?

ROSMER. That may be. We shall never escape them—we who live in this house.

REBECCA. Then stay, John!

ROSMER. Man and wife should go together.

REBECCA. But first tell me this. Is it you who are going with me? Or I with you?

ROSMER. That we shall never know.

REBECCA. I should like to know.

ROSMER. We go together, Rebecca. I with you, and you with me.

REBECCA. Yes. I think you are right.

ROSMER. For now we two are one.

REBECCA. Yes. Now we are one. Come! Let us go gladly!

They go out hand in hand through the hall, and turn to the left. The door remains open behind them. For a few moments the room is empty. Then MRS. HELSETH *opens the door right.*

MRS. HELSETH. Miss—the carriage is—! (*Looks round.*) Not here? Out together at this hour? Well, I must say! Hm! (*Goes out into the hall, looks round and comes back again.*) They're not on the seat. Well, well. (*Goes to the window and looks out.*) Blessed Jesus! What's that white thing over there—? Upon my soul, if they're not both standing on the bridge! God forgive the sinful creatures! If they're not putting their arms round each other—! (*Screams aloud.*) Ah! They've fallen—both of them! Into the mill-race! Help! Help! (*Her knees tremble; she holds on, shaking, to the back of the chair, hardly able to speak.*) No. No help. The dead mistress has taken them.

NOTE ON THE TRANSLATION

A Doll's House and *An Enemy of the People* present fewer problems to the translator than any other of Ibsen's plays. They are simply and directly written, and for nearly all the time the characters say what they mean, instead of talking at a tangent to their real meaning. Torvald Helmer utters several stuffy Victorianisms, and Krogstad sometimes speaks the language of melodrama, but both work well in performance. Here, as in all the plays, I have retained certain turns of phrase which look Victorian on the printed page but are effective in the theatre when spoken by an actor or actress in nineteenth-century clothes in a nineteenth-century room.

In one or two instances I have, as any honest translator must, allowed myself a small amount of licence. For example, in *An Enemy of the People*, when Dr. Stockmann likens aristocrats of the intellect to pedigree dogs, Ibsen makes him name the poodle as an example of refinement and intelligence; but poodles, at any rate in England, today have rather the wrong kind of associations, and I have altered this to "greyhound." This involves, in performance, cutting the reference to the dogs being able "to perform the most amazing tricks"; but in any case this section of the play needs to be reduced in performance. When Stockmann speaks of his hatred of *ledende maend* (literally "leading men"—in the political, not the theatrical sense, though he knew a thing or two about the latter kind also), I have translated the phrase as "politicians." Ibsen means by *ledende maend* anyone who leads other men by the nose, which is a pretty accurate definition of a politician.

An Enemy of the People is, with the single exception of

The Wild Duck, the longest of Ibsen's mature prose plays, and is usually cut in performance. Stockmann's address in the fourth act contains a certain amount of red herringry which it is no great loss to shed; and the opening of the final act, with its repetitious insistence on "not daring," and the closing minutes, both profit, in my opinion, by judicious thinning.

Unlike *A Doll's House* and *An Enemy of the People, Ghosts* is oblique, sometimes even opaque in its dialogue, most noticeably when Mrs. Alving and Manders are speaking together. In common with the leading characters in the later plays, such as *Little Eyolf,* these two spend much of the time circling around a subject which they dread referring to directly. Manders is particularly awkward to render. His verbosity and pompousness must not be exaggerated; he has not much more of either than a television cleric (or, for that matter, a television politician). It is hardly necessary to add that he should be played straight, not as a caricature; a glance through the reviews of past London productions shows how often a "character performance" has hampered the suspension of disbelief. He should, moreover, be a handsome man; otherwise Mrs. Alving's youthful infatuation with him becomes difficult to credit. Similarly, Mrs. Alving should be under fifty and still beautiful; it is of the essence of her tragedy that a third of her life still lies before her.

The Norwegian title *Gengangere* corresponds closely to the French *Les Revenants.* It really means "The ones who walk again," and Ibsen, even with his very limited knowledge of English—he could hardly write a sentence of it without making some elementary howler—questioned the adequacy of *Ghosts* as an accurate translation of the title. But there is no better alternative, and the word has become so much a part of English theatrical history that it seems scarcely desirable to change it now.

Rosmersholm is, for three quarters of its length, directly written; the remainder consists of that same kind of weighted and evasive dialogue which Mrs. Alving and Pastor Manders speak. Ulrik Brendel is an extravagant talker in the mould of Hilmar Toennesen of *The Pillars of Society,* and Hjalmar

Ekdal of *The Wild Duck*. It, like them, is a baroque part for a baroque actor. One may perhaps add that the play and its ending make sense only if Rebecca is acted (as she is written) as a deeply passionate woman; just as Rosmer, beneath his inhibitions and frightened at the suggestion of it, is a deeply passionate man. If Rebecca is played as an intellectual bluestocking and Rosmer as a sexless parson, the last act makes nonsense. Why should such a couple kill themselves for love? It is only Rebecca's enemy, Dr. Kroll, who calls her an intellectual. Of course she has an intellect, but that is another thing; Ibsen, like George Eliot, knew well the predicament of the woman of intellect whose passions can find no outlet. Rebecca and Dorothea Brook of *Middlemarch* have a good deal in common.

My thanks are due to Mr. Casper Wrede for many invaluable suggestions and criticisms in connection with the translation of *Ghosts*.

M. M.

ANCHOR BOOKS

ART AND ARCHITECTURE